FAMILY ORIGINS *and* OTHER STUDIES

PUBLISHED BY

Constable & Company Limited
London W.C. 2

·

BOMBAY
CALCUTTA   MADRAS

Oxford University
Press

·

TORONTO

The Macmillan Company
of Canada, Limited

·

NEW YORK

Richard R. Smith Inc

J. Horace Round

FAMILY ORIGINS

and other Studies

by

the late

J. HORACE ROUND
M.A., LL.D.

Edited with a

Memoir and Bibliography

by

WILLIAM PAGE, F.S.A.

LONDON
CONSTABLE & CO LTD
1930

PRINTED IN GREAT BRITAIN BY ROBERT MACLEHOSE AND CO. LTD,
THE UNIVERSITY PRESS, GLASGOW.

PREFACE

THE papers which are printed in this volume were written by Dr. Round before 1922, after which date his health prevented him from devoting much continuous time to historical research. Dr. Round's original purpose was to bring out two volumes—the one to contain genealogical papers and to be entitled ' Family Origins,' and the other to be a volume of historical studies. The material for the former was left in a more or less complete condition, and is here printed as he prepared it ; besides the papers included in this volume, however, he proposed to reprint certain articles from the *Ancestor*, but owing to the want of space this has not been done. The papers for the volume of historical studies were, unfortunately, largely left in an unfinished state, and some of them have had to be pieced together from scattered fragments found after Dr. Round's death. It has thus been difficult to gather these fragments together into a connected form, particularly in the case of the article on ' Reliefs,' which seems to have been taken up at various times covering an extended period. One or two articles intended by Dr. Round for the volume are either out of date or too fragmentary for inclusion.

I wish to express my indebtedness to Dr. Round's old friends Sir Henry Maxwell Lyte and Dr. R. Lane Poole for reading the proofs of this volume ; to Prof. James Tait for advice on certain points relating to the article on ' Burh-bot and Brig-bot ' ; to Mrs. Shaw-Kennedy and Mr. Geoffrey Ellis for information relating to the Memoir. I have also to acknowledge the frequent help and many suggestions from Mr. Charles J. Round and Mr. Arthur G. L. Gamlen, executors of the late Dr. Round, at whose desire this volume has been prepared and published.

The Bibliography is partially based on a bibliography compiled by the librarian of the Public Record Office Library, the use of which has been of great assistance in making the more complete bibliography which is here printed. In the compilation and checking of this I am indebted for assistance from Mrs. B. Shewell.

WILLIAM PAGE.

ASHMERE CROFT,
MIDDLETON, NEAR BOGNOR.

CONTENTS

vii

FAMILY ORIGINS AND OTHER STUDIES

MEMOIR OF DR. J. HORACE ROUND

ACCORDING to the researches made by Horace Round regarding the history of his family, his ancestors obtained their name from the manor of Rounde, now corrupted to Rowde, near Calne in Wiltshire. A branch of the family settled at Alcester in Warwickshire at the end of the sixteenth century and from thence went to Stratford-on-Avon. Here we find John Round, an attorney, two of whose sons sought their fortunes in London. John, the elder, became solicitor for the City of London and married Mary, daughter and co-heir of Matthew Lister, a first cousin of the beautiful Duchess of Tyrconnell and the famous Sarah, Duchess of Marlborough. James, the younger son, prospered as a bookseller in Exchange Alley, at a time when London merchants lived in the City and treated their bookseller as their friend and literary adviser. He became Master of the Stationers' Company, and in 1724 he purchased Little Birch Hall in Essex. He died unmarried in 1745, leaving Birch Hall to his nephew William, son of his brother John Round, who had died in 1718. William practised as a solicitor in London and had three sons. The eldest, James, who became a partner in the Colchester Bank and succeeded to Birch Hall, married Thamar, daughter of Peter Creffield, by whom he acquired Colchester Castle, the Holly Trees, Colchester, and property at Mersea Island. The second son, William, died unmarried in the Black Hole of Calcutta in 1756, and a third son, John, of St. Martin's House, Colchester, great-grandfather of Horace Round, was called to the bar and became recorder of Colchester. His wife, Catherine, was the daughter of Edward Green of Lawford Hall and widow of the Rev. Richard Daniell. Their only child, John Round, had a distinguished career. He was educated at Balliol College (1803-8), and the University of Oxford gave him in 1814 an honorary degree of D.C.L. He was a J.P. and D.L. for the county of Essex, member of parliament for Ipswich (1812-20) and for Maldon (1837-47), high steward of Colchester and high sheriff of Essex (1834). He married Susan Constantia, daughter of George Caswell of Sacombe Park, Herts, who brought him the manor of West Bergholt, Essex. It was through this lady, who in 1839 was burnt to death in a fire at a hotel in Albemarle Street, that Horace Round claimed a descent from the first three Edwards, Kings of England, through Anne Wilmot, daughter of John, second Earl of Rochester.

John Round died in 1860, leaving three sons and two daughters. John, the eldest son, was the father of Horace. Frederick Peel, the second son, was gentleman usher of the Green Rod, and Edmund, the third son, was in his early days in the Colchester Bank and later a successful barrister. Both the latter died without issue. John who was educated at Harrow and Balliol College, lived most of his time at 15 Brunswick Terrace, Brighton, which his father had bought in 1827. It was at Brighton that he met his wife Laura, youngest of the three gifted daughters of Horace Smith, joint author with his brother James, of the well-known *Rejected Addresses*. After his retirement from business, Horace Smith settled at Brighton in 1823 where he entertained and corresponded with most of the writers of that brilliant literary period. His sound common sense was constantly requisitioned in literary quarrels and his pocket was never appealed to in vain by literary brethren in distress. Lord Lytton, writing in 1891 to Miss Eliza Smith, recalls ' the old days when your dear father and mother were alive and Laura only just out, and Rose the belle of Brighton, and I a little boy at Mrs. Walker's and all of you so kind to me, they sometimes seem to me much nearer and I think I remember them better than all the days between them and now.'

John Round and Laura Smith were married in 1853 and on 22nd February, 1854, John Horace Round, the subject of this memoir, was born at Brunswick Terrace, Brighton. Two daughters were afterwards born. On the death of his father in 1860, John Round let his house at Brighton and went to Paris, where he and his family lived for four years. Here Horace obtained a knowledge of the French language that was so valuable to him in after years. On 7th April, 1864, the elder of John Round's daughters, Laura Constance, a particularly engaging child, died, and on 27th August in the same year his adored wife also died at the early age of thirty-six. Her death was mourned by a large circle of friends. Bulwer Lytton in a letter of condolence to Miss Rosalind Smith wrote, ' In spite of endless absence from old friends I have ever felt the deepest interest in and truest affection for your poor sister whom I was truly in love with, when I was a little boy and she a little girl.' Thackeray, too, had a great admiration for her, and Laura in *Pendennis* is said to have been named after her. Horace Round owed much to his mother's family. It was probably from her father that he inherited his ready wit, quick perception, and clear brain together with his marvellous memory and facile pen.

After the death of his wife, John Round returned to Brighton with his two surviving children, John Horace and Violet Grace, who later married Frederick David Shaw-Kennedy, but he never recovered from his double loss. He had studied art abroad and painted in water colours, principally sketches of Italian, Swiss or French scenery ; his interest flagged, however, when he lost the inspiration of his clever little wife. He seemed to lose all motive in life and the house at Brighton became a somewhat melancholy home for his young and delicate children. Fortunately their mother's sisters, Miss Eliza and Miss Rosalind Smith, always welcomed them at their house at Silwood Place, Brighton, and their father's brothers took a keen interest in their welfare.

Horace was sent to a preparatory school at Brighton, kept by Mrs. Cook. He was a delicate boy, subject to severe headaches. He was studious and his studies were allowed to wander in any direction that took his fancy. Even at this early date history and genealogy engaged his attention. His father encouraged him to draw and he could make clever caricatures.

John Round became more and more of a recluse. His brother saw how cramped the life at Brighton was becoming for young Horace, and in 1868 urged that he should be sent to Harrow. The family physician thought, however, that he was not strong enough for public school life and so a tutor was engaged and his name was put down for Balliol College. His uncle, Edmund Round, wrote urging that Horace should 'go through Oxford somehow (honours would be out of the question) but the object is to make a man of him, expand his ideas and get him out of the narrow groove in which from unavoidable circumstances he moved.' His health seems at this time to have improved and he went up to Oxford in 1874 when he was twenty-one, an age which his uncle considered rather old for entrance, but added, 'his youthful appearance will always avail him for his age.'

It is remarkable how easily young Horace settled down to college life considering his upbringing. In a letter to his father he bewailed the absence of public school traditions and friendships, which as a matter of fact affected his character even more than he then knew. That he should be the object of a certain amount of ragging was inevitable, but he took it in good part and was able to hold his own against the wilder spirits with whom he associated. He won a pot at a college regatta and occasionally coxed the college fours or eights but was too heavy for coxswain. He proudly records the vaulting of the six feet horse at the gymnasium, a feat, he wrote, which only two or three other men could do. Long walks and regular exercise made his time at Oxford probably the healthiest and happiest of his life. 'I am getting to like the Oxford life very much,' he wrote to his father in his first term, 'my mathematical tutor is the only shadow.' This shadow was shortly removed and he took classics alone which, he said, were plain sailing for him, while mathematics became more and more distasteful.

For Jowett, his college head, Round had little liking or respect. He gave his views of the Master of Balliol in a letter to his father. ' The great fault of Jowett,' he wrote, ' seems to be rather one of omission than of commission. The age at which men come up to Oxford and the age in which they live, are both conducive to scepticism. Now it is the undoubted duty of Jowett to counteract this tendency by sound outspoken doctrine. But on the contrary he developes it by the uncertain sound of his sermons and by refusing to admit anyone into his chapel who is not of the same way of thinking as himself. You yourself heard him last time declare that miracles were not a fundamental point of faith, that they were prima facie impossible and if possible were not established.' Jowett himself had qualms as to the effect of his religious doctrines. ' I sometimes feel,' he wrote to his friend Morier in 1875, ' that the want of religion is destructive to Idealism and elevation of character ; but then again the disregard of truth seems to be equally destructive. I cannot tell you how the question presses on me at times in reference to undergraduates and young fellows in Balliol. I seem to see so clearly what is right and to have so little power of impressing it on others.' [1]

Round took no part in the religious movements which were engaging the attention of men like Arnold Toynbee, Argles and Gore, who were his contemporaries at Balliol. His views were not theirs and although he occasionally mentions them in his letters, he had no close association with them. He was punctilious in his attendance at chapel and studious in his observance of all college rules. On Sunday evening he wrote to his father a criticism of the ser-mon he had heard during the day. Thus we have his views on many prominent preachers. Jowett had entered keenly into the conflict between science and religion. His friend Tyndall, in 1874, gave his celebrated inaugural address at

[1] Abbott and Campbell, *Letters of Benjamin Jowett,* 77.

the British Association, claiming that Science must be left free to deal with its subjects as it chose. Jowett took the opportunity to preach a sermon in the college chapel, which Round describes as the broadest and boldest ever preached by him or any other man in Oxford. The burden of his sermon was the mechanical uniformity of the laws of nature. ' By insisting on these laws being unalterable he practically proved that the laws were superior to Him Who made them —a rather awkward conclusion. He thus, by implication, denied the omnipotence of God and the efficacy of prayer, a sure result of the doctrine. In denying the principle of the efficacy of prayer, he could not avoid denying the power.'

On another Sunday he wrote, ' the freethinker,' Jowett, was in his element having succeeded in getting that ' arch heretic Colenso ' to preach, notwithstanding the Bishop had forbidden him to preach in Carfax church. Colenso, he said, had a powerful, earnest delivery and his sermon was admirable at first, but he soon got astride his favourite hobby and violently denounced the Flood. ' He ended with a word of encouragement to the wicked, that is, a pious hope in the impossibility of eternal punishment. Of course he went in for Jowett's hobby of the fixed law, setting Nature well above Nature's law.'

Dean Stanley was another of the Sunday preachers who came under Round's criticism. ' I had imagined him,' he wrote, ' a genial middle-aged man, with a commanding presence and I found a little wizen old man with a broken delivery.' He had always believed that Stanley had learned the secret of being charitable to other men's beliefs without of necessity abandoning his own. He was certainly far above Jowett for he knew what he believed and Jowett did not. ' Still they have this in common that though their watchword is to be charitable and liberal, two more bitterly personal preachers were never heard ! ' Bradley of University College, afterwards Dean of Westminster, on another occasion preached ' a dreary sermon ' at St. Mary's in which he gave some hard raps at Jowett. He denounced all innocent amusements which are wasteful of time or money, ' a point in which I quite agree with him. They may do no harm, but do they do any good ? '

Even at this early date Round was nothing if not logical, a point upon which he later prided himself. Although he had little in common with Pusey and the high church party, he respected their positive doctrines, but for what he considered the confused arguments of Jowett and Colenso he had no tolerance.

Round was fortunate in his tutors. Evelyn Abbott, who took him in classics, was a man of attractive personality and of strong influence. He had been an athlete, but owing to an accident his lower limbs were paralysed. Even in this crippled state he became a great classical scholar and Jowett's right hand. He urged Round not to read too hard and to take more physical exercise, advice which Round followed, much to the improvement of his health. For history he worked under the Rev. James Franck Bright, a sympathetic tutor, who at once recognised Round's literary ability but said he ' must put him down to bald questions although he admired his essays.' It was not until later that Stubbs became his history tutor. Round was on friendly terms with the Rev. Thomas K. Cheyne, fellow and librarian of the college, a great Hebrew scholar, who considered Colenso too orthodox. According to Round, he was reported to have said at a Divinity lecture, ' If any gentleman is present who does not believe that Abraham was a solar myth, let him understand that I am not lecturing to him.'

In 1876 Round took a second in classical moderations which was a disappointment attributable as he thought to the illegibility of his handwriting. There was an improvement in this respect for a time, but those who have to decipher his later manuscript, have a sympathy with his university examiner.

In the following year, the allotted time for his residence having expired, he pleaded unavailingly to retain his rooms in college. Jowett thought he was less likely to get into mischief in lodgings than some of his wilder seniors, and so he had to move into rooms at 43 Broad Street. In 1878 he took a first class in the Final History Schools. It was during this later time at Oxford that Stubbs, then his tutor, obtained so great an influence over him and his work. He gave him an outlook beyond mere pedigree-making and opened out the value of genealogy in historical research. A life-long friendship was started between tutor and pupil. Although the pupil made corrections on several important points in his former tutor's *Constitutional History*, they were made and taken in good part so that the friendship was never marred by any controversy or quarrel.

After leaving Oxford in 1878, Round spent some time in visiting his relatives in Essex and took keenly to lawn tennis which had lately come into fashion. His father's failing health, however, recalled him to Brighton and the nature of his father's illness necessitated his constant attendance on him. He seems at this time to have had the idea of taking up journalism as a profession, but bad health, the care of his father and the lack of necessity to earn a living, deterred him from being more than a free lance in literature. Apparently his first attempt at journalism was an article for the *Saturday Review* of 20th December, 1879, on Burke's *Landed Gentry*. He took the opportunity afforded by a review to give a scholarly essay on the rise and fall of ' the untitled nobility ' of the land. The article is written in his best style, before he had acquired a controversial habit, and shows the result of wide reading.

Round did not immediately follow up this article, but from the beginning of 1881 there is a continual flow from his pen of articles, reviews, letters and notes on historical, genealogical and political subjects to the London, Essex and Sussex press, and the antiquarian and historical magazines. Editors began to clamour for his readable and rather pungent articles. For some reason he sought anonymity at this time for his more important work. In May 1881, he issued anonymously and apparently privately a pamphlet called *The*

Coming Terror, which later he described as his first effort at political writing. It treats of the tendency of Socialism towards repression instead of freedom, and calls attention to the two great schools into which all politicians were being rapidly, though perhaps unconsciously, divided. The one school allowed the fullest freedom to the working of natural laws and was founded on non-interference, while the other aimed at checking and restricting the working of these laws and consequently was founded on repression.

Politics, however, were only side issues of his life's work ; and such controversies as ' the Hove rates,' ' Landlordism ' and ' the Congregational Union,' into which he had been drawn, gave place to a series of articles on the ' Domesday of Colchester ' in the *Antiquary*. In these he showed the important distinction between the *burgus* and *civitas* and that the latter included not only Colchester within the walls but a large urban district outside. These articles were followed by a small volume entitled *The History and Antiquities of Colchester Castle*, published anonymously in 1882, which evoked a good deal of local criticism. The denial of the long cherished legends of a Roman or Saxon origin for the castle, the general discarding of Camden's theories and the criticism of those of the Rev. Henry Jenkins and Clements Markham led to a long controversy. In this, Round, in reply to one of his critics, said he was perfectly aware that Camden placed Camulodunum at Maldon ; he was also aware that Camden believed the earth to be stationary and the sun to circle round it, but he should not dream of ' labouring hard,' as it had been suggested, to disprove either the one proposition or the other.

Round's historical work drew him in the early eighties to the Public Record Office where he made many friends. The Public Record Office then bore little resemblance to its present state. The old Rolls House and Rolls Chapel were still standing, and the cobbled courtyard behind the eighteenth century residences facing Chancery Lane with the Virginia creeper covering their back walls, formed a picturesque piece of old London. The records had been brought together from repositories scattered over London, from the Tower, the Chapter House, Westminster, Carlton Ride, the State Paper Office and elsewhere. A few of the older members of the staff who had been drafted in with the records under their charge, formed rather an eccentric group of officials, some of them affecting the dress of an earlier generation. Of the younger members of the staff, Round associated chiefly with Walford D. Selby, then in charge of the Literary Search Room, and Hubert Hall, who was becoming recognised as an authority on the ancient practice of the Exchequer. The searchers in the Literary Search Room were largely genealogists : General Wrottesley, compiler of *Pedigrees from the Plea Rolls* ; James Greenstreet, editor of the *Lincolnshire Survey*; John A. C. Vincent, the genealogist, were habitual attendants ; whilst Dr. Furnivall, Dr. Stubbs, Bishop of Chester and later Bishop of Oxford, Father Gasquet, Charles Gross, Father Stevenson and Prof. Maitland, among many others, made occasional searches for historical purposes. The Legal Search Room was frequented by record agents who prepared the ancient evidence in such legal cases as it was required. They were successors to the officials who at one time were allowed to undertake this work. Stuart Moore, formerly assistant to Sir Thomas Hardy, who practised as a record agent before he was appointed deputy-keeper, became famous for his book on the *History of the Foreshore*, and went to the bar late in life, creating for himself an excellent practice in foreshore and fishery disputes. R. E. G. Kirk, his partner, had been assistant to Mr. Brewer, editor of the *Letters and Papers, Henry VIII* ; Henry Hewlett, keeper of the Land Revenue Records, who undertook searches for the Crown, while his more famous son, Maurice, practised in partnership with his cousin, W. O. Hewlett, author of a work on Peerage Law and later a master in chancery. Maurice Hewlett afterwards succeeded his father but abandoned record searching for poetry and fiction. My partner and brother-in-law, W. J. Hardy, was son of Sir William Hardy and nephew of Sir Thomas Hardy, both deputy-keepers. Other searchers also favoured this room, such as General 'Plantagenet' Harrison of the Peruvian army, a giant, wearing a cowboy hat, who claimed against many impediments to be Earl of Lancaster, and two strange Welsh gentlemen who periodically retired to worship on the Welsh mountains and returned in unsavoury sheepskins.

Into this family party Round entered as an historical and genealogical searcher and a pioneer in a new school of historical genealogy. The prosperity of trade at this time brought much work to the Record Office, claims to mineral and other rights were worth disputing and peerage claims were frequently made. It was with regard to the latter that I first came into touch with Round. Further, it was a period of activity in the study of records and Round threw himself with his accustomed enthusiasm into the various enterprises which were then started. Mr. (later Sir) Henry Maxwell Lyte, who succeeded Sir William Hardy as deputy-keeper in 1886, brought about many long delayed developments in the administration of the Record Office. Besides the rebuilding of a great part of the office which he induced the Treasury to undertake, he introduced more scholarly methods in making the records available to students, and his name will always be associated with the systematic calendaring of the documents under his charge. The energies of the previous deputy-keepers had been absorbed by the sortation and arrangement of the records, but now the officials who had come from the scattered repositories were fast retiring and with them passed the traditions of other days and other conditions. The changes penetrated into the search rooms, the eccentricities were dying off and retiring, and historical students with broader views and lady searchers (previously almost unknown) were taking their places.

Besides the greater facilities for searching at the Public Record Office, numerous record societies were springing up.

Round took a special interest in the Pipe Rolls Society, for printing the early rolls of the Exchequer, which was started in 1884, mainly by Selby and Greenstreet. He was for many years one of the auditors of the Society and in 1888 edited for it a volume of early charters ; in 1913 the ' Rotuli de Dominabus,' and from 1904 to 1915 he wrote an introduction to each of the Pipe Rolls printed. He was on the council of the Archaeological Congress and did much to establish the separate committees on Earthworks, Parish Registers and Place Names. He helped also on the Index Library which developed into the British Record Society ; the Selden Society for printing documents illustrative of the history of English law, and the Canterbury and York Society for printing episcopal registers.

From 25th to 29th October, 1886, the commemoration of the eight hundredth anniversary of the completion of the Domesday Survey was held under the auspices of the Royal Historical Society. Round, who represented the Essex Archaeological Society, took a prominent part in its organisation and prepared three papers for it, namely, ' Danegeld and the Finance of Domesday,' ' Notes on Domesday measures of land ' and ' Early references to Domesday.' Owing to the lack of time, only the first of these was actually read and discussed. He, however, established a reputation as one of our foremost students of the Domesday Survey at this meeting, his papers being the most important of those printed in its proceedings.

Besides his work for these record societies and meetings, Round was writing articles for most of the historical and genealogical magazines. A friendship with Joseph Foster was started in 1881 over the royal descent that Round claimed through his grandmother, which was entered in Foster's *Royal Lineage of our Noble and Gentle Families*. Foster stayed at Brighton and found Round's genealogical knowledge of incalculable assistance for the Peerage on which he was then at work. Round subsequently became a regular contributor to the *Collectanea Genealogica et*

Heraldica, edited by Foster, and although they had serious differences over the Roll of Baronets, which will be referred to later, a friendly correspondence was maintained until Foster's death in 1905. He was also a constant contributor to the *Genealogist*, to the editorship of which Walford D. Selby had succeeded Dr. Marshall, and to the *Antiquary*, edited by Edward Walford and later by H. B. Wheatley. Articles, reviews and notes from him also appeared in most issues of the *Athenaeum*, the *Academy* and the *St. James' Gazette*, then under the editorship of Frederick Greenwood and later of Sir Sydney Low.

These somewhat concentrated activities, together with the constant care of his invalid father, were a severe tax on Round's nervous and delicate constitution and he was frequently laid up with attacks of nervous prostration. Apparently the numerous and lengthy controversies upon which he entered at this time were not so exhausting to him as they might have proved to others, they even acted as a tonic and were looked upon as a pastime. ' I have to let off steam occasionally,' he wrote at a later date, ' and even waltzing on (Reginald) Sharpe and (W. W.) Skeat and polking on Gardiner and Firth is insufficient.' He had complete confidence in himself and his own judgment, and consequently spoke with assurance. As we look back we see that many of his points of controversy were trivial and perhaps not worth the time and trouble that their corrections involved. A friend once remarked that if he would cease killing flies, what valuable work he would do. Nevertheless his destructive criticisms have usually left us a constructive theory, or failing that, are suggestive of a new line of investigation. It will be impossible to refer in detail to all the controversies which arose about this time. Those relating to Colchester have been already mentioned, others with W. A. Lindsay on the translation of ' dux ' in Anglo-Saxon charters (1884); with E. C. Waters about the date of the Lindsay Survey (1885); with J. Cordy Jeaffreson on the Leicester records (1886); with H. B. Wheatley on

' Londinium ' (1887) ; with the Rev. W. Loftie on the first mayor of London (1887) ; with O. C. Pell on the Domesday hide (1888) ; and with R. E. G. Kirk on the Countess Lucy (1888), are only instances of many of a like kind. The two outstanding controversies, namely, those on the accuracy of the works of Prof. Freeman and Dr. Hubert Hall, acrimonious as they both were, stimulated his investigations into matters that have added much to our historical knowledge and so cannot be passed over.

Round, like other students, had been greatly attracted by the wide scope and apparent erudition of Prof. Freeman's *Norman Conquest*. In his article on the ' Domesday of Colchester,' printed in the *Antiquary*, he expressed the view that ' we are fortunate in possessing such a guide for our labours as the invaluable *Norman Conquest*, perhaps the noblest monument of modern historical literature.' Beyond some minor criticisms in historical articles he made no general attack until Freeman published his pamphlet on *The Nature and Origin of the House of Lords*, just after his appointment as professor of Modern History in 1884. The unfortunate habit which Freeman had of colouring his historical work with his political views, was particularly apparent in this book. Round was writing a series of articles in the *Antiquary*, on the House of Lords, and in one of them which appeared in April 1885, he called attention to the gross partiality displayed in Freeman's work. This was followed by a letter in the *St. James' Gazette* of 24th June of a more scathing nature. In it he accuses Freeman of having ' ingeniously and unscrupulously perverted both the actions and motives of the Lords ' over their attitude towards the admission of Lord Wensleydale into the House as a life peer. ' If Freeman's charges were true,' he adds, ' they could only be described as indecent and could only ' have been employed with the deliberate object of inflaming the passions of the populace.' The next attack was in the June number of the *Antiquarian Magazine and Bibliographer*, where he argues with considerable force that Freeman was wrong in attributing the building of Colchester Castle to Eudo Dapifer and shows fairly clearly that it must have been the work of the Conqueror.

His aunt, Miss Smith, obtained an introduction for him to the editor of the *National Review* through Lord Lytton, who wrote on 25th August that he had asked the editor ' to make a ring for the fight between Mr. Round and Freeman who will I hope be well punished by your nephew, for he is a pretentious fellow and a bad writer, though I suppose strong on his own special ground.' But the editor thought the time had gone by for a criticism on Freeman's book on the House of Lords.

The attack was followed up by a very cleverly worked out article in the *Antiquary* for August showing that Freeman's account of the attack on Dover by Count Eustace of Boulogne in 1067, was based on an erroneous translation of the word 'oppidum' used by Ordericus, which, as Round showed, referred to the castle and not to the town, a point which vitiated the whole story as given by Freeman. To Round's intense disappointment, Freeman made no reply to these attacks. ' I do wish Freeman would reply in the *Times* . . . but they say he is fairly afraid of me now,' he wrote at this time. Mr. Reginald Lane Poole gave an answer regarding the Dover incident, but admitted the error which he said had been corrected in a subsequent edition of the *Norman Conquest*. At the end of the year and during 1886 Round continued the attack in a series of letters to the *Antiquary* and the *Antiquarian Magazine*, in which fresh errors were pointed out. It was useless, however, to continue an attack to which there was no defence, and so for a time it ceased. Freeman must have had some sense of humour, for in the midst of the assault, Round was approached to write the history of Colchester for the Historic Towns Series of which Freeman was editor. The proposal was indignantly declined.

A fresh controversy at once engaged Round's attention. In 1886 he published a little book called the *Early Life of*

Anne Boleyn. In it there was an attack upon the late Mr. Brewer, editor of the *Letters and Papers, Henry VIII,* published by the Record Office, and on James Gairdner his collaborator. Round claimed that there had been a confusion in the ages and consequently in the lives of the two sisters, Anne and Mary Boleyn, and in the descent of the Boleyn estates. Gairdner, the most amiable of men, at once assumed responsibility for his dead colleague, and admitted in the *Athenaeum* of 20th March, 1886, that it would be childish to complain of observations which were on the whole perfectly just. The mistakes, he confessed, he had 'too readily followed both in editing Brewer's *Reign of Henry VIII* and in an article in the *Dictionary of National Biography* on Anne Boleyn.' He only ventured to plead in mitigation of Mr. Round's censure—'not for myself who am likely to go on blundering yet for some years, but of Mr. Brewer who can err no more—that though, as he says, our best criticism may be inferior to that of the Germans in accuracy, the extent and width of research should also be taken into account.'

Between the times occupied by these controversies and a very full year of literary work, Round took a part in the political turmoil consequent on the two elections of 1886. In the campaigns previous to both of these elections he canvassed the Harwich division of Essex on behalf of his cousin, James Round, the Conservative candidate. Throughout November 1885 and in February 1886 and again in July following after Mr. Gladstone's defeat on the Irish question, he organised and spoke at meetings at Colchester and throughout the constituency. He was a keen fighter and his speeches were always good and telling, though frequently rather over the heads of his audience. His delivery, however, was nervous and his speech too quick. In the former campaign he spoke mostly against the disestablishment and disendowment of the Church, and in the latter the main purport of his speeches was in favour of the maintenance of the Empire. 'For my part,' he said, 'I believe from the bottom of my soul that England has a mission upon earth, and that her mission is to fill in these latter days, the part which Rome and her Empire filled in the ancient world . . . yes, her mission was to rule the nations and to spread throughout the world the reign of peace, of order and of law.' [2]

Besides his political work in Essex, Round was taking a keen interest in Essex history. In 1884 he gave a lecture at the Colchester Town Hall on the Battle of Colchester, in aid of the Essex and Colchester Hospital. About this time he also began to write papers for the Essex Archaeological Society and stimulated others to undertake useful work for the Society. In 1886 he printed for private circulation an account of St. Helen's Chapel, Colchester, which his cousin, Mr. Douglas Round, had purchased. At Brighton he formed a friendship with Halliwell Phillipps whom he often visited at Hollingbury Copse and helped with his History of the Drama.

In May 1887, his father died after a long and distressing illness. Round had been a devoted son and his father's death was a great shock to his nervous temperament. ' One consolation, however, you must have,' wrote his friend, Sir George Douglas, ' the greatest in a case like this, the recollection of what I had so often noticed, so often heard alluded to by friends of us both, your great care and perfect conduct to your father.' After his father's death, Round let his house at Brighton and went to live in furnished rooms at 31 Alfred Place West, South Kensington.

From this date he travelled abroad almost every year. During the winter of 1890-91 he took an extended tour to the East, visiting Egypt, India and Burma, going up the Irrawaddy as far as Bhamo towards the Chinese frontier, and spending a fortnight in King Thebaw's palace at Mandalay. His visits abroad, however, at this time were usually to France for the purpose of collating and transcribing charters for his *Calendar of Documents preserved in France*,

[2] *Essex Standard*, 17th July, 1886.

which he edited as one of the Public Record Office Calendars. This work which is invaluable for the eleventh and twelfth century history of this country, was not authorised by the Treasury until 1894, but it is clear he was engaged on a calendar of this nature some time before that date. He visited at his own expense, all the principal French repositories of records and got into touch with many of the continental historians such as Bémont of the *Revue Historique* and Liebermann. He encouraged, if he did not initiate, a scheme for an Anglo-Norman Record Society, with a view to printing the chartularies of some of the French monasteries that had cells and possessions in England. W. A. Lindsay, late Norroy king-of-arms, strongly supported the proposal, and a meeting was held at Norfolk House to inaugurate the society, but nothing apparently materialised.

Round's visit to the East seems to have improved his health and he returned to London to carry on his literary work with renewed energy. Besides his regular contributions to the *St. James' Gazette* and other newspapers and magazines, he was working on his most consecutive piece of history, *Geoffrey de Mandeville : A Study of the Anarchy*, which was published in 1892. He also took an active part in the election of that year on behalf of his cousin, James Round, the sitting member for the Harwich division of the county of Essex. He presided and spoke at a dinner of the West Bergholt Conservative Association and canvassed the constituency, speaking at many meetings. His work in the county was rewarded by Lord Rayleigh, the Lord Lieutenant, appointing him a deputy-lieutenant on 2nd December in this year.

With *Geoffrey de Mandeville* off his hands he made a fresh attack on Freeman's *Norman Conquest*. Freeman had died in Spain on 16th May, 1892, and in the *Quarterly Review* of July following, appeared a criticism of his work, which Round had written long before but the publication had been delayed. The controversy that followed is said to have been the fiercest of this generation.

The principal point in dispute was the conduct of the Battle of Hastings. Firstly he challenged the name of Senlac which Freeman had given to the battle, and then he repudiated the theory of the ' palisade ' which Freeman stated was adopted by Harold ; at the same time many minor errors were indicated. A number of Freeman's followers at Oxford, principal among whom were Mr. T. A. Archer and Mr. (now Sir Charles) Oman, resented the attack upon their late chief and put up a strong defence, but the tone of this second controversy as to Freeman's accuracy, was more conciliatory than the earlier attack. The controversy was carried on in the *Quarterly Review*, the *Contemporary Review*, the *English Historical Review*, the *National Review*, the *Academy*, the *Athenaeum* and other magazines. It lasted nearly six years, and on the main points Round may be said to have been victorious.[3]

In 1895, in the midst of the Freeman controversy, Round published *Feudal England : Historical Studies in the Eleventh and Twelfth Centuries.* The first part of this work deals with the Domesday Book and the kindred surveys and brings out his great discoveries of the five-hide and six-carucate units of assessment. The second part largely goes over the ground of the Freeman controversy and gives various other essays. He was urged to publish this volume by Prof. Maitland who was much impressed by his papers for the Domesday Commemoration, printed in *Domesday Studies.* Prof. Maitland wrote to him in 1892, ' As you say, there is not much encouragement for work on Domesday, but I cannot help thinking that a book by you would have a very fair sale—not of course the sale of a fourth-rate novel, but still enough to cover expenses.' Maitland, himself, had been working on Domesday but

---

[3] A Bibliography of the whole controversy will be found as an appendix to a paper on ' The Battle of Hastings,' by Round, in the *Sussex Archaeological Society's Collections*, vol. xlii. There was a further controversy between Round and Dr. W. R. W. Stephens, Dean of Winchester, in the *Athenaeum* of 25th May, 1st, 15th, 29th June, 6th July, 1895.

'did not wish to collide with Round,' he wrote to Dr. Poole. He was, however, persuaded to give light to his studies in 1896 under the title of *Domesday Book and Beyond*,[4] a truly monumental work, much appreciated by Round and all historical students.

Round's most intimate friend at this time amongst the officials at the Record Office was Walford D. Selby. In 1885 Selby was authorised to edit the 'Red Book of the Exchequer,' for the Master of the Rolls Series, a work in which Round was profoundly interested. Mr. Hubert Hall had for some time contemplated editing the 'Dialogus de Scaccario,' which Sir William Hardy, then deputy-keeper, and others thought should form a part of the 'Red Book.' 'De Aula,' the name by which Selby and Round referred to Hall, was, as they said, ready to relinquish this part of the work and 'take a back seat.' The point was not settled at the time of Selby's death in 1889, but the 'Dialogus' was left to be edited at a later date with great scholarly care by three other officials of the Record Office. On the death of Selby, Hall urged Round to apply for the editorship of the Red Book, but he hesitated, and so Hall himself applied and afterwards induced Round to make an application also. A difficulty seems to have arisen about giving the work outside the Office, but the matter was eventually compromised in the early part of 1890 by the Treasury appointing Round and Hall as joint editors.

It is impossible to pass over the long and embittered controversy that ensued over this subject, as it coloured the after years of both parties. With an opponent like Freeman, the disputants would probably be equal, but between men of such opposite dispositions as Round and Hall it was a very different matter. As early as June 1890 there were differences of opinion about the accuracy of Alexander de Swereford, the mediaeval compiler of part of the 'Red Book,' and in August Round resigned the editorship ostensibly on account of health. He gave a hint, however, to the officials

[4] H. A. L. Fisher, *F. W. Maitland*, p. 86.

at the Record Office that he had not confidence in the methods of his collaborator. A second editor to take his place was talked of, but Hall opposed the suggestion and nothing was done. Proofs of the volumes were sent to Round, but, as he afterwards said, he felt no obligation to correct anything beyond what he suspected, particularly as he was much abroad at the time.

After many delays the volumes were published in April 1897, although dated 1896. A little before their publication there appeared a long anonymous review of Round's books, *Geoffrey de Mandeville* and *Feudal England*, in the *Quarterly Review* for July 1896. The style and matter gave no doubt as to the authorship of the article, and Hall admits that he wrote it. The article strongly criticised Round's views of Alexander de Swereford, which Round resented. He expressed this annoyance to Prof. Maitland, who, foreseeing trouble, wrote on 7th September that although he agreed that the reviewer had a weak spot in his love for Swereford, yet it could do no harm to anyone. Further, he wrote, there were few people who were 'such right good sorts' as the reviewer, and he hoped Round would let the matter rest. The *Quarterly Review* article produced a correspondence in the *Athenaeum* in which Round accused Hall of having charged him with misstatement of facts and demanded an apology. At this point the correspondence was stopped by the editor. This was followed by articles by Round, attacking Hall's preface to the ' Red Book,' in the *Genealogist* and the *Genealogical Magazine*[5] and an adverse criticism in the *Athenaeum*. A review by Prof. Tout in the *English Historical Review* of January 1898 acknowledged the difficulties of the work and pointed out some of its failings. Here the matter rested for a time, as editors were unwilling to open their doors further to what was likely to be a lengthy and acrimonious controversy. As a

[5] See ' The Surrender of the Isle of Wight ' in the *Genealogical Magazine* for May 1897, vol. i, p. 3, and correspondence on pp. 112, 185, 224.

consequence, in the summer of 1898, Round published for private circulation, a little book entitled *Studies on the Red Book of the Exchequer*. This was a bitter attack upon Hall and a merciless criticism of his work. It also attacked Prof. Tout for his review of Hall's work.

Up to this point Hall had remained silent. As a civil servant he was under the disadvantage of having to refrain from public controversy on his official work, but a little later in the year he issued a privately printed reply. Although he argued his view of the credibility of Alexander de Swereford, he mainly harped on the point that ' his adversary was one who had been, so to speak, *de familia nostra*, a colleague, a collaborator, and a once intimate friend.' Mr. Poole was appealed to by both parties for space in the *English Historical Review*, which he could not see his way to grant. He himself, however, gave a review of the two privately printed books. He kept his criticism to the points of error of which Round accused Hall, and came to the conclusion that Prof. Tout had ' pronounced a favourable judgment to which it (the Red Book) was not entitled,' and that Round had proved his case. Thereupon Hall printed an open letter to Dr. S. R. Gardiner, then one of the editors of the *English Historical Review*, deprecating the unfairness of Mr. Poole's conclusions, about which he felt very bitterly. Finally, Round printed another pamphlet giving a résumé of the controversy and maintaining that, as a specialist on the subject, he felt it a public duty to publish the criticisms he had made in order to save historical students from endless error.

Here the matter ended as far as concerned Hall, who from this time abandoned mediaeval history. Round continued for many years to revert to the subject. Prof. Maitland, to whom Round sent a copy of his little book on the *Studies on the Red Book of the Exchequer*, voiced the opinion of many in a letter of thanks, dated 31st August, 1898 : ' My first lucid interval,' he wrote, ' shall be given to the Red Book. I shall learn much, though I expect to feel in my proper person some of the blows that you inflict upon H. H. I fear that what I shall read will be all too true, and yet of the said H. H. I am fond.'

Before the disputes with Hall were completed Round threw himself into the political and religious controversies of the end of the last century. He was a strong protectionist and among his regular contributions to the *St James' Gazette* was a signed article on the ' Collapse of Cobdenism ' (7th Aug., 1894). In this article, which caused some sensation, he pointed out how free trade was leading to war and to sweating, for the buying in the cheapest market was the root of the sweating system and the ruin of agriculture. The article elicited refutations of his contentions in the *Daily Chronicle* (8th Aug.) and in the *Spectator* (11th, 12th Aug., 1st Sept.). It was followed by another article in the *St. James' Gazette* (16th Aug.) called ' the Legacy of Cobden,' and correspondence in the same paper and the *Essex County Standard* through September.

The religious controversy of the time received greater attention from Round. Although there is a strong Protestant bias throughout his numerous essays on this subject, yet, like his friend, Prof. Maitland,[6] his interest lay not in religious doctrines but in historical accuracy. ' I don't care which conclusion proves to be the right one, but I do care most earnestly for the truth,' he wrote to me at a little later date. Some of his critics called in question his frequent references to his old tutor, Stubbs, then Bishop of Oxford. On 13th May, 1896, the Bishop wrote to him, ' I am amused with what you tell me of the view the critics have taken of your kind regard for me. I almost wonder that they do not charge you with sacerdotalism. No doubt they would if they knew you had been looking up Martin *v.* Mackonachie. Seriously these ritual matters are terribly convincing of the weakness of human nature and of the perversity with which good men are tempted to hinder their own good work.'

[6] H. A. L. Fisher, *F. W. Maitland*, p. 100.

As in most of Round's work, the articles upon which he now became engrossed are based on the criticism of current literature. In this case the selected works were *The Introduction to the History of the Church of England* by H. O. Wakeman and *The Church and Her Story* and *A Popular Story of the Church of England*, both by G. H. F. Nye, and articles by Gladstone and George W. E. Russell, all high churchmen. The points against which Round contended were the continuity of the mass in the communion service of the Church of England, and the use of the term altar as the correlation of the mass. The controversy was continued throughout 1897 and 1898 in *The Nineteenth Century* and *Contemporary Review*. (*See* Bibliography.) In the following year an article by Round in the latter, entitled 'As Established by Law,' attacked Sir George Arthur, Canon Gore, later Bishop of Oxford, and the English Church Union, for their denial of the right of the Crown or Parliament to determine the doctrine, discipline and ceremonial of the Church of England. The bitter hostility which pervades these articles, as his opponents stated, detracted from their value, for, whether agreeing or not with the conclusions arrived at, the arguments are supported by so much authority that they must be consulted by all who study the subject. The articles attracted a good deal of attention not only in the English Church papers but also in the Roman Catholic press. The *Weekly Register* (8th May, 1897) greeted his arguments as to the mass, saying that ' Mr. Round makes very evident that of doctrinal continuity there is none ' in the English Church.

Round contemplated editing a volume of essays on the ' True Theory of the Reformation and its antecedents ' with the view probably of reprinting the substance of these articles. He tried to organize a team of workers and asked Prof. Maitland and Prof. Tout to undertake sections. Both of them, however, were too busy, and so the scheme fell through. In the summer of 1899 he wrote that some ' wicked publishers ' were bent on decoying him from

' Domesday ' to the ' Reformation ' as he put it, but, he added, ' personally I prefer family history.' To genealogy and family history he now devoted his attention to the abandonment of church history. He was working at this time on his *Studies in Peerage and Family History*, which came out in 1901 and was the first of his books on purely genealogical subjects.

Round, about this period, began his connexion with the Home Office, which later developed into more intimate relations with the Treasury Solicitor's Department. The question of the rights of the Baronetage had for some time been in a state of confusion and the matter was brought to a head in 1897 by an order for the precedence of the children of legal life-peers above baronets, which the baronets resented. For a long time people to the number, it was estimated, of no less than fifty, had been wrongfully assuming the title of baronet, and there seemed to be no remedy. The inconvenience of this state of affairs was emphasised owing to an old undertaking by the Crown to bestow the honour of knighthood upon the eldest sons of baronets of ancient creation, and the Crown had knighted the eldest son of a man who had assumed the dignity of a baronet without warrant. Joseph Foster, the genealogist, wrote to the *Morning Post* suggesting the formation of a committee to vindicate the rights of baronets, and obtained the adherence of a good many of the order. In the meantime Sir Lambton Loraine, Sir Charles Rich and Capt. Fletcher-Vane, heir to Sir Henry Fletcher-Vane, formed a Baronets' Protection Society. The latter association obtained Round's help towards its organisation and possibly towards the union of the two bodies. It was not long before Round found a weak point in his opponents' programme. One of its demands was that the Royal Warrant of 3rd December, 1783, should be revised in so far as it ordained that each baronet on succeeding to his title should establish his descent from his last recorded ancestor. Round, however, discovered that the Royal Warrant in question contained no such provision. This ' bomb shell,' as he called it, and his propaganda in the press at the end of 1897 destroyed Foster's society. The Provisional Committee of the Baronetage was formed, which developed in 1898 into the Honourable Society of the Baronetage, and later into the Standing Council of the Baronetage. Matters moved slowly, but in 1905 a departmental committee was appointed to report upon what steps should be taken to safeguard the status of baronets, with the Earl of Pembroke as chairman. Round gave evidence before this committee, strongly urging for a close scrutiny of the right to the title in every case, but the committee leaned towards leniency, much to his disappointment. The committee recommended that an official roll of baronets should be kept at the Home Office. To the preparation of this roll Round devoted much time. Doubtful cases were submitted to him and he gave an immense amount of assistance which is acknowledged in the report accompanying the first list of baronets, issued in 1913. He strenuously opposed the inclusion of many who desired to be entered on the roll, pointing out the weakness of their claims, particularly in the case of some Scottish claimants, but too careful a scrutiny of their titles was not thought desirable.

Round took a leading part in launching the enterprise for a uniform series of county histories which later, by command of Queen Victoria, took the name of the ' Victoria History of the Counties of England.' He gave the work his sane guidance and help from its beginning in the early part of 1899 to the time of his death. In drawing up the prospectus of the scheme he gave considerable assistance, which reminded him, he said, that a relative once cruelly observed that he would have made an admirable advertising agent. He attracted what sympathy he could to the History from Oxford and other centres of learning, and gave a standard of work for the articles on the Domesday Survey throughout the series. For the next two years he did little else but work for the ' Victoria County History.' With others he found it irksome to complete his articles to a given date, but unlike them he always admitted the necessity of keeping to time in a work of the kind. 'You must not blame yourself for my being overworked,' he wrote to H. A. Doubleday, one of the editors of the History, 'You have simply to do with a scrupulous and very anxious contributor who worries himself if he has not time for exhaustive research in his theme, and still more if he is behindhand. When I was at Balliol I was the only man whom Jowett had to warn against overwork and whom he had to send away for week-end holidays forbidden to all others. . . . I still hope (with the help of strychnine and quinine) to let you have the paper by the end of the week.' He was interested in the extension of the History to Scotland and Wales and was in touch with the Duke of Argyll and Sir Herbert Maxwell with regard to the History of the former country, but nothing further was done. A committee was formed for the History of Wales, of which the late Lord Kenyon was chairman, but the inability to carry the work beyond England resulted in the appointment of the Royal Commissions on Ancient and Historical Monuments for England, Scotland and Wales.

The death of Queen Victoria on 22nd January, 1901, brought Round's historical knowledge prominently into view. In the *Contemporary Review* for April he had an article on the ' King's Protestant Declaration,' in which he traced the history of the Declaration, from its institution under the Bill of Rights (1689). He repeated his arguments on the doctrine of the mass and ended with an appeal for the maintenance of the Declaration ' not for the purpose of insulting the Roman Catholic religion but for that of pre-serving, against the present avowed attacks on it from within, the historic and protestant position of the Church of England.' This article was reprinted with additions by the Church Association and sold in great numbers.

The accession of King Edward brought into existence the Court of Claims for coronation services, and the cases for the decision of this court necessitated a considerable amount of historical research. The particular claim most difficult to decide was that to the office of Lord Great Chamberlain, which was referred by King Edward to the Committee for Privileges of the House of Lords. Round's unique knowledge of the peerage was apparently brought to the notice of the Treasury Solicitor, Lord Desart, by the Duke of Argyll. His assistance in this complicated case was at once requested. The claimants in the case were the Earl of Ancaster, the Duke of Atholl, the Marquess of Cholmondeley and Earl Carrington, who claimed to represent co-heiresses of the Veres, Earls of Oxford. The question involved raised points of considerable interest and importance regarding the great offices of state, and Round gave a series of most learned and valuable memoranda, the titles of which are set out in the bibliography of his works. On 30th June, 1901, he wrote to the Duke of Argyll,[7] ' that the case for the Crown in the matter of the Great Chamberlain has grown still stronger in my hands and has fully justified my original suggestion that the Crown should claim the office. I am handing in to-morrow a further memorandum showing that the title of all its holders since the latter part of the sixteenth century originated in wrongful usurpation and that, as in the cases given in my recent *Peerage Studies*, the Crown, as I had always suspected, was simply imposed upon. I have also drawn the attention of the law officers to an opinion of their predecessors in 1821, the existence of which appears to have been unknown, and in which, the co-heirs, then as now, being unable to agree upon a deputy, they advised His Majesty King George IV that he was entitled to select a person himself to officiate at his coronation.'

Round attended the Court of Claims and the Committee for Privileges in the beginning of 1902, an exhausting matter for those in the best of health. After one of these attendances he wrote, ' I reached home very bad and had to go to bed and was too ill to get up this morning. No one

[7] Draft of letter among Dr. Round's papers.

realises how delicate I am, as I always have been.' The Committee for Privileges was strongly influenced by his views on the Lord Great Chamberlain case. It was decided that the rights of the co-heiresses had been inherited by the Earl of Ancaster, the Marquess of Cholmondeley and Earl Carrington, in whom the selection of a deputy vested, subject to the King's approval, and in the event of want of agreement among all the co-heirs, the King should appoint whom he would.

His association with the law officers of the Crown in this and subsequent occasions placed Round in a somewhat anomalous position. Before the hearing of the case of the Lord Great Chamberlain, he raised the question as to the method to be adopted to acknowledge his help, whether by being called as a witness for the Crown or by an acknow-ledgment before the committee. Lord Desart urged him to accept a fee, but he declined, saying, that 'when he originally approached the Treasury Solicitor's Department, it was solely with a view of bringing to the knowledge of the Crown certain material facts, which might otherwise have been overlooked, and with no idea of rendering other than voluntary service.' His friend, George Edward Cokayne, Clarenceux king-of-arms, pressed him to ask the Duke of Norfolk to make him a herald extraordinary. He answered, 'I reply, No, I will take nothing but a Deputy-Kingship, *pro hac vice.*'

Shortly after the death of his aunt, Miss Smith, in July 1903, under whose will he benefited, Round returned to 15 Brunswick Terrace, Brighton. On 10th September he wrote that he was looking forward to settle down there— 'I can see what a boon it will be to have my working books handy round me. At present the problem of finding room for them is even here insoluble. On the whole I am very hopeful at present as to my move. The flood of light and air about me and proper food, making me, I think, better than in town, certainly up to now in any case.' The improvement in health, however, to which he looked forward did not come. The air of Brighton never agreed with him. He was ill throughout the winter of 1903-4 and on 4th February he wrote that he had been already condemned to spend all next winter abroad. His London doctor protested that he must give up Brighton and return to live in town, 'a nice look-out just when I have had all the expense and trouble of settling in here.' His friends, also, urged him either to return to London or to go to his house at West Bergholt, near Colchester, but he would not listen to their advice. With his genealogical leanings he clung to the associations of the Brighton house. It was to him the home of his grandfather and his father, and his own birthplace ; there he had arranged his library, his family portraits, his old china and other treasures. Those who visited him at this time may perhaps recollect how after an abstruse and exhausting discussion in his somewhat dreary library, he would suddenly suggest luncheon or tea and proceed to slide down the baluster rail of the long flight of stairs to the ground floor, and with a boyish whoop, leap into the hall.

With his residence at Brighton, his work became more restricted, the number of articles for the press and magazines became fewer but his time was fully occupied on work for the *Victoria History of the Counties of England*, the *Complete Peerage* and the various peerage cases and disputed claims for admission to the Roll of Baronets. Each year until the time of the war he spent some part of the winter or spring abroad, in France, Italy or Switzerland, which braced up his nervous system for the summer and early autumn. When his health permitted, he often visited London until his old lodgings in Kensington were given up in 1907, when his visits became less frequent and only for the day.

It was a great satisfaction to him and his friends that the University of Edinburgh granted him the honorary degree of LL.D. in February 1905. It was the only honorary academic recognition conferred upon him. He later declined the fellowship of the British Academy and would not allow his name to be brought forward for fellowship of the Society of Antiquaries. In 1909, Sir Alfred Scott Gatty tried to obtain for him a companionship of the Bath, but he was then on the wrong side of politics and the appeal was unsuccessful. At the end of the year Round was asked to deliver the Ford Lectures at Oxford for 1910-11 but he had to decline on account of ill health. His health, however, seems to have improved in 1907 when he took part in the Sussex Amateur Art Society's Exhibition at Brighton and was responsible for its catalogue. In the following year he was instrumental in getting Princess Louise to open the new buildings of the Essex County Hospital at Colchester and was able to take part in the ceremony. He was ailing again in 1910 and tried a treatment of Swedish exercises without much result. The waters at Harrogate did him no good in the following year.

Notwithstanding his continued ill-health it is marvellous the amount of work he was able to accomplish. He was deeply occupied with peerage cases and articles, but yet in 1910 he found time to publish his *Peerage and Pedigree* : *Studies in Peerage Law and Family History* in two volumes. These contained a series of essays, the most important being styled ' The Muddle of the Law,' which dealt with the long-felt confusion in peerage law. These volumes were followed in the next year by *The King's Serjeants and Officers of State with their Coronation Services*, which is the last book he published.

It was at this time that Sir Henry Maxwell Lyte contemplated re-editing the *Testa de Nevill*, published by the Record Commission in 1807, a piece of work which Round had long urged. In answer to a letter from Sir Henry on the subject, he wrote on 28th October, 1910, 'With regard to the *Testa* on which I have worked for many years, the two things needed for its successful editing are (1) a thorough grasp of our feudal system, (2) an exceptional knowledge of our feudal genealogy. Without the latter it is impossible to trace the devolution of baronies and fees, their fissure and their accretion. The problem is further complicated by grants *in maritagio*, which upset all calculations. Good reading is of course essential but the text is so corrupt and the minims so ambiguous that it is not sufficient.' He gave occasional help in the editing of this work until it was completed.

The number of peerage cases on which he was consulted by the Solicitor's Department of the Treasury was increasing and in 1911 both the Law officers of the Crown and Round himself agreed that some public recognition of his services should be made. He would like to have been made a peer that he might have had a seat on the Committee for Privileges, failing that to be a privy councillor. The former of course he could not expect, and with regard to the latter there were insuperable difficulties. The matter was delicate, as he only wanted a position which would regularise his work on peerage cases. He did not wish for an ordinary distinction which was suggested as an alternative, and was indignant at the idea of a reward for the cash value of his services rendered. ' There are many of us,' he wrote, ' who feel strongly on the present prostitution of honours, and we at least of the county families leave their purchase to *nouveaux riches*, by whom they are sought with clamour. . . .' It was difficult to arrange what he wanted, as the Attorney-General was official adviser to the Crown on all peerage cases. Although Sir John Simon, then Attorney-General, was sympathetic, he could not delegate his responsibilities. Eventually a form of acknowledgment was agreed upon and the following announcement was made in *The Times* of 30th January, 1914—' The Attorney-General, with the approval of His Majesty, has appointed Mr. John Horace Round, D.L., LL.D., to be Honorary Historical Adviser to the Crown in peerage cases.' With this he expressed himself satisfied.

Round took a leading part at the International Congress of Historical Studies held in London in April 1913. Many of his friends from France and Germany were present and he read two papers, ' Historical Genealogy ' and ' The

Garrison Theory of the Borough,' the former of which is printed for the first time in this volume.

The registration of the Smith-Carrington pedigree at the Heralds College caused Round considerable indignation at this time. He claimed that the pedigree was accepted without any proof of an affiliation in the sixteenth century. A long correspondence on the subject followed with the College of Arms.

Although he seldom went to London, the papers in peerage claims were submitted to him and he carefully followed the reports of them. On 18th May, 1914, he wrote to Mr. Geoffrey Ellis,[8] ' Strabolgi was allowed after all, partly because Cozens Hardy argued the case so admirably and partly because the Attorney wandered away from a line I had originally taken, and introduced a lot of weak matter, so that at the end of it all the Lords hardly knew what our contention was. Halsbury was boss and wished from the first to allow it. A curious point has arisen about Martin. After the House had actually passed the Resolution to be submitted to the King, I discovered that there was an attainder, which had never been reversed, and that there had not even been restitution of blood, so a formal Resolution of the House has now been passed, quashing the former one, and referring the matter back to the Committee for Privileges who will hear it on Wednesday, and will then try to finish St. John. After that we shall have to deal with Ferrers and Wharton, the latter of which will involve for me much work and trouble. All this means that my own book is once more postponed.'

The Treasury Solicitor was very anxious to receive Round's report on the Wharton case, which was postponed in order to give him time to write it. He took considerable trouble about the case and was much disappointed regarding his treatment over it. On 22nd February, 1916, he wrote, ' You will probably have seen that the Wharton case about which I spoke and wrote to you, has had a rapid and

[8] Taken from draft of letter among Dr. Round's papers.

to me, scandalous termination. There was absolutely no question that the barony was created by patent with limitation to heirs male of the body, and I spent enormous time and toil in working out the proof of this. Unfortunately I was too ill to meet the Attorney-General in consultation or to attend the hearing, and he and his junior being utterly new to peerage law, . . . seem to have practically thrown my report aside and offered no resistance to the claim. As the claimant has been summoned to the House at once in consequence of the result, the matter is by far the most serious with which I have had to deal.' In spite of the efforts of the Treasury ' to smooth him down,' he asked to be excused from acting as Adviser so long as the then Attorney-General remained in office. 'After such treatment,' he added, ' this was inevitable—all that the Treasury can plead is that by some oversight, the Attorney-General had not been told how great an authority I was ! '

With the war, historical work largely came to an end. Documents from the Record Office and British Museum were moved to the West of England away from the danger of air raids. The *Victoria County History* and the *Complete Peerage* fell into abeyance, but Round continued to correspond with Sir Henry Maxwell Lyte about his new edition of the *Testa de Nevill*, which emerged later as the *Book of Fees*. This was a relaxation to them both from the anxieties of the war. Round, however, became much worse in health in the autumn of 1914 and his medical advisers recommended an internal operation, which was performed at a nursing home at Brighton in March of the following year. He never fully recovered from the operation and became more or less a permanent invalid.

Like others he felt the strain of the war, but an added sorrow befel him at the end of 1916 by the death of his cousin, Mr. James Round, P.C. In his younger days Round spent much time with his cousin at Birch Hall, the family seat, and frequently helped him in his parliamentary candidature for the Harwich division of the county. He had a sincere

xlii

regard and affection for him and summed up his character in the obituary notice he wrote for the Transactions of the Essex Archaeological Society, in which he referred to his ' singularly unassuming nature, his entire devotion to duty and his unvarying kindness [which] endeared him to all his friends.'

Round continued to make reports on peerage cases and was called upon to assist the select committee of the House of Lords to whom the bill on the ' Titles, etc., held by Enemies ' was committed in 1917. He submitted some valuable observations based on historical research, for which the committee expressed their indebtedness in their report of 21st May of that year.

With the end of the war the number of peerage cases increased ; frequently the work was urgent and Round could not at once attend to it on account of his health. This became a cause of worry to him. Besides the peerage work, the Attorney-General proposed that he should prepare a memorandum on the constitutional aspect of the Reform of the House of Lords to assist the committee under the chairmanship of Lord Curzon, to which the Bill on the subject had been referred. With his declining health his medical advisers in the spring of 1921 recommended him to relinquish his work on peerage cases. He continued it, however, during the summer, but in the autumn he became too ill to attend even to correspondence, and on 22nd January, 1922, he definitely resigned his office of Historical Adviser to the Crown. On the following day Sir Gordon Hewart, then Attorney-General, wrote accepting his resignation with deep regret, adding, ' the services which you have rendered during so many years have been of highest importance, and looking to your pre-eminent authority in respect of the matter upon which you have been accustomed to advise, and to the learning and research which you have devoted to the examination of peerage cases, I cannot but feel that the loss of your assistance to the Crown is a very serious one ; much of the work you have done has, I fear, been accomplished under the grave disadvantage of continued ill-health, and in expressing as Attorney-General my high appreciation of your great services, I wish also to pay a tribute to the public spirit which has led you, throughout, to place them without remuneration at the disposal of the Crown, and disregarding all difficulties to continue to do so until this has become unfortunately no longer possible. I can only add the very cordial hope that relief from official work may result in such an improvement in your health as will enable you to turn again to those literary labours which must have suffered so much interruption.' Sir John Mellor, the Treasury Solicitor, also wrote in a like strain.

Although Round retired from the post of Historical Adviser, queries were sent to him from time to time, and he took a keen interest in the case of the Dukedom of Somerset to which his old college friend, Mr. Henry Sidney Seymour, was a claimant. It was thought that possibly some honour would have been offered him although it is quite likely he would have refused it. A friend wrote to him at the time, ' the greater honours (so called) to-day are political gifts, the smaller are hardly worth your notice and certainly would not be commensurate with all the voluntary labour you have done for the Crown.'

As his friend, Mr. Geoffrey Ellis, has pointed out, his evident feeling that he had not been sufficiently recognised did nothing to abate his interest in peerage work, so far as health allowed, in the remaining years of his life. Often one went down to see him at Brighton and for half-an-hour, or so long as his whipped energy would allow, all his stored knowledge came out to elucidate some knotty point. But in those days he seldom gave one a final conclusion. He felt, he said, it would not be fair. He could call on his memory and it never failed, but latterly he distrusted his own judgment. He was particularly interested in the abeyance alleged to exist in earldoms and particularly fierce against a certain *nouveau riche* who through marriage had, he said, fastened himself on to an ancient stock and wished for his progeny to appropriate in one line all the ancient co-heirships to long-forgotten historical titles. It was a joy to him that these claims were subsequently withdrawn, but he said more than once, even in his best days, that the whole question was very involved. If one admitted honours in fee, and allowed baronies in fee, the main distinction appeared to be that the abeyance of baronies had become an established rule by a process of legal interpretation on doubtful historical evidence. Historically, an earldom in fee had never been regarded as capable of becoming abeyant since the end of Plantagenet days, until Queen Victoria, without consulting the House of Lords, assumed and allowed an abeyance in the Earldom of Cromartie, created by herself. The Report of the Lords Committee on Abeyance, which recommended certain restrictions in the termination of abeyance in relation to future claims, he regarded as shutting the stable door after the horse had escaped ! To him all Peerage Law was history. He never believed in following a learned lawyer, however great—unless facts justified the conclusion. Hence his tilt, and a very successful one, at taking Coke at face value. Had he lived to read later cases he would have been overjoyed to note how much the Committee for Privileges went back to first principles, and demanded careful history to justify theories and conclusions.[9]

Round had had an almost lifelong connexion with the Essex Archaeological Society and on 17th May, 1916, he was elected its president. As it was understood he would be unable to attend the meetings, the Bishop of Barking undertook to act as his deputy. During the time of his presidentship which continued until 1921, he contributed many valuable papers to the transactions of the Society. He had been interested also since its foundation, in the Pipe Roll Society, which became dormant during the war. With the encouragement which he, Dr. William Farrer and Sir Henry Maxwell Lyte gave to Prof. and Mrs. Stenton, the

[9] For the substance of this paragraph I am indebted to Mr. Geoffrey Ellis.—W. P.

Society was resuscitated and brought up to its present state of efficiency.

Notwithstanding his ill-health Round did not lose his powers of controversy. In the *English Historical Review* for October 1918, he had an article entitled ' Barons and Peers,' in which he strongly disputed the conclusions of Mr. H. A. Doubleday, editor of the *Complete Peerage*, regarding the thorny questions of Abeyance and Barony by Writ.[10] In the same Review for January 1922, in an article on the ' Legend of Eudo Dapifer,' he made an equally violent attack on the late Mr. Walter Rye. For his research on these articles and all his other work, which hitherto he had always conducted himself, he had now to rely on the help of friends, chiefly the late R. C. Fowler of the Record Office, but occasionally Major D. Warrand and myself. Handicapped as he thus became, he was able to continue his contributions to the *English Historical Review* until 1923, but from this time his health gradually became worse and he was seldom able to leave his bedroom. He had two resident nurses whom he trained to find what books he wanted from his library. But his work was now almost wholly confined to writing papers for the Essex Archaeological Society of which, finished and unfinished, there were over sixty awaiting publication at the time of his death. It was a great blow to him when a few months before his death both his nurses left. ' I am in disgrace with everyone for my inability to do anything, I used to be so punctilious,' he wrote on 6th April, 1928.

During the last few years of his life he was a somewhat pathetic figure, his health, his nature and his pursuits made him a lonely man. He had few friends at Brighton and his health being so uncertain, friends from a distance were never sure of being able to see him. When well enough to see visitors, however, he gave them a hearty welcome and was delighted to discuss new historical schemes or the

---

[10] See *Complete Peerage*, vol. iv, appendix. Mr. Doubleday replied in a privately printed pamphlet.

progress of old schemes. One of the principal of the former was Prof. Allen Mawer's enterprise for a systematic study of the place-names of England, county by county. Round, who was a pioneer in this subject, had drawn up a report on the classification and study of place-names which was brought before the Archaeological Congress in 1899. In 1923 he was to have written a section on Feudal place-names in the introductory volume of the Place-Name Society, into which Prof. Mawer's scheme developed, but his health compelled him to relinquish this task. He continued to work up to a day or two of his death which occurred on 25th June, 1928.

Round had the advantage of a marvellous memory; he forgot nothing that he read and thought accurately and logically. In a critical review of his work in the *English Historical Review* for October 1928, Prof. Tait remarks that Round's mind was more critical than constructive. It is true that much of his work was based on criticism of the work of others, but his criticisms almost invariably reconstructed the problem under discussion from fresh evidence, or shed a new light upon the material already collected. Although many of his published criticisms are very bitter, yet it will be remembered by many that when he thought a work worthy of his attention, he would not spare himself in correcting and criticising it in a friendly spirit. His corrections, however, had to be adopted without argument, otherwise the luckless author would lay himself open to some of those flashes of caustic and cynical wit, which he directed against those who persisted in their errors. During the twenty-five years and more that I was associated with him over the *Victoria History of the Counties of England*, I found him an inspiring help and an unfailing support, never weary of giving sound advice in historical questions or on matters of business. His bitterness in controversy was largely the result of his health and upbringing. He had been a delicate child, missing the formation of character which a public school gives and for which a university career was no substitute. Being of a studious and intellectual nature, he thus became somewhat self-centred. His aunt, Miss Eliza Horace Smith, writing to him in 1888, referred to his 'sad secluded life,' and called him ' a very solitary though perhaps self-sufficing individual.' Nevertheless he enjoyed the society of his intimate friends and was a good conversationalist. Paradoxically few men were more open to flattery, yet no one was less influenced by the opinion of others. His health made him incapable of long sustained effort, hence his work was more that of an historical essayist than an historian. Genealogy had been his study from his childhood and it was only for the years over which the influence of Stubbs lasted that he worked, and worked brilliantly, on constitutional history. With failing health at the beginning of the present century he returned to the study of genealogy and topography, for the former of which he found a most useful outlet through his connexion with the Committee for Privileges. He made for himself a position among historical scholars which, perhaps, will never again be filled.

A BIBLIOGRAPHY OF THE WORKS OF
DR. J. HORACE ROUND

SEPARATE PUBLICATIONS

The Coming Terror. Brighton, 1881. Pamphlet. 8vo.

History and Antiquities of Colchester Castle. (Published anonymously.) Colchester, 1882.

The Early Life of Anne Boleyn. London, 1886. 8vo.

St. Helen's Chapel, Colchester. 1887. Pamphlet. 8vo.

Domesday Studies. [1888.] 25 copies for Private Distribution only.
> (1, Danegeld and the Finance of Domesday; 2, Notes on Domesday Measures of Land; 3, An Early Reference to Domesday.)

Domesday Commemoration, 1086-1886: Domesday Studies. Ed. P. E. Dove and H. B. Wheatley. 2 vols. 1888, 1891.
> (Vol. I, Danegeld and the Finance of Domesday, p. 77; Notes on Domesday Measures, p. 189. Vol. II, An Early Reference to Domesday, p. 539.)

Geoffrey de Mandeville: a study of the Anarchy. London, 1892. 8vo.
> (I, The Accession of Stephen, p. 1; II, The First Charter of the King, p. 37; III, Triumph of the Empress, p. 55; IV, The First Charter of the Empress, p. 81; V, The Lost Charter of the Queen, p. 114; VI, The Rout of Winchester, p. 123; VII, The Second Charter of the King, p. 136; VIII, The Second Charter of the Empress, p. 163; IX, Fall and Death of Geoffrey, p. 201; X, The Earldom of Essex, p. 227.
>
> *Appendices* :—A. Stephen's Treaty with the Londoners, p. 247; B. The Appeal to Rome in 1136, p. 250; C. The Easter Court of 1136, p. 262; D. The 'Fiscal' Earls, p. 267; E. The Arrival of the Empress, p. 278; F. The Defection of Miles of Gloucester, p. 284; G. Charter of the Empress to Roger de Valoines, p. 286; H. The 'Tertius Denarius,' p. 287; I. 'Vicecomites' and 'Custodes,' p. 297; J. The Great Seal of the Empress, p. 299; K. Gervase de Cornhill, p. 304; L. Charter of the Empress to William de Beauchamp, p. 313; M. The Earldom of Arundel, p. 316; N. Robert de Vere, p. 326; O. 'Tower' and 'Castle,' p. 328; P. The Early Administration of London, p. 347; Q. Osbertus Octodenarii, p. 374; R. The Forest of Essex, p. 376; S. The Treaty of Alliance between the Earls of Hereford and Gloucester, p. 379; T. 'Affidatio in Manu,' p. 384; U. The Families of Mandeville and De Vere, p. 388; V. William of Arques, p. 397; X. Roger 'de Ramis,' p. 399; Y. The First and Second Visits of Henry II to England, p. 405; Z. Bishop Nigel at Rome, p. 411; AA. 'Tenserie,' p. 414; BB. The Empress's Charter to Geoffrey Ridel, p. 417.
>
> *Excursus* :—The Creation of the Earldom of Gloucester, p. 420.)

Family Origins

Feudal England : Historical Studies on the Eleventh and Twelfth Centuries. London, 1895. Reprint 1909. 8vo.

PART I.—*Territorial Studies.* Domesday Book, p. 3 ; Nature of the *Inquisitio Com. Cant.* p. 6 ; Criticisms of the Domesday Text, p. 16 ; ' Soca ' and ' Theinland,' p. 28 ; The Domesday ' caruca,' p. 35 ; The Domesday hide, p. 36 ; The five-hide unit, p. 44 ; The six-carucate unit, p. 69 ; The Leicestershire ' hida,' p. 82 ; The Lancashire ' hida,' p. 86 ; The Yorkshire unit, p. 87 ; General Conclusions, p. 91 ; The East Anglian ' Leet,' p. 98 ; The words *Salinum* and *Solanda*, p. 103 ; The ' Firma unius noctis,' p. 109 ; ' Wara,' p. 115 ; The Domesday ' juratores,' p. 118 ; The *Inquisitio Eliensis*, p. 123 ; The Ely Return, p. 133 ; First Mention of Domesday Book, p. 142 ; The Northamptonshire Geld-roll, p. 147 ; The Knights of Peterborough, p. 157 ; The Worcestershire Survey (Hen. I), p. 169 ; The Lindsey Survey (1115-1118), p. 181 ; The Leicestershire Survey (1124-1129), p. 196 ; The Northampton-shire Survey (Hen. I-Hen. II), p. 215 ; The Introduction of Knight Service into England, p. 225 ; The *cartae* of 1166, p. 236 ; The ' servitium debitum,' p. 246 ; Scutage, aid, and ' donum,' p. 262 ; The total number of Knights due, p. 289; The normal knight's fee, p. 293 ; The early evidence, p. 295 ; The Worcester Relief, p. 308.

PART II.—*Historical Studies.* Normans under Edward the Confessor, p. 317 ; Mr. Freeman and the Battle of Hastings, p. 332 ; The name of ' Senlac,' p. 333 ; The palisade, p. 340 ; Mr. Freeman's authorities for it, p. 343 ; My argument against it, p. 348 ; The shield-wall, p. 354 ; The disposition of the English, p. 359 ; The Norman advance, p. 368 ; The fosse disaster, p. 374 ; The great feigned flight, p. 380 ; The Relief of Arques, p. 382 ; Summary, p. 387 ; Conclusion, p. 394 ; Master Wace, p. 399 ; Wace's meaning, p. 400 ; Wace's authority, p. 403 ; Wace and his sources, p. 409 ; Note on the Pseudo-Ingulf, p. 419 ; Regenbald, Priest and Chancellor, p. 421 ; The Conqueror at Exeter, p. 431 ; The alleged Destruction of Leicester (1068), p. 456 ; Ely and her Despoilers (1072-75), p. 459 ; The Lords of Ardres, p. 462 ; Early Irish Trade with Chester and Rouen, p. 465 ; Walter Tirel and his Wife, p. 468 ; Waldric, Warrior and Chancellor, p. 480 ; A Charter of Henry I (1123), p. 482 ; The Origin of the Nevilles, p. 488 ; The Alleged Invasion of England in 1147, p. 491 ; The Alleged Debate on Danegeld (1163), p. 497 ; A Glimpse of the Young King's Court (1170), p. 503 ; The First known Fine (1175), p. 509 ; The Mont-morency Imposture, p. 519 ; The Oxford Debate on Foreign Service (1197), p. 528 ; Richard the First's Change of Seal (1198), p. 539 ; Communal House Demolition, p. 552 ; The Cinque Port Charters, p. 563.

Studies on the Red Book of the Exchequer. 1898. 8vo. 120 copies only. Printed for private circulation.

I, The Antiquity of Scutage, p. 1 ; II, The Red Book of the Exchequer, p. 17 ; III, Alexander Swereford, p. 67.

Calendar of Documents Preserved in France, Illustrative of the History of Great Britain and Ireland. A.D. 918-1206. (Public Record Office Publication.) 1899. 1 vol. 8vo.

The Commune of London, and Other Studies ; With a Prefatory Letter by Sir Walter Besant. London, 1899. 8vo.

(I, The Settlement of the South-Saxons and East-Saxons, p. 1 ; II, Ingelric the Priest and Albert of Lotharingia, p. 28 ; III, Anglo-

Norman Warfare, p. 39 ; IV, The Origin of the Exchequer, p. 62 ; V, London under Stephen, p. 97 ; VI, The Inquest of Sheriffs (1170), p. 125 ; VII, The Conquest of Ireland, p. 137 ; VIII, The Pope and the Conquest of Ireland, p. 171 ; IX, The Coronation of Richard I, p. 201 ; X, The Struggle of John and Longchamp (1191), p. 207 ; XI, The Commune of London, p. 219 ; XII, The Great Inquest of Service (1212), p. 261 ; XIII, Castle-ward and Cornage, p. 278 ; XIV, Bannockburn, p. 289 ; XV, The Marshalship of England, p. 302.)

Notes on the Systematic Study of our English Place-Names [1899]. Pamphlet. 8vo.

The King's Protestant Declaration. Pamphlet, reprinted in part, with additions from the *Contemporary Review* of April 1901.

Studies in Peerage and Family History. London, 1901. 8vo.
(I, The Peerage, p. 1 ; II, The Origin of the Stewarts, p. 115 ; III, The counts of Boulogne as English Lords, p. 147 ; IV, The Family of Ballon and the Conquest of South Wales, p. 181 ; V, Our English Hapsburgs, p. 216 ; VI, The Origin of the Russells, p. 250 ; VII, The Rise of the Spencers, p. 279 ; VIII, Henry VIII and the Peers, p. 330 ; IX, Charles I and Lord Glamorgan : Part 1— Glamorgan's Dukedom, p. 367 ; Part 2—Glamorgan's Treaty, p. 396 ; X, The Abeyance of the Barony of Mowbray, p. 435 ; XI, The Succession to the Crown, p. 458.)

Peerage and Pedigree : Studies in Peerage Law and Family History. London, 1910. 2 vols. 8vo.
(Vol. I, The Willoughby d'Eresby Case and the rise of the Berties, p. 1 ; The Barony of Delawarr, p. 55 ; Peerage Cases in the Court of Chivalry, p. 69 ; The Muddle of the Law, p. 103 ; Tales of the Conquest, p. 284 ; The House of Lords, p. 324. Vol. II, Some ' Saxon ' Houses, p. 1 ; The Great Carington Imposture, p. 134 ; The Geste of John de Courcy, p. 258 ; Heraldry and the Gent. p. 307).

The King's Serjeants and Officers of State, with their Coronation Services. London, 1911. 8vo.
(Preface ; I, Introduction, p. 1 ; II, Serjeanty and Knight-Service, p. 21 ; III, Some Features of Serjeanty, p. 35 ; IV, The King's Household, p. 52 ; V, The King's Sport, p. 268 ; VI, Coronation Services, p. 318.)

THE ACADEMY

Henry I as an English Scholar.   13th Sept. 1884.
The First Mayor of London.   12th Nov. 1887.
Countess Lucy.   10th Dec. 1887.

THE AMERICAN HISTORICAL REVIEW

The First Whig.   Vol. I, 533 (Ap. 1896).   R.
Die Schlacht von Hastings.   Vol. II, 512 (Ap. 1897).   R.
Feudal Relations between the
  Kings of England and Scotland
  under the Early Plantagenets.   Vol. III, 707 (July 1898).   R.
The Foundations of England.   Vol. V, 112 (Oct. 1899).   R.
The Commune of London.   Vol. VI, 181 (Oct. 1900).
The Early Norman Jury.   Vol. IX, 412 (Jan. 1904).

Family Origins

THE ANCESTOR

THE ANTIQUARIAN MAGAZINE AND BIBLIOGRAPHER

Bibliography

Curiosities of Elizabethan Nomenclature and the Irish Calendar.	Vol. V, 49 (1884).
' Port ' and ' Port-Reeve.'	Vols. V, 247, 282 (1884) ; VI, 23, 159, 299 (1884).
Ports and Chesters.	Vol. VI, 96, 202 (1884).
The Viscounty of Cullen.	Vol. VI, 45 (1884).
A Fourteenth Century Library.	Vol. VII, 64 (1885).
' Port or Gate ? '	Vol. VII, 94 (1885).
More Curiosities of Official Scholarship.	Vol. VII, 254 (1885).
Professor Freeman on his Defence.	Vols. VII, 264 ; VIII, 69 (1885).
Professor Freeman and J. H. Round.	Vol. VIII, 197 (1885).
Brighthelmstone and Brighton.	Vol. IX, 95 (1886).
The Essex Archaeological Society.	Vol. X, 47 (1886).
Sir William Dugdale.	Vol. X, 141 (1886).
' Ancient ' and ' Modern ' History.	Vol. X, 141 (1886).
The ' Jus Primae Noctis.'	Vol. X, 144 (1886).
Proof of Age.	Vol. X, 285 (1886).

THE ANTIQUARY

The Webster Papers.	Vols. IV, 259 (1881) ; V, 279 (1882).
Traditions about Old Buildings.	Vols. IV, 279 (1881) ; V, 278 (1882).
Archaic Land Tenure in Domesday.	Vol. V, 104 (1882).
The Domesday of Colchester.	Vols. V, 244 (1882) ; VI, 5, 95, 251 (1882).
Footsteps of the English in Germany.	Vol. VI, 229 (1882).
The Great Case of the Impositions.	Vols. VI, 182, 277 (1882) ; VII, 182 (1883).
The Pole Family.	Vol. VI, 229 (1882).
Colchester Keep and Mr. G. T. Clark.	Vol. VII, 45, 157 (1883).
The Book of Howth.	Vols. VII, 196 (1883) ; VIII, 21, 116 (1883).
Whitsun Ales.	Vols. VII, 34 (1883) ; XIII, 183 (1886).
The Hide of Land in India.	Vol. VIII, 181 (1883).
Succession through Females.	Vol. VIII, 183, 270 (1883).
St. Christopher as portrayed in England during the Middle Ages.	Vol. VIII, 271 (1883).
That Detestable Battle of Lewes.	Vol. IX, 14 (1884).
British or Roman Remains near Bicester.	Vol. IX, 45 (1884).

ARCHAEOLOGIA

Bibliography

Giarnier de Nablous, Prior of the Hospital
in England, and Grand Master of the
Order of St. John of Jerusalem.   Vol. LVIII, 383.

ARCHAEOLOGICAL JOURNAL

Origin of the Mayoralty of London.	Vol. L, 247 (1893).
Introduction of Armorial Bearings into England.	Vol. LI, 43 (1894).
The Family of Clare.	Vol. LVI, 221 (1899).
Castle Guard.	Vol. LIX, 144 (1902).
The King's Pantler.	Vol. LX, 268 (1903).
The Chronology of Henry II's Charters.	Vol. LXIV, 63 (1907).
The Essex Sackvilles.	Vol. LXIV, 217 (1907).

THE ARCHAEOLOGICAL REVIEW

The Cornish Acre.	Vol. I, 60 (1888).
Richard the First's Change of Seal.	Vol. I, 135 (1888).
The Sussex Rapes.	Vol. I, 229 (1888).
Domesday Measures of Land.	Vols. I, 285 (1888) ; IV, 130, 391 (1889).
The Suitors of the County Court.	Vol. II, 66 (1888).
The South Porch.	Vol. II, 215 (1888).
Widowhood in Manorial Law.	Vol. II, 267 (1888).
The Norman Exchequer.	Vol. IV, 78 (1889).
The Hundred of Swanborough.	Vol. IV, 223 (1889).
Communal House Demolition.	Vol. IV, 366 (1889).

COLLECTANEA GENEALOGICA

Rachel, Lady Kingston.	Vol. I, 17 (1881).
The Barony of Arklow.	Vol. IV, 42 (1881).
Burke's 'Dormant and Extinct Peerage.'	Vol. IV, 49 (1881).
Isabella Howard.	Vol. IV, 52 (1881).
Spurious Coat Armour.	Vol. IV, 53 (1881).
Ulster before ' My Lords.'	Vol. IX, 77 (1882).
The Earldoms of Ormond in Ireland.	Vol. IX, 84 (1882).
The Peerage of Scotland in the House of Lords.	Vol. IX, 108 (1882).
Are there two Earls of Mar ?	Vol. XII, 146 (1883).
The Barony of Ruthven of Freeland.	Vol. XIII, 167 (1884).

THE CONTEMPORARY REVIEW

Church Defence.	No. 395, p. 702 (Nov. 1898).
As Established by Law.	No. 402, p. 814 (June 1899).
The King's Protestant Declaration.	No. 424, p. 514 (Ap. 1901).
A New Anglican Argument.	No. 517, p. 75 (Jan. 1909).

Family Origins

Bibliography

Clare, Richard de, Founder of the House of Clare.	Vol. X, 389.
Clare, Richard de.	Vol. X, 389.
Clare, Walter de, Founder of Tintern Abbey.	Vol. X, 397.
Courci, John de.	Vol. XII, 330.
Despenser, Hugh le, Justiciar of England.	Vol. XIV, 412.
Ferrers, Henry de, Domesday Commissioner.	Vol. XVIII, 385.
Ferrers, Robert de, warrior.	Vol. XVIII, 386.
Fitzailwyn, Henry, First Mayor of London.	Vol. XIX, 85.
Fitzalan, Thomas, Earl of Arundel and Surrey.	Vol. XIX, 100.
Fitzalan, William, rebel.	Vol. XIX, 103.
Fitzcount, Brian, warrior and author.	Vol. XIX, 108.
Fitzhubert, Robert.	Vol. XIX, 176.
Fitzjohn, Pain.	Vol. XIX, 184.
Fitzosbern, William, Earl of Hereford.	Vol. XIX, 188.
Fitzosbert, William.	Vol. XIX, 189.
Fitzwilliam, Roger, alias Roger de Breteuil, Earl of Hereford.	Vol. XIX, 229.
Gloucester, Miles de, Earl of Hereford.	Vol. XXI, 438.
Mandeville, Geoffrey de, Earl of Essex.	Vol. XXXVI, 22.
Marshal, John, warrior.	Vol. XXXVI, 221.
Nigel, Bishop of Ely, statesman.	Vol. XLI, 60.
Randulf, called Le Meschin.	Vol. XLVII, 284.
Randulf, called De Gernons.	Vol. XLVII, 286.
Redvers, Family of.	Vol. XLVII, 385.
Reginald, Earl of Cornwall.	Vol. XLVII, 422.
Ridel, Geoffrey, judge.	Vol. XLVIII, 274.
Robert, the Staller.	Vol. XLVIII, 359.
Tirel or Tyrrell, Walter.	Vol. LVI, 414.
Urse d'Abetot, Sheriff of Worcestershire.	Vol. LVIII, 52.
Vere, Family of.	Vol. LVIII, 219.
Vere, Aubrey de, great chamberlain.	Vol. LVIII, 220.

THE ENCYCLOPAEDIA BRITANNICA

Abeyance ; Aids ; Baron ; Bayeux Tapestry ; Castle ; Chamberlain, Great ; Domesday Book ; Earl ; Ferrers (Family of) ; Fitzgerald Family ; Hereward ; Knight Service ; Mar (Earldom of) ; Mandeville, Geoffrey de ; Mowbray (House of) ; Nevill of Neville (Family of) ; Percy (Family of) ; Plantagenet; Scutage (or Escuage) ; Serjeanty ; Stafford (Family of) ; Stewart ; Talbot (Family of) ; Vere (Family of) ; Viscount.

ENGLISH HISTORICAL REVIEW
(*Articles*)

Molmen and Molland (an explanation of these tenures).	Vol. II, 103 (1887).
The ' Virgata.'	Vol. III, 329 (1888).
The Great Carucage of 1198 (on the discovery of some fragments of the assessment of this aid).	Vols. III, 501 (1888) ; IV, 105 (1889).

Bibliography

The Early Charters of St. John's Abbey, Colchester.	Vol. XVI, 721 (1901).
The Colchester Mint in Norman Times.	Vol. XVIII, 305 (1903).
Some English Crusaders of Richard I.	Vol. XVIII, 475 (1903).
Decies and Desmond.	Vol. XVIII, 709 (1903).
The Officers of Edward the Confessor.	Vol. XIX, 90 (1904).
King John and Robert Fitzwalter.	Vol. XIX, 707 (1904).
The Burton Abbey Surveys.	Vol. XX, 275 (1905).
A Plea Roll of Richard I.	Vol. XXII, 290 (1907).
The Origin of Belvoir Castle.	Vol. XXII, 508 (1907).
The Domesday ' Ora ' : [on the value of the Danish coin].	Vol. XXIII, 283 (1908).
The Weigher of the Exchequer.	Vol. XXVI, 714 (1911).
The Debtors of William Cade.	Vol. XXVIII, 522 (1913).
The Domesday Hidation of Essex.	Vol. XXIX, 477 (1914).
John Doreward, Speaker (1399-1413).	Vol. XXIX, 717 (1914).
The House of Lords and the Model Parliament.	Vol. XXX, 385 (1915).
Date of the Grand Assize.	Vol. XXXI, 268 (1916).
The Saladin Tithe.	Vol. XXXI, 447 (1916).
Bractoniana.	Vol. XXXI, 586 (1916).
Knight Service of Malmesbury Abbey	Vol. XXXII, 249 (1917).
' Barons ' and ' Peers.'	Vol. XXXIII, 453 (1918).
The ' Tertius Denarius ' of the Borough.	Vol. XXXIV, 62 (1919).
The Staff of a Castle in the Twelfth Century.	Vol. XXXV, 90 (1920).
Castle Watchmen.	Vol. XXXV, 400 (1920).
Early Sheriffs of Norfolk.	Vol. XXXV, 481 (1920).
' Shire-House ' and Castle Yard.	Vol. XXXVI, 210 (1921).
The Dating of the Early Pipe Rolls.	Vol. XXXVI, 321 (1921).
A Butler's Serjeanty.	Vol. XXXVI, 46 (1921).
The Legend of ' Eudo Dapifer.'	Vol. XXXVII, 1 (1922).
' Domesday ' and ' Doomsday.'	Vol. XXXVIII, 240 (1923).
Robert Aylett and Richard Argall.	Vol. XXXVIII, 423 (1923).
An East Anglian Shire-moot of Stephen's Reign.	Vol. XXXIX, 568 (1924).

ENGLISH HISTORICAL REVIEW

(Reviews)

Select Pleas of the Crown.	Vol. III, 788 (1888).
Select Pleas in Manorial and other Courts.	Vol. V, 586 (1890).
Records of the Borough of Nottingham.	Vol. VI, 606 (1891).

Bibliography

Calendar of Inquisitions Post-Mortem and other Analagous Documents. Vol. IV.	Vol. XXIX, 155 (1914).
Regesta Regum Anglo-Normannorum.	Vol. XXIX, 347 (1914).
Calendar of Inquisitions.	Vol. XXIX, 561 (1914).
The Book of the Bayeux Tapestry.	Vol. XXX, 109 (1915).
Catalogue of Ancient Deeds.	Vol. XXXI, 177 (1916).
Catalogue of English Coins in the British Museum : The Norman Kings. By G. E. Brooke. 2 vols.	Vol. XXXII, 430 (1917).
Calendar of Inquisitions Post-Mortem preserved in the Public Record Office.	Vol. XXXII, 453 (1917).
Le Strange Records. By Hamon Le Strange, F.S.A.	Vol. XXXII, 599 (1917).
The Normans in European History. By Prof. Haskins.	Vol. XXXII, 616 (1917).
Histoire féodale des Marais, Territoire et l'Église de Dol. Par Jean Allenon.	Vol. XXXIII, 260 (1918).
Calendar of Inquisitions, Miscellaneous (Chancery).	Vol. XXXIII, 395 (1918).
Feudal Cambridgeshire.	Vol. XXXVI, 249 (1921).
Calendar of Inquisitions.	Vol. XXXVII, 273 (1922).
Final Concords of the County of Lincoln.	Vol. XXXVII, 426 (1922).

ESSEX ARCH. SOC. TRANSACTIONS

(New Series)

Some Documents relating to Colchester Castle.	Vol. III, 143.
Who was Alice of Essex ?	Vol. III, 242.
Origin of St. Botolph's Priory, Colchester.	Vol. III, 267.
Rayleigh Mount.	Vols. V, 41 ; VIII, 228.
St. Botolph's Priory, Colchester.	Vol. V, 69, 103.
Pleshy.	Vols. V, 83 ; XVI, 268.
Halstead Church.	Vol. V, 103.
Nonconformity in Essex.	Vol. V, 104.
Some Essex County Families.	Vol. V, 131.
Abbeys of Coggeshall and Stratford Langthorne.	Vol. V, 139.
Stifford Church.	Vol. V, 182.
Witchcraft in Essex.	Vol. V, 182.
Essex Clergy in 1294	Vols. V, 182, 244 ; VI, 346.
Harwich and the Siege of Colchester.	Vol. V, 191.
The Oldest Essex Charter.	Vol. V, 243.

Family Origins

Bibliography

Family Origins

Bibliography

Jarvis in Bemfleet.	Vol. XVIII, 229.
The Harvest Horn.	Vol. XVIII, 229.
Horlock.	Vol. XVIII, 296.
Clements in Navestock.	Vol. XVIII, 297.
Ramsey Tyrrell's.	Vol. XIX, 51.
Bocking and Stisted.	Vol. XIX, 51.
Henry III in Essex.	Vol. XIX, 126.
Cesterwald.	Vol. XIX, 170.

NOTE.—The following papers, prepared by the late Dr. Round, will be printed in forthcoming volumes of the Essex Archaeological Transactions.

The Essex Possessions of St. Martin le Grand.
The Advowson of Rainham (with Norman descent of manor).
Shallow Bowells and the Willingdales (including Spayn family).
The Mantels of Little Maldon.
The Hockesleys of Little Hockesley.
Braiswick, Lexden and East Donnyland.
Sturmer Manor and Advowson.
The Early Lords of Toppisfield.
The Belchamps.
Stratford Langthorne and Stratford atte le Bow.
Origin of the Teys.
Wallfleet.
Sir Lewis John.
The Bruces in Essex.
The Ockendons and their Churches.
Forest Notes.
Maskelsbury in White Roothing.
Beckett's Sisters.
St. Clair's Hall, St. Osyth.
An Early Eyre in Essex.
The Essex Eures.
Stanstead Mount Fichet.
The Mildmay Family.
Inning the Essex Marshes.
Fulling in Essex and Spains Hall.
Holy Trinity and Bere Church, Colchester.
Two Hornchurch Charters.
The Churches of Feering and Boxstead.
The Hanningfields of East Hanningfield.
Cattiwade Bridge.
Maldon Grammar School.
Presbyterian Essex.
Maldon.
The Original Colchester.
Horsepits in West Bergholt.
Note on Morant's Essex.
Porters in Stebbing.
Scarlets in West Bergholt.
Rivers Hall in Boxted.
The Thurrocks.

Family Origins

The Forestership of Essex.
Spain of Spains Hall.
Witham and its Burh.
Sandon (Bedenesteda).
The Manor of Bendish.
The Family of Hodillow.
The Borough of Colchester To-day.
Parishes and Churches (Colchester).
Colchester as a Hundred.

THE GENEALOGIST

(New Series)

Bibliography

Lord Adam Lisburn.	Vol. X, 255.
Pedigree of Wegg.	Vol. XI, 19.
Pedigree of Barker.	Vol. XI, 65.
Sir William Stewart of Jedworth.	Vol. XI, 127.
Trotter ' of Byers Hall.'	Vol. XI, 129.
Origin of the Thynnes.	Vol. XI, 193.
Earldom of Leicester.	Vol. XI, 63.
Faramus of Boulogne.	Vol. XII, 145, 288.
Pedigree of Baynard.	Vol. XII, 211.
Le Poher Family.	Vol. XII, 216.
Origin of the Lindsays.	Vol. XII, 75.
De ' Poher.'	Vol. XIII, 15.
The Red Book of the Exchequer.	Vol. XIV, 1.
Creffield Family.	Vol. XIV, 80.
Earldom of Glamorgan.	Vol. XIV, 213.
Barons of the Naas.	Vol. XV, 1.
Heirs of Richard de Lucy.	Vol. XV, 129.
Origin of the Swintons.	Vol. XV, 205.
Marriage entry in 1526.	Vol. XV, 192.
Families of St. John and of Port.	Vol. XVI, 1.
Notes on Anglo-Norman Genealogy.	Vol. XVII, 1.
Sir Thomas Rolt, ' President of India.'	Vol. XVII, 145.
Earldom of Worcester.	Vol. XVII, 224.
Origin of the Stewarts and their Chesney connexion.	Vol. XVIII, 1.
William Bentinck, first Earl of Portland.	Vol. XVIII, 36.
The Ports of Basing and their Priory.	Vol. XVIII, 137.
Countess of Ireland.	Vol. XVIII, 166.
Pedigree of Ringesdune.	Vol. XVIII, 216.

THE MONTHLY REVIEW

The Companions of the Conqueror.	Vol. III, 91 (No. 9, June 1901).
Coronation Peerages.	Vol. VI, 65 (No. 17, Feb. 1902).
The Lord Great Chamberlain.	Vol. VII, 42 (No. 21, June 1902).
The Bayeux Tapestry.	Vol. XVII, 109 (No. 51, Dec. 1904).

THE NATIONAL REVIEW

The Protectionist Revival.	Vol. XXV, 497 (No. 148, June 1895).
The Battle of Hastings.	Vol. XXVIII, 687 (No. 167, Jan. 1897).

THE NINETEENTH CENTURY

The English Libro D'Oro.	Vol. XXXV, 796 (No. 207, May 1894).
A Visit to Queen Elizabeth.	Vol. XL, 619 (1896).
The Elizabethan Religion.	Vol. XLI, 191 (No. 240, Feb. 1897).
The Sacrifice of the Mass.	Vol. XLI, 837 (No. 243, May 1897).
Historical Research.	Vol. XLIV, 1004 (No. 262, Dec. 1898).

NOTES AND QUERIES.

The Carucate.	6 Series, Vol. VI (1891).
The Ruthven Peerage.	6 Series, Vol VII (Mar. 3, Ap. 14, May 19, 1883).
The Ruthven of Freeland Peerage.	6 Series, Vol. VIII (July 14, 1883).
Turstin de Wigmore ; Turstin Flandrensis.'	10 Series, Vol. X.
' The Norman People.'	11 Series, Vol. XII.

PIPE ROLL SOCIETY

Introduction to the Pipe Roll of 22 Hen. II.
,, ,, ,, ,, 23 Hen. II.
,, ,, ,, ,, 24 Hen. II.
,, ,, ,, ,, 25 Hen. II.
,, ,, ,, ,, 26 Hen. II.
,, ,, ,, ,, 27 Hen. II.
,, ,, ,, ,, 28 Hen. II.
,, ,, ,, ,, 29 Hen. II.
,, ,, ,, ,, 30 Hen. II.
,, ,, ,, ,, 31 Hen. II.
,, ,, ,, ,, 32 Hen. II.
,, ,, ,, ,, 33 Hen. II.

Preface to Vol. X, p. v. (Ancient Charters previous to A.D. 1200).	1888.
Rotulus de Dominabus.	1913.

THE QUARTERLY REVIEW

Professor Freeman.	No. 349, p. 1 (July 1892).
The Battle of Hastings.	No. 353, p. 73 (July 1893).
The Peerage.	No. 354, p. 386 (Oct. 1893). R.
English Castles.	No. 357, p. 27 (July 1894). R.
English Surnames.	No. 359, p. 207 (Jan. 1895). R.
County Families.	No. 409, p. 531 (Oct. 1906). R.
Recent Peerage Cases.	No. 444, p. 49 (July 1915). R.

THE SUSSEX ARCHAEOLOGICAL COLLECTION

Some Early Grants to Lewes Priory.	Vol. XL, 58.
Holmwood, East Grinstead.	Vol. XL, 280.
Early History of Rotherfield Church.	Vol. XLI, 49.
Battle of Hastings.	Vol. XLII, 54.
Some Early Sussex Charters.	Vol. XLII, 75.
Rape of Pevensey.	Vol. XLII, 237.
Henry I at Burne and Burneham.	Vol. XLII, 238.
Withyham.	Vol. XLIII, 278.
Note on Sussex Domesday.	Vol. XLIV, 140.
Stigand, Bishop of Chichester.	Vol. XLVI, 234.

Bibliography

An Earl of Arundel in France, 1188.	Vol. XLVI, 235.
Chichester Inquest, 1212.	Vol. XLVII, 113.
Benton's Place in Shipley.	Vol. XLVIII, 152.
A Sussex Knight's Fee.	Vol. LIII, 183.
Echingham of Echingham.	Vol. LIII, 276.
The Stophams, the Zouches, and the Honour of Petworth.	Vol. LV, 19.
Descent of the Manor of Eastbourne.	Vol. LV, 307.
Early History of North and South Stoke.	Vol. LIX, 1.
The Hundred of Eastbourne.	Vol. LIX, 126.
The Lords Dacre and their Hoo Quarterings.	Vol. LIX, 128.
The Norman Seats of the Families of Buci and Covert.	Vol. LXI, 142.
Lord Poynings and St. John.	Vol. LXII, 1.
The Early History of Ovingdean.	Vol. LXII, 197.
The Glass in Chichester Cathedral.	Vol. LXII, 203.
The Family of Alard.	Vol. LXII, 204.
New Shoreham Church.	Vol. LXII, 206.
Radynden.	Vol. LXIII, 226.
The Knights Hospitallers.	Vol. LXIII, 227.
The Origin of the Finches.	Vol. LXX, 19.

NOTE.—The following paper by the late Dr. Round will be printed in a forthcoming volume of the Sussex Archaeological Collections.

Sussex in the Pipe Rolls of Henry II.

THE VICTORIA COUNTY HISTORY

Introduction to the Bedfordshire Domesday.	Bedfordshire, Vol. I, 191.
Introduction to the Berkshire Domesday.	Berkshire, Vol. I, 285.
Introduction to the Buckinghamshire Domesday.	Buckinghamshire, Vol. I, 207.
Introduction to the Essex Domesday.	Essex, Vol. I, 333.
Text of the Essex Domesday.	,, Vol. I, 427.
Ecclesiastical History. (Dr. Cox and J. H. R.)	,, Vol. II, 1.
Political History. (Miss E. Stokes and J. H. R.)	,, Vol. II, 203.
Introduction to the Hampshire Domesday.	Hampshire, Vol. I, 399.
Text of the Hampshire Domesday.	,, Vol. I, 448.
The Winchester Survey.	,, Vol. I, 527.
Introduction to the Herefordshire Domesday.	Herefordshire, Vol. I, 263.
Introduction to the Hertfordshire Domesday.	Hertfordshire, Vol. I, 263.

Family Origins

MISCELLANEOUS PAPERS

Bibliography

DR. ROUND'S REPORTS ON CLAIMS TO PEERAGES, BARONETCIES, ETC.

NOTE.—These Reports have been deposited in the Library of the House of Lords. Those contained in Volumes I and II may be inspected by students and others upon permission to use the Library. Those in Volumes III and IV are placed under the particular care of the Librarian, and access to them cannot be had without his special permission and he will consult Counsel to the Treasury for the time being before granting it.

VOLUME I

The Lord Great Chamberlainship

lxxi

Family Origins

Appendices : (A) The Formula of Creation.
(B) The Earldom of Oxford
Case in 1626.
(C) The Earldom of Oxford
in the Lords' Report
on the dignity of a
Peer.
(D) The Third Penny.
(E) Sir Harris Nicholas and
Lord Chelmsford.

VOLUME II

Reports, etc., on Claims to Peerages

VOLUME III

Reports, etc., on Claims to Peerages, Deprivation of Titles, etc.

Surrender of Peerage Dignities.
    Report.   [1917 ?].
Memoranda.
    (1) Deprivation of Peers' Titles.   [1917 ?].
    (2) The Right to Sit and Vote.
    (3) The double status of peer and
        foreign sovereign.
    (4) Alien Peers.   [1917 ?].
Memorandum.   Princes and Royal Dukes.   [1917 ?].
Memorandum.   Titles, etc., held by
    Enemies Bill.   [1917 ?].
Letter.   The reversal of Attainders.   Undated.

VOLUME IV

Reports, etc., on Claims to Baronetcies

Cox.   Extract from a letter.   Undated.
Cope. Letter to Mr. Robert Froding
    Reynard.   4th Dec. 1911.
Hamilton of Preston.
    Letter to Mr. R. F. Reynard.   Undated.
    Letter to Mr. R. F. Reynard.   13th Feb. 1911.
    Report.   Undated.
Hamilton of Silverton Hill.
    Report.   Undated.
Mansel. Letter to Mr. R. F. Reynard.   16th June, 1912.
Richardson of Pitfour. Report.   Undated.
Roberts of Glassenbury.
    Letter to Mr. R. F. Reynard.   26th Nov. 1911.
    Letter to Mr. R. F. Reynard.   29th Nov. 1911.
    Letter to Mr. R. F. Reynard.   29th Nov. 1911.
    Letter to Mr. R. F. Reynard.   1st Dec. 1911.
    Letter to Mr. R. F. Reynard.   3rd Dec. 1911.
Sinclair of Mey. Report.   Undated.
Turing.
    Extract from letter.   Undated.
    Letter to Mr. R. F. Reynard.   14th June, 1912.
    Letter to Mr. R. F. Reynard.   18th June, 1912.
    Letter to Mr. R. F. Reynard.   18th June, 1912.
    Letter to Mr. R. F. Reynard.   18th June, 1912.
    Report.   Undated.
    Letter to Mr. R. F. Reynard.   Undated.
Wardlaw of Pitreavie.
    Letter to Mr. R. F. Reynard.   15th Dec. 1910.
    Report.   13th Jan. 1911.
Note relating to Charles II Baronets.

HISTORICAL GENEALOGY [1]

' HISTORICAL GENEALOGY' is a title which might have three meanings. Genealogy as a branch of historical study, Genealogy based on the same principles as those of historical research, Genealogy in its own historical development— these are the three meanings which the title I have chosen might suggest. And on all three of these subjects I hope to touch.

Let me confess, as an ardent genealogist, that the service which this branch of study can render to the general historian, can easily be overrated. When Palgrave, who had the passion of his race for adopting the name of an English house, wrote in the stilted language of the time, that ' the fortunes and changes of one family, or the events of one upland township, may explain the darkest and most dubious portions of the annals of a realm,' he was exaggerating that service. In Stubbs we have an illustrious historian who was also a devoted genealogist. Read his preface to Hoveden's chronicle and note his marvellous knowledge of the families of Hugh de Puiset, the princely bishop of Durham, or of William Longchamp, the low-born bishop of Ely. And yet, if he acquired this knowledge, it was not because it was requisite for his work, but because he was a born maker of pedigrees and loved the study for its own sake.

For the illustration of Domesday Book, genealogy, of course, is essential ; it is the key that opens many a door. For the history of the feudal baronage as affecting the history of the nation, its use is very great : it enabled me, for instance, to show that in the struggle for the Great Charter,

[1] Paper read before the International Congress of Historical Studies held in London in April 1913.

Robert Fitz Walter was a noble of greater power and influence than historians had realised, and that his family connections also are evident in the Charter group. In later and post-Tudor days the historian has still something to learn from the relationships of our great houses whether under Queen Elizabeth or even under George the Second. Between the members of a governing group there was, at times, the tie of marriage or of blood.

But if for political or national history genealogy can only be of slight service, for topographical history it is of supreme value. The topographer should always have a pedigree by his side, and the genealogist a local map. When you have once grasped the method of combining the two studies, you will be surprised at the results. The history of a manor, though a blank for generations or even for centuries, can be traced, by the help of genealogy, with precision, through the history of another manor in what may be a distant county. What is required is a knowledge of your men and a sound grasp of the feudal system.

In what we may term the feudal period, the period of territorial baronies, the importance of a noble depended on his lands, and we have to study the descent of families and of fiefs jointly. There is here a great field of study for those who are able to employ genealogy and topography in conjunction. The scheme I would propose is based upon the feudal system alone. It would, therefore, discard the Old English divisions, the County, the Hundred, even the township, and would restrict itself to that newer and rival system, which had for its units the baron's fief, the knight's fee, and the manor. We should take, as Dugdale did, for our starting-point the great Domesday fief and should endeavour to link it up with the returns of 1166. The great Inquest of Service in 1212 would afford us our next fixed point. This, in turn, we should link up with the surveys under Henry III, and so we should reach open country, first with the ' Inquisitions post-mortem ' and then with ' Feudal Aids.' Another valuable source of information is found in the partitions between co-heirs and even the assignments of dower, both of them enrolled on the Close Rolls. As to the great fiefs that were forfeited or were, for temporary causes, in the King's hands, they preserved their individual existence as ' Honours ' and their tenants are even easier to trace owing to the entry of their reliefs. Other sources of information now available to all are the splendid Calendars of documents and rolls for which we are indebted to the Public Record Office, and the publications of the Pipe Roll Society. We have also, now, the publications of many local Societies, especially cartularies and county fines. The great value, for this purpose, of monastic cartularies is that they not only prove the descent of the founder's heirs, but give us, at the darkest period, the names of their knightly tenants, witnessing their charters or, often indeed, making grants to their lord's foundation.

By thus working on feudal lines it will be possible to reconstruct the great network of tenure that the system had spun about the land and to base upon the sound footing which is afforded by that tenure the pedigrees not only of the tenants-in-chief but of their under-tenants. But the student must ever keep in view that long chain of sub-infeudation, the ignorance or forgetfulness of which has often puzzled or misled writers of local history. For monographs such as I suggest on the English barons and their fiefs, we may hope, perhaps, to be indebted to some of those American students whose dissertations have already done so much for our early history.

From this sphere of ' Historical Genealogy ' I pass to that post-mediaeval period when the downfall of the old nobility, which owed its greatness to its lands, opened the way for the new families which rose to wealth under the new dynasty that was founded on Bosworth Field. This is the beginning of that family history which is unconnected with the tenure of land. Genealogy now becomes a study based on other sources than the records of manorial descent.

This phase of the study, which is that of genealogy to-day,

has made it, to many minds, a subject of ridicule and of scorn. When I was at Balliol under Jowett and stood at the seat of judgment, the historical tutor told him that I was too fond of pedigrees. ' You should read,' said Jowett, ' Freeman's article on " Pedigrees and Pedigree-Makers." ' [2] Now that article was a bitter, I might even say a savage, attack on Sir Bernard Burke and his *Peerage*. But it was richly deserved. Freeman assailed Burke's *Peerage*, not because of pedigrees historically false, but because it asserted those pedigrees to be true. This is still the ground on which the historian must protest against Burke's *Peerage* and Burke's *Landed Gentry*. Many of their fabulous pedigrees I have myself slain, but yet they are repeated.

Now Freeman was careful to explain that he was not denouncing genealogy. ' Let no one deem,' he wrote, ' that because a false pedigree is a thing to be eschewed and scouted, therefore a true pedigree is a thing to be despised. . . . It is only the false imitation of the true which is to be despised.' Stubbs went further : ' the expansion,' he wrote, ' and extension of genealogical study is a very remarkable feature of our own times.' ' There is,' he added of those who try to trace their pedigrees, ' nothing in this that need be stigmatised as vain and foolish ; it is a very natural instinct, and it appears to me to be one of the ways in which a general interest in national history may be expected to grow.' Personally, however, I cannot accept as a true student of genealogy one who cares for nothing but the pedigree of his own family.

Let me now trace the growth of English genealogy. Although the causes of the new development are to be sought under the early Tudors, the great age of the pedigree-makers, of whose concoctions not a few have survived to the present day, extended, roughly speaking, from the middle of the sixteenth to the middle of the seventeenth century. This was also the period covered by the heralds' visitations—though these overlapped it. It is, probably,

[2] *Contemporary Review*, vol. xxx.

no mere coincidence that the heralds, who appear to have increased their influence under Henry VIII, and whose first incorporation was only a year before his father's accession, received their college and a fresh incorporation in 1554. For their influence is thenceforth seen not only in the decadence of heraldic art, but in the more commercial aspect of the process of granting arms, and above all in those armorial scrolls, with the names of heralds at their foot, which provided for the new nobility pedigrees, if not from the Conquest, at least from illustrious sires.

It was under Elizabeth and her successor that the craze reached its height. The Queen herself had set the example with a Tudor pedigree deduced from Adam. The great Burghley was pedigree-mad and sought for the upstart Cecils' ancestors in all directions. Sir Christopher Hatton, that comely person who danced himself into Elizabeth's favour and became her Lord Chancellor, was fitted with a pedigree tracing his family to ' Yvon, a Norman noble, who came in with the Conqueror,' which was duly ' seen and registered ' by that notorious herald, ' William Dethick, Garter.' To support one of Burghley's ancestries there was forged a document in old French of the days, it was alleged, of the third Edward ; to support Hatton's there was duly produced a whole galaxy of charters and seals, which remind us that in these cases we have to walk warily. For the pedigree-maker stuck at nothing ; he forged documents, not only in Latin, but in Old English and Old French, and these he showed to the heralds, by whom they were greedily swallowed. These frauds I have set myself to expose with infinite labour, nailing them up one by one, as a gamekeeper nails his vermin, and trying to place the critical study of genealogical evidence on a sound and historical basis.

Elizabeth's example was followed by James, who, in 1610, received, to his delight, his own pedigree ' from Brute, the most noble founder of the Britains ' and caused it to be prominently displayed. Right through Charles' reign the demand for ancestry persisted ; Domesday Book was beginning to be searched and provided, ready to hand, a Norman or a Saxon patriarch as preferred. Even after Charles had lost his head, the quest was not over ; men were solemnly making oath to the genuineness of charters and of seals, of monuments and of glass windows, all of which were of their own invention. Bysshe, Garter King-of-Arms, fitly crowned the edifice under Cromwell's Protectorate, by inventing for himself a spurious descent and setting up in stained glass the arms of his alleged ancestors. That memorial glass I have myself seen.

But the school of historical genealogy had already come to the birth. While the learned Selden was writing on the baronage, Sir Robert Cotton forming his collections, and Dodsworth working on the Pipe Rolls and transcribing monastic charters, there was an outburst, in England as in France, of antiquarian research. Duchesne had already led the way, in 1619, by printing the Norman chronicles, and in 1624, by his *Histoire généalogique de la maison de Montmorency*. In England the public records in the Tower were searched with such assiduity that the knowledge of their contents under Charles the Second becomes absolutely astounding when we remember the difficulties under which they had been consulted. Private muniments were examined, registers of wills ransacked, and when, entering into Dodsworth's labours, Dugdale published the first *Monasticon* in 1655, it became possible to compile his great work on the Baronage, of which he issued the first volume twenty years later.

In the history of English genealogy this work is a landmark. It is so because it is inspired by the true historian's spirit. Although himself a King-of-Arms, Dugdale deliberately ignored the work of his predecessors and his colleagues ; I have found him significantly guarded in his language as to certain spurious descents which had official heraldic authority, and the only herald whose manuscript collections he used and used largely, was ' the learned and judicious Robert Glover, Somerset Herald,' as he styles him, who seems entitled to honourable distinction among his Elizabethan brethren for the care and faithfulness of his work. Let me illustrate his ideal. He speaks, on the opening page of his preface, of Smyth's great work on the Berkeleys as written ' in an historical way '—you should observe that phrase—' which I heartily wish may be a pattern for some others to follow, it being faithfully extracted, partly out of public records and partly from the great mass of antient charters and other memorials still remaining in Berkeley Castle.' There you have the ideal for which I stand to-day, ' historical genealogy ' in the sense that it is written on historical principles.

No doubt, his critical ability was not up to our own standard, but he stood for honesty, he strove for truth. And it is perhaps his supreme merit that for every statement, he gives his reference so that we can test it for ourselves. For the real student of genealogy that is the essential point and, if only for this, Dugdale deserves our gratitude. I must not linger further over the *Baronage of England*, but I may warn you that its weakest point is his acceptance of monastic statements as to the founder's family. These are, too often, the origin of persistent error and show the danger of departure from primary evidence as his source. Yet even here he is far superior to the French genealogist, La Roque, whose great *Histoire de la maison d'Harcourt*, published some years earlier, was constructed on the same principles, but whose *Preuves* are a lamentable jumble of evidence and of mere assertion.

From Dugdale I pass to Collins, who wrote under George the Second, and whose genealogical peerage is important, not only because it dominated the eighteenth century, but also because it became the basis of the well-known Burke's *Peerage*. Industrious and well-qualified though he was, Collins was fatally lacking, possibly from his want of means, in that manly independence which made Dugdale refuse to flatter family pride. His work is crammed with ludicrous genealogy, taken from the old heraldic pedigrees in the

7

possession of ennobled houses. Thus began those wild stories in the pages of Burke's *Peerage* which move historians to contempt and scorn. The historical statement, for instance, at the head of Lord Bolingbroke's pedigree, that his ancestor, William de St. John, ' came into England with the Conqueror, as grand master of the artillery and supervisor of the wagons and carriages, whence the horses' hames or collar was borne for his cognizance,' is taken bodily from Collins, who took it from a pedigree in the private possession of the great Bolingbroke himself. The St. Johns, as I have shown, did not even arrive in England until a later period.

English genealogy had fallen back into the old, bad, despicable groove, and, in spite of Garter Anstis, on whom Pope's epigram is harsh,[3] Blackstone, in the third quarter of the eighteenth century, could charge the heralds with ' such falsity and confusion in their records ' that ' now even their common seal will not be received as evidence in any court of justice in the kingdom.'

I pass to the era of the Great Reform Bill, from which period we may clearly distinguish the existence of two rival schools. On the one hand was that of the complaisant herald, typified by successive publications bearing the name of ' Burke ' and flooding the market with gorgeous pedigrees of new or old invention. The other, the critical and historical school, had a more limited public. Founded by John Gough Nichols with his valuable periodicals, which came to an end with the *Herald and Genealogist* in 1878, its work was successfully carried on by the *Genealogist*, in spite of the small demand for work of this character. It has been vigorously supplemented by the twelve volumes of the *Ancestor*, a publication definitely intended to deal with genealogy and heraldry on historical lines and enjoying the advantage of its editor's learning and singularly brilliant style. You will also find examples of the best modern

---

[3] A man of wealth is dubbed a man of worth,
Venus shall give him form, and Anstis birth.

methods in *Northamptonshire Families* and *Hertfordshire Families*, the two great folios produced by the ' Victoria County History.' I would further mention the *Complete Peerage*, especially the new edition, on account of its value for historical students, for here also the principles of our school are being rigidly enforced. In these days of widely scattered archaeological work one cannot enumerate all those who are helping on the cause, but I ought to mention the attempt of the late Mr. Joseph Foster, whose great *Alumni Oxonienses* should be known to every genealogist, to produce a peerage similar in scope to that of Sir Bernard Burke, but historically truthful in its family pedigrees. In that respect, at least, it was remarkably successful.

Many will, I know, sympathise with those who are striving to place genealogy on an historical basis, the more so because they work in the teeth of much discouragement. It is no easy or popular task to cleanse it of fiction or of folly—indeed it is far easier to construct a spurious pedigree than to demolish the imposture. Only the expert knows the time and labour it may cost to detect the falsehood of a pedigree, especially if its compiler has been careful to conceal the fatal flaws by adducing no evidence or none, at least, that can be tested.

The serious thing is that there is not any means by which the public, the uninitiated, can distinguish between the work of these rival schools. If it has been impossible, as it has been till now, to know even if a man were a genuine baronet or not, who can be expected to distinguish the true genealogy from the false. ' Mais où sont donc vos chancelleries ? ' a Frenchman once exclaimed to me. Well, we have now a *Chancellerie* for our rapidly increasing orders, but for pedigrees there has always been only the Heralds' College. Ought we to accept the fact that a pedigree is ' recorded,' as they call it, at the Heralds' College, as proof that it satisfies the requirements of the modern critical school ? Is the existence of a pedigree among the ' records '

of the College the real test of its truth ? If not, you have
no standard ; you have only individual opinion.

Well, however excellent its methods, however learned its
members may be, you must first remember that the College
has a ' past ' ; and its ' records,' dating from that ' past '
are, I believe, valid. By ' records ' it means its canonical
scriptures as distinct from its apocrypha, but I find it sometimes difficult to learn what is actually *de fide*. In the
second place, an old corporation has, of necessity, traditions ;
it cannot, without difficulty, radically change its methods.
Here and there, at least, old methods may survive. Let me
prove my point. A member of the College whose family
had been traced, on historical lines, by record evidence,
back to its modest origin in the fourteenth century, published
some years ago, an account of it on the old lines, deriving
it from a knightly ancestor under Henry II ' on record,'
with a predecessor under William Rufus. And, in the
grand Elizabethan manner, he endowed these mythical
forebears with no less mythical wives.

Again, a pedigree of the Trafford family by a member of
the College, which describes itself as ' compiled from the
Records of the Heralds' College, Record Office, Probate
Registries and other reliable sources,' opens thus : ' Ran-
dolph, Lord of Trafford. This Thane lived in the reign of
King Canute, and died about 1050.' This ' thane ' we
further learn, was succeeded by a son, Ralf, and by a
grandson, Robert, of whom the latter was ' born about
1045.' We historians, of course, know that this *must* be
false, because Lancashire ' thanes,' who were born long
before the Conquest, did not receive Norman names
generation after generation.

Another pedigree here begins with a ' cousin-german ' to
William the Conqueror, who marries a ' daughter of Walter,
son of Wolfred, lord of Hatton, co. Chester.' But, two
pages further on, this ' Wolfred ' reappears as ' Wolfayth
de Hatton,' son of ' Yvon, a noble of Normandy.' Blissfully unconscious that these names represent the same

creature, the compiler first makes him exist before, and then after the Conquest. ' Yvon,' of course, is a lady's name and is, therefore, as absurd for ' a noble of Normandy ' as is ' Wolfayth ' for his son. But the name is precious, for it tells the expert whence this nonsense is derived, namely, that old Elizabethan pedigree concocted for Sir Christopher Hatton, which, you may remember, began with ' Yvon, a Norman noble who came in with the Conqueror.' Here then, we have again a survival of the old methods.

The expert will also recognise the true Elizabethan touch in the wondrous tale of Mr. Richard Smith, with which I have dealt at great length in my *Peerage and Pedigree* (vol. ii, pp. 134 *et seq.*). In a similar case, under Queen Elizabeth, Robert Cooke, Clarenceux, announced, in inimitable language in the case of the Mildmay genealogy, that—

' As it is dayly seen that tyme (Destroyer and Consumer of all thinges) throwes downe and extinguishes many auntient and honorable families, or by altering and translating their houses and habitations, obscures their worthy races and extractions that thereby God's justice may be felt and man's patience tryed. So comes it to passe as often that the same tyme (mother of truthe) bringeth to light and discovereth to be gentlemen of Longe and Auntient contynuance dyvers whose auncestors (sondry yeares beffore) were not reputed of such Antiquitie, that thereby the same God's mercie may be sene and his bountie praysed.' [4]

The same providential discovery was made in the case of Mr. Smith, a successful business man, of whom it was no secret that his father was of lowly origin. Suddenly, in Burke's *Landed Gentry* (1894) it was revealed to the world that he had a gorgeous pedigree, beginning at the Norman Conquest, and that he was heir-male of the body to Sir Mychell de Carington, Standard-bearer, on crusade, to King Richard the First. Here, you observe, we touch history. The same work was able to announce, four years later (1898), that ' the descent is recorded in the Heralds'

---

[4] (A.D. 1583) *Misc. Gen. & Her.*, ii, 193.

College in an unbroken line for over 700 years.' The great history of the family, published more recently, explained that the earlier ancestors of those *before* the standard-bearer had failed to satisfy the strict tests now required by the heralds. ' There is somewhere,' said Freeman of Sir Bernard Burke, ' a last straw that breaks the back even of a King-of-Arms.'

But the standard-bearer, at least, was proved. Well, it is my painful duty to assure you that no such person is known ; in the chronicles and records of the time you will search for him in vain. His existence rests wholly and solely on a gross Elizabethan forgery, which appears to have been accepted as genuine by Dethick, Garter King-of-Arms and Robert Cooke, Clarenceux, which is just what we should expect of those two wretched heralds.

Until the officers of the College are wholly freed from Elizabethan influence we cannot accept their verdict on a pedigree as, in every case, decisive. We, the advocates of historical methods, are, happily, under no necessity of pouring our new wine into old Elizabethan bottles. In us the word ' tradition ' excites no reverence, for the expert knows that those who appeal to it do so in default of any proof for the origin they seek to claim. Show us the evidence—valid evidence, such as historians would accept—and we will gladly admit a pedigree from the Norman Conquest, its splendour increased by the very methods which have enabled us to purge genealogy of its dross and to give you its ore alone.

AN APPROVED PRECONQUEST PEDIGREE

THERE are more methods than one of constructing for one-self a pedigree. To some, ' tradition ' is a sufficient warrant for a vague but lengthy descent, although there is, perhaps, no ' authority ' so unworthy of credit.   Indeed, the so-called ' tradition ' is really, in most cases, the guess of some speculative antiquary or even of a member of the family itself, at no remote period.[1] Others, again, appear to be blissfully unaware of the need for evidence and for proof : to them one statement is virtually as good as another : of a very different school are those who would disarm the critic by actually insisting on that need, and proclaiming that the pedigree has been proved.   Dr. Copinger, for instance, in his vast *History . . . of the Smith Carrington Family* asserted that

There are not many pedigrees which can be taken back like that of Smith-Carrington in the *direct male line* to the Conquest. Each descent is fully verified, etc., etc.

With that alleged pedigree from the Conquest—of which the earlier portion I have shown was a ' late Victorian addition ' —I have fully dealt in *Peerage and Pedigree* (ii, 143 *et seq.*). Shortly after the appearance of Dr. Copinger's work,[2] Mr. George Grazebrook published, in *Miscellanea Genealogica et Heraldica* (4th series, vol. ii), his descent in the male line

[1] See *Peerage and Pedigree*, i, 296, 302, 315, 317 ; ii, 45, 72-3, 83, 91, 108, 118.   Compare the observations of a very sound antiquary, Mr. A. N. Palmer.   ' Is there not shown, in the history of the Broughton and Wyke families, how untrustworthy, how contrary to truth, is much that passes under the name of " tradition " ? . . . there are people who . . . are blind to improbabilities, have no conception of the nature of evidence, and never think of subjecting any statement, especially if it be once printed, to due examination.'   (*Y Cymmrodor*, ix, p. 71.) See also p. 100 below.

[2] In fact they seem to have been both published in 1907.

from an even earlier period. This he entitled ' Pedigree of the Family of Grazebrook with ample proofs for every generation from 1035. . . .'

The pedigree then given to the world was only, however, the coping-stone to that which Mr. Grazebrook had published several years before. This latter traced his family ' since their settlement at Shenston, co. Stafford in 1204,' [3] and with that portion of the pedigree I am not here concerned. Of it I will only say that Bartholomew, with whom it begins, was father of Robert, living at least as late as 1300, and that I can find no proof of the date ' 1204.' One notes also of John ' Gresbrook,' temp. Henry VIII, through whom the descent is traced, that even Burke's *Landed Gentry*, which does not err on the side of scepticism, asserts that ' his parentage has not been ascertained,' while Mr. Grazebrook's argument on the subject strikes one as an unconvincing piece of special pleading. There was also a mysterious change of coat in the eighteenth century, the author's ancestors then adopting arms quite different from those of the earlier Grazebrooks.

It is, however, with the earlier pedigree—a quite distinct production—that I am here concerned. A descent in the male line from 1035 would indeed be a *rara avis*, and even if it only reached the Conquest, it is, as its author observes, ' hardly ever possible to prove a descent for two or three generations after the Conquest as we (*sic*) have done.' Mr. Grazebrook, not only parades his proofs ; he is justly sceptical of those descents which are not duly proved. He speaks of the ' contemporaneous documents from which our accurate pedigree has now been impregnably proved ' ; [4] his principle is ' make good everything as you go along . . . like clinching down the points of nails';[5] and he sternly writes:—

I frankly confess that, after years of examination, I refuse to

[3] *Misc. Gen. et Her.* (1899).

[4] George Grazebrook, *Pedigree of the Family of Grazebrook* (Reprint), p. 57.

[5] *Ibid.* p. 21.

accept any early pedigree which is not provided with dates and references to where the proofs may be seen. This is a great innovation, I know, as such skeletons have passed current for centuries, but now they are quite inadmissible. The records are collected together and open to everyone. . . . I prefer to leave my work, like that famous castle of Wark, small and compact, and quite impregnable.[6]

This, no doubt, is most impressive, and the principle expressed admirable. But when the expert examines the pedigree and tries to find the proofs to make it thus ' impregnable,' he is driven almost to distraction. Different pedigrees, different generations, are jumbled up together, and record evidence is intermingled with what is mere assertion. I had to complain of similar methods in Dr. Copinger's volume, methods which would baffle any but an expert, in trying to test the pedigree. And the expert has just cause for complaint, when the task involves so needless a waste of time. But if he has the necessary patience, he will at length discover that the vital parts in Mr. Grazebrook's case are two. The first is that Bartholomew ' de Gresbroc,' who founded the Staffordshire line, was a younger son of ' Robert, son of Roger de Gresbroc ' in Yorkshire.[7] The second is that this ' Roger de Gresbroc ' was ' Roger de Busli III, who had settled his residence at Gresbrook and so taken that name.'[8] After close and repeated study of Mr. Grazebrook's paper, I have failed to discover any proof whatever of either of these points. They rest, so far as I can find, on his own assertion alone. And yet he declines, in another case, to give the names of possible cadets on the ground that he will not do so ' without absolute evidence.'[9]

With regard to the first, I have always held, as a canon of genealogical research, that alleged descent from a cadet should be viewed with some suspicion. In the old days of pedigree-making it was a favourite device, to assert such descent, but the expert knows the extreme difficulty of finding any proof of it. And in this case, the alleged cadet

[6] *Ibid.* p. 72. [7] *Ibid.* p. 69. [8] *Ibid.* p. 63. [9] *Ibid.* p. 43.

is found in another county. The second point is also one that urgently requires proof. Mr. Grazebrook, naturally, is anxious to claim that the name of ' Gresbroc ' was actually borne by his alleged ancestors, the Buslis, before Bartholomew de Gresbroc turns up in Staffordshire ; he asserts that Roger de Busli ' resided at Gresbroc . . . and so became " de Gresbroc " after 1130 '[10] . . . ' having settled his residence at Gresbrok and so taken that name.'[11] Again, ' he was generally called ' de Gresbroc, as explained.'[12] Of his son also, Mr. Grazebrook states that ' after his father's death in 1156 ' he ' left Scauceby and took up his residence at Gresbroc and used that name as his father had done.[13] For all this, there is not offered even a vestige of proof ; nay, Mr. Grazebrook actually produces a goodly number of documents in which Roger or Robert is named, and in not a single one is either of them styled ' de Gresbroc.' In view of his ' vaunted proofs for every statement ' that he makes, the revelation is astounding.

The house of ' Busli '—of which the Grazebrooks were, according to him, not only the descendants, but actually the heirs male—was founded here by Roger de ' Busli,' one of the magnates of the Conquest, of whose vast fief, afterwards known as the ' Honour ' of ' Blythe,' Tickhill Castle, was the head. Roger had a younger brother, Ernald, who held Kimberworth, Scawsby, and other knight's fees, and it is from him that the author claims to be descended in the male line. The heirship, both of Roger and Ernald, is very well and clearly set out for several generations in Mr. Holm's valuable *Chartulary of St. John of Pontefract*,[14] and, for excellent reasons, as we shall see, Mr. Grazebrook's alleged ancestor is not to be found.

It is not an infrequent delusion that because the forms of names, whether of persons or of places, were not originally

---

[10] George Grazebrook, *Pedigree of the Family of Grazebrook* (Reprint), p. 84.

[11] *Ibid.* p. 63.   [12] *Ibid.* p. 64.   [13] *Ibid.* p. 66.

[14] *Yorks. Arch. Soc. Rec. Ser.* vol. xxx, pp. 608-9.

stereotyped as they are at present, we can therefore treat as identical, names that were wholly distinct. By this ingenuous method, we find the ' Busli ' pedigree is here constructed, with such resultant confusion that even the author himself finds it impossible to explain. Now there are cases in which, no doubt, names are easily confused ; the Gresleys, for instance, who took their name from Gresley in Derbyshire, are, at times, difficult to distinguish in records from the Nottinghamshire Greasleys of Greasley, or from that family of Gresle or Grelley, which had its seats at Manchester, and at Swineshead in Lincolnshire.[15]   But with the house of ' Busli ' there should be no such difficulty ; it is admitted on all hands that this name represents what is now Bully, just to the west of Neufchatel in the far east of Normandy, and the name repeatedly occurs in Yorkshire charters as ' Bulli.' [16]   But there is a wholly distinct name, viz. ' Buissei,' [17] which would seem to represent some such place (in Normandy) as Boissei, or Boissy, or Boissey. Now Mr. Grazebrook has constructed his pedigree by mixing up the bearers of these two distinct names as if they were one and the same.

A single instance will suffice to prove my point. In *Bracton's Note Book* (ed. Maitland), there is a plea (No. 1085) concerning William de Bussey, nephew and co-heir of Walter Espec, a well-known baron. This is the William ' de Busseio ' of the Pipe Roll of 1160 (p. 37). Now Mr. Grazebrook, dealing with this record, calmly transforms the ' de Bussey ' into ' de Busli,' [18] yet on reverting later to this plea, he duly gives the name therein as ' de Bussey.' [19]

[15] See my paper on ' The origin of the Shirleys and of the Gresleys,' in the *Derbyshire Arch. and Nat. Hist. Soc. Journ.* 1905.

[16] See, for instance, the *Chartulary of St. John's, Pontefract* (ed. Holmes).

[17] In 1179, it is ' Bussei ' on the Pipe Roll and ' Boissei ' on the Chancellor's Roll. It occurs twice, as ' Buissei ' on the Pipe Roll of 1178 and also as ' Busseia ' and ' Bussei ' on the Chancellor's Roll of that year ; on the Pipe Roll of 1160 it is latinised as ' de Buisseio.' On those of 1156 and 1157 it is ' Buissei.'

[18] Geo. Grazebrook, *op. cit.* p. 26.   [19] *Ibid.* p. 33.

But, not content with this confusion, he even annexes the third family, the well-known Lancashire house of Bussel of Penwortham as ' Buslis,' and states that ' Mr. Farrer shows many Busseis (*sic*) occurring in his Lancashire Records of the twelfth century.' [20]   It is bad enough to introduce such wanton confusion, but it is far worse to accuse of ignorance those who are not guilty of these inaccuracies and blunders. Mr. Grazebrook does this [21] when he rebukes the learned and laborious editor of the Pontefract Cartulary, for being unacquainted with ' the Lancashire branch ' of the ' Buslis.'[22]

I will now show in detail how Mr. Grazebrook has constructed his (alleged) early pedigree, by mixing up the house of ' Busli ' with that of ' Buissey.'   Mr. Holms gives the pedigree of the younger line of ' Busli ' as follows :

Ernald of Kimberworth, etc.,
|
Jordan (Pipe Roll of 1120)
|
Richard
(A founder of Roche Abbey in 1147)
|
Richard de Builli,
succeeded in 1165

This last Richard's succession is proved by the Pipe Roll of 1165 (11 Hen. II), on which we find him as ' Ricardus de Builli,' charged with ' relief ' for six knight's fees of the honour of Tickhill (p. 55).   It should be noticed how distinct is the name ' Builli ' from that of ' Buissei.'   These 6 knight's fees were the holding (Kimberworth, Scawsby, etc.) of the cadet branch of the ' Buslis ' founded by Ernald.

The other family, that of ' Buissei,' succeeded to a portion

---

[20] See index to *Lancashire Pipe Rolls and Early Charters* (ed. Farrer), pp. 453-4.

[21] Geo. Grazebrook, *op. cit.* p. 19.   [22] *Ibid.* p. 68, note.

of Walter Espec's barony as his senior co-heirs. The
relationship was this

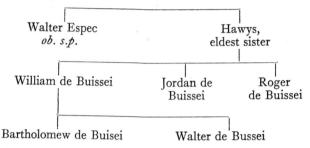

Walter Espec | Hawys,
ob. s.p. | eldest sister

William de Buissei | Jordan de Buissei | Roger de Buissei

Bartholomew de Buisei | Walter de Bussei

Mr. Grazebrook calmly transforms these Busseis into
Buslis, and finally, as I have said, asserts that Roger, the
youngest son, took the name of 'de Gresbrok.'

The pedigree which he thus constructed runs thus [23] :—

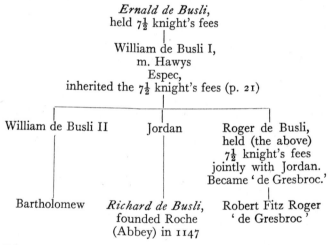

Ernald de Busli,
held $7\frac{1}{2}$ knight's fees

William de Busli I,
m. Hawys
Espec,
inherited the $7\frac{1}{2}$ knight's fees (p. 21)

William de Busli II | Jordan | Roger de Busli,
held (the above)
$7\frac{1}{2}$ knight's fees
jointly with Jordan.
Became 'de Gresbroc.'

Bartholomew | *Richard de Busli*,
founded Roche
(Abbey) in 1147 | Robert Fitz Roger
'de Gresbroc'

The only real members of the Busli family in this pedigree
are those whom I have italicised, namely Ernald and
Richard : the others have all been pitchforked in from outside by Mr. Grazebrook. The connecting link, which he
tries to establish is the holding of $7\frac{1}{2}$ knight's fees by

[23] *Ibid.* pp. 35, 55, 84.

Ernald and his heirs [24] in Kimberworth, Scawsby, etc., which is ' a sufficient proof of the direct male descent,' and he repeatedly asserts that Jordan and his brother, in this pedigree, are recorded as paying relief for these knight's fees on the Pipe Roll of 1156 (2 Henry II). The actual entry on the Roll is professedly printed on p. 41 and we are told that they ' inherited jointly the original $7\frac{1}{2}$ knight's fees ' and paid ' this very large sum which was their " Relevium " on the change of ownership and by it we see that the original $7\frac{1}{2}$ fees from gradual diminutions were then accepted as only 5 feoda and one third.' When we turn to the printed text of the Pipe Roll, we discover, with natural astonishment, that the passage really runs :—

' Et Jord[ano] de Buissei et Rog[er]o [fratri] eius xxvi li. xiii s et iiii d.' Not a word about ' relief,' nor any possibility of its being ' relief,' for the payment is made *to* the brothers *by* the ' sheriff.' [25] To crown all, the name we see is not Busli, but ' Buissei.'

Further, having first stated that the $7\frac{1}{2}$ fees were reduced to $5\frac{1}{3}$ fees, and then that ' henceforth these estates were to be taken as knight's fees only,' he finds them afterwards paid for as 6 fees and says, ' I cannot account for these discrepancies.' [26] Of course he cannot, if he first invents the figures $5\frac{1}{3}$ and 5, from inability to understand records.

Again we find him writing :

It strikes me as rather unusual that Richard and his wife should found Roche Abbey in 1147, when he was 31, and his father and uncle both alive and in joint possession of the family estates, which they held for 10 years afterwards.[27]

The explanation is, of course, that Jordan and Roger de ' Buissei ' were not the father and uncle of Richard de ' Busli,' but were of a different family and that they were not in possession of the (' Busli ') family estates (i.e. the 6 or $7\frac{1}{2}$

[24] Geo. Grazebrook, *op. cit.* pp. 8, 9, 10, 17, 21, 41, 42, 45, 55, 56, 63, 84.

[25] See also ' Et Jordano de Buisseio et Rog[er]o fratri ei[us] X. m. arg. per breve Regis ' (*Pipe Roll, Rec. Com.* 2, 3, 4 Hen. II, p. 85).

[26] *Ibid.* p. 43.   [27] *Reprint*, p. 44.

knight's fees). One of the quotations that Mr. Grazebrook selects to place at the head of his production is, ' Daylight and truth meet us with a clear dawn.'

Is it, one is asked, worth while to spend time and toil on exposing such productions ? That it is a shocking waste of both, one may at once concede. But there are features of this pedigree which makes its exposure a necessity. In the first place it is published to the world in a genealogical organ ; in the second it is compiled with the sole object of enabling its author to boast of descent in the male line from a great Conquest house ; third, it is a brand new compilation, without even the excuse of tradition, being similar in this respect to Dr. Copinger's Carington compilation[28] for the Norman period ; in the fourth it is distinguished by its ' vaunted proof ' of each step in the descent and its author's loud insistence on its ' impregnable ' character. When a writer takes his aim from Cicero, as being ' to show clearly what is true and accurate,' when he sternly refuses to accept ' any early pedigree ' that is not supported by references and proofs, he cannot complain if his own tests are applied to his own pedigree or feel surprised if it calls for a more severe exposure than those which are put forward with no such assurance of ' proof.'

[28] See p. 13 above.

THE ORIGIN OF THE CAVENDISHES

APART from fortunate marriages, the leading English families have mainly owed their rise to three great sources : successful trade, the law, and the spoils of monastic houses. Nor have they always owed it to one source alone. Even the Howards, although they attained their great position by marriage, were originally founded by a judge, who raised their name from obscurity. But the house of Cavendish perhaps enjoys the singular distinction of combining all four of these sources in its origin. Now that its Fitz Gernon descent has been practically discarded, its accredited founder is Sir John Cavendish, that hapless chief justice who was put to death by a Suffolk mob in 1381. But its great upward leap was due to that William Cavendish, who, though a cadet, was fortunate enough to obtain, as a young man, the significant appointment of a Commissioner for visiting and taking the surrenders of certain religious houses. This start on the road to fortune, it is fairly assumed, he owed to the influence of his elder brother, George, the gentleman usher, biographer, and devoted servant of Wolsey.[1]

Obviously, one of those Tudor officials who made the most of their opportunities when opportunities were great, William became an auditor of the Court of Augmentations and then treasurer of the Chamber to Henry VIII, Edward VI, and Mary, obtaining, in due course, not only grants of lands, but the spoils of the monasteries in many places. He did not, however, neglect the chances offered by marriage. In the words of Collins, the peerage writer, ' the greatest

---

[1] It was formerly supposed that William himself was the biographer of Wolsey, but this error was exposed in 1814.

addition to his fortunes was made by a prudent and happy match with Elizabeth, his third wife.'[2] This was the famous ' Bess of Hardwick,' who brought him a fortune, derived from her first matrimonial adventure as well as from her own family, a fortune which enabled her to build Hardwick, to found Chatsworth, and to leave such wealth to her sons that it secured for one of them a peerage as first Earl of Devonshire.

The family obtained its barony (1605) and its earldom (1676) at the very time when the pedigree-maker was eager to provide with Norman descent, houses founded in Tudor times ; and one of them must have selected the Cavendish family as his prey. Why he should have pitched upon Gernon as the name of their Norman ancestors has never been ascertained, nor is it worth while wasting time over his gross concoction. He took the Robert Gernon of Domesday, made him into Robert de Gernon, and dragged in Ranulph de ' Gernon,' earl of Chester, as probably of the same lineage with ' Robert.' Then he introduced Ralf de Gernon (d. 1248), founder of Lees priory in Essex, as son of another Ralf. Possibly he wished to annex this pious founder because he was also Lord of Bakewell in the Peak ; but in any case his pedigree is wrong, for I have elsewhere shown that the true name of Ralf's father was Osbert de Gladfen.[3] Finally he made a Roger de Gernon of Grimston Hall, Suffolk, marry the heiress of the manor of Cavendish, also in that county, by whom he left ' Sir John Cavendish ' and younger sons, one of whom, Stephen Cavendish, became Mayor of London.[4]

The credit of exposing this concoction is originally due to a country gentleman, Mr. Thomas Ruggles, F.S.A., who in 1712 proved from deeds that the chief justice acquired

[2] *Historical Collections*, p. 15, and *Peerage*.

[3] *Essex Arch. Trans.* (N.S.), xii, 91.

[4] The whole of this preposterous pedigree will be found in Collins' *Historical Collections* (1752), pp. 1-4, and his *Peerage* (1768), i, 279-283. His authorities are a family *stemma*, Seager's MS. *Baronagium* (Seager was Garter) and Cott. MS., Julius, F. 11.

the manor of Cavendish Overhall from John d'Odding-selles in 1359, so that he cannot have taken his name from it, as alleged, owing to his father having married its heiress.[5] It is a singular fact that Sir John Cavendish, in all his dealings with Suffolk lands, is usually associated with Alice, his wife.

Mr. Ruggles also printed from Cottonian MS., Julius, F. xi, the pedigree to which Collins refers, and which he himself styled ' a very imperfect sketch.'[6] It is this.

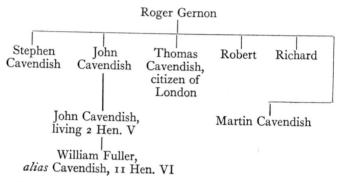

The Gernon pedigree being fictitious,[7] the parentage of the chief justice remains to be discovered. This, so far as I know, has not yet been done. I propose, however, to show that there is some reason to connect the origin of the ducal house with the family of mercers and drapers in the city of London. Collins, we have seen, was willing to allow that Stephen Cavendish, who rose to be Mayor of London, was a younger brother of the chief justice, and, as such, a Gernon by birth ; but his parentage can be proved and was very different. When we examine the admitted

---

[5] *Archaeologia*, xi. *The Dict. Nat. Biog.* (ix, 353) suggests a marriage settlement, see also Rye's *Suffolk Fines* (Suffolk Inst. of Arch.), p. 218. Sir John Wingfield and Gilbert de Denham join with Sir John Cavendish and Alice his wife in the transaction.

[6] *Archaeologia*, xi, 52.

[7] It is now left doubtful in Burke's *Peerage* whether ' Sir John Cavendish was or was not the son of the member of the baronial family of Gernon.'

pedigree, we find that Thomas Cavendish, of the King's Exchequer, father of that William who raised the fortunes of the house, desired in his will, dated 13th April, 1524 (15 Henry VIII), to be buried in the church of St. Thomas of Acres, . . . in the North Isle of the Quere, next unto my grandfather, William Cavendish, if it may conveniently be.' And his said grandfather had similarly desired in his will (1433) to be buried ' in the church of St. Thomas the Martyr of Acon.' Now this was the burial place of mercers subsequently known as the Mercers' Chapel, and this William Cavendish is actually styled ' mercer.' [8] Stephen Cavendish, the Mayor, had similarly desired by his will (1372) to be buried in the quire of the same church.[9] He was a draper,[10] but he can be shown to have been a son of Thomas Cavendish, mercer or draper (*mercerus seu pannarius*),[11] who, in his will (1348), similarly desired to be buried in the same church.[12]

His parentage is proved, not merely by the fact that he names his father Thomas in his will, but by the fact that he bequeathed ' rents in augmentation of a chantry founded by his father in the church of " St. Mary de Colcherche." ' For Thomas, the testator of 1348, held houses in that parish and left rents ' subject to a charge for the maintenance of chantries in the parish church of St. Mary de Colcherche.' Moreover, in or about 1358, we have a reference to ' the chantry of Thomas de Cavendish, draper, in the church of St. Mary ' de Colcherche.' [13] This is decisive. We have now, therefore, placed Stephen Cavendish in a nest of mercers and drapers. His brother, John, was a mercer,[14] with a shop in Soper Lane, and he himself in his will names a nephew, Thomas ' Pyek,' who was clearly Thomas Pyke,

---

[8] *Calendar of Letter Books*, K, p. 127.

[9] Sharpe, *Calendar of Wills*, 749.

[10] *Calendar of Letter Books*, F, *passim*.

[11] His son John describes him as a mercer, and his son Thomas as a draper.

[12] Sharpe, *Calendar of Wills*, i, 547-8.

[13] *Calendar of Letter Books*, G, p. 118.   [14] *Ibid.* F, p. 95.

draper,[15] afterwards Alderman and Sheriff. He also leaves a reversionary interest to Richard, son of Richard Cavendish, who occurs as an orphan, a city ward, son of Richard Cavendish, ' late draper,' 30th November, 1365, and 5th February, 1375-6.[16] But the Mayor is also found as Stephen Cavendish of London, party to a fine relating to Reydon, Suffolk, in 1363.[17]

Passing to the Mayor's father, Thomas, we gather from his will (dated 30th October, 1348),[18] that he was a wealthy man, but in another quarter we make the unexpected discovery that he was not by birth a Cavendish nor even a Suffolk man. An entry early in the year 1312 records his admission thus : ' Thomas de Cavendish, the son of William atte Watre de Ewelle, late apprentice of Walter de Cavendish, mercer, who had served with him eight years.[19]

This entry is confirmed by the fact that Ewell Church (Co. Surrey) is the only one outside of London to which he makes a bequest for a chantry.[20]

A short chart pedigree of these City Cavendishes can now be put together and may be profitably compared with that in Cotton MS., Julius, F. 11.[21]

It will be observed that the elder Thomas and his sons, John and Thomas, must have died within a few months of each other, which is of special interest in view of the fact that this was the time when the Black Death was raging among the citizens of London.

There is no proof that Sir John Cavendish, the chief justice, was of this family, however probable it may be ; but then there is also no proof that he was, as alleged, the direct ancestor of the ducal house of Cavendish. The only indication, so far as I can find, that he was even connected

[15] 9th March, 1377-8 (*Ibid.* H, p. 76).

[16] *Ibid.* G, p. 201 ; H, p. 21 ; Richard the father appears as living and a draper, 15th August, 1353, and 1356-7 (*Ibid.* G, p. 13 ; F, p. 39).

[17] Rye, *Suffolk Fines*, p. 229.   [18] Sharpe, *Calendar of Wills*, i, 547-8.

[19] *Calendar of Letter Books*, D, pp. 167-8.

[20] Sharpe, *Calendar of Wills*, i, 548.   [21] See p. 24 above.

with them, is that the widow of his son and heir, namely, Rose—who, I find, was a daughter of Adam de Bury, Mayor of London—named as her executors in 1419, William and Robert Cavendish, who were brothers, of whom William was, without doubt, their ancestor.

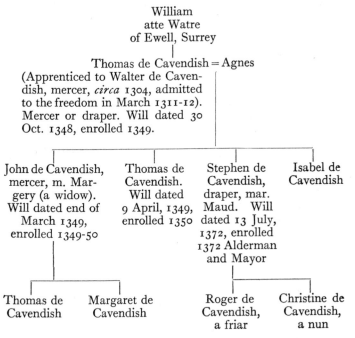

William
atte Watre
of Ewell, Surrey

Thomas de Cavendish = Agnes
(Apprenticed to Walter de Cavendish, mercer, *circa* 1304, admitted to the freedom in March 1311-12). Mercer or draper. Will dated 30 Oct. 1348, enrolled 1349.

| John de Cavendish, mercer, m. Margery (a widow). Will dated end of March 1349, enrolled 1349-50 | Thomas de Cavendish. Will dated 9 April, 1349, enrolled 1350 | Stephen de Cavendish, draper, mar. Maud. Will dated 13 July, 1372, enrolled 1372 Alderman and Mayor | Isabel de Cavendish |

Thomas de Cavendish — Margaret de Cavendish

Roger de Cavendish, a friar — Christine de Cavendish, a nun

The connecting link with the chief justice is alleged to be one John Cavendish, or, as Burke's *Peerage* styles him, ' Sir John Cavendish,' esquire of the body to King Richard II, who was his younger son and who left three sons, the above William (of London, mercer) and two others. But there is no proof of this affiliation. The chief justice mentions in his will his son and heir, Andrew, with Andrew's wife, Rose, and daughter, Margaret, but not a son John.[22] This may be only negative evidence, but we can go further.

[22] Collins, *Hist. Coll.* 4 ; *Peerage,* i, 283-4 and *Test. Vet.* i, 110.

The very existence of this John rests upon three statements : (1) that, as an esquire of the King's House, it was
he who slew Wat Tyler at Smithfield in 1381 ; (2) that he
' or another of his name (which in that age was wrote
Caundish) served under King Henry V, in his wars in
France and was in the famous battle of Agincourt, 1415 ' ;
(3) that, in 4 Henry V, the King gave him ' the office of
Brouderer of his wardrobe, to act by himself or deputies,'
etc.[23]   We may, in the first place, dispose of John Caundish,
' The Brouderer,' who did receive the office as stated, and
who was sworn joint master of the ' Brawderers,' 26th
November, 1431.[24]   But this John is fully accounted for ;
he made his will, 8th May, 1433, as John Caundish,
' brouderer,' and the wife and sons whom he names are all
entirely different from the wife and sons assigned to John,
the alleged son of the chief justice.[25]   Worse still, we find
that Collins, a few pages earlier,[26] had actually made John
Cavendish of the ' Embroiders' Company ' to be quite
another person, being second son of Roger Cavendish.   As
far as the mention of a John Cavendish as present at the
Battle of Agincourt, Collins could only cite a MS. catalogue
of peers, from the reign of Stephen to that of Henry VIII,
in the library of John Anstis, which is obviously no
authority.

There remains only the chief achievement of this alleged
John, the only one which has found its way into Burke's
Peerage, namely, his infliction on Wat Tyler of his mortal
wound at Smithfield, a service for which he was knighted

[23] These are not set forth by Collins in *Hist. Coll.* p. 5 and *Peerage*, i,
234-5.

[24] *Letter Books of the Corporation.*

[25] Sharpe, *Calendar of Wills*, ii, 472-3. He names Matilde his late
wife, Alice his then wife, and Thomas, Rowland, and Henry, his sons
(the sons assigned in Burke to John, the alleged son of the Chief
Justice, are William, Robert, and Walter).   The ' brouderer ' does not
mention the Essex manor of Strethall, but it is afterwards found in
possession of Thomas Cawndishe, his son and heir and Agnes, his wife.
It was subsequently held by Augustine Caundish (Morant's *Essex*).

[26] *Peerage*, i, 281.

28

and given £40 a year in lands.[27]   This statement appears
to be derived from Stow's *Annals*, and Burke's *Peerage*
follows Collins in asserting that 'the mob . . . being
incensed in a more than ordinary degree against the chief
justice, Cavendish, his son John, having killed the notorious
Wat Tyler,' dragged him into Bury market-place and there
had him beheaded.   This statement, the reader will
observe, confirms in a striking manner John's alleged
paternity.   Unfortunately, the Chief Justice was beheaded
by the mob (not at Bury but on the extreme north-west
border of Suffolk) on 14th June, while Wat Tyler was not
killed till the day *after* (15th June).   So the sequence of
events is fatal to the story that the mob were avenging the
action of his ' son.'

When we come to examine the story of John's exploit, we
find a perfectly simple, if somewhat startling, explanation.
The very valuable ' Anonimal Chronicle,' published by Mr.
George Trevelyan in the *English Historical Review*, tells
us that Wat Tyler was mortally wounded by one of the
King's household, but does not mention the name.
Froissart, who comes so generally to grief over our English
names, calls him ' messire Jehan Standuick,' in which he is
followed by Holinshed, but Knighton mentions him as
' Ralph Standiche.' [28]   It was reserved for Stow to convert
this ' esquire of the King's House ' into ' John Cavendish,'
and to state that he was knighted for his exploit and given
lands worth £40 a year.

One often finds that what at first sight might be deemed
an enquiry of genealogical interest has a wider and instructive bearing.   In this case we may learn at once how
strangely stories arise and how lightly errors are repeated
in the absence of intelligence and care.   For instance, to
take recent learning, Prof. Sir Charles Oman, who has made
a detailed study of the crisis,[29] states that the ' squire of John

[27] Mr. Ruggles accepted this in his paper (*Archaeologia*, xi, 56).

[28] Or ' de Standyche.'

[29] *The Great Revolt of* 1381 (Clarendon Press), 1906.

Standwick ' was one of those rewarded on the field by knighthood,[30] and explains that the third of the ' citizens of London ' who were knighted on the field ' was John Stand-wyche ' (*sic*).[31] It would seem, however, that the squire's name was not John Standwick (or Standwyche), nor was he one of the three citizens who were knighted on the field.

When ' the Anonimal Chronicle ' tells us that in addition to the Mayor, the King made ' three other Knights from among the citizens of London,' it should be clear to those of intelligence that the one whose name it omits would hardly be a squire of the King's Household ; as a matter of fact, it was an Alderman, Robert Launde.[32] Nor is there any difficulty about the squire's name, for the Patent Rolls show us Ralf Standish as a squire of the King's Household.

It is both amusing and instructive for the student of genealogy to trace the rival claims to the squire in question as an ancestor. In Burke's *History of Commoners*,[33] he is confidently identified, on the authority of Froissart and Holinshed, with John Standish, a cadet of the ancient house of Standish of Standish, which identification was continued in Burke's *Landed Gentry*, while Burke's *Peerage*, as we have seen, makes him to be John Cavendish. Both versions, of course, are wrong, for the squire's name was Ralf Standish, which is duly found in the Standish pedigree.

There is no proof, therefore, that this alleged John was either a son of Sir John Cavendish or indeed even existed. Collins vouches Weever for the fact that his wife was Joan, daughter of Sir William Clopton of Clopton in Suffolk, who was buried at Clare, but Weever only speaks of a ' Jone Candishe, daughter of Clopton,' without naming her husband.[34] For the parentage of William Cavendish, mercer, the proved ancestor of the family, we are dependent

---

[30] *The Great Revolt of* 1381 (Clarendon Press, 1906), p. 79.

[31] *Ibid.* p. 203.

[32] *Letter Book*, H, fo. 133 ; Weever, *Ancient Funeral Monuments*, p. 410.

[33] *Op. cit.* ed. 1835, ii, 65.   [34] *Funeral Monuments*, p. 742.

on the *Inquisition post-mortem* on his brother Robert, who died 17th March, 1438-9. The return to this inquisition gives his heir as ' Alice, wife of John Neel, daughter of John, grandfather of Robert,' [35] but this, it will be seen, does not enlighten us as to who was the *father* of William and Robert. That they were brothers is quite clear, for William, in his will (dated 5th January, 1432-3), names his brothers, Robert and Walter, and appoints the former guardian to his son Thomas.

To make the matter clearer, I here append a pedigree of these later Cavendishes.

William Cavendish of London, mercer, d. 1433	Robert Cavendish, Sergeant-at-law, d. *s.p.* 1439	Walter Cavendish

Thomas Cavendish
(in ward to Robert)
of Cavendish
Overhall, esq.

Thomas Cavendish
of Cavendish Overhall,
Clerk of the Pipe
in the Exchequer

George Cavendish of Cavendish Overhall	William Cavendish, Ancestor of the Dukes	Mary Cavendish

The obvious difficulty is caused by the finding in the inquisition that the heir of Robert Cavendish was not his brother's son, Thomas, but his aunt (grandfather's daughter) Alice Neel. This would seem to indicate that William was only his brother of the half-blood. In any case there is nothing to show what was their father's name, and if ' John,' Robert's grandfather, was indeed the Chief Justice, there is at least nothing to prove it. The daughter-in-law of the Chief Justice did indeed, as I said above, make them her

[35] *Archaeologia*, xi, 58.

executors (in 1419), and as early as 1411-12, William Cavendish, grandson and heir of the Chief Justice, had passed to them by fine the manor of Cavendish Overhall.[36]

In Mr. Ruggles' paper there is an engraving of the manor house, which was probably never of much consequence. The manor was sold by the head of the family, William Cavendish, son of George, in July 1569, and it is curious that this cousin-german of the first Earl of Devonshire, is styled at the time ' William Cavendish of London, mercer.' [37] He had reverted, therefore, to the ancestral occupation.

To sum up the results of our enquiry, so far as it has been carried, the pedigree of the ducal house is not proved, at present, further back than William Cavendish of London, mercer, who d. 1433. But it is very possible if not actually probable that this William was of the same family as Sir John Cavendish, the Chief Justice, and as those Cavendishes, mercers and drapers in the fourteenth century, one of whom Stephen Cavendish was Mayor of London in 1362. In the latter case, their earliest ancestor was William atte Watre of Ewell, Surrey. It would seem likely that the records of the Mercers or the Drapers' Company might throw further light on the early pedigree of the house.

[36] There were fines from him to each of them (Rye's *Suffolk Fines*, p. 282).

[37] *Archaeologia*, xi, 59.

THE ORIGIN OF THE CHURCHILLS

It is a singular fact that the Spencer-Churchills, Dukes of Marlborough (1702) and Lords Spencer of Wormleighton (1603), bear the names of two families for each of whom there was invented a splendid but a fabled origin.[1] With ' The Rise of the Spencers ' I have dealt in my *Studies in Peerage and Family History* (pp. 279 *et seq.*), and have there exposed that false descent from the noble house of Despencer which is still the root of their coat of arms. In the present paper, I shall briefly deal with the pedigree invented for the Churchills, a pedigree of even greater splendour, but one that is easier to destroy.

It is probably a widespread belief that the Dukes of Marlborough are true Churchills, descendants in the male line of the illustrious Duke. Yet, not only are they Spencers, but as Spencers they held the Dukedom for more than eighty years. It is indeed less than a century since, of their own volition, they adopted the name and arms of Churchill in addition to their own. They were under no compulsion to do so, nor were they even the senior representatives of John, Duke of Marlborough.[2] The history of four centuries is bridged, when in his admirable pamphlet on ' The Land,' the present Duke—' anxious to see repatriated on the soil that population which now has left it '—announces his intention of turning into ploughland the broad acres of Blenheim Park ' to make the countryside more prosperous and contented.' For it was the founder of his house, of whom he is the heir-male, John Spencer of Hodnell, who

[1] Both the fabulous pedigrees were set forth in full by Collins in his well-known *Peerage*, vol. i.

[2] That representation is vested in the heirs of his eldest daughter, who inherited his dukedom.

made his fortune as a rich grazier by turning into pasture for sheep the ploughlands of midland villages, who was one of those that in More's words, ' Leave no ground for tillage ; that enclose all into pasture, and throw down houses ; that pluck down towns, and leave nothing standing, but only the church to be made into a sheep house.'

History, as it used to be taught, was a dry and dreary thing, and yet the problems of the past were sometimes those of the present, and it binds together the present and the past when, in 1913, we find the Duke of Marlborough employing the same arguments as those which were brought against his ancestor, four centuries ago. When John Spencer acquired Wicken in 1512, he promptly extended its park, and turned arable into pasture. ' In 1514 a proclamation against ingrossing farms recited that the prevalent scarcity of grain and victuals was due to the ingrossing of farms and of the conversion of arable to pasture,' and the reconversion to arable was ordered. But this and the act of 1515 to the same effect were alike powerless to arrest the economic change.[3] Two years later, the inquisitions on the subject enlighten us as to John Spencer, and we have the result in his petition that if his land ' should be put in tyllage . . . yt shuld be to his uttour undoyng, for his livyng ys and hathe byn by the brede of cattell in his pastures.' [4] The aim, at that time, of the government was that which is described by the present Duke as

' The aim of every patriot, to see more people placed back on the soil . . . it takes more men to look after ploughland than it does to look after cattle pasturing in green fields, so that the success of any policy must be measured by the possibility of turning back into corn-land, some, or all of the land which has lapsed into pasture.'

But the key of the position is the price of wheat, and if land is used for pasture instead of for the growth of wheat, it is now, as under Henry VIII, simply because the economic law requires that it must be put to its most profitable use.

---

[3] *The Domesday of Inclosures*, pp. 8-9.   [4] *Ibid.* p. 487.

That is why, as an old Protectionist [5] (not Tariff Reformer), I have maintained that the national gain from substituting arable for pasture must far outweigh the difference in price of a very few shillings a quarter, which represent the whole difference between growing wheat at a loss and at a reasonable profit. Such a proposition is far simpler than the very complicated problems raised by ' Tariff Reform.'

Let us turn to the Churchills. Obscure as is their early history they were no mere Tudor upstarts ; a John Churchill, we shall find, was already styled ' gentleman ' in the days of Henry VI. But they wanted, of course, more than this. In the days of the great quest for a noble Conquest ancestor, there was invented for them a descent from a great Domesday baron, for whom, further, a noble grandfather was discovered beyond the sea. Sir Winston, the father of the great duke, shall tell the tale in his own words, but let me first explain how he came to tell it.

If the second Charles squandered his treasure in the wrong quarters with a lavish hand he displayed a perfect genius for economy in rewarding those who fought and bled in his own and his father's cause. Titles cost him nothing, but not even they were needed. Augmentations to a coat of arms—' augmentations of honour '—were deemed sufficient guerdon for the loyal cavalier who had not only fought for his King but had suffered loss in his cause. A lion of England, a lily of France, the national crest of St. George, such were some of the charges granted in an ' augmentation.' Thus it was that Sir Winston Churchill obtained as his first reward,[6] when the King had come to his own again, an ' augmentation of honour ' in the form of a canton on his shield, representing England's ancient flag, the cross of St. George on its ' silver field.' But when this was granted him by the King's sign-manual (5th December, 1661) he received with it the singular permission ' to leave

---

[5] See my article on ' The Protectionist Revival,' in *National Review* for June 1895.

[6] He had not then been knighted.

out the bend ' from his shield. The Churchill coat had been till then, sable, a lion rampant argent ; but with a bend over the lion. Sir Winston seems to have felt that this spoilt his coat, but its removal can only have been sanctioned on the ground that his coat would thenceforth be sufficiently distinguished from others by the added augmentation. This was, apparently, the view taken, and rightly taken (as it seems to me), by the heralds. But it was not that of Sir Winston. He wrote to ' Bluemantle ' at the Heralds' Office, 22nd June, 1686, from Mintern, his family seat.

I doe not suspect in the least my tytle to the ancient armes (as you call it) should be forgotten or questioned, since the monuments of my ancestors will clear that dispute . . . besides the very grant itselfe, by which I am licensed to beare, the lyon without the bend, evinces that till the tyme of the grant, it was borne with the bend.

And as to the canton, I take it not to be given me as any essentiall part of my coate (for so I refused to accept it), but (as 'tis expressed in the grant) as an augmentation of honour, and if my son think it not so, I know ' not ' but that he is at liberty to omitt it and beare the lyon without it.

After replying to the heralds' objection that, ' that were to assume the coate of divers other families,' by asserting ' that divers families may give one and the same armes, and why not mine as well as others, deriving my authority from the same fountaine (the King),' the knight boldly asserts that his descent entitles him to bear the simple lion of his pre-conquest ancestor.

I must further tell you (as I have formerly) that I take not this as a grant of new armes, but a restoration to the old, for however you call the lyon under the bend the ancient bearing (which is indeed very ancient) yet it is not the ancientest, the originall coate being only ' sable,' a lyon rampant argent, which was the coate of Otho de Leon . . . castelan of Gisor (whome we call our common ancestor) and of whom we have this account. The said Otho had two sons, Richard, Lord of Montalban and Wandrill, Lord of Courcelle. Richard had issue by his wife Yoland, countess of Grimburg, Claud, whose posterity continued the name of Leon. Wandrille had issue by his wife Beatrice de

The Origin of the Churchills

Tria, Raoule and Roger, who tooke the surname of Courcelle : Roger, the youngest brother came into England with William the Conqueror and had by guift from the sayd King the forfeited estates of B[r]ictic and Bond, two Englishmen of great note in the west ; he maryed the lady Mabel de Solariis by whome he had issue Roger, commonly called the blind Baron of Soleigny, who tooke the surname of Fitz Roger and gave his mother's armes quarterly argent and gules : he had issue by his wife, Gertrud, daughter of Sir Guy de Torbay, three sons, Roger, Hugh, and John. From Roger (who was the second Baron of Soleigny), descended the Fitz Rogers ancestors to the families of Clavering and Fitz Roger in the North. Hugh, the second brother, was lord of Corfeton in Dorcetshire (so 'tis called in the Domesday Book), which for ought I know was Corton ; who having the estate of the above said Bond given to him in franch mariage with his only daughter, his posterity assumed the name and armes of the sayd Bond, who was lord of Fisherton in Somersetshire, viz. in a feild sable a fess or : John the third brother was Lord of Currichill or as 'tis in divers records Chirechile, since called Churchill in Somersetshire, who marrying the lady Joan de Kilrington, had issue by her Sir Bartholomew de Churchill, a man of greate note in the tyme of King Steven, for whom he defended the castle of Bristow against the Empress Maud, and was slaine afterward in the warr.

This tangle of statements requires a chart pedigree.

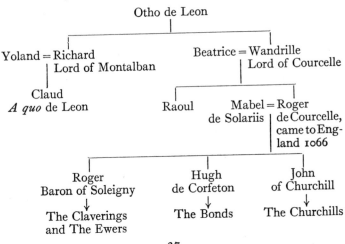

37

Family Origins

The chief value of Sir Winston's narrative is that it carries back the existence of the fabulous pedigree considerably beyond the date of Anderson's *Royal Genealogies* (1732),[7] from which Collins, in his *Peerage*, avowedly took it. Anderson cited no authority, but the character of the concoction suggests to us the early part of the seventeenth or possibly the end of the sixteenth century. There is not a complete concordance between the two accounts : Anderson makes the patriarch of the race to be ' Gitto ' de Leon, and styles Yoland, his daughter-in-law, Countess of Luxemburg, not of Grimburg ; but Sir Winston was growing old and may have made some slips. The strange thing, however, is that he seems to derive the name of his house from Churchill (' Currichill '—' Chirechile ') in Somerset, though the whole pedigree was really based on the blundering notion that Churchill derived its name from the ' Courcelle ' family. This is clear from Anderson's statement as to ' Roger de Courcil,' that ' the Lordship of Churchill in Somersetshire was so called from him, being the place of his abode.' Now Roger de Courcelles, Corcelle, or Curcelle,[8] appears to have taken his name from Courseulles (Calvados) on the coast (NNW. of Caen), a name very different from Churchill, which Domesday renders (in Oxfordshire and Devon) as Cercelle. It is shown in the present work (p. 61), that the Thynne pedigree was similarly constructed by confusing families which took their names from Botfield in Shropshire and Boutteville in Poitou, and that Mr. Grazebrook has constructed his genealogy by confusing those which were named from Bully and from Boissey in Normandy. It might in that case perhaps be claimed for Churchill that there was a superficial resemblance sufficient to excuse the confusion.

But Collinson clearly showed in his *Somerset*[9] (1791) that Roger cannot have held Churchill (Somerset), for at the time of Domesday it was an unnamed portion of the

---

[7] Ed. 1736, pp. 580-581 (Table cccxxxviii).   [8] Domesday.
[9] Vol. iii, p. 588.

bishop's manor of Banwell. Eyton [10] observes that Collinson ' dissipates the fable which connected Roger de Corcell with the name and manor of Churchill, neither of which had existence at the date of Domesday.' Sir Winston, we saw, asserted that Roger was given ' the forfeited estates of Bictric (*sic*) and Bond, two Englishmen,' which seems to show that some one or other had been looking up Domesday Book. But Roger only held a few of Briktric's manors and only one that had been held by ' Bond ' [11] in Fisherton, Wilts. Sir Winston contradicts himself, for he makes the ' Bond ' estate at Fisherton come to Roger's grandson, Hugh, by marriage, and places it wrongly in Somersetshire. The arms he blazons are those of the Bonds of Creech Grange in the Isle of Purbeck, for whom a Cornish origin was claimed and who had nothing to do with Fisherton. With regard to the alleged descent of the Claverings and Ewers from Hugh's elder brother Roger, those two families both differenced by a bend sable, that ' quarterly or and gules ' coat, which was connected, as I have shown,[12] with the coat of Mandeville, Earl of Essex, not with that of the Domesday Roger's alleged mother, Mabel ' de Solariis,' who, indeed, could not at that time be entitled to any arms.

Roger de Courcelle's alleged youngest son, John, had a son, we see, ' Bartholomew de Churchill, a man of great note in the tyme of King Stephen, for whome he defended the castle of Bristow against the Empress Maud, and was slaine afterward in that war.'

Here we have at length definite information, which is confirmed by Collins' *Peerage*, where we read of ' Sir Bartholomew de Chirchil, a great warrior and celebrated in ancient songs, who held the castle of Bristol for King Stephen, and died fighting in his cause.' It is unfortunate for this gallant knight, the only early Churchill who made

[10] *Somerset Domesday*, i, 60.

[11] This represents the name Bondig or Bundig, not ' Bond,' which merely denoted a bondman.

[12] *Geoffrey de Mandeville*, p. 392.

for himself a name, that history shows us Bristol as the stronghold, not of Stephen but of his foes : its castle knew Stephen only as a futile assailant and as a captive. But if of Sir Bartholomew history knows nothing, if his sole exploit is one that could not have taken place, he was at least, Collins tells us, ' celebrated in ancient songs.' This is clearly a reference to one of those amusing forgeries, which are recognised by the critical genealogist as the pillars of a ' faked pedigree.' Collins, in his *Baronage* (another work), states that Sir Bartholomew ' was a man of great powers as this old epitaph informs us ' (pp. 126-7). It runs thus :

Who comon here into this Isle,[13]
    Pray ye for the spirit
Of good Sir Barthol. de Cherchile
    That most renowned knight ;
Arrayed in sooth as he was
    With tabard in fashion,
A sword bright as his burnd Brass
    And eke a light Gipion.
Into the Battail for to fight,
    He then did make his way ;
Ne was there founden any Wight,
    So stout as might him stay :
But as midst Gleves began to thrike
    And Glisames thick eft soone
He felt, I wis, a deadly prick
    That pierc'd his heart too soon.
Now failed been his Sprite and Breath
    And dusken been his Eye,
Wo worth that while, yt in geud Faith,
    Tis certes he mought dye.
Wi boateth it he was so good
    They laft tholk [14] Feild,
Where thick then his deerest Life Blood
    Was, I trou, fouly spill'd.
And night thik Place, a tyny Ville
    Now standeth, and there is,
Me clypeth it right sooth *Cherchile*
    After his name, I wiss.

[13] i.e. aisle.   [14] ? the ilk.

This clumsy doggerel reminds one of that similar imposture in prose, on which rests the existence of Sir Michael Carington, standard-bearer to King Richard I, the ancestor in whom every Smith who has persuaded himself that he is a Carington, fondly sees his own. Of that imposture such a scholar as Mr. W. H. Stevenson made for me short work.

'It is the grammar that makes it impossible. There are forms and usages in it that never existed, or could have existed, in any English dialect at any period, and it is impossible to explain them upon any other hypothesis than that they are the products of a person unskilled in Middle English, who was trying with a most extraordinary lack of grammatical power to concoct a narrative that should seem from its deviations from the language of his time, to be the product of a couple of centuries or so, earlier. It is a most clumsy performance.' [15]

The metre, on the other hand, of the Churchill epitaph resembles that of the rhymed pedigree, composed for the Stauntons by Robert Cade.

> O champion cheefe and warlike wight
> Of Staunton's stock the pryme
> The[e] and thy sequel I must blase
> And pedegrewe define
>
> *   *   *   *   *
>
> The first Sir Mauger Staunton Knight
> Before Williame came in,
> When this realme into one monarche
> Did conquer it and winne.

In that case, however, the absurd faking of the language used is absent.

Archdeacon Coxe, in his well-known *Memoirs of John Duke of Marlborough*, was loth to part from Sir Bartholomew : ' Gitto de Leon ' is still found at the head of the great Duke's pedigree and we duly find ' Sir Bartholomew de Churchill killed in the wars, between Stephen and Maud.' [16] It is only fair to add that the warrior is now dropped ; the

[15] *Peerage and Pedigree*, ii, 174-5.   [16] Vol. i, pp. i-ii.

pedigree, indeed in Burke's *Peerage*, begins only with William Churchill of Rockbear, Devon, early in the fifteenth century. This deprives it of its only interest, the preposterous epitaph on Sir Bartholomew, which illustrates even better than the exploded Carington document the gross daring of the pedigree-maker.

The true pedigree of the Churchills was singularly undistinguished down to Sir Winston himself ; they seem to have been ' gentlemen,' but not ' esquires.' Sir Winston was admitted to St. John's, Oxford, as son of John Churchill ' of Wootton Glanville, gent.,' but this John raised his position by successful practice at the bar and by his lucky marriage with a daughter and co-heir of Sir Henry Winston. It is noteworthy that such little information about the early Churchills points to Devon rather than Somerset as the district where they originated, and an authentic record shows us a ' John Churchull ' at or near Alverdiscot, Devon, in 1428.[17] Now Alverdiscot is only a few miles SSW. of Barnstaple and it seems to me not improbable that they really sprung from a little place called Churchill, in the East Down, about the same distance NNE. of it.[18] In that case their alleged connection with, and possession of, the Somerset Churchill was invented only to support the story that they had for their illustrious sire that great Somerset Domesday baron, Roger ' de Curcelle ' (or ' Corcelle ').

---

[17] *Feudal Aids*, i, 463.

[18] It is a singular fact that ' Jocelin de Churchilla ' and William, his son, are found, in the days of Henry II, attesting a charter of Alice de Nonant (Cartulary of Buckfast). But this was a *south* Devon Charter.

THE ORIGIN OF THE WALPOLES

NORFOLK and the history of Norfolk families are the recognised preserves of Mr. Walter Rye. Of his genealogical ardour and of his amazing industry there is ample proof in the 'list of publications' from his busy pen, extending over more than fifty years.[1] These labours were crowned by the publication of his *Norfolk Families*, 1913, a work of eleven hundred pages in which are seen the fruits of a lifetime's labours.

We are reminded by the preface to that production that Mr. Rye's critical work is that of which he was proudest; he justly denounces 'flamboyant nonsense' on the subject of family antiquity and recurs to the mythical pedigrees of his county which he has 'exposed successfully.' It is this critical attitude in the matters of genealogy which gives special importance to Mr. Rye's admission, and indeed assertion, of a pedigree from the Conquest period in the case of the family of Walpole. His actual words are these:

> This is the only Norfolk family which could show a probable male descent from approximately the time of the Conquest, and which recently held property which it held eight centuries ago. In fact I may go so far as to say, that their pedigree is the only one in the county which bears the impress of honesty on it and is practically capable of being proved up to the hilt, though legal proof of some of the descent . . . is still wanting. Whether they were here before the Conquest . . . is another matter.[2]

Pedigrees extending, or alleged to extend, back to the Norman Conquest have been with me an object of special

[1] See the appendix to *Cal. of Norwich Deeds*, issued by him in 1910. This essay was written before Mr. Walter Rye's death.

[2] Rye, *Norfolk Families*, pp. 974-5.

43

study.[3]   And I was consequently led to examine the proofs of a descent asserted in this emphatic fashion by one who is before all a critical genealogist.   The interest in the case is increased by the fact that in Burke's *Peerage*, where one might expect to find the Conquest pedigree, the lineage is not carried back to beyond the days of Henry III.

The sheet-anchor of the early descent, as found in Mr. Rye's book, is :

Sir Henry de Walpole, living in the reign of Henry II (1154-1188), who married Elizabeth de Wahull, and held one knight's fee in Houghton of the fine (*sic*) of Blauminster of (*sic*) the Honour of Wormegay.[4]

For the period of a century, more or less, between Sir Henry and the Conquest, we are dependent on a single document, described as ' an undated and therefore very early charter in the family's possession,' which mentions a Reginald de Walpole and his sons, Geoffrey and Reginald. A footnote refers us for further details to *Norfolk Antiquarian Miscellany* I, where we read :

as such deeds are undated, it is supposed that this Reginald and his sons must have been anterior in date to the Sir Henry de Walpole hereafter referred to, who is the earliest dated person in the pedigree [5] (p. 268).

That is to say that this deed, because it was undated, must have been anterior to ' the reign of Henry II.'   I need scarcely say that such deeds continued to be undated for a considerable time *after* that reign.   There is, therefore, nothing to show that the deed was so early in date, while its nature makes a later date infinitely more likely.

We are left therefore with ' Sir Henry de Walpole ' living in the reign of Henry II as the earliest known ancestor.

[3] e.g. *Studies in Peerage and Family History*, pp. 46-67 ; ' Companions of the Conqueror,' *Monthly Review*, June 1901, pp. 91-111.

[4] Rye, *op. cit.* p. 975.

[5] This idea was stated by Collins, who begins the pedigree with ' Reginald de Walpole,' living about the time of the Conquest, on the strength of this ' deed without date.'

His importance for the early descent of the house is due not only to the fact that his date, we see, is given, but also to his tenure of Houghton, the ancestral home of the Walpoles, which they held, Mr. Rye tells us, ' eight centuries ago.' Now it struck me that this tenure, as it is given by Mr. Rye, is not at all suggestive of the days of Henry II. Moreover, I sought in vain for any mention of such tenure in the records of that reign. I therefore referred here again to Mr. Rye's earlier article in the *Norfolk Antiquarian Miscellany*,[6] where I discovered it to be stated with more accuracy, and to be taken ' Ex libro Ms. voc. Antiq. Tenor. de Com. Norf.' (quoted by Collins *ut supra*, p. 578). Here, then, we trace the statement to its source ; it is taken straight from Collins' *Peerage*, that eighteenth century work which Mr. Rye has elsewhere denounced as no authority at all. And having so taken it, he has in his later work converted ' fee ' into ' fine ' and left out the essential words ' and the fourth part of a Knight's fee ' before ' of the Honour of Wyrmegey.'[7]

We can identify without difficulty the entry which Collins quotes, but it is taken from a record, not of the twelfth but of the fourteenth century. A return of 1302 contains the entry :

Henricus filius Henrici de Walpole tenet tenementa sua in Houton per servicium j feodi de feodo de Blawmouster.
Idem Henricus tenet in Houton unum quarterium feodi militis de feodo de Wyrmegeye.[8]

This is the entry which, following Collins, Mr. Rye relies on as ' the reign of Henry II.' Exit, therefore, Sir Henry de Walpole, holder of Houghton under Henry II, the sole prop of the early pedigree.

Although, therefore, we read that this pedigree is ' practically capable of being proved up to the hilt,' it

[6] ' Evidences of the early pedigree of the family of Walpole of Houghton.'

[7] ' One knight's fee in Houghton of the fee of Blauminster and the fourth part of a Knight's fee in the Honour of Wyrmegey.'

[8] *Feudal Aids*, iii, 404.

collapses like a house of cards. The strange part of the business is that between the appearance of its alleged proofs in Mr. Rye's earlier paper and its assertion on the strength of those proofs, now in the *Norfolk Families*, we find the following passage in the author's entertaining treatise on *Norfolk songs, stories and sayings* :

> Another good later family, whose earlier pedigree is all moon-shine, is that of the Walpoles. Collins and Burke gave them an ante-Norman descent, but their pedigree is not provable, at Houghton at all events, before 1286. The fact that there were people living earlier who took their name from the place of Walpole being of no value as evidence.

This is a very different story, which seems to err, if at all on the side of excessive caution. The closing sentence is extremely sound as genealogical criticism. But when the passage continues :

> though in all probability, they came from Henry de Walpole of Walpole temp. Henry II.[9]

one has to observe that Henry de Walpole was, according to the author himself, *not* ' of Walpole ' but ' of Houghton,' and that he lived much later than the days of Henry II.

Even when we come to his real occurrence as the holder of Houghton, viz. in 1302, Mr. Rye has confused the pedigree, although the deeds cited by Collins are in harmony with the return, which, we have seen, makes him the son of another Henry. Mr. Rye makes him the son of John. Although the public records before the reign of Edward the Second are almost silent as to Walpoles,[10] the private deeds to which Collins refers contain much information and enable us to reconstruct the pedigree under Edward I. Of the first Sir Henry de Walpole Mr. Rye observes that, ' he must have been dead by 1311, when his second wife, Isabel Fitz Osbert, then Jernegan, had a third of Houghton

[9] This passage is quoted from chapter viii (' smiles on their claims of long descent '), p. 99.

[10] It is evident from Collins' work that they had been assiduously examined.

in dower.[11]   But he must have died a good deal earlier, for Isabel was already the widow of her second husband, Walter Jernegan, early in 1306.[12]

The deeds cited by Collins may be fairly held to show that John (or Sir John) de Walpole was living, under Henry III, about the middle of the thirteenth century, and was father of ' Sir Henry de Walpole,' who with his said father and his own son Henry, is mentioned in a deed of 25 Edward I (1296-7) relating to Walpole.   The elder Henry appears to have died a few years later, leaving a widow, Isabel, who died *circ.* 1311, when Henry, son of Henry Walpole is found holding Houghton.   This younger Henry was coroner for Norfolk in 1311 and knight of the shire in 1316 : from whom descended the long line of the Walpole squires of Houghton, eventually Earls of Orford (1742).

The tenure of Houghton by the Walpoles was undoubtedly of great antiquity, but how or when it began is not easy to say.   In my paper on ' Historical genealogy ' I drew attention to the importance of combining genealogy with topography and of studying together in feudal times the descents of families and of manors.   The two Walpoles, from which undoubtedly the Walpoles derived their name, lay some eight miles to the west of King's Lynn, down in the marsh land, with the head of the Cross Keys Wash between them and Lincolnshire.   Houghton, on the other hand, lay to the east-north-east of the borough, at least twelve miles from it as the crow flies, in the heart of the north-west shoulder of the county.   In early days the Walpoles were connected with both places ; in later times it was King's Lynn which gave to Sir Robert Walpole for forty years his seat in the House of Commons.

It was at Houghton that he built his great house, that ' heavy, ugly, black building,' and lived, as First Lord of the Treasury, a hard-drinking, hard-riding squire.   In 1731, at the time of his supreme power, they were hunting

[11] *Norfolk Families*, p. 976.   [12] *Cal. of Inq.* iv, 392.

six days a week, three days with his own harriers and three with his son's fox-hounds,[13] while at Rainham, another barrack of a house, six miles away, his brother-in-law, Lord Townshend, whose resignation had left him supreme, was associating his name for ever with the triumphant turnip.[14] Houghton was held in the feudal period, partly of the great Warenne fief, of which Castle Acre was, in Norfolk, the head, and partly of the local Honour of Wormegay, at which place its *caput* was a small fenland fortress. But this we should not learn from the entry above (p. 45), where the former (and larger) portion is stated to be the fee of ' Blanmuster ' : There are records which need their Daniel. This fee of ' Blanmuster ' (or ' Blaumuster ') which occurs four times in the Norfolk returns,[15] is officially identified as ' Whitechurch,' [16] but this hardly assists us.

It is now well known to experts that, in Shropshire, Whitechurch and Oswestry were both Latinized in records as *Album Monasterium*, which corresponded with a French ' Blancmester.' Thus ' Blancmester in the march of Wales,' which occurs on the Patent Rolls in 1266, is officially identified as ' Oswestry or Whitechurch.' [17] But, in the same volume, the castle *de Albo Monasterio* is rendered ' the Castle of Whitechurch ' in June 1260 and the Castle of Oswestry in the following month.[18] It is clear, however, that this castle was really of Whitechurch, and it was held of the Warennes by a certain William ' de Albo Monasterio,' who evidently took his name from it. This William died in or just before 1260, leaving as his co-heirs four daughters, of whom Bertreia was the eldest.[19] It is this

---

[13] *Hist. MSS. Com.* Fifteenth Report, app. vi, p. 85.

[14] ' Why of two brothers, rich and restless one,
Plows, burns manures, and toils from sun to sun.
The other slights, for women, sports, and wines
All Townshend's turnips and all Grosvenor's mines.'

(Pope.)

[15] *Feudal Aids*, iii, 404, 518, 578, 637.   [16] *Ibid.* p. 817.

[17] *Cal. of Patent Rolls*, 1258-1266, pp. 672, 700.   [18] *Ibid.* pp. 77, 102.

[19] *Ibid.* p. 80. The Inq. p. m. on her in 1281 shows that she inherited

William who gave its name to the Norfolk fee of ' Blan-muster,' [20] and who appears in 1246-8 as William de Blanc-moster, holding at Manuden, Essex, from Warenne.[21] It is important to observe that his undertenant at that place is Baldwin de Rosey, under whom was John de Rosey. It is in Essex also that his name survived in the two manors of ' Blamsters ' in Halstead and in Great Easton.

I have been thus particular in identifying this man, because he forms the clue to the descent of Houghton. One of the most regrettable gaps in the *cartae* of 1166 is that of the return for the Warenne fief ; in its absence it is difficult to trace the great tenants of the earls. But this tenancy we can reconstitute. In the *Book of Fees* (pp. 904, 906) ' Houeton ' is our Houghton, and when we find Baldwin de Rosey entered as holding 1¼ knight's fees there and one at Rockland of Earl Warenne, we may be sure that William de Blancmuster's name as mesne tenant is omitted, for these manors with North Barsham were held by him of the Earl. Moreover, we have seen that at Manuden (Essex) William was similarly mesne tenant between Baldwin and the Warennes. Conversely, when Henry de Walpole is found subsequently holding at ' Houghton,' of the fee of ' Blan-muster,' we may be sure that the name of the Warennes, as the tenants-in-chief, is omitted.

In the same place, Henry de Walpole is entered as holding a quarter fee in Houghton of the Honour of Wormegay. In this also he appears to have been preceded by Baldwin de Rosey. An important but unindexed entry not under Norfolk, but under Cambridgeshire runs thus :

Baldewinus de Rosey tenet in Enhale insimul cum terris suis in ' Houcton,' Crek et Gidesterne in Norff feodum j militis de honore de Wrmegay.[22]

a fourth part of Whitechurch (' Blancminster ') and the lands in great Easton and Little Canfield, Essex, all held of Warenne (*Cal. of Inq.* ii, No. 387).

[20] See for him and his heirs as its holders, *Feudal Aids*, iii, 406, 422, 550.

[21] *Book of Fees*, ii, 1161. [22] *Ibid.* 923, cf. 928.

There was clearly a quarter fee in each place. In the Wormegay return in the *Red Book* (p. 744) we have clearly the same entry in the form, ' Baldwynus de Rosey, j feodum in Torhal (*sic*) et Houton,' where ' Torhal ' must stand for ' Enhal ' (Yenhall, Cambs.). According to a deed of 4 Edward II (1310-11), the elder Henry de Walpole had acquired of ' Asceline, daughter of Hugh de Laverd,' lands in Houghton of the fee of Wormegay : these may well have been the quarter fee in question.

The upshot of this enquiry is that there seems to be no proof of the Walpoles holding Houghton before the closing years of the thirteenth century, when its holder was the first Henry de Walpole, whose widow was dowered out of the manor. Also that they seem to have been preceded there by the Rosey family, who held, as they did afterwards, of that ' Blanmuster ' fee which was held of the Earls Warenne and of the Honour of Wormegay. This would give them a tenure of some five centuries, which, although notable, no doubt is far short of that antiquity which Mr. Rye would claim for it.

I am not sure, however, that the pedigree he claims for the Walpoles is not surpassed by the statement of their origin which is found in Mr. Evelyn Shirley's *Noble and Gentlemen of England*.[23] Here is Mr. Shirley's version :

Walpole in Marshland in this county, gave name to this Historical family, and here ' Joceline de Walpole ' was living in the reign of Stephen. Reginald de Walpole in the time of Henry I, seems to have been lineal ancestor of the house. He was father of Richard, who married Emma, daughter of Walter de Hawton or Houghton, which at a very early period became the family seat (p. 147).

The facts are, that ' Joceline de Walpole ' was living, not under Stephen, but in the thirteenth century ; that Reginald was not the ' lineal ancestor ' and did not live under Henry I, and that Richard's wife had nothing to do with Houghton.

The connexion of the Houghton Walpoles with Walpole is not easy to determine. Of the deeds cited by Collins, the

[23] Third edition, corrected, 1866.

first which connects them with Walpole is of 1305. Regarding John Walpole, who died seised of Houghton in 1494,[24] Mr. Rye states :

This is, of course, the amplest evidence of his descent from Henry de Walpole, who after 1154 held a knight's fee in Houghton of the honour of Wormegay (*sic*),[25] and his tenure of land in ' Walpole ' itself is also strong proof of the truth of the earlier statements in the pedigree (p. 977).

The above Sir Henry is he whom Mr. Rye erroneously supposes to have held Houghton between 1154 and 1187. As for Walpole, the Inquisition of 1494 states that John Walpole held some tenements there of the Bishop of Ely, ' service unknown.' Unless these tenements can be shown to be identical with those held by an alleged ancestor at an early date, they cannot afford ' strong proof,' or indeed any proof at all. Now the one early Walpole who had a traceable holding there is a ' Joceline de Walpole,' who is made by Mr. Rye a direct ancestor of the house ; with him he deals fully (pp. 975-6) as living under John and as holding a twelfth of a fee in Wisbeach, and a half of a knight's fee in Walpole [26] of the Bishop of Ely.

If that half fee in Walpole can be traced as descending to the Walpoles of Houghton, then there is proof of the descent. If not there is none. Under Norfolk in *Feudal Aids* no Walpole can be found holding land in Walpole by knight service ; there were two half fees there held of the Bishop of Ely, but one of them was held by the Colvilles, who were still holders in 1494,[27] and the other was held by three co-heirs.

[24] See *Cal. of Inq.* Henry VII, i, No. 1019.

[25] It was held, we saw, of the fee of ' Blawmester,' and so late as 1428 Henry de Walpole was returned as holding a knight's fee in Houghton ' de Blawmester.' *Feudal Aids*, iii, 576.

[26] Mr. Rye first dates this holding 1211-2 and then, in the *Testa de Neville*, as 1216-1272. This is because he does not understand the *Testa* and has been misled by its title-page. Both entries (the right references are *Red Book of the Exchequer*, p. 526, *Testa de Neville*, p. 359, and corrected entry in *Book of Fees*, ii, 628-9) relate to the returns of 1212.

[27] *Cal. of Inq.* Henry VII, i, No. 2021.

We fail, therefore, to find either at Houghton or at Walpole any proof of the Walpole pedigree before John de Walpole, who was living apparently about the middle of the thirteenth century. For, as Mr. Rye himself observes, ' the fact that there were people living earlier, who took their name from the place of Walpole ' is ' of no value as evidence.' [28] And so we have demolished the statement in *The Dictionary of National Biography* that the family ' since the early part of the 12th century had possessed a competent estate in the fen country of West Norfolk and North Cambridgeshire.' (LIX, 176).

It has been my intention in this paper to illustrate two points. The first is that in early genealogy the feudal evidence of the tenure and of the descent of land is that which affords the best and most decisive proof of pedigree. Many a pedigree which has been compiled by merely stringing together the bearers of a certain surname could be shattered at once by this test, which the publication of our national records now enables us to apply. The other is, that a few pedigrees carefully tested and worked out are to be preferred to many hundreds hastily put together from unchecked evidence and unproved descents. Work of the latter character is not merely valueless, it is actually misleading. To ensure accuracy, patient labour and no small expenditure of time are, no doubt, required, and that is why the careful genealogist must limit his field of work. Mr. Rye, however, would have had at his disposal more time for such investigation if he had devoted less to his arduous endeavours to discover whether this or that family had ' bought and paid for ' a coat of arms.[29] It is obvious that the fact of their having done so, to which he appears from his preface to attach enormous importance, cannot affect in any way either their social position or their genealogical status. It is to be regretted that, by making this his test and dividing line, he should bolster up the false idea,

[28] See p. 46 above.

[29] The phrase is taken from his own Preface (p. iii).

the somewhat vulgar conception, that such a purchase raises a man into a class distinguished and apart.[30] It is very difficult to understand Mr. Rye's standpoint. On the one hand he makes ' Heralds' College the sole arbiter of arms borne since its creation,' and is actually inclined to recognise the ' false ' arms of the Bacons as validly borne, because confirmed by the heralds in 1569. On the other, he goes dangerously far in asserting that ' until about a hundred years ago, many of the heralds were venal in the extreme, and used to fudge pedigrees as boldly as the advertisers of to-day.'

[30] Mr. Rye announced his work as an ' account of the descents and arms of such residents in the county of Norfolk who (*sic*) are entitled to bear arms, and of those who use them improperly.' His Preface speaks of the ' sheep ' (the former) being formerly separated from ' the goats,' and describes the latter as deserving public contempt (p. i). He accordingly divides his families into two classes. With his denunciation of those who usurp the arms of another family of the same or similar name, I am of course in entire agreement, but that is another matter.

NEVILLE AND BULMER

AMONG the miscellaneous returns in the *Red Book* and the *Testa de Nevill* are two lists of knight's fees for the Yorkshire portion of the great fief held by the house of Mowbray. Mr. Hall, the editor of the former, dates the list in the *Testa* (pp. 363, 366) as ' older ' than that in the *Red Book* (p. 734). It is, however, quite certainly the later of the two.

The most interesting result of comparing the parallel entries in these lists is that the *Red Book* fee of ' Robert filius Mendre,' (*sic*) is held in the *Testa* list by ' Robert de Neville.' For who was the former Robert ? We have but to change ' Mendre ' into ' Meudre ' by reading ' n ' as ' u,' and then to treat ' u ' as equivalent to ' l ' [1] in order to produce Robert Fitz Meldre[d], the well-known founder of the house of Neville. Is this doubted ? Then I cite at once the Patent Roll of 22 Hen. III with its entry that, at the beginning of 1238 the administrator of the bishopric of Durham was ' commanded to take with him Robert son of " Meaudre " and Geoffrey son of Geoffrey,' to hear a plea in the court of the said bishopric.[2] We can now advance to a record of 1242, known to us only from the Chancery Roll of Bishop Matthew in 1598, of which we read :

In 1242, Robert Fitz Murdras, Walter de Merton, etc. . . . were justices itinerant in the palatinate. Of Robert nothing is known, but Walter de Merton is familiar to every student of English History.[3]

[1] e.g. in records, ' Aldelin ' for ' Audelin,' ' Baldricus ' for ' Baudricus,' ' Balduinus ' for ' Baudouin,' ' Bealmont ' for ' Beaumont ' ; (*Pipe Roll*, 12 Henry II), ' Fulgeriae ' for ' Fougere,' ' Malduit ' for ' Mauduit,' etc.

[2] *Cal. of Patent Rolls*, 1232-47, p. 209.

[3] See Prof. Lapsley's valuable monograph on the *County Palatinate of Durham*, 1900 (*Harvard Hist. Studies*, viii), p. 195.

Robert Fitz ' Murdras ' is, I hold, Robert Fitz ' Meudre ' further disguised by an Elizabethan scribe. His grandson and namesake, Robert de Neville is found acting in the same capacity, 1278-9, when he seems to have been the principal justice in the palatinate.[4]

As for Robert Fitz Meudre, he had succeeded his father, ' Meldred ' Fitz Dolfin, of Raby,[5] as early as 1195,[6] and must, therefore, have been advanced in years in 1242.[7] In the second of our two lists, that in the *Testa*, he has at length assumed the surname of Neville, as he also has in the return of his own fees.[8]

I now propose to connect the earlier and the later return of the Mowbrays' Yorkshire fees with the far earlier return of 1166,[9] by tracing back the fee held by Robert Fitz Meudre.[10] This I detect in that which William de ' Bolemer ' was holding of Roger de Mowbray at that date. This is the only place in which William is mentioned in the *Red Book*, but his name affords the clue to a very important descent. On the whole family of Bulmer, Dugdale was hopelessly at sea.[11] So also was Courthope's *Nicolas* (1857), Burke's *Extinct Peerage* (1866), etc., as they merely followed Dugdale. Thus it was that Prof. Lapsley was altogether misled when he had to deal with the barons of the palatinate of Durham. The whole family were named from Bulmer in the North Riding of Yorkshire, but the line with which we are concerned is that to which the great inheritance passed, through a succession of two heiresses,

---

[4] *Ibid.* pp. 176-7. Prof. Lapsley observes, somewhat strangely, that ' Neville belonged to an important north country family, but nothing more definite can be said of him.'

[5] See my paper on the origin of the Nevilles in *Feudal England*, 488-490. He is ' Mildred filius Dolfini ' in the Bolden Book.

[6] *Pipe Roll*, 7 Ric. i.

[7] The span, indeed, is unusually long, but there is no reason to doubt the correctness of the pedigree here.

[8] *Testa de Neville*, p. 364 (*Book of Fees*, ii, 1097). It has been supposed that his son Geoffrey was the first to assume it. Both these returns appear to belong to the so-called ' Scutage of Gascony ' (1242-3).

[9] *Red Book of the Exchequer*, pp. 418-421.

[10] *Ibid.* p. 420.   [11] *Baronage*, i, 592-3.

to the Nevilles.   A chart pedigree is requisite to explain the actual descent.

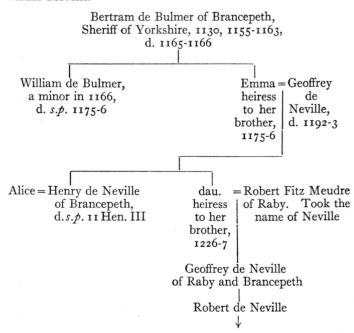

Bertram de Bulmer of Brancepeth,
Sheriff of Yorkshire, 1130, 1155-1163,
d. 1165-1166

William de Bulmer,
a minor in 1166,
d. *s.p.* 1175-6

Emma = Geoffrey
heiress   de
to her   Neville,
brother, | d. 1192-3
1175-6

Alice = Henry de Neville
of Brancepeth,
d.*s.p.* 11 Hen. III

dau.   = Robert Fitz Meudre
heiress | of Raby.   Took the
to her | name of Neville
brother,
1226-7

Geoffrey de Neville
of Raby and Brancepeth

Robert de Neville

' Bulmer of Brancepeth,' says Prof. Lapsley, was certainly one of the three ' most prominent ' lay barons of the Durham palatinate.[12]   Bertram, who heads my pedigree, was styled, as he observes, ' baro episcopi ' by Symeon of Durham in 1144, but he adds :

In 1162, the Bulmers are described as barons by tenure of the King.   In Edward I's reign, they certainly owed to the Crown, the services of tenants in chief, but were summoned to Parliament first in 1327 and last in 1349.   Banks describes them as ' reputed barons of the County of Northumberland.'[13]

He then proceeds :

From this collection of facts . . . it is clear why these . . . barons were prominent in the palatinate . . . Bulmer and Hilton

[12] Lapsley, *op. cit.* p. 64.   [13] *Ibid.* p. 65.

had both been summoned to Parliament . . . when the practise of summons to Parliament begins to define and restrict the title, there is a kind of recognition of the social or aristocratic claim to its use made by the representatives of such families as Hilton and Bulmer in the inconsistent and arbitrary summonses occasionally addressed to them. . . . It is not fantastic to suppose that . . . his claim to that dignity was justified by his possessions in the palatinate.[14]

All this is at once disposed of by the fact that the writer's facts are wrong. No Bulmer of '*Brancepeth*' was ever summoned to Parliament, for the sufficient reason that the Bulmers of Brancepeth became extinct in 1175-6.[15] Their whole inheritance with the status it involved passed, we have seen, to Robert Fitz Meudre and to his descendants, the Nevilles. To historians, surely, the case is a warning that they cannot afford to dispense with the help of genealogy, Cinderella though she be, among their auxiliary sciences.

Bertram de Bulmer, who was sheriff of Yorkshire before and after Stephen's reign, was already holding, under Henry I, lands which we can identify with considerable precision. In Yorkshire he held of the King more than three knight's fees, in which two were in Sutton in the Forest,[16] to the north of York, and Raskelf (in Easingwould) to its north-east, and another in Terrington (adjoining Bulmer) and Kirkby Misterton. Of Mowbray he held a fee in Kepwick (in Over Silton), at the foot of the Hembleton Hill, about a dozen miles south of the Durham border. But his most important holding was that under the Bishop of Durham, of whom he held five fees, which must have included not only Brancepeth but Sheriff-Hutton in Yorkshire, just between Bulmer and Sutton in the Forest, where

---

[14] *Ibid.* pp. 66-7.

[15] The Bulmers so summoned were those of Wilton (near Redcar), where they flourished till the Pilgrimage of Grace wrecked their fortunes.

[16] All this we learn from the list of Robert de Nevill's holdings in *Testa*, pp. 364, 367, collated with that of Bertram in the *Red Book*, pp. 428-9, where he is expressly said to have held, in the time of Henry I, Sutton, which is styled in the *Testa* 'Sutton sub Galtris,' i.e. Sutton in the Great Forest of Galtres.

the ruins of his castle still stand. For we find his name associated with it in the days of Stephen, and his shrievalty is said to be the origin of its distinctive name.

Sheriff again from Christmas 1154 [17] to Michaelmas 1163, he was still living two years later,[18] but died before the following March (1166). This we knew from the *Cartae Baronum* which were then sent in. I state the facts in this detail, because Dugdale made here his fundamental error. He alleged that Bertram was succeeded by his son *Stephen*. This Stephen de Bulmer, who was not his son, made, on the contrary, his own return under Northumberland [19] and also held one fee of the Bishop of Durham.[20] His son Thomas succeeded him. The name of Bertram's son was *William*, though the *Cartae* only give it for his holding on the Mowbray fief.[21] The Bishop of Durham returns him only as ' filius Bertram de Bolemer,' and he is not even mentioned in the return for Bertram's fief, which was made by one of its smaller tenants, David the Warden (of the forest of Galtres).[22] But the Chancellor's Roll of two years later (1168) records ' William son of Bertram de Bulemer ' as accounting for the aid upon his fief.[23]

This William was in turn succeeded in 1176 by his sister and her husband Geoffrey de Neville, of whom we read in the Pipe Roll for that year that he is responsible for Bertram's debts, being in possession of his daughter and inheritance.[24]

Geoffrey was succeeded by his son Henry, whose sister and heir brought Brancepeth and Sheriff-Hutton with the rest of the Bulmer heritage to Robert Fitz Meudre, who himself held in the palatinate the famous Castle of Raby. Thus were founded the fortunes of the great house of

[17] *Red Book of the Exchequer*, p. 652.   [18] *Pipe Roll*, 11 Henry II.

[19] *Red Book of the Exchequer*, 439.

[20] *Ibid.* p. 417. This entry is not indexed. It is probable that the Bulmer connexion with the Bishops arose from Bulmer adjoining the Yorkshire holding of those prelates.

[21] See p. 56 above.   [22] See for him, *The King's Serjeants*, p. 242.

[23] *Pipe Roll*, 14 Henry II, p. 88.

[24] ' habet filiam ejusdem Bertrami cum hereditate ' (p. 700).

Neville ; nor was their doubtful origin forgotten in later days. When Neville of Raby was at strife with his Lord, the Prior of Durham, in 1331, he was reminded that his ancestors ' were not such great men,' when they held but Raby ; for Brancepeth and Raskelf came to them since by marriage, as also other lands.[25]   But the Nevills were not unmindful of their Bulmer forefathers. At Raby, their memory was preserved not only by the ' Bulmer and the Raskelf ' towers, but by the emblematic bull carved upon the castle barbican, and the initial ' b,' carved upon its towers.   That initial figures also in Nevill seals and coats. And to this day the bull's head crest, and the bull ' supporters ' of Lord Abergavenny recall, in the tongue of medieval heraldry, the name of Bulmer of Brancepeth.[26]

[25] Dugdale, *Baronage*, i, 293.

[26] This article is apparently unfinished.—W. P.

THE MILDMAY MYSTERY

A PECULIAR feature of Tudor heraldry, to which I have
devoted great attention, and which I was apparently the
first to note, was the bearing of a double coat by a family of
recent origin. Its explanation, as I have shown, is that the
new coat, granted to a *novus homo*, was found to be an
awkward fact when it was ' discovered ' at a later date that
he came from an ancient stock. The device adopted for
overcoming this obvious difficulty was the addition to this
coat, in the form of a separate quartering of what was alleged
to be ' the " ancient " coat ' of his house, concurrently with
the concoction of a pedigree that proved his right to bear it.
These coats were often called the ' ancient ' and ' modern '
arms of his house [1] and they have, as a rule, descended in
conjunction to the present day.

To the Warwickshire family of Spencer, enriched by sheep
farming and grazing, grants of arms were made by heralds
in 1504 and 1560. But when that rascal Lee, Clarenceux
King-of-Arms, certified them in 1595 to be of the lordly
stock of the Despencers, Earls of Gloucester, the granted
coat of the Spencers of Althorpe—the male ancestors of the
Dukes of Marlborough, the Earls Spencer, and the Lords
Churchill—was relegated to the second quarter, and a
differenced coat of Despencer usurped its place in the
first.[2] There they have been, says Baker,[3] ' uninterruptedly
borne by his noble descendants under the sanction of the
College of Arms.' Peter Temple, of yeoman stock, whose

[1] *Peerage and Pedigree*, ii, 210.

[2] See my *Studies in Peerage and Family History*, pp. 279 *et seq.*, and
Peerage and Pedigree, ii, 210.

[3] *History of Northamptonshire*, i, 106.

forefathers had farmed abbey lands, had his grant of arms in 1567 ; but when there was invented for the Temples that wildly fabulous descent from the Saxon Earls of Mercia, his granted coat was ousted by their alleged eagle, which is proudly displayed to this day in the first quarter of their arms.[4] Barker, Garter under Henry VIII, made a grant of arms to Sir John Smith of Cressing, Essex, Baron of the Exchequer ; but when, by the help of a forged document, there had been invented for the family a descent in the male line from the ancient Cheshire house of Carington, Sir John's grandson, Henry Smith, relegated the coat to the second quarter and installed a new one in the first.[5] To these instances I have now been able to add the case of Sir John Thynne, who similarly had a grant of arms, but for whose family it was subsequently discovered that they were originally Poitevin Bouttevilles, with the result that a ' Botteville ' coat has since been quartered with that of Thynne. In this case, however, the Botteville occupies the second quarter.[6] Finally Mr. Rye, in his *Norfolk Families* (p. 109), cites Blomefield (ix, 238) for the fact that Robert Coke of Mileham had a grant of arms in 2 and 3 Philip and Mary (1555-6), viz. 'Argent a chevron engrailed gules between three tigers' heads erased sable, dented argent and langued of the second, collared or,' but that his son, the great Sir Edward Coke (d. 1634), bore the far finer and earlier-looking coat, ' Per pale argent and gules, three eagles displayed azure,' [7] which seems to be that borne by his descendants in the female line, the present Earls of Leicester.

I have been thus particular in illustrating this process, not only for the reason given immediately below but also because it seems to be connected with a development in heraldry thus described by Sir William St. John Hope in his small but important manual, *A Grammar of Heraldry* (1913):

After 1570, for some occult reason, there was for a consider-

[4] *Peerage and Pedigree*, ii, 15-17.   [5] *Ibid.*
[6] See the paper on ' The Origin of the Thynnes.' *Genealogist*, xi, 1195.
[7] Rye, *Norfolk Families*, p. 22.

able time, a marked reversion in grants to arms of simpler character and better taste (p. 89).

The reason I would suggest may not be ' occult.' The worst Elizabethan pedigrees, I think, date from after 1570, ' an age of heraldic scandals, and it was not, surely, from any love for a purer or simpler pedigree that the character of grants changed.' ' The over crowded shield,' of which Sir William Hope speaks as characterising the grants of the period immediately preceding, may have been purposely designed to distinguish the coats of Tudor *novi homines* from those of older families, and if so, the reversion to arms of an earlier and more feudal type may have been dictated by reasons obvious rather than ' occult.'

Now that the existence of this practice has been sufficiently established, one may fairly ask whether we have but another instance of it in the ' restitution ' at the same period to the Essex family of Mildmay of their alleged ancient arms. Like the Essex Smiths and Sir John Thynne, the Mildmays rose to wealth on the spoils of monastic houses, and their rise was very rapid. The father of the brood was Thomas Mildmay, yeoman and merchant of Chelmsford, Essex, who had a stall in Chelmsford market and died in 1547. Two of his sons were fortunate enough to be employed in that Court of Augmentations, which was also the happy hunting ground of Sir John Smith's family.[8] The ' augmentation ' of the King's revenue seems to have involved that of their own. The eldest son, Thomas Mildmay, appears as an officer of the Court of Augmentations so early as 1536,[9] and was one of the King's Commissioners who ' visited ' the Essex religious houses in the same year.[10] In 1539 he took a lease of the dissolved home of the Black Friars in Chelmsford.[11] Moulsham, a Westminster Abbey manor, adjoining Chelmsford, was acquired by him the next year, and it was there that—long before

---

[8] See *Peerage and Pedigree*, ii, 206.

[9] *Essex Arch. Trans.* (N.S.), ix, 292 ; x, 16.

[10] *Ibid.* ix, 280 *et seq.*   [11] *V. C. H. Essex*, ii, 180.

his father's death—he began the great house which became the seat of himself and his immediate ancestors.

It is alleged, as we shall see below, that his father obtained a grant of arms,[12] and this allegation which is made by Cooke, Clarenceux King-of-Arms, is supported by the fact that the arms in question appear not only on his own monument,[13] which at his death in 1566 he ordered to be erected, but also, it is said, on a seal used by his younger brother Walter in 1556.[14] I would, however, suggest that in accordance with a practice which has lasted, I believe, to our own time —the arms were really obtained by the son in the father's name, in order that he might claim to have inherited them from his father.[15] I have made a similar suggestion in the case of Richard Bertie, a contemporary of the Mildmay brothers, to whose father arms were granted in 1550.[16]

But a real difficulty is caused by a fresh grant of arms to the younger brother of Thomas Mildmay, the enriched auditor, namely, Walter. This Walter, who had similarly begun his official life in the Court of Augmentations, quite outstripped his elder brother in his rise under the Crown, and made a much more influential marriage, his wife being the sister of Elizabeth's minister, Walsingham. He must have been quite a young man when he was knighted by Edward VI in 1547. Under him and under both his successors he was employed in a financial capacity and rose to high office, probably by his own ability. There is much

[12] Foster's *Grantees of Arms*, edited by Mr. Rylands for the Harleian Society in 1915, gives this grant as by Hawley a patent of arms and crest, 15th May, 1542, 34 Henry VIII, to Thomas Mildmay of Mursey (? Mersea Island), Essex. But the son also was named Thomas.

[13] See Mr. Chancellor's work on Essex monuments.

[14] They appear also as the arms of Thomas in the 1552 Visitation of Essex, according to the Harleian Society's edition (i, 11), where, however, they are not identified, and are blazoned ' Per fess nebule argent and azure, three antelopes' heads erased counter-charged collared gules spotted or.

[15] At the time of the grant (1542) his son Thomas was already in possession of Moulsham and must have been in a better position than his father.

[16] *Peerage and Pedigree*, i, 28-32.

about his grants of arms in Foster's *Grantees of Arms* (ed. Rylands, p. 171). He is there stated to have received a grant (as of Essex) from Barker in 1546, the year before he was knighted, and another from Dethick in 1559. On 20th May, 1552, he obtained a grant of arms from Dethick, Garter, the only record—or at least public record—of which appears to be in Camden's ' Heraldic Collections (Cotton MS. Faustina, E. 1), whence it is printed in *Miscellanea Genealogica et Heraldica*, ii, 261. This, as I have said, was essentially a *new* grant and speaks of the grantee as ' Sir Walter Mildmay, knyght of the countye of Essex,' who ' ys desended of a howse unedefamyde,' significantly omitting the clause as to the house ' bearing arms.' [17]

Why should Sir Walter wish to discard his father's coat and even to ignore the fact that a coat of arms had been granted him ? The only suggestion I can make is that he thought the new one simpler and finer in design ; but this does not strike one as quite a sufficient explanation. The blazon, modernised, was ' Azure, on a bend silver a horse with wings courant sable langued gules.' In any case there seems to be no evidence that this new coat was ever used by Sir Walter.

More than thirty years elapsed after this before the ' restitution ' to Sir Walter of that alleged ancestral coat which was then discovered for him. Of what took place on that occasion (1583) two versions are preserved. The documents granted by the heralds to the family descended with Sir Walter's seat, Apethorpe, to his heirs, the Earls of Westmorland, till they parted with Apethorpe, not long ago, when they passed, I believe, by purchase to the Fanes of Fulbeck. The other is a transcript of those documents in Harl. MS. 245, which is printed in *Miscellanea Genea-logica II*, 192-196. The former of course are not accessible, but appear to contain a very important ' codicell,' by which Robert Cooke, Clarenceux, who ' restored ' the alleged ancient arms to Sir Walter and his heirs and to the heirs of

[17] See *Peerage and Pedigree*, i, 29-30.

his father,' recited that a fresh grant (as stated above) had been made by his predecessor to the said father and entitled his sons to the arms then granted. They were therefore declared to be entitled to bear this 'newe' coat quarterly with the 'oulde.' To this point I shall return. But the vital question is that of the evidence adduced for the existence of the 'oulde' coat, and for the descent of Essex Mildmays from those alleged to have borne it.

So far as one can say without seeing the documents, there seem to have been (A) The 'Restitution' of the 'old' arms by Robert Cooke, Clarenceux, and (B) a great illuminated pedigree thoroughly typical of the period, attested like the preceding document by Robert Cooke, Clarenceux, on the same day (20th August, 1583). But the pedigree was also signed by the Earl Marshall himself, George, Earl of Shrewsbury, eight days previously. By the side of each generation in the pedigree is an abstract of the deed or documentary evidence, proving the descent, with a note in some cases of the seal thereof. It describes them as 'dyvers aunctient Evidences and other Recordes, the Copies wherof with a signification of their severall seales is heerin truly mentioned.' In addition—apparently a separate document—there was (C) a repertory to the pedigree, consisting of 'Brief notes howe to prove the pedigree of the family of Mildmay by the Evidence enclosed.'

This 'Repertory' refers, by their numbers, to the *original* charters (cartae) on which the whole story is based. In his 'Restitution' Cooke refers to them thus :

For proof whereof this day hath his (Sir Walter's) sonne and heir apparant Anthony Mildmay . . . shewed unto me (in the presence of dyvers other Heralds) such auntient credible and authenticall deedes, charters, Records, wrytinges, evidences and letters, some sealed with seals of Arms, as well of ther Ancestors as of dyvers noble Erles Barons and other great personages of this land. . . . I have subscribed a pedigree (bearing this date) wherein orderly and verbatim be inrolled all ye said deedes, Charters, Wrytings and muniments *in ye custody* (as is aforesaid) of ye said Sir Walter.

It is important to observe that we are not in this case dealing with transcripts of alleged documents or drawings of alleged seals. The documents and seals themselves were actually produced to the heralds and they have been seen and inspected in our own time. Either, therefore, they are genuine, or they are deliberate forgeries. Other alternative there is none.

To decide the question without seeing them and with only abstracts of their contents before one puts the critic on his mettle. In default of such obvious and gross flaws as would settle the question at once, he must first consider their *provenance*. It is singular that the evidence necessary to prove the pedigree and the right of the family to arms should all be found in its own possession, the more so, as Sir Walter and his father cannot have known that they possessed it when they respectively obtained new grants of arms. Also, one would rather have expected to find it in the possession of Sir Walter's elder brother, Thomas. In the solemn and delightful rigmarole already quoted (p. 65) Clarenceux endeavoured to gloss over the difficulty.

But although oblivion might cause a family, as it sank in the social scale, to be ignorant of its own origin, this will obviously not explain the case of a house that carefully preserved the evidence required to prove its former importance and its arms. When Thomas Mildmay took his stand in Chelmsford market under Henry VIII, he must have known, if the story is true, that he possessed ' a most friendly and familiar letter ' to Thomas Mildmay senior, his grandfather and namesake, from no less eminent a person than the King-maker himself, ' labouring him to stand his good freend, . . . written all of yᵉ Erles own hand and sealed with the beare and Ragged staffe.' But of his evidences and seals of arms he can have told the heralds nothing.[18]

When his pedigree was carried back in 1583 as far as

[18] It might be suggested, on behalf of the Mildmays, that a few of the evidences produced in 1583 might have come to light through the Court of Augmentations. But even this unlikely suggestion will not account for the others.

The Mildmay Mystery

Stephen's days, it cannot have been easy work. For there was no recorded family of the name with which connexion could be claimed and the public records were singularly destitute of any reference to Mildmays. None, indeed, of the proofs adduced is derived, apparently, from that source. The result of a modern search among them revealed only a 'Walter Mildmay, keeper of the park of Morlewode,' who is found in 'Ancient Deeds, A. 886,' acknowledging, 12th June, 1484, 30s. 4d. for his fee as the keeper of the park, from the receiver of 'the lordship of Thornbury.' This evidence, though it supports the family tradition that they came from Gloucestershire under the Staffords (who became lords of Thornbury), illustrates their true social position at the time.

Of the charters produced the earliest belong to 'the Church of Osoluester,' that is Ouston Priory on the eastern edge of Leicestershire. Earl Simon, 'at the petition of Robert Mildmay,' knight, the sonne of Hugh Mildmay, grants (i.e. confirms) Robert's gift to it. This charter was assigned to the reign of Henry II, in which case the style of 'knight' is a distinct anachronism. Later on, this wandering house appears in Herefordshire and Gloucestershire, but from Gloucestershire (or Worcestershire) it was necessary to bring them *per saltum* to Essex. The migration was plausibly explained. It was alleged that a Walter Mildmay was an officer in the house of Anne duchess of Buckingham (d. 1480) at Writtle in Essex, ' as appeareth by the household Booke of the sayed Duchess,' and that he was father of Thomas Mildmay of Chelmsford. This of course, is quite possible, for he may have been only the ' yeoman ' of some office such as the buttery or the pantry. But it was also claimed that he ' was the first of that family that came out of the West and settled to dwell in that Countey.' His family were represented as serving the Staffords, Dukes of Buckingham, from whose western lands they had come.

The explanation, however, is not quite satisfactory, for

Walter is described as with the Duchess at Writtle under Edward IV, and indeed she died in 1480. Yet his father is represented as giving to the Abbot of Evesham, in 2 Henry VII (1486-7), a receipt for the annual corredy due to himself and to Walter, his son, as if they were still resident in the West. Again, it was to this Thomas (the father) that the Kingmaker as ' deputie of Callis in E 4 reigne wrote a most frendly and familier letter, labouring him to stand his good freend, as he had done before often to ye Lord his Maister,' who is taken to be the Duke of Buckingham.[20] The Earl of Warwick did indeed become Captain of Calais in 1467, but the Duke of Buckingham who succeeded his grandfather in 1460 was only born in or about 1454.

It will be seen that in the absence of full transcripts of the documents it is not possible, as I explained above, to say with absolute certainty whether any or all of them are forgeries, and it is greatly to be wished that transcripts may be published, or better still, the documents themselves submitted to an expert examination. On the one hand it is *prima facie* improbable that a forger would produce a series of documents so disconnected in character and locality. On the other, apart from suspicious features, it is practically certain that the family cannot have obtained them by inheritance ; for most of them ought to have been found in the custody of other persons. I am myself guided by what, I suppose, one must call the higher criticism in looking with the gravest suspicion on the evidence produced to the heralds. Those who have not made a special study of the subject might well doubt if it would be possible to produce such elaborate forgeries, or at least to persuade the heralds that they were genuine documents. But it was this same Robert Cooke, Clarenceux, who certified, as I have elsewhere shown, at about this time, to that ' antient manuscript ' which was alleged to prove the descent of the Essex Smiths from the Cheshire Caringtons, but which was a gross forgery.[21]

[20] *Misc. Gen. and Her.* ii, 196.   [21] *Peerage and Pedigree*, ii, 211.

The Mildmay Mystery

The documents, which in the next century—and indeed, down to our own times—were believed to prove the descent of the Feildings in the male line, are now known to have been forged, and, as a crowning instance, the outrageous Lambert forgeries were solemnly recognised as genuine by the highest officers in the College. Camden, as Clarenceux, wrote :

oculis meis vidi evidentias et chartas antiquas ex quibus haec genealogia autentice probatur, quod non potui non testari eandemque manus mea subscriptione approbare.

St. George, Norroy, was equally positive :

vidi et perlegi scripta autentica *cum sigillis appensis* antiqua hujus familia (*sic*) et nominis Lambertorum tangentia, in fide et attestatione quorum manum meam apposui.

Treswell, Somerset herald, bore similar witness :

genealogiam hanc antiquae Lambertorum familiae (*sic*) et specificatas evidentias quam verissime approbatam attestor.

Segar himself, as Garter, saw and ' approved ' the pedigree. Yet the deeds on which it rested have been shown by me to be forgeries.[22]

But the main object of the Mildmays, in producing these documents to the heralds in 1583, was to obtain a recognition of their right to an ancient coat of arms, used, as they alleged, by their ancestor, Henry ' de ' Mildmay, under Edward III and by his great-grandfather before him. They put in, accordingly, a document sealed by the younger Henry, and another sealed by Henry, his great-grandfather. Each of these deeds is alleged to have been ' sealed with 3 lyons rampant.' Even if this was so, we must naturally ask how Clarenceux King-of-Arms, can have known that the field was ' silver ' and the lions ' azure.' His assertion is that it is :

manifest by y[e] severall two seales . . . fayre and whole at their deeds . . . that an auncient cote of Armes pertayneth properly to y[e] same house and family, for these two, being great grand-

[22] *The Ancestor*, iii, 26-32.

father one to another, beares therein their Scoutchions, circum-
script with their proper names and surnames, 3 lyons rampynge,
wch be *azure in a feild silver*, for none els in this land gyves the
same : as by most diligent searche made in ye oldest and newest
Recordes and Register of myne office is to be seene and prooved.

This may possibly mean that no other house bore three
rampant lions *azure* in a *silver* field, and that this, therefore,
was the only combination available for the shield shown on
the shield.   But it reveals the fact that he could not find in
his office any record of a coat anciently borne by Mildmay,
and had therefore to guess at the tinctures.

Moreover, there are other difficulties.   The *later* of the
two sealed charters does give us something tangible ; for
it purposes to be a gift from Henry de Mildmay of ' Stonehouse, Gloucestershire,' of ' all his goods within the manor
of Stonehouse ' to two chaplains, evidently feoffees.   But
Gloucestershire histories, as far as I know, have nothing to
say of any Mildmays at Stonehouse.

The *earlier* of the two sealed charters presents a different
difficulty.   It is of great importance to the pedigree, for it
proves three generations in the alleged descent.   The
version before me runs :

I, Henry de Mildeme, son of Roger de Mildeme give and by
present charter confirm to Ranulphe (*sic*) de Mildeme my son
all my lands in Hereford (*sic*) which I held of the Dominus
Reginald Fitz Herbert, Miles, etc.

It is evident from the pedigree that the ' dominus ' here
mentioned was Reginald Fitz-Peter, or ' Piers,' as he was
invariably styled at the time ; Fitz-*Herbert* is the name
which has been loosely given to his family as a whole.
Moreover, although this Reginald held land in several
counties, his *Inquisitio post mortem* reveals no lands held of
him in Hereford[shire ?].   Lastly, it is at least a very
singular coincidence that this Reginald bore on his shield
' 3 lions rampant,' which are said to be the charge on the
seal affixed to this document and the first occurrence of the
coat afterwards allowed to the Mildmays.   Is it possible
that we have here the origin of the pretended coat allowed

to the Mildmays as that of their ancestors, two of the rampant lions from which were included in the new arms granted to the borough of Chelmsford in 1889.

In any case, the King-of-Arms formally restored the coat, which he caused to be depicted in the margin of the document, though only to Sir Walter and ' his heirs and to yᵉ heirs of his father.' And he further stated at the foot of his ' Repertory to the pedigree,' that the Mildmays, ' may lawfully beare (as their ancesters did beare) Argent (*sic*) 3 lions rampinge Asure, as more playnly is specified in the restitution of Armes made to Sʳ Walter Mildmay, and to Sʳ Thomas Mildmay his nephewe.' In accordance with this restitution, Cooke, somewhat later in the reign, when compiling his great armorial pedigree of the Sydney family, assigned to Sir Walter Mildmay's daughter the newly ' restored ' coat.[23]

It will be remembered, however, that Cooke, by a ' codicell,' sanctioned the bearing of the ' new ' coat, granted to Thomas Mildmay, the father, quarterly with the alleged ' ancient ' one which he restored to the family.[24]

Actual instances of this being done are found in the funeral certificates of Sir Walter Mildmay of Sawbridge-worth (1606), a nephew of Sir Walter, and of his cousin Sir Anthony Mildmay (1617), the elder Sir Walter's son, preserved at the College of Arms.[25] But as with the true coat of the Spencers, charged with its seamen's heads, so this true Mildmay coat, charged with its greyhounds' heads, after being relegated to the second quarter, was allowed to drop out of sight, precisely as was the case with the coat granted to Sir John Smith,[26] when the visitation of Essex was made in 1634, the Mildmays were only assigned the coat ' restored ' to them by Cooke in 1583.[27] But not only had the ' new ' coat dropped quietly out of their shield : it had been replaced by an early coat representing, it is said,

[23] *Miscell. Gen. et Her.* ii, 165. [24] See pp. 64-5 above.

[25] *Ibid.* ii, 267, 268. [26] See p. 61 above.

[27] *Misc. Gen. et Her.* ii, 197, 198, 200.

Rous, in virtue of an alleged match between Sir Robert Mildmay (? temp. Henry II) and the ' daughter and heir to Le Rowse.'

These coats, be it remembered, are found in the records of the College of Arms, and are such, therefore, as Mr. Fox Davies, Mr. Phillimore, and their school, would exalt as genuine and official. As for the ' ancient ' Mildmay coat, which was borne after the restitution by the spreading branches of that house, it is now part of the arms of the St. John Mildmay family under the royal licence of 1790. The College may wish to dissociate itself from the doings of Elizabethan heralds, but as I have previously pointed out, their handwork permeates its ' records.' However careful it may now be, its members are bound by these ' records,' and only those who are not so bound can give us such pedigrees and heraldry as are based on modern research alone.

THE LORDS OF KEMES [1]

In my book, *The King's Serjeants and their Coronation Services* (1911), I spoke of the novel claim, unsuccessfully advanced before the ' Court of Claims,' to carry the King's silver harp, at his Coronation (pp. 331-6). I also glanced at the claim of the petitioner, Sir Marteine Lloyd, to be the last of the Lords Marcher and to have inherited the barony of Kemes from his ancestor, Martin de Turribus, who had accompanied the Conqueror to England and had won the barony by the sword. On his petition coming before the Court of Claims :

Mr. Llewellyn Williams, who appeared in support of the claim, recited the petition, which set out, that the petitioner was a descendant of Martin de Turribus, a Norman knight, who conquered the cantref of Kemaes, in Pembrokeshire, one of the earliest marches formed in Wales, about the year 1100.[2]

The Norman Martin similarly figures in Burke's *Peerage and Baronetage* at the head of the family pedigree. We there read (1911) :

Sir Marteine Owen Mowbray Lloyd is by right of tenure, 24th Lord of the Barony of Kemes, co. Pembroke, in hereditary descent from Martin de Tours, one of the Companions in arms of William the Conqueror. . . .
Lineage. Martin de Tours, a Norman, who accompanied the Conqueror to England, having, as one of the Lords Marchers acquired by conquest, etc.[3]

Although I denied in the above work that the Owens of

---

[1] The correct Welsh name seems to have been ' Cemais ' ; Kemmeas, etc., are other forms.

[2] *Morning Post,* 28th Jan., 1911.

[3] So also in Debrett, Sir Marteine is representative of Martin de Tours, who accompanied the Conqueror to England.

Henllys can, as alleged, have succeeded Sir Marteine's ancestors (in the female line), ' by right of inheritance,' to the old lordship of Kemes (p. 334), I could not, for want of space, give the evidence in detail as I shall now proceed to do.

The pedigree which I shall here demolish does not depend for its sanction upon the heralds of a distant past, nor has it merely floated down from the harps of flattering bards.[4] It has for its origin a Welsh antiquary and for its sponsors at the present day two of the Welsh members of that Royal Commission which has been appointed to deal with the subject of our national records, Mr. Henry Owen, D.C.L., and Mr. Llewellyn Williams, B.C.L., who, as we have seen, supported as counsel before the Court of Claims the descent of Martin de Turribus.   Moreover, the enquiry will, I hope, illustrate the value of Welsh genealogy, with its fatal reliance on ' tradition ' and the use it makes and is likely to make of our national records.

Martin, the founder of the Lords of Kemes, was undoubtedly a real man, whose name gave rise to that of his descendants, the Lords Martin, and is preserved in Combe Martin (Devon), in which county they were great barons, and in Compton Martin (Somerset).

It has also, one gathers, been revived in that of Sir Marteine Lloyd, ' Marteine ' being the form found on that ' Battle Abbey Roll,' which is still quite seriously cited by some benighted persons.

---

[4] It is observed by a Welsh expert no less competent than Mr. Gwenogvryn Evans that, ' According to Sion Tudyr, the bards were prone to fabricate ancient pedigrees for upstart families, and to praise all and sundry for a consideration ' (p. 185b).   There is also a much older allusion to ' the manner of the bards ' differing from that of History (p. 63, i, 21).   But this is not enough to account for the sad and evil days which Simwnt Vychan laments as having fallen on the bards (p. 250k).   The Lords Marcher and those in authority spoke English ; the more influential families in Wales, consequently gave up speaking Welsh more and more, and thus gradually but surely lost touch with their surroundings, and, therefore, their sympathies with the ancient ways and customs.   They could no longer understand the eulogies of themselves, but they did understand that the bards were numerous and their fees grievous.   ' Report on Manuscripts in the Welsh Language.' (*Hist. MSS. Com.*), vol. i, p. xiii.

But Martin's alleged surname of 'de Tours,' for 'de Turribus,' does not occur, so far as I can find, in any contemporary source.[5] Indeed I have suggested, in my *Calendar of Documents preserved in France*, that he may be that Martin 'of Wales' (de Walis), who occurs in an early charter. It was Martin's son Robert who founded in his Lordship of 'Kemeys' the Abbey of St. Dogmaels, as shown in the above *Calendar*.

I must here say something of *The History of St. Dogmael's Abbey*, a work which was published in 1907 and formally dedicated, as dealing with the house founded by the Martins, 'to their present worthy descendant, Sir Marteine Lloyd, Bart., Lord Marcher of Cemaes.' In this strange book, we learn a great deal about the original Martin. The brief introduction is devoted almost entirely to Blaeu's map of Pembrokeshire, a reproduction of which is issued with the volume. Blaeu, by whom the map was published in 1648, placed above it what he termed 'Penbrochie comitum insignia,' that is to say, the arms of the successive families on whom the Pembroke title had been conferred, ending with those of William Herbert who had been created Earl of Pembroke in 1551, and whose family continued to hold the title in 1648, as indeed they do still. Nothing could be clearer or simpler.

The authoress, however, explains that, 'Edward Prince of Wales' (who received the earldom in 1479) was 'doubtless' the Black Prince (who never received it) and observes of the coats that :

The most remarkable is that of Anne Boleyn—why her arms should figure on this map is strange, and stamps the date of the original map, from which this was copied, as about 1534, the date of the signing of the Acknowledgment of the King's Supremacy, when Anne Boleyn was still in full favour.

[5] It is found, temp. Henry VIII, in Leland's *Collectanea*, where we read that ' The chaunter of St. David's told me that one Martinus de Turribus, a Norman, wan the countrey of Kemmeys in Wales about the tyme of King William the Conqueror and that this Martinus founded the Abbey of St. Dogmaels in Kemeis.' (Dugdale, *Mon. Angl.* iv, 128-9.)

The discovery so confidently announced is, of course, a mare's nest; Anne's arms 'figure on this map,' in due chronological sequence, because she was created Marchioness of Pembroke in 1534. The next coat is that of the next holder of the 'Pembroke title,' William Herbert (1551), of whom we read that 'his coat of arms' is 'twice inscribed on the map.' This may be 'specially interesting to Pembroke-shire folk,' but is contrary to the fact, the other and different coat being that of the William Herbert to whom the Earldom of Pembroke had been granted in 1468.

This is an ominous beginning which prepares us for the further discovery that Martin 'of the Towers' is the right rendering of Martinus de Turribus (pp. 9, 22, 24, 26), and that he was so called from the three towers blazoned on his shield and banner, and not because he came from Tours in Touraine or any other Tours in France, no town in France bearing crests (*sic*) anterior to A.D. 1200 (p. 22). One sometimes finds, at seaside resorts, their coats of arms on teacups described as 'crest china'; but it is, I imagine, generally known that coats of arms are not 'crests.' More-over it was quite impossible for Martin himself, as for the city of Tours, to possess an armorial shield or banner in the days of William I, or indeed of his successor. If he was really styled 'de Turribus' it can, at that period, have had nothing to do with heraldry, and must have been from his place of origin.

The account of 'Martin' is so exhaustive in the book of which I speak, that we are surprised to find that the fact 'that he came over with William the Norman' can be asserted to rest only on the long discredited Battle Abbey Roll (pp. 22-3, 56, 59, 61). But the authoress, who accepted without question this supposed proof, was worried in her anxiety to be accurate by one seeming discrepancy. Martin, we read :

had come over in his (the Conqueror's) train, as is seen by three of the Battle Abbey Rolls, though his name is not found inscribed in the roll of those who set sail from Dives, near Caen, in Normandy, with William the Conqueror. Still, he is in three lists of those who fought with William at the Battle of Hastings, so it may have been that he sailed from a different port (p. 22).

The same difficulty occurs on p. 56, where we read that 'oddly enough he is not mentioned in the list, which is still in existence at Dives, near Caen, in Normandy, and it is from Dives that William the Conqueror is known to have sailed.' Finally, we are reminded on p. 61, that 'If Robert [6] had come from Tour, near Bayeux, his name would certainly have been in the Dives Roll, as this Tour and Dives are both in the same department.' This imaginary difficulty is of her own making. The very work on which she relies, namely, ' The Duchess of Cleveland's *Battle Abbey Roll* ' (p. 56), explains fully that the old lists, which are styled variants of the Battle Abbey Roll, have nothing in the world to do with the modern compilation described as ' the Dives Roll.' This list, of which the authoress speaks as ' still in existence ' :

Is modern, having been inaugurated at the celebration of the eighth centenary of the battle (1866) when it was solemnly affixed on a tablet in the ancient Church of Dives. . . . It is entitled " Companions of William the Conqueror at the conquest of England in 1066 " : and was compiled with much care and labour by M. Leopold Delisle, the greatest antiquarian authority in France, who professes to give no name that is not vouched for by some deed or document of the period (p. ix).

The reason why Martin's name is not found in this list is precisely because it is not vouched for by any deed or document of the Conqueror's reign or that of his son.[7]

The fact is that everything points to Martin having ' flourished,' as the saying is, at a date later than that of William's coming. If ' his grandson William built Newport

---

[6] ' Robert ' is obviously an error for ' Martin.'

[7] Although we read (p. 23) that ' happily it is proved, both by the Domesday Book and by many other sources, that the Norman knight Martin lived there (in Devon),' Domesday does not prove it, nor were there Martins whom ' further researches in the Domesday Book reveal ' in Buckinghamshire and in Lincolnshire identical with him as alleged (pp. 60-61).

Castle in the thirteenth century ' (p. 25), it is obvious that Martin is not likely to have shared in the Conquest of England so far back in the eleventh. The fact that his son, Robert Fitz Martin, was an active supporter of the Empress in 1141, points in the same direction.[8] One reason for dealing critically with this history of the abbey is that both the introduction and the text of my *Calendar of Documents preserved in France* have been duly drawn upon (pp. 41, 44-5, 57-8) without availing in any way to check the repetition of unsupported statements.

Robert Fitz Martin is a well-known man as compared with his father ; we have abundant evidence of his marriage and his benefactions.[9] From him descended the Martins lords of Kemes and of Somerset and Devon manors. Nicholas Martin greatly increased the wealth and importance of his house by marriage with an heiress who brought him her share of the important barony of Barnstaple. To this Nicholas I now pass, for he is the turning-point in the pedigree of the lords of Kemes. The true pedigree of his descendants presents no difficulty ; the false pedigree was asserted in the teeth of record proof.

The vital record is the Inquisition taken after his death, which proves that he died early in 1282, and that his heir was his grandson William, son of his son Nicholas.[10] This William was summoned to Parliament in 1295 and is proved to have sat there in 1320, which facts were recently established before the Committee for Privileges.[11] The

---

[8] This fact is duly taken from my *Geoffrey de Mandeville*, p. 59.

[9] His charter granting Teignton to Montacute mentions his mother, Geva. This very distinctive name was also that of the wife of Geoffrey Ridel (*d.* 1120), who was a daughter of Hugh, earl of Chester. As the above grant was for the souls of Hugh Earl of Chester and his wife and the welfare of Ranulf Earl of Chester and his wife *inter alios*, and as Robert and his wife held at Veregsons (Normandy) of Richard Earl of Chester (*d.* 1120), Hugh's son, it seems possible that Geva, his mother, was connected with the Earl's family.

[10] *Cal. of Inquisitions*, ii, 263 ; *Cal. of Fine Rolls*, i, 160.

[11] On 2nd, 3rd, and 5th March, 1914, ' Willelmus Martyn Dominus de Camesio ' ; he is one of those whose name appears on the ' Barons' letter to the Pope ' early in 1301.

78

barony thus created was petitioned for by two of his direct descendants, as co-heirs to the dignity, one of whom has inherited as his seat William's manor of Tawstock. Accompanying their petition and case [12] was a printed chart pedigree bearing at its foot the signature of Mr. A. C. Fox-Davies. This pedigree ran thus :

William Martin of Kemeys co. Pembroke, and Lord of the manor of Tawstock, co. Devon, Lord Martyn . . . he died 1325	= Eleanor, daughter of William de Mohun

William Lord Martin. . . . He died unmarried 1326, when the barony fell into abeyance between his sisters	Nicholas, Lord Audley (1st husband) =	Joane,[13] co-heir to the barony of Martin = Henry de Lacy, Earl of Lincoln (2nd husband)

On this pedigree a genealogist would offer these criticisms :

(1) The first William did not die in 1325, but in 1324.[14]

(2) He did not marry ' Eleanor, daughter of William de Mohun,' [15] but 'Eleanor, late the wife of the said William de Mohun.'

(3) The second William did not die unmarried, but left a widow Margaret, who held his manor of Tawstock in dower for many years. She was remarried to Robert de Wateville before 1st June, 1326.[16]

(4) His sister Joan did not marry Nicholas de Audley as her first husband and the Earl of Lincoln as her second, but on the contrary the Earl as her first and Nicholas as her second husband.[17]

[12] These came before me as Honorary Historical Adviser to the Crown in Peerage cases.

[13] I omit the other sister and co-heir as not affecting the descent.

[14] *Cal. of Inquisitions*, vi, p. 358.   [15] *Ibid.* ii, p. 333.

[16] *Cal. of Close Rolls*, 1323-7, pp. 483, 595, 600-2.

[17] *Cal. of Inquisitions*, vi, p. 42 ; *Cal. of Close Rolls*, 1307-1313, p. 535 ; Dugdale's *Baronage*, i, 748 ; *Complete Peerage*, etc., etc.

From the Lords Audley, the true heirs [18] of that Nicholas Martin whom I have termed the turning-point in the pedigree, we will now pass to his ' bogus ' heirs—to employ the word dear to the heart of Mr. Fox-Davies. According to the purely fictitious pedigree put forward by George Owen in the days of Queen Elizabeth and repeated by Dr. Henry Owen,[19] Nicholas was succeeded, not by his grandson (as the Inquisition proves he was), but by the son of his brother ' Colonett.' Nicholas, however, had left, according to this story, a daughter ' Ales,' from whom George Owen was descended [20] and in right of whom his father, ages after her death, claimed and ' won back ' Kemes. From the Owens Kemes passed with an heiress in the eighteenth century to the Lloyds, and this is how Sir Marteine Lloyd is representative of Martin de Tours [21]—as he would be if the pedigree were true. But, as we have seen, it is not true. Even in Burke's *Peerage* it is thrown overboard and the true pedigree of Martin is substituted for it, with the result that the Audleys are shown to be the true heirs of Kemes. Yet this is followed by the absurd statement—based upon the false pedigree—that ' in the family of Audley, the barony of Kemes continued vested for several successive generations until it passed *by right of inheritance*[22] to the Owens of Henllys, descended from the Martins, ancient Lords Marcher of Kemes.

We will now see further, how Doctor Owen deals with the details of the alleged descent, and what he makes chronologically of the Owen and the Martin pedigrees. Let us first take this passage from Dr. Owen's Preface (p. vii) on the origin of the Owens of Henllys :

Philip ap Riccard, an ancestor of the Owens, had married (temp. Henry III) Nest the heiress of Henllys, the only daughter of Llewelyn ap Rhydderch, who was descended in the direct male line from Rhys ap Tewdwr, the last King in South Wales. The father of this Philip had married Ales, the only daughter of

---

[18] i.e. his senior co-heirs in blood and his actual successors in Kemes.

[19] Owen's *Pembrokeshire*, i, 491. It is duly found also in the *Hist. of St. Dogmael's Abbey* (p. 57).

[20] Owen, *Pembrokeshire, ibid.*   [21] Debrett.   [22] The italics are mine.

Nicholas Martin, the Lord of Kemes, an event of no small importance to the future historian.[23]

That is to say that Philip, the grandson of a man who died in 1284, was himself married under Henry III (i.e. 1216-1272).

But let us continue. ' The father of this Philip,' a footnote informs us, was himself ' grandson of Lucas de Hoda, a knight in the train of Martin de Tours,' which Martin, as we read on the same page, came to Kemes ' in the reign of William Rufus.' [24] Dr. Owen, therefore, gives us this gorgeous anachronism :

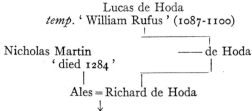

Does it arouse in him the slightest doubt ? None whatever. There is nothing of my own invention about the above pedigree. The ' emblazoned ' pedigree of 1677 preserved at Bronwydd gives it as on p. 82.[25]

Here, it will be seen, the same space is covered by two generations of Hoods as by five generations of Martins. We may note in passing that ' Ales,' the alleged heiress through whom (according to Dr. Henry Owen) the Owens claimed descent from the Martins, here becomes ' Nesta.' [26]

[23] See chart pedigree of the Martins below.

[24] It is a very interesting fact that this family, I find, derived its name from Hood in Rattery, co. Devon, where Jordan de Hode held half a fee of Nicholas Martin 1243 (*Testa de Nevill*, p. 178b) ; cf. Mr. Reichel's paper on ' The Hundred of Stanborough,' in *Trans. of the Devonshire Assoc.* xlv, p. 175). The earliest gift of the Martins in Devonshire to St. Dogmael's appears to have been at Rattery. So the families were associated there, as in Kemes.

[25] This pedigree is printed to face p. 136 of the *Baronia de Kemeys* (*Cambrian Archaeol. Assoc.*).

[26] In the *Hist. of Dogmael's Abbey* (1907) the same pedigree, with its wondrous chronology, reappears : ' Martin's great-great-great-granddaughter, Ales or Nesta, married Richard de Hoda, the grandson of this young Norman knight, and through her, the Barony of Cemaes

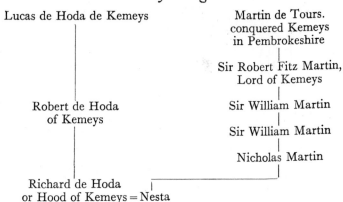

Lucas de Hoda de Kemeys

Martin de Tours.
conquered Kemeys
in Pembrokeshire

Sir Robert Fitz Martin,
Lord of Kemeys

Robert de Hoda
of Kemeys

Sir William Martin

Sir William Martin

Nicholas Martin

Richard de Hoda
or Hood of Kemeys = Nesta

Let us turn to Dr. Owen's pedigree of the Martins, lords of Kemes (p. 491), and similarly test its chronology. It runs thus :

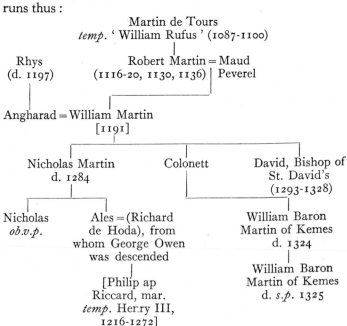

Martin de Tours
temp. ' William Rufus ' (1087-1100)

Rhys
(d. 1197)

Robert Martin = Maud
(1116-20, 1130, 1136) | Peverel

Angharad = William Martin
[1191]

Nicholas Martin
d. 1284

Colonett

David, Bishop of
St. David's
(1293-1328)

Nicholas
ob.v.p.

Ales = (Richard
de Hoda), from
whom George Owen
was descended

William Baron
Martin of Kemes
d. 1324

[Philip ap
Riccard, mar.
temp. Henry III,
1216-1272]

William Baron
Martin of Kemes
d. *s.p.* 1325

descended to their son Philip ' (p. 25). This last statement is an added error, for Cemaes never passed to the Hoods, but, as the authoress admits (p 57), ' to the Audleys.'

The Lords of Kemes

Thus is the chart pedigree actually given by himself to show ' the devolution of the barony of Kemes through the Martins, Audleys, and Touchets, to John, Lord Audley, from whom William Owen won it back for the old Pembrokeshire family in 1543.' The dates which I have added within brackets are, for any competent genealogist, its sufficient condemnation. But Dr. Owen himself gives 1328 as the date of Bishop David's death and yet makes him, without hesitation, grandson of a man who was married and was already Lord of Kemes more than two centuries before.

It seems to be one of the qualifications required for a Welsh genealogist that he should always be ready to take leave of his senses. Their pedigrees at times will not stand even the simplest tests. I have dealt in another place with their venerable absurdities [27] and observed that they have good reason to pray, from all facts and dates, ' Good Lord, deliver us.'

As a matter of fact Bishop David was not even the son, as alleged in the pedigree, of William Martin, but of that Nicholas Martin whom the pedigree makes his brother. This I prove from the Register of Bishop Bronescombe of Exeter, where we find this Bishop writing to the Bishop of St. David's, 3rd May, 1276, about the presentation to Bratton Fleming (in N.E. Devon), by Richard le Fleming, of David, then a subdeacon, ' Nati Nobilis Viri, Domini Nicholai filii Martini, de diocesi vestra oriundi,' and admitting him on the 10th May following. David resigned this living in 1280, having been made rector of Ermington.[28]

But let us return to the alleged marriage of George Owen's ancestor with ' Ales, the only daughter of Nicholas Martin, the Lord of Kemes, an event of no small importance to the future historian.' Why was it of no small importance ? Because the historian's father, William Owen, is alleged to have recovered the barony of Kemes in 1543 as the heir of this marriage, from the Audley family which had held it

---

[27] *Ancestor*, No. 5, pp. 47-51.
[28] *Bronescombe's Register*, ed. Hingeston-Randolph, pp. 117, 134.

till then as the heirs of these Martins. In Dr. Owen's words :

The barony of Kemes was won back to the old Welsh house by William Owen, the father of the author, who claimed it as a descendant [29] of the above-mentioned ' Ales,' the daughter of Nicholas Fitz Martin. William's suit against Lord Audley lasted nineteen years, and in 1543 ' Johannes Dom. de Audley relaxavit et quiet' clamavit predict' William (*sic*) Owen et heredibus totum jus suum ' : a result which bears no small testimony to the legal ability and perseverance of the Pembrokeshire lawyer (p. viii).

That is to say (as will be seen on referring to the chart pedigree above) that the Owens won back the lands on the ground that they had descended wrongly for two and a half centuries.

But had they descended wrongly ? Dr. Owen's pedigree, we saw, makes Nicholas Martin leave at his death, in 1284, a daughter ' Ales,' through whom this claim was made. The old emblazoned pedigree in the possession of the family at Bronwydd [30] made that daughter *Nesta* (see p. 82 above). [31] But George Owen himself, her alleged heir, asserts in this very work (p. 454) that :

Aboutes this tyme, (vizt) 1284, the saied Nicholas Martin died haveinge noe issue of his body.

What has Dr. Owen to say to that ? Let us, however, continue the quotation :

whose enheritaunce fell to his brother *Colonet's* sonne, called William Martin that succeeded him in the lordship of Kemeys. . . . His elder (*sic*) brother *Colonett* was stiled *Valectus domini Regis*, and his younger brother David was bishop of Menevia (i.e. St. David's).

[29] Dr. Owen must have meant ' the heir,' not ' a descendant.'

[30] See p. 81, note 25.

[31] In the *Hist. of St. Dogmael's Abbey* (p. 25) she is ' Ales or Nesta.' The reader should compare the ' Nesta ' or ' Vesta ' of a Welsh pedigree and its ' Momea, rather Rohesia,' in my paper on ' The origin of the Carews,' together with Mr. Wood's admission that in Welsh pedigrees ' little attention is paid to the Christian names of women ' (*Ancestor*, No. 4, p. 48).

Now it is proved by record evidence that the inheritance of Nicholas Martin did not fall to a son of his brother, Colonet,' but to his own grandson William, whose father, Nicholas, had died in his lifetime (see chart pedigree above).[32] This is proved, as we saw, by the Inquisition post-mortem on the elder Nicholas and also by the Fine Roll of 10 Edward I (m. 15) and the Pipe Roll of 14 Edward I, which latter records William's 'relief.' The second and third of these records were known to the admirable Dugdale, who gave the succession correctly.[33] This passage in his work was actually known to Dr. Owen,[34] and yet he rejected the evidence of public records cited by the English writer and adopted the erroneous genealogy of the Elizabethan Welshman.

There is more, however, to come. As Nicholas Martin (d. 1282)[35] was succeeded not by his nephew, but by his son's son, it follows that his daughter, if she existed and if she was ancestress of the Owens, cannot possibly have given them any right to the barony. Therefore, the whole story that they claimed it successfully in right of her, under Henry VIII, cannot be correct. Yet Burke's *Peerage*, as I showed[36] in its pedigree of Sir Marteine Owen Lloyd, while actually admitting that Nicholas Martin was succeeded by his son's son, asserts that 'Kemes passed by right of inheritance to the Owens of Henllys,' an assertion which that admission proves to be contrary to fact.

[32] Although my paper does not clash with that of Sir Henry Maxwell Lyte on the families of Burci, Falaise, and Martin—our subjects being different—we both mention 'Colonet,' or 'Colinet,' as he styles him. I am bound, therefore, to point out that Sir Henry treats him as identical with the younger Nicholas (who died in his father's lifetime), while I, on the contrary, make him a separate person, who was uncle to this Nicholas. Of course we are both in agreement as to the true pedigree ; but it is of great importance to grasp the exact form of the spurious version. For the whole story of the rightful heir being supplanted by 'Colonet' and his heirs till the days of Henry VIII rests entirely on the allegation that 'Colonet' was only a younger brother of the Nicholas Martin who died in 1282.

[33] *Baronage* (1675), i, 729.

[34] *Op. cit.* p. 491.

[35] Dr. Owen gives the date as 1284.

[36] See p. 82 above.

The astonishing thing is that Dr. Owen had before him George Owen's own ' bref note of the order of the *pourchase* of the lordship of Kemes from John Lord Awdeley, Mary his wiffe, and George Awdeley, his sonne and heir,' which recites, we find, nine deeds including ' a bargain and sale of the barony to the plaintiff,' ' a recovery suffered by the defendant,' ' a fine with relese and duble warranty,' etc., etc. (p. viii). He had also George Owen's statement in a Star Chamber suit, under Elizabeth, that his father ' did *purchase* a manor called the barony of Kemes ' from Lord Audley, and his further statement that he had been made to produce the ' purchase ' deeds, ' being in number about threescore several peeces ' (p. 511). All this evidence he gets over by interpolating the gloss ' acquisition,' ' acquire ' for ' purchase,' though he himself adds the definition of purchase.—' In law to obtain land by one's own act, not by descent ' (p. 511). Just so, William Owen did not obtain the baronage as alleged, ' by descent,' or inheritance, but by a bargain and sale of the barony . . . with a condition of redemption on payment of £300 (p. viii). This appears to have been an ordinary Welsh mortgage of former days.[37]

As for the tale that William Owen, who significantly enough was a Tudor lawyer, proved his right by a descent from a daughter of Nicholas Martin,[38] it is, we have seen, demolished by records and, indeed, now abandoned, while Dr. Owen himself admits that it first appears in the 1607 edition of Camden's *Britannia*, and ' does not appear in any previous edition ' (p. ix), and Camden was merely told the tale (' me docuit ') by his friend George Owen. And yet Dr. Owen swallows it without hesitation. Indeed, it is

[37] George Owen himself speaks of ' an obligation from the morgagee to the morgager for redemption of the landes, which often times bredd much lawe and descord and wrested the meaning of the parties to wrong ' (p. 181), and Dr. Owen comments in a note (p. 182) that ' In a Welsh mortgage formerly much used in Wales, the estate was conveyed absolutely to the creditor, without any condition, but was redeemable at anytime on repayment of the loan.'

[38] ' Regnante Henrico Octavo Guilielmus Owen, qui genus deduxit a filia Nicholai Martin Militis, jus suum longa liti persecutus tandem obtinuit.'

again repeated by the latest historian of Pembrokeshire (1909), who writes :

The male line of the Martins of Kemes had ended with the death of William Martin, who died in 1326, when the barony of Kemes passed to his nephew, James Lord Audley, son of his sister Joan. . . . The barony of Kemes was ultimately won back by William Owen of Henllys, himself a descendant of Nicholas Martin, Lord of Kemes, the grandfather of William Martin.[39]

The reader, I hope, will by now have grasped the fact that the whole story of Nicholas Martin (d. 1282) leaving as his rightful heir a daughter, whose rights passed to her heirs, the Owens, is a fiction of the Tudor period. But further proof that this was so, though quite unnecessary, is afforded by the descent of that great Devonshire inheritance, which came to Nicholas with his wife. This inheritance is duly found in the hands of the later Martins, who could only therefore be descended from herself and not, as alleged, from her husband's brother. The story is as clumsy as it is false.

To sum up the result of my investigation of the pedigree, there is no question whatever as to the true descent. Nicholas Martin, Lord of Kemes, who died in 1282, was succeeded by his son's son, William Martin, who was summoned to Parliament, and whose lineal heirs have recently been ascertained by the House of Lords. From these Martins, the lordship of Kemes passed to the Lords Audley, as their senior co-heirs. Thus far, the lineage as now given in Burke's *Peerage* is quite correct, but after this the lordship of Kemes passed from the Audleys to the Owens, under Henry VIII, not, as alleged in Burke's *Peerage*, ' by right of inheritance '—which, on its own showing could not be the case—but by purchase. The purchaser's son, George Owen, an Elizabethan herald, concocted a pedigree to prove that his family were the rightful heirs of the Martins and had proved, as such, their hereditary right to Kemes,

---

[39] *Hist. of Pembrokeshire* (Rev. J. Phillips), p. 399.

which they had thus regained. To prove this, he falsely alleged that Nicholas Martin (d. 1282) had been wrongfully succeeded by a brother's son though he had left a daughter (whose name is doubtful), who should have succeeded to Kemes as his rightful heir (or co-heir), and whose representative he (George Owen) was. The whole of this story is completely disposed of by the fact (proved by the public records) that Nicholas was, on the contrary, succeeded by his son's son, who was his rightful heir, in 1282.[40] George Owen, however, palmed off his spurious pedigree on his friend, Lewis Dunn, the herald depute in 1591, and subsequently on that credulous *antiquary* Camden. I have shown that since then it has been persistently repeated without the slightest suspicion that it was sheer falsehood.

We have now reached the point at which it is possible to set forth the true pedigree of the Martins at the essential period.

The True Pedigree.

Rhys ap Gruffyd of Dehenbarth,
captured Kemes in 1191, d. 1197

Angharad = William Fitz Martin
of Kemes

Sir Nicholas Fitz Martin =
recovered Kemes from
the Welsh but lost it
(1257) for a time. d. 1282

Nicholas Martin,
ob.v.p.

Sir William Martin,
heir to his grandfather
in 1282 (see p. 85)

David Martin,
Rector of Ermington
(Devon) 1280; Bishop of
St. David's 1293

[40] *Cal. of Fine Rolls*, i, 144-5.

But we must go a step further.   That the Owens were not descended from a daughter *and heir* of Nicholas is, we have seen, proved, but were they even descended from a daughter ? There are, we saw, three versions : (1) that in the narrative of George Owen, namely, that Nicholas Martin ' died haveinge noe issue of his body ' [41]; (2) that in the emblazoned pedigree of the family at Bronwydd, namely, that *Nesta*, a daughter (not styled heir) of Nicholas Martin, married ' Richard de Hoda (or Hood) of Kemeys,' the Owens' ancestor ; (3) that of Dr. Henry Owen, namely, that Ales, daughter of Nicholas Martin, was the Owens' ancestress.[42] When we remember that it is almost impossible to prove a marriage of this kind in the thirteenth century, unless the wife was an heiress who brought lands to her husband, we naturally ask whether there is any proof at all to this marriage.   And we are given absolutely none.   It follows, therefore, that the Owens of Henllys and their modern descendants have not a proved descent from the Martins, Lords of Kemes.   Their root of title is a ' purchase ' by their ancestor in the days of Henry VIII, and their pedigree in earlier days rests, not on records, but on that vague jumble of traditions of which Welsh genealogy consists.

We have seen the chronological absurdities of the early Owen (Hood) pedigree as given in the pedigree at Bronwydd and repeated by Dr. Owen ; but even that exposure does not stand alone.   Dr. Owen writes that George Owen

belonged to the ancient house of Henllys, near Newport, Pembrokeshire.   Of Henllys, the author [43] says that it did not appear that any other family or person than his ancestors had ever lived there (p. vi).

[41] Owen, *Pembrokeshire*, p. 454.

[42] *Ibid.* p. 491.   Her name, I find, must be taken from Lewis Dunn's *Heraldic Visitations of Wales* (ed. Meyrick), i, 156-7, where we read that ' Rickard ap Luwcas Hood, Frank,' married ' Ales v. koeres Nicklas ap Sir William Martynn Argylwydd y Kemes marchog.'   But this statement heads the pedigree signed by George Owen, 21st Sept., 1591, when he duly paid his friend, Lewis Dunn, the deputy herald, his fee for entering it (see Meyrick's edition of Dunn, pp. xxv ; i, 157).

[43] i.e. George Owen.

Family Origins

The 'emblazoned pedigree' at Bronwydd no doubt carried back the possession to his ancestor, Sir Meredith ap Griffith, who died in 1188, but Dr. Owen's own volume contains a note (p. 144) that the fair and market at Henllys 'were granted by Edward I (*sic*), not to any Owen but to John de Langton, on the 18th of June 1284' (*sic*), and adds that, 'The deed is printed with the *Baronia*,' pp. 76-7. We turn to the place cited, only to discover that the charter is there headed in full, 'Ex rotulo Cartarum de anno duodecimo regni Regis Edwardi Tertii.' This date is confirmed by the names of the witnesses, and we thus discover that the grant was actually made by Edward the Third in the year 1338.[44]

Apart from the question of date it is to be observed that John de Langton received this grant for a fair and market, to himself and his heirs for ever, 'at his manor of Henllys' (*apud manerium suum de Henles*), a grim comment on the statement as above, by George Owen, that 'it did not appear that any other family or person than his ancestors had ever lived there.'

Welsh heraldry can fairly claim to be even more grotesque than Welsh genealogy. For, however fantastic the latter may be, the former, before the days of Richard I, must be absurd fiction.[45] But a Welsh antiquary should at least be able to play his own foolish game. Let us see what Dr. Owen makes of George Owen's arms. On p. xiii of his preface, he quotes Dineley (*Beaufort's Progress*) to the effect that 'the Field Gules, a Boare Argent armed grisled

[44] Dr. Owen's treatment of this record is precisely parallel to that passage in his *Old Pembrokeshire Families* (p. 13), where he writes of the Carews that, 'Other (*sic*) soon after his father's death (1173) . . . obtained from Henry II the manor of Brampton, co. Oxon (*sic*), so long as the Welsh held Emlyn.' The reference given for this statement is '*Pipe Rolls*, 2 Henry II' (1156), where there is not, and could not be any such entry. The entry required is on the *Pipe Roll* of 20 Henry II (1174), where we read (p. 89) that Odo, not Other, received as compensation £20 a year from the manor of Brampton, co. Devon, not Brampton, co. Oxon.

[45] See pp. xii-xiv of my *Studies in Peerage and Family History* for the proved and recorded coats of arms by Coel Godebog and Beli Mawr.

collared and chained Or, tyed to a Holly-Bush on a Mount in base, both proper, was the paternall coat armor of George Owen Esq. deceased.'   On this he comments : ' These were the arms of Llwch Llawenvawr, Lord of Kilsant in Pembrokeshire in the early part of the 11th century, whose daughter and heiress married Cadivor Vawr, from whom George Owen was descended (see Lewys Dwynn, i, 156-7).' We learn then in the first place that Dr. Owen believes arms to have been borne ' in the early part of the 11th century.' On such a statement in these days I need make no comment. But he might at least have played properly the Welsh heraldic game. In the great heraldic pedigree of 1677, preserved by the family at Bronwydd,[46] among what he terms ' the invaluable archives ' there placed at his disposal,[47] we find (1) that the arms in question are, on the contrary, derived from Lucas de Hoda, the alleged patriarch of the Owens ; (2) that they are not the arms assigned to Llwchllawen Vawr, the field of whose coat was sable, not gules, while the boar was ' headed gules ' and the tree ' argent ' ; (3) that it was not George Owen, but his wife who ' was descended from Llwchllawen Vawr through his daughter,' so that ' the parental arms of George could not be those of Llwchllawen.' [48]

With regard to the claim that Sir Marteine Lloyd is ' the only Lord Marcher in the Kingdom,' I have already dealt with it in my book, *The King's Serjeants* (pp. 331-4), where I have cited Dr. Owen's contention that ' the Lords Marcher were in theory and in practice sovereign princes,' whose powers were greater than those of ' the Earls Palatine,' which he illustrates in detail.[49]   That this position and the powers he names are not held by Sir Marteine Lloyd there is, of course, no question ; but it is further very doubtful

---

[46] See p. 81.   [47] Owen, *Pembrokeshire*, i, xxvii.

[48] The two coats are treated as distinct by Lewis Dunn (i, 157) to whom Dr. Owen refers.

[49] *Y Cymmrodor*, vol. xiv, pp. 17-8, 22.

whether the ancient Lords of Kemes enjoyed that measure of independence which was essential, it is recognised, to the status of a Lord Marcher. George Owen argued desperately and strove, under Elizabeth, for many years to prove that they had that *status* and that he was entitled to revive it.[50] It was a lawyer's quibble ; he contended that, as Kemes was no part of the old county of Pembroke, and was not mentioned among the lordships which were added to that county to make up the new shire, his baronial rights were left untouched.[51] But on the general question Dr. Owen has observed that :

The prerogatives of the Lords Marcher were vested in the Crown by Henry VIII. . . . The prerogatives of the Marches had been absorbed and Wales had been annexed to England. . . . The act for recontinuing the liberties in the Crown (27 Henry VIII, cap. 24) . . . had discrowned the Marchers. . . . The act of Union (27 Henry VIII, cap. 26) united Wales to England, made the Marches shire ground, abolished the civil and criminal jurisdiction of the Lords Marcher.[52]

[50] See his argument, ' that Kemes is a Lordship Marcher,' in *Baronia de Kemeys*, pp. 7 *et seq.*, ' and Prooffes that Kemes is an aunciente Lordshippe Marcher ' (*Ibid.* pp. 37-42).

[51] Owen, *Pembrokeshire*, pp. x, xxiii. Prof. Tout, in the paper cited below, disposes of this contention by his observation that the ' lordships that make up the modern shire,' of which Kemes is one, ' were annexed to the county of Pembroke. The other lordships Marcher of the south were joined to the old Welsh shires of Cardigan and Carmarthen ' (p. 221). The essential point to be remembered is that a ' Lordship Marcher,' from its very nature, could not form part of a shire. On its being incorporated into a shire, it ceased to exist as a ' Lordship Marcher,' and without a Lordship Marcher there could not be a ' Lord Marcher.'

[52] *Y Cymmrodor*, vol. xiv, pp. 2, 9, 11, 23. This, indeed, does but repeat what had been said by Prof. Tout, an historian specially qualified to speak on this subject, in a paper read in 1888, before the Society of Cymmrodorion. Of the abolition by Henry VIII of the *status* of the Lords Marcher he observed :

' In a series of great statutes he incorporated England and Wales into a single whole with equal rights and similar laws. This union of England and Wales involved the extension of the shire system to all Wales. The palatine jurisdiction of the Marcher was abolished and the lord of the March reduced to the humble position of the lord of an English manor. The Lordships Marcher were either incorporated into existing shires or aggregated into new ones.' *Ibid.* vol. ix, part 2, p. 220.

The Lords of Kemes

On the ancient status of Kemes in particular, Dr. Owen very justly admits that :

The truth seems to have been that, although the Kings of England had been willing to allow that the lords of Kemes, as all others who had won lands in Wales by the sword, held of the Crown *in capite*, the great earldom of Pembroke in time over-shadowed the lordship, and the Kemes lords were unable to maintain their independence.[53]

So early as 1277 there was concluded and sealed at Pembroke a formal agreement, unknown apparently to George Owen and all others who have written on the subject, between William de Valence, ' Dominus Penbrochie,' [54] and Joan his wife, heiress of Pembroke, on the one part, and ' Nicholas filius Martini ' on the other.[55] This agreement takes the form of a grant from William and Joan to Nicholas of a certain jurisdiction, together with the right of ' wreck,' within the ' land ' (*terra*) of ' Kemmeys,' reserving to them-selves pleas of the Crown, and even the right to fine Nicholas if he could not clear himself of allowing a thief to escape, within it. To the legal antiquary this document should be of much interest, while for our present purpose it is of special importance for its allusion to ' the men of Kemmeys ' serving in the host, not under their alleged Lord Marcher, but under the Lord of Pembroke. It still bears the seals of William and Joan.

Again in 1282, as is proved by record evidence, we find Newport Castle, the ' caput baroniae ' of Kemes, returned as ' held of the earl Marschall ' [56] in the Inquisition on Nicholas Martin's death. ' His successor,' wrote George Owen, ' did very much endeavour in his youth to withdraw his suite and service, from the Lorde, castle and honour of

[53] *Ibid.* p. x.

[54] This style is of some importance in view of the doubt as to the date at which he was recognised as Earl of Pembroke.

[55] It is printed in full in Jeayes, *Catalogue of the Muniments at Berkeley Castle*, pp. 142-6.

[56] ' His castle of Newport in Camays in the Marches of Wales in co. Panbroch . . . held it of the earl Marschall.' (*Cal. of Inquisitions*, ii, 263, No. 440.)

93

Pembroke, desereinge rather to hold his Lordshippe of Kemeys of the principalitie of Wales or of the King in capite than to be subject to the jurisdiction of the Lordes of Pembroke, which did begett some striffe between the both Lordes toucheinge their tenures and jurisdictions.' [57] This, it will be seen, is an admission that Kemes had rendered suit and service to the Lords of Pembroke and been subject to their jurisdiction.

The great ' composition ' which followed became the governing instrument on these vexed relations. It is described by George Owen as ' the greatest matter that the adverse parte hath to urge against the lordshippe of Kemes to be a lordshippe marcher.' [58] He gave its Latin text in his ' Register Book of Kemeys ' [59] and in his history of ' The Lordes of Kemes.' [60] Its date was 5th November, 1290 (18 Edward I), and it was enrolled on the Close Roll in January following. The contents of this document are absolutely fatal to the view that Kemes possessed the independence essential to the status of a lordship Marcher. In the official calendar the abstract runs thus :

Sir William Martyn, lord of Kemmeys . . . acknowledges and grants that he and his heirs are bound to do suit at the county (court) of Pembroke for the land of Kemmeys for ever. He also grants that William de Valencia and Joan his wife,[61] and Joan's heirs shall have in all the land of Kemmeys, cognisance of rape, arsons in time of peace, forestall, treasure trove, and cognisance of appeals of homicide, and of any other felony without mainour, etc., etc. . . . He also grants that (they) shall have cognisance of injuries and trespasses of William Martyn and his baliffs there, and pleas of fresh force both of ferms and of free tenants, and the running (*cursus*) of all writs by the seal of the chancery of Pembroke, with the execution thereof and with all things pertaining to them.[62]

[57] Owen, *Pembrokeshire*, p. 455. See further on this point, *Rot. Parl.* (Rec. Com.), i, 29, 68, where this contest is dealt with and William de Valence shown to have secured, as Lord of Pembroke, his jurisdiction over the barony of ' Cammeys.'

[58] *Baronia de Kemeys*, p. 20.   [59] *Ibid.* pp. 61-2.

[60] Owen, *Pembrokeshire*, pp. 455-6.   [61] Lord and Lady of Pembroke.

[62] *Cal. of Close Rolls* (1904), 1288-1296, p. 188.

The Lords of Kemes

In return for these sweeping concessions William Martyn was granted the cognisance of all [other][63] pleas arising within the precinct of the whole land of Kemmeys that may be duly determined in his court of Kemmeys, unless it be through the default of William Martyn or his bailiffs, where they have been remiss in doing justice or have denied justice, in which case, William de Valencia and Joan and her heirs shall apply correcting hands to such cognisances.

This agreement was reaffirmed by Richard II as Lord of Pembroke, and Nicholas de Audley, on payment of a fine of £25, was pardoned for his offences against it, as Lord of Kemes, 12th July, 1378.[64]

In spite of the decisive character of this great ' composition ' the death at Arras, 16th April, 1575, of John (Hastings), Earl of Pembroke, who left an infant heir, led to a fresh effort on the part of the Lord of Kemes to assert his independence of Pembroke. The King, as guardian of the infant heir, claimed to stand in the Earl's shoes, which brought him into conflict with Nicholas de Audley, acting as Lord of Kemes. Nicholas was most vigorously brought to book and forced to abandon his claim to the jurisdiction which he had exercised within the lordship of Kemes. The King successfully took his stand on the above great ' composition,' which was recited in full.[65] It appears that Nicholas and Elizabeth his wife had refused to make suit and had hindered the King and his ministers from exercising the liberties and privileges contained in the composition and agreements, whereat the ' King is moved to anger.' [66]

[63] This essential word, unfortunately, is actually omitted in the printed *Cal. of Close Rolls* and the whole meaning thereby obscured. The text runs ' omnium *aliorum* placitorum.'

[64] *Cal. of Patent Rolls*, 1377-81, p. 261, cf. p. 215.

[65] Document of 4th July, 1376, in *Cal. of Close Rolls*, 1374-7, p. 386. The official who prepared the text of this volume for press appears to have been unable to supply the date of the real composition, for he leaves the year blank.

[66] Close Roll, 50, Edw. III, p. ii, m. 18 ; *Cal. of Close Rolls*, 1374-7, p. 386. So far back as 15th June, 1374, it was stipulated that ' a writing indented ' should be given up to Nicholas and his wife Elizabeth (pp. 79, 80, 547).

Nicholas had, it seems, been outlawed as the result of his prosecution in the county court of Pembroke and only obtained pardon on his abject submission. On 30th April, 1377, the steward and sheriff of Pembroke were ordered to stay until further order the publication of outlawries and exigents against him.

On the same date Nicholas bound himself to abide the judgment and order of the King and council concerning all things which affect the jurisdictions and claims . . . within the precinct of the lordship of Kemoys.' [67]   Particular attention should be given to the phrase ' their liberty of Kemoys, which is in the said county ' ; for it was the fundamental contention of George Owen that his lordship of Kemes was *not* within the county of Pembroke and that it consequently was and remained a Lordship Marcher.

It is pointed out very fairly by Dr. Henry Owen that the Inquisition on the death of Lawrence de Hastings, Earl of Pembroke, 31st May, 1358, shows him to have been duly seised of suit from James de Audley in respect of ' Kemmeys ' and of liberties therein in respect of his earldom of Pembroke.[68] This further illustrates the dependent position of Kemes and directly impugns George Owen's contention.

So far as any of the jurisdictions of undoubted Lords Marcher can be said to have survived the acts of Henry VIII, those of the Welsh bishops have a claim, we find, to be considered. ' The Welsh bishops,' Dr. Owen writes, ' so far as their dioceses lay in the Marches, were, also Lords Marcher,

[67] Close Roll, 50, Edw. III, p. ii, m. 18 ; *Cal. of Close Rolls*, 1374-7, p. 540.

[68] ' De secta Jacobi Daudeleye Militis pertinente ad predictum Comitatum Pembr' ratione Dominii sui de Kemmeys et de aliis libertatibus prenominatis infra Dominium de Kemmeys tanquam pertinentibus ad Comitatum predictum ' (Owen, *Pembrokeshire*, p. 385). See also *Cal. of Inquisitions*, ix, p. 128 (No. 118), where we find that the ' libertates prenominate ' are very fully defined. The lord of ' Kemmeys ' with all his tenants were bound to assist the said earl and his ministers of the County of Pembroke, when summoned, at the county court and castle gate court of the earl, and the sheriff of Pembrokeshire held his tourn twice a year wherever he wished in the lordship, and attached ' those indicted before him and took them to Pembroke castle, there to be judged, etc.' Dr. Owen seems to have overlooked all this.

as were also other ecclesiastical personages.' ... 'The bishops of St. David's led their "subjects" to war. ... The bishops [of Llandaff] had *jura regalia*.' [69] Profits from forfeitures were reserved, by Statute 1 and 2 Philip and Mary, cap. 15, to 'bishops and other ecclesiastical persons being Lords Marcher.' [70] The point, however, that has to be grasped is that the alleged unique position of Kemes as a Lordship Marcher rests on George Owen's contention that it was not 'part of the old county of Pembroke,' and was not included by name in the new shire, so that its lord retained the baronial rights of wardships and of inflicting imprisonment.[71] I need hardly add that these rights were not upheld and are not claimed.

It would seem, however, that fresh claims may now be made in addition to that of being the last of the Lords Marcher. In the *Weekly Despatch* of 13th December, 1914, there appeared a special despatch from Newport, headed ' Cat to be honoured with a monument.' In it one reads of ' Sir Marteine Owen Mowbray Lloyd, Bart., the chief Commoner of Wales, and the last of the Norman Lords of the Marches' (*sic*), that 'he is hereditary standard-bearer of Wales and the last of the Norman Lords of the Marshes' (*sic*).

One has heard the speaker of the House of Commons described as ' the first Commoner of England,' but I cannot conceive what is meant by ' the chief Commoner of Wales.' In England, the office of hereditary standard-bearer has been claimed without foundation by more than one family ; in Scotland the right to it has been established after much litigation ; but this is the first that I have ever seen of a claim to such an office within that portion of the kingdom of England which is popularly termed ' Wales.' [72] There appears to have been a ' banner of Wales ' borne at the coronation of Queen Elizabeth, the last of the Tudor dynasty, but the arms upon it were those of the ancient princes of

---

[69] *Y Cymmrodor*, xiv, pp. 20, 22.   [70] *Ibid.* p. 15.

[71] Owen, *Pembrokeshire*, p. x.

[72] For the union of Wales to England by Henry VIII, see p. 92 above.

Wales (i.e. without the Marches), and its bearer was
' Viscount Bindon ' (i.e. Lord Howard of Bindon).[73]

I do not know to whom is due the revival in our own time
of George Owen's exploded claim that ' Kemes is a Lordship
Marcher.' But even he, one gathers, would never have
contended that if it could not claim that position with the
amazing privileges that this would imply, he would still
himself be a Lord Marcher and the only surviving specimen
of that ' genus ' in the country. Yet this claim, which has
not lacked ' publicity,' appears to have enjoyed quite a
vogue among the archaeologists of Wales. When the
Cambrian Archaeological Association held its annual
meeting at Fishguard in 1883, the President informed its
members that at Newport ' they would see one great Castle
rich in memories of a mighty past, where the lords of
Cemmaes held state, little less than regal,' etc., etc.[74] At
Newport they learned that this castle ' remains still in the
possession of a descendant of its founder, William, son (*sic*)
of Martin de Tours.' [75] But the tale, left thus imperfect,
was adorned by a correspondent whose amazing information
was duly printed in the organ of this learned body. Newport, we read, ' is the principal town of the Barony of Kemes,
this latter (*sic*) being a feudal tenure (*sic*) of a most peculiar
character, the last and only Lordship Marcher now in the
Kingdom.'[76] The writer's grammar is, indeed, ' of a most
peculiar character,' but his statements are even more so.[77]
They are elaborated as follows :

' The feudal barony of Kemes is co-extensive with the modern

[73] This appears in the ancient drawings, reproduced as the frontispiece to Lewis Dunn, *Heraldic Visitations of Wales*, and also in Joseph
Foster, *Some Feudal Coats of Arms*, p. 224.

[74] *Arch. Camb.* Fourth Ser. vol. 14, p. 334.   [75] *Ibid.* p. 342.

[76] *Ibid.* p. 331.

[77] It was at this Fishguard Congress that the tale of the famous
French landing was told once more, and a member of the Editorial sub-
committee of the Association added the story of ' Lord Cawdor '
visiting the French prisoners in Porchester Castle, and how some of
those who were kept on short commons ' took his horse and *eat* (*sic*)
it ' (raw ?), ' leaving him only the saddle and bridle ' (p. 340). One can
hardly imagine this tale being told even to ' the horse marines.'

hundred of that name, and embraces within its limits twenty-five parishes, is divided into several manors and lordships, and measures in circumference some sixty miles.

Kemes was erected into a Lordship Marcher by Martin de Tours, one of the principal companions in arms, who obtained it by conquest from the Welsh. Martin and his descendants, the Lords of Kemes, sat in Parliament (*sic*) for several generations as Peers of the Realm by tenure, the same as (*sic*) the Lords Berkeley and Arundel. . . .

These noblemen enjoyed several peculiar privileges as Lords Marchers, of which a few are still exercised by their descendant and representative (*sic*), Sir Marteine Owen Mowbray Lloyd of Bronwydd, the twenty-fourth Lord of the Barony of Kemes, who still holds his Baronial Courts ' (!) . . .

Sir Marteine, we have seen, can scarcely be the representative ' of the noblemen ' described ; nor has any proof been shown that he is even descended from them. That shadowy personage ' Martin de Tours ' cannot have sat under ' William the Conqueror in a non-existent Parliament ' ; nor did his descendants ever sit there ' as Peers of the Realm by tenure of the Barony of Kemes.' The implication that Sir ' Marteine ' is ' Lord of the Barony of Kemes . . . a feudal tenure of a most peculiar character ' is emphasised by the assertion that he ' still holds his Baronial Courts ' for the whole territory described. What are these courts and what is the alleged ' feudal tenure ' ?

The same writer asserts that the castle at Newport ' was first erected by Martin de Tours ' (p. 332), though, as we have seen, the members of the Congress had been informed that its founder was ' William (*sic*), son of Martin de Tours ' (p. 342), whose existence is unknown. Both statements are hopelessly wrong, for it is known that the earliest *caput* of the barony of Kemes was at Nevern, and that it was not till its lords were expelled thence by the Welsh under Rhys, in 1191, that they founded Newport and its castle. That castle in turn was seized by Llewellin ap Gruffyd in 1257, when the Welsh under him again overran Kemes.

The only remaining point is the claim that the Lords of Kemes are entitled to carry, at a coronation, ' the King's silver harp.' According to the *Morning Post* report (28th January, 1911), Mr. Llewllyn Williams, who appeared for Sir Marteine Lloyd before the Court of Claims, alleged that 'the ancestors of the petitioner on divers occasions attended at Coronations as bearers of the king's silver harp.' As nothing, it would seem, is known of any such appearance in any chronicle or record, and as benighted Englishmen had never heard of the 'King's silver harp,' counsel was naturally asked for his evidence. He is reported as making the strange reply that 'he had no documentary evidence in proof of the claim, which rested on tradition.' [78] Here, then, we have again that Welsh reliance on 'tradition,' which to the scholar of to-day, who works from evidence and from records, comes with something of a shock. Even in their own antiquarian organ, the English point of view has thus found expression.

Is there not shown in the history of the Broughton and Wyke families, how untrustworthy, how contrary to truth, is much that passes under the name of 'tradition' . . . there are people who . . . are blind to improbabilities, have no conception of the nature of evidence, and never think of subjecting any statement, especially if it be once printed, to due examination.[79]

English Coronations have formed the subject of such meticulous research that the strange phenomenon of a 'Lord Marcher' bearing in the solemn procession 'the King's silver harp' could not have escaped attention. This statement could only be questioned by those who, in the words of Mr. Palmer, 'are blind to improbabilities.' But we can go further. 'Is there not shown,' by this example, 'how untrustworthy, how contrary to truth is much that passes under the name of "tradition"?' For, as so often is the case, the alleged tradition proves to be a mere unauthorised development of what was the old belief. That belief will be found set out in George Owen's paper,

[78] *Arch. Camb.* Fourth Ser. vol. 14.

[79] Mr. A. N. Palmer in *Y Cymmrodor*, ix, 71. See p. 13 n. above.

The Lords of Kemes

' De Dignitatibus baroniae de Kemes,' [80] where the ' silver harp ' clause runs thus :

Citherae argenteae dispositio ad istam pertinet Baroniam, quasi ad mansionem principis, quem (*sic*) in absencia domini ad monasterium suum custod' traditur.[81]

Though George Owen was here striving to exalt the privileges of Kemes, there is not a word, we see, about the King's Coronation ; and indeed, to any one conversant with Welsh institutions it will, of course, be obvious that ' the disposal of the silver harp ' had nothing to do with the Coronation, but refers to the Eisteddfod.[82] In a document of George Owen's day (1594) we read of ' severall sylver prises . . . as for poetrie, the sylver chayre for harpeinge the silver harpe,' etc.[83] And even before he made the above assertion, the famous Commission for the Caerwys Eisteddfod (1568) had announced that the President and Council of the Marches of Wales

had perfect understanding by credible report . . . that William Mostyn Esquior and his auncestors have had the gyfte and bestowing of the sylver harpe appertayning to the cheff of that facultie (i.e. mynstrelles and musicions).[84]

Clearly, therefore, it was to the Mostyns of Mostyn Hall that belonged ' the disposal of the silver harp ' within the Principality of Wales.[85]

---

[80] Printed in *Baronia de Kemeys*, pp. 39-40, and also in Owen, *Pembrokeshire*, pp. 500-502.

[81] Dr. Owen gives a marginal translation of the eighteenth century : ' The disposal of the Silver Harp belongs to this Barony as to ye Palace of the Prince, which in ye Absence of the Lord is delivered to the Monastery of St. Dogmaels for safe Custody.'

[82] In the romancing communication to 'Archaeologia Cambrensis' (1883), of which I have spoken above, it is claimed that the ' Lords Marchers of Kemes enjoyed the privilege of giving the silver harp as a prize at the Eisteddfodan . . . and in their absence the abbots of St. Dogmaels presided ' (p. 332).

[83] ' Report on MSS. in the Welsh language ' (*Hist. MSS. Com.*), i, 293.

[84] *Ibid.* p. 291.

[85] i.e. the counties of Anglesey, Carnarvon, Merioneth, Denbigh, and Flint (*Ibid.* p. 292).

Family Origins

Referring to the above Commission the authors of *The Welsh People* [86] (1900) observe that ' This silver harp is in the archives of Mostyn Hall and was kindly exhibited to members of the Welsh Land Commission by Lord Mostyn on the occasion of their visit ' (p. 519). Mr. Gwenogvryn Evans, who reported in 1898 on the MSS. in the Welsh language at Mostyn Hall, describes the ' silver harp ' there as that which was won at the Caerwys gathering of 1568.[87] In any case, it has now been clearly shown (1) that the ' silver harp ' was connected with the Eisteddfod alone and had nothing whatever to do with the King's Coronation ; (2) that the story of its disposal belonging to the Lords of Kemes is traceable to that Elizabethan romancer, George Owen ; (3) that its disposal within the Principality of Wales was formally established, under Elizabeth, to be vested in the Mostyns of Mostyn Hall.

[86] Messrs. Rhys and Brynmor-Jones.
[87] *MSS. in the Welsh language*, i, xiii.

THE BRODRICK CHARTERS

AMONG concocted pedigrees supported by fictitious documents, that which was constructed in or about the year 1649 for the Brodricks, now Lords Midleton, is entitled to a high pre-eminence. Its date is of interest to the student as proving that, as I have contended, the great breeding time of these concoctions extended from the middle of the sixteenth to the middle of the seventeenth centuries. They did not proceed only from ' Elizabethan heralds,' for Garter Segar and Garter Bysshe, to say nothing of Philipot, the herald, carried on the evil work. In the barefaced character of its fiction, in its extraordinary daring, and in the fact that the alleged documents, together with the alleged monuments, were formally deposed to on oath, the performance has much in common with the famous Coulhart imposture.

To the student, again, the pedigree affords a valuable illustration of the co-existence at the College of Arms of what one may perhaps term ' canonical ' and ' apochryphal ' pedigrees. The ' recorded ' pedigree of the family at the College is that which appears in the peerage-books ; it begins only with ' Sir Thomas Brodrick of Wandsworth, co. Surrey,' who was knighted in 1625 and was buried there early in 1642, aged 46.[1] Of his parentage it asserts nothing. But there was ' communicated ' by Lord Midleton in 1876, as ' copied from the original pedigree in the College of Arms,' the amazing production, which carries the family back to the days of William Rufus.[2] In whatever way it may have entered the College this pedigree was not, we shall see, the work of an officer of arms. Of its origin the College is guiltless.

[1] *Misc. Gen. et Her.* ii, 364.   [2] *Ibid.* pp. 359-363.

The real founders of the Brodrick family were Alan, and his younger brother St. John, sons of Sir Thomas of whom the *Dictionary of National Biography* observes that they ' greatly profited by the forfeitures in Ireland.' It was evidently for Alan, who was then of Gray's Inn and afterwards obtained an appointment and a grant of lands in Ireland, that this pedigree was concocted. As he was born 28th July, 1623, he can only have been twenty-five at the time.

In accordance with general practice we have first the pedigree in chart form and then the proofs thereof in the form of eighteen abstracts of charters and deeds, which are accompanied by six drawings of alleged seals appendant to them. It is a clumsy performance. In the first place it is of course obvious that the name ' Brodrick ' represents the Welsh ' Ap Rodric,' even as ' Bevan ' is Ap Evan, ' Bethal ' is ' Ap Ithel,' and so on. Yet, to invest the name with territorial dignity, its form was here given as ' de Brodrick ' as late as the days of Henry VI. The patriarch of the family under William Rufus was given the wildly improbable Christian name of George ; [3] and his son, by an equally unlucky shot, is given as Edward. To prove this portion of the pedigree, a charter granted by Walter, alleged son of Edward, is cited. In it of course Walter mentions the names of his father and grandfather, in that convenient fashion which should set the expert on his guard. In fact the charter serves to prove four generations. The appearance of a Percy, a Neville, and a St. John, as witnesses, was obviously meant to show that the Brodricks, under the second Henry, moved in the best society.

The pedigree was also illumined by a really brilliant match in the days of Henry the Sixth. For Thomas

[3] An even wilder development is found at a date considerably later, when we read in Archdall's *Lodge* (1789), that ' his Lordships family came from Normandy to England so early as the reign of King William II in the person of George de Brodrick, son of Sir Richard, descended from Rodolphus Count of Hapsburg, second brother to Henry, Duke of Germany. Which George was lineal ancestor to Sir Thomas Brodrick,' etc., etc. (v, 159).

Brodrick then married ' Alice, daughter of Ralph de Nevile and co-heir of her brother, Robert de Nevile,' whereby the famous Nevile coat came as a quartering to the house.   For proof of this alliance there were three documents and a seal.   By the first of these documents Robert, son of Ralph de Nevile, assigns to John, son of Thomas de (*sic*) Brodrick, his brother (*fratris mei*), his right in certain lands.   Stately are the names of the first witnesses, Hugh de (*sic*) Talbote, Geoffrey de Vernon, and Henry de Ferrars, while the charter is granted at Middleham itself—the favourite seat of no less a person than ' the Kingmaker,' Nevile.   Then we have the seal of Alice, the widow of Thomas, as appurtenant to another deed.   Its ' legend ' is prudently omitted but the lady herself is shown with the Brodrick shield in her right hand and that of Nevile in her left.

The places named by this alleged heiress, Richmond, Hudswell, (North ?) Allerton, Ne[a]sham, and Middleham, give us—with Middleton (Tyas)—the scene of action selected by the pedigree-maker ; but histories of Richmond-shire will be searched in vain for corroboration of his statements.   As was frequently the case, he had studied to good purpose the *formulae* of genuine charters and knew that the last of the three Edwards should be styled ' third after the Conquest,' but when he dated a charter of the days of Richard II ' anno regni regis Rich'i *sec'di post conquestum* quarto,' he at once overreached himself, and proved that his document was a fraud.

I have now said more than enough to show that this pedigree was an elaborate tissue of falsehood.   But I desire to draw special attention to the last of the appended proofs, because of its unusual character and the inference to be drawn from its contents.   Even the immediate ancestry of the family seems to have been obscure, for the ' recorded ' pedigree begins only with Alan Brodrick's father.   The fictitious pedigree assigns him for grand-father ' William Brodrick, his Majesties imbroderer,' whom it makes the son of ' Edward Brodrick ' ; but for the parentage of this Edward no evidence is given and, indeed, for his very existence there is only this document :

Alan Brodrick, of Gray's Inn in Com. Midd, Esq., by his Indenture dated xxiiiito Car. Regis (1648-9) sold unto George Marshall of Com. Eborum landes belonging to the Mannor and Lo'pp of Hudswell in Com. Eborum praed. with warrantie against all claymeinge under Sir Tho. Brodrick his father, William his grandfather, of Edward Brodrick of Richmond aforesayd his great grandfather.

As I have before observed, it is a sound canon of criticism that when a document goes somewhat out of its way to afford the genealogical information that a pedigree-maker requires, it is, on that account, open to some suspicion. And, when, as in the present instance, such a document is found in the company of forged deeds, that suspicion is intensified. It is certainly my own impression that this conveyance, by Alan Brodrick—which belongs to the very time at which the pedigree was concocted—had no other purpose than that of stating that his great grandfather was Edward Brodrick of Richmond, whose existence, as I have said, is not otherwise proved. There is no question here of the document having been forged, for its date is within a year or so of that at which this pedigree was deposed to on oath : my suggestion is that Alan Brodrick was induced to execute this deed with the warranty as given, to support the pedigree which the pedigree-makers were then constructing for him. It was only for him, I think, that they can have constructed it, as his father had been dead for some years and he was the eldest son.[4]

Of course this suggestion of mine represents only my own impression. The point is not of much importance so far as the pedigree is affected. For the deed's evidence, even if accepted, would not carry the family further back than Edward. Its interest lies in its possible execution for pedigree purposes alone and in the part played, in that case, by Alan Brodrick himself.

[4] He had been admitted to Gray's Inn in May 1642, after his father's death, being then eighteen.

The Brodrick Charters

It may perhaps be asked why I should revive the facts of this imposture when neither in the ' records ' of the College of Arms nor in the present Peerage books is the false pedigree to be found. It is, I reply, of real importance for the critical study of genealogy, to collect and set on record, cases in which evidence has been forged or falsely alleged to exist, for the purpose of affording proof of a wholly fictitious pedigree. It was a relatively easy matter to concoct a fabulous pedigree unsupported by proof, but this was a comparatively venial offence when we set it by the side of such forging of evidence as might indeed be deemed incredible if the fact were not demonstrated over and over again. Here for instance are Thomas Clarke and William Smith thus attesting their Brodrick evidences :

These seaventeene deeds above written were diligently and faithfully coppied and examined by the originals, and the Coat of Brodrick with the six other Coates found with the same beareinge and Collo^{rs} in severall auncient glasse windowes and monumentes by us.

Who could suppose that the original documents, the monuments and the glass windows, were all alike fictitious ? Yet the audacity of these rascals was no greater than that of ' Messrs. Cheyne and Knowles,' who concocted, two centuries later, the notorious Coulhart pedigree, perhaps the most brazen of all these impostures. Did not Mr. George Parker Knowles assert that ' the transcribing and translating of the old deeds, wills, charters, pedigrees, marriage settlements,' etc., on which their concoction rested, had been accomplished by Mr. Alexander Cheyne, although the latter was found to have evolved them from his own fertile brain ? [5]

The parallel goes further. Perjury itself had no terrors for the makers of the Brodrick pedigree who solemnly ' made oath ' that the whole of its contents were true.

For the further probat of this pedigree William Smith gent., aged about twentie five yeares, and Thomas Clarke esq., aged

[5] See Mr. Barron's article on this amazing imposture in *The Ancestor* (1903), No. IV, pp. 63-77.

'bout thirtie seaven yeares, make oath that these seaventeene
extracts of deeds doe exactly agree with the originalls both in
names dates and seales as they are expressed in this roll of
parchment and the seaven coats quartered in this shield are the
same in the Chardge (and) in color with those that have been
aunciently graven and painted on the monumentes and glasse
windowes belongeinge to this family.

Jurat' decimo quarto Aprilis 1649.

Robt Aylett.

Robert Aylett, who took their oaths, was a rather interesting man.[6]   An ecclesiastical lawyer and a Doctor of Laws,
he had acted in Essex as Commissary to the Bishop of
London and Judge of the Commissary Court.   On him fell
the difficult task of enforcing in that county Laud's reforms
and innovations.   He is met with in probate and admiralty
cases and eventually became a master in Chancery.   His
recreation was ' sacred verse,' marked by ' pious aphoristic
thought.'   History repeated itself when, in Victorian days,
a similar device was employed to give the Coulhart pedigree
a cloak of official respectability.   The Mr. Coulhart, for
whom it was compiled, ' insists,' we read, ' before putting
his family history into type, that Mr. George Parker Knowles
shall solemnly sign and attest his work in the presence of
the Lord Bishop of Manchester and of the incumbent of
St. Matthew's, Manchester.[7]   Mr. Knowles was equal to the
task : he assumed full responsibility in his work for the
statement that ' an uninterrupted male succession from the
era of Julius Agricola . . . is clearly traceable ' by documents and ' ancestral muniments,' the whole of which
existed only in his fertile imagination.

[6] See my paper on ' Dr. Robert Aylett,' with pedigree, portrait and
facsimile of autograph, in *Essex Arch. Trans.* (N.S.), x, 26-34.

[7] *Ancestor*, No. IV, p. 67.

A HUGUENOT HOUSE

OF the two great immigrations of Protestant refugees which added so valuable an element to our native population, that of the French Huguenots in the seventeenth century was, in many cases, drawn from a higher social stratum than that of the industrious Flemings who, under Queen Elizabeth, fled from the Low Countries to escape from Alva's persecutions. The latter, though, of course, vastly superior to the Jewish immigrants from Eastern Europe who have flocked hither in our time, were probably more akin in status to our own Puritan emigrants who settled in New England. But in France, where the reformed faith had an aristocratic following, it could still number among its adherents, if not nobles, at least gentry in the English sense of the word, when the Edict of Nantes was revoked (1685). From those who fled to this country there descend, as is well known, families of good position, and among them some can boast of pedigrees which Englishmen would reckon long.

A proved pedigree in the male line from the fifteenth century is a thing by no means common in England, although the uninstructed doubtless think otherwise. But two families of Huguenot descent, though holding English baronetcies, can lay claim to that distinction; they are those of Portal, a Languedoc house, which can prove its descent from at least the year 1456, and of Champion, now 'Champion de Crespigny.' I employ this phrase for the latter sonorous name, not merely because, according to Burke's *Peerage*, the immigrant himself was the first Champion who added 'De Crespigny' to his name, but also because a document recorded in the College of Arms proves that his sons as well as himself, after the family had settled in England, were still named Champion only, so that they cannot have added the aristocratic suffix till after they had left France. This document is given in the extract which follows :

Peter, Thomas, and Gabriel Champion de Crespigny, (who are mentioned in the text) were made free denizens of England, by an act passed March 5th 1690 ; and, by order of chapter held at the College of Arms, in London, August 27th 1696, the following extract of the records of the court of Aides, in Normandy, (dated 15 August 1674) was permitted to be entered in the records of the same college : ' The said Champions are issued of a noble and ancient family, wherein their noble quality and filiation are justified from Herbert Champion, who lived in the year of our Lord, 1463, down to Claude Champion, Escuier, sieur de Crespigny, father to the said Peter, Thomas, and Gabriel Champion.' It is also certified by the said college, that ' we have seen and perused an old book of the pedigree of the said Champion, from Messire Maheus Champion, Knight, who lived in the year of our Lord 1350, down to the said Claude Champion, their father, deceased in the aforesaid city, (London) the 10th of April 1695, and buried in Maribone, in the county of Middlesex '—Testified at London, 4 May 1697.[1]

The object of this quotation is to afford proof that the immigrant himself was styled ' Claude Champion ' only down to the time of his death. In Burke's *Peerage* he is described as ' Claude Champion *de Crespigny*, Escuier, Sieur de Crespigny,' but it will be seen, on comparison with the quotation in the above extract, that the words which I have here italicised are not found in them. This founder of the family in England is stated to have been ' an officer of high rank in the French service ' and afterwards a colonel in the British Army. Two of his sons also were English officers.

The Denization referred to above [2] is dated 5th March, 1690-1. Here again the names are ' Gabriel, Thomas, and

[1] I am indebted for this quotation to the vast tomes of Playfair's *Baronetage of England*.

[2] Patent Roll, 3340 (3 William and Mary, pt. 1), No. 8.

A Huguenot House

Peter Champion . . . Jane Champion,' there is nothing about ' De Crespigny.' As British officers, however, the family adopted the name Crespigny, but without ' De.' Gabriel Crespigny ' had a commission in the Foot Guards, 23rd October, 1691 ; ' Thomas Crespigny ' became a cornet in Lord Cardross' Scottish regiment of Dragoons so early as 7th August, 1689, and held commissions afterwards as Captain-Lieutenant in Dragoon regiments and Captain in a regiment of foot (1710). Far into the eighteenth century Crespigny, without the ' De,' remained the family name ; the first baronet's father and mother are so named in their obituaries.[3]

It should be observed that the ' court of Aides,' according to the quotation above, only certified the descent from ' Herbert Champion,' who lived in the year of the Lord, 1463, although there was produced, to the College of Arms, ' an old book of the pedigree . . . from Messire Maheus Champion, Knight, who lived in the year of our Lord, 1350,' and who is stated to have been great-grandfather of the above Herbert. If this descent could be proved, it seems strange that the Cour des Aides should only have carried back the pedigree to Herbert, who is stated to have purchased the estate of La Fleurière in 1463. The point, however, is of small consequence as compared with those to which we are coming.

In the first place it is somewhat startling to find that, though the Champions are alleged to have been certified, in 1674, as of ' noble quality and filiation,' an official record of no more than seven years earlier proves that the first immigrant and his father were found to be usurpers of nobility and were actually fined as such. This record runs as follows :

Richard Champion et Claude, son fils, le premier de la paroisse de St.-Jean-le-Blanc, élect. de Vire, le second de la paroisse de Vierville, élect. de Bayeux, condamnés, le 20 septembre (ou octobre) 1667, chacun à 300 livres d'amende. . . . Descendus

---

[3] ' Musgrave's Obituary ' (*Harl. Soc.*), ii, 102.

III

de Michel Champion frère de Jean anobli en 1470 et non pas le dit Michel dont les consanguins ont été condamnés par arrêt de la Cour des Aides, en 1622, confirmatif d'autre arrêt de 1591, dans lesquels arrêts il y a des rôles à taille induits sur lesquels les veuves et enfants d'Antoine et Rault, aïeul et bisaïeul des produisants, sont compris. Ledit Richard même, produisant, a reconnu devant les Élus, à Vire, le 8 avril 1622 (alias 1652) qu'il est imposé en la paroisse de Vassy; pour quoi défenses lui ont été faites de prendre à l'avenir la qualité de *noble*, a peine d'amende.[4]

This is a record which requires explaining. No mere empty claim to social status was at stake. The distinctive and substantial privilege enjoyed by the members of the French *noblesse* was their exemption from payment of the *taille*, to which *roturiers* were subject. The Crown and its officers, therefore, had to be ever on their guard against the usurpation of noblesse and of the valuable privilege it conferred. As the editor of Chamillart's record has observed :

afin de réprimer les usurpations que les faisaient de la noblesse et de ses priviléges, nos Rois, à diverses époques, ordonnerent qu'il serait fait des recherches de ces usurpations et que tout individu se disant noble serait tenu de justifier de cette qualite par titres authentiques.

Thus it was that the Champions had already been decreed not to be ' noble ' and to be, therefore, liable to the *taille* in 1591 and 1622.

Chamillart, as the local ' Intendant,' was ordered to conduct this fresh enquiry for the ' Généralité de Caen ' in 1666 and the following years. His report is divided into six sections, in five of which the local *noblesse* is classified according to its antiquity. The sixth section is devoted to ' Usurpateurs en la généralité de Caen,' and it is among these that the Champions are found. Record proof that the family had been subject to payment of the *taille* was, of course, fatal to their claim, and they were forbidden, under penalty, to style themselves ' noble ' in future.

It has always been a difficult matter for Englishmen to

---

[4] Chamillart, *Recherche de Noblesse en la généralité de Caen*, p. 776.

understand the principle of nobility abroad, owing to the English 'peerage' differing so widely from the Continental *noblesse*. The latter was composed of *gentilshommes*, not of a titled aristocracy, and its distinctive mark was not the use of the prefix de—as is here widely supposed—but the right to a helm or crest (*timbre*) above its coat of arms. Chamillart recorded the arms of those who proved their *noblesse*, but allowed none to the *usurpateurs*. One is naturally reminded of our heralds' visitations and their 'disclaimers' by some features of these *Recherches*, and, indeed, amusing efforts have been made, in this country, to claim that the grant of a coat of arms conferred nobility—of some kind—or, at least created a gentleman. In France it was because a man was a *gentilhomme* that he was entitled to heraldic distinction ; it was not because he bore arms that he was reckoned a *gentilhomme*.

After this decisive proof that, in 1667, the family were judicially found to be liable, as *roturiers*, to payment of the *taille*, and, therefore, not to be entitled to use such arms as the *noblesse*, it is strange to read the alleged finding, in 1674, of the 'Cour des Aides.' Some families, whom Chamillart had rejected, made good their claim subsequently, but neither he nor his editor speak of the Champions as doing so. We will pass, however, to the second point.

It is, as I observed, of little consequence whether the family can be carried back to 1463 or to 1350, but very different is the claim advanced in the long and involved statement with which the ' lineage ' is introduced in Burke's *Peerage*. This statement leads up to the astonishing conclusion : ' the male representative of the Marmions of Urvyle et Fonteneys (*sic*) le Marmion being Sir C. le (*sic*) Champion *de Crespigny*.' We owe it, no doubt, to Sir Walter Scott that the Marmions of ' Fonteneys le Marmion ' enjoy a romantic renown.

> Two pursuivants, whom tabarts deck,
> With Silver scutcheon round their neck
> Stood on the steps of stone,

By which you reach the Donjon gate,
And there with herald pomp and state,
 They hailed Lord Marmion :
They hailed him Lord of Fontenaye,
Of Lutterward, and Scrivelbaye,
 Of Tamworth tower and town ;
And he, their courtesy to requite,
Gave them a chain of twelve marks weight,
 All as he lighted down.
' Now largesse, largesse, Lord Marmion,
Knight of the crest of gold !
A blazon'd shield in battle won
Ne'er guarded heart so bold.' [5]

' Largesse ' the heralds still expect, though in the more prosaic form of fees paid in hard cash, for a shield, which, to put it mildly, is not ' in battle won.'

But if Scott's ' Lord Marmion,' who had fought at ' Bosworth Field ' (1485) was a wholly imaginary personage, there were real Marmions, at an earlier time, who were lords, in Normandy, of Fontenay-le-Marmion and, in England, of Tamworth and Scrivelsby ; and these Marmions owe their fame to the contest between their heirs for the well-known office of King's champion at the coronation of English kings. They have been dealt with at some length in Stapleton's valuable *Observations on the great rolls of the Exchequer of Normandy* and in various English publications. The last Marmion who held these lands died so far back as 1291, and to claim the male heirship of so famous and ancient a house is no light matter. It is a claim which certainly invites critical investigation.

The lengthy statement of which I have spoken begins with this assertion :

Chamillart in 1666 describes the extinct Comtes de Cicé—related to the Champions de Crespigny of Vierville near Fonteneys—as taking their name from their office.

Chamillart's ' Recherche de la Noblesse faite par ordre du roi en 1666 et années suivantes ' lies before me, but in

---

[5] *Marmion*, canto I, verse xi.

that work, at least, I can find no such statement.   Moreover, Vierville, which is here described as ' near Fonteneys ' (i.e. Fontenay), figures in the next column as ' near Bayeux,' that is, some thirty miles, ' as the crow flies,' from Fontenay. The quotation I have given from Chamillart's work shows that the latter statement is right and the previous one wrong. Again, Crespigny itself is first spoken of as ' near Aunay, Lower Normandy,' and then, in the very next paragraph, as ' in the parish of Vierville,' which was far away both from Fontenay and from Aunay.   As a matter of fact, it lay in the parish and commune of St. Jean-le-Blanc, some five miles to the south of Aunay and nowhere near either Vierville or Fontenay (le Marmion).   One need not pursue this wild geography further than to point out that ' the Abbey of *St. Barberie*, founded by Robert Lord Marmion, in 1140, occurs three times in the story.   There is, of course, no such saint.   The truth is that the Marmions were benefactors to two religious houses, the Abbey of Fontenay (le Marmion) near the junction of the Orne and the Laize, and St. Mary's Abbey *at Barbery*, some five miles to the south of it, with the Forêt de Cinglais between them. The grotesque conversion of the latter abbey into that of ' St. Barberie ' stamps the whole story.

The confusion in the early genealogy is as great as in the topography.   Just as it used to be the aim of all English genealogists to trace their patrons' pedigree up to the Norman Conquest, so have French genealogists striven to place a crusading warrior at the top of the family tree.   We read, therefore, in Burke that ' Jordan and Thomas de Fonteneys (*sic*) served in the first crusade and Robert of Urvyle et (*sic*) Moulins in that under St. Louis at Aigues Mortes.'   But it is difficult to see, even if this were so, what it has to do with the Marmion or Champion families.   One can only surmise that ' Richard of Urvyle . . . Vicomte of Vire . . . in 1220,' from whom, apparently, descent is claimed, is identical with Richard de Fontenai, who was bailiff of Coutances, Vire and Mortain at an earlier date, and

who has been described by Professor Powicke as ' perhaps
the most important local official in Normandy during the
last year of John's rule.' He continued to act as a Norman
official after the loss of the duchy. But he is not known to
have been a member of the Marmion family and Fontenay
is a not uncommon place-name in Normandy.

Apart from the confused introduction, the actual pedigree
' in Burke ' is traced only up to ' Guillaume, Baron
d'Urvyle,' who, in 1181, assisted his near relation (*sic*)
Lord (*sic*) Marmion of Tamworth, Scrivelsby, and Fonteneys, in endowing the abbey of St. (*sic*) Barberie.' But
how this ' Baron d'Urvyle ' was related to ' Lord Marmion,'
or why his heirs, if his heirs they are, should be heirs male of
the Marmions, we are not told. Again, this William, who
was living in 1181, is made great-grandfather of Maheu
(' Maheas ') Champion, the earliest possible ancestor of the
Champions (of Crespigny), who was living in 1350. The
wild character of this chronology is obvious. Nor is there
any proof or explanation of the alleged fact that this Maheu
was a younger brother of Robert Bertrand ou Urvyle,
Bretvyle and Fonteneys.[6] The ancestry of Robert Bertrand and the way in which Fontenay descended to him
are both of them quite different from the story in Burke's
Peerage. It is there vaguely stated that ' in the 13th
century the Urvyle branch succeeded to Fonteneys (*sic*)
le Marmion,' but the actual successor to Fontenay, after
Philip Marmion, was, on the contrary, Jeanne, one of the
daughters and co-heirs of Ralf Tesson, a well-known
Norman noble, who had brought to her husband, Robert
Bertram, baron of Bricquebec in the Cotentin, the fief of
Thury, and who, in 1264, was a benefactress to the Marmion
foundation at Fontenay and Barbery. Her sons were
Robert and William Bertram.[7] These facts, it will be
found, make short work of the pedigree given in ' Burke.'

There appears to be no reason to doubt the pedigree as it

---

[6] i.e. Urville, Bretteville, and Fontenay-le-Marmion.

[7] Stapleton's *Rot. Scacc. Norm.* II, cvii, ccx.

used to be given, which gave these Champions a proved descent from Herbert Champion, the purchaser of La Fleurière in 1463, and a possible descent from Maheu Champion, living in 1350. But the parentage and ancestry now assigned to this Maheu Champion are not merely without proof but are a wild concoction.

The fact that the whole story of the Marmion ancestry of the Champions must have evidently been suggested by the supposition that the Marmions held the office of ' Champion ' to the Norman dukes and the further supposition that a family which had Champion for its surname must have derived it from holding that romantic office.[8] I have elsewhere dealt with what I term ' some of the delusions on the subject ' of the king's champion.[9] Even in England the service of champion, in spite of persistent statements that it dates from the Norman Conquest, cannot be traced any earlier than 1326. As to Normandy no evidence has ever yet been produced to show that the Marmions or anyone else held this office under the Norman dukes. Indeed, it is difficult to see how it could have existed where there was no king and, therefore, no ' coronation.'

Nor is there any evidence to show that any Marmion ever took the name of Champion. The name is not a rare one, either in England or in France, and though it certainly does not denote descent from those who, at coronations, held the office of ' king's champion,' it is believed to be derived from acting as hired ' champion ' in the days when ' trial by battle ' was still a judicial proceeding. The virtually ornamental office of ' king's champion ' at coronations was, of course, derived from the same source. Mr. Neilson, whose *Trial by Combat* (1890) is the standard work on the subject, aptly cites a passage from the Barnwell Priory

[8] We meet with ' Thomas, the king's champion ' (*Campio Regis*), under Northumberland, in 1163, but, as he was evidently in receipt of threepence a day pay (*Pipe Roll,* 9 Hen. ii, p. 43), he was clearly a hireling with a regular retaining fee. The King's approvers (*probatores regis*) had only a penny a day (*Ibid.* 11 Hen. ii, p. 32) two years later.

[9] *The King's Serjeants,* pp. 381-3.

book at the time of the Barons' War (1267), when a big violent man ' named ' Philip le Champion behaved like a Prussian officer towards the unfortunate canons.[10] Even earlier we meet with a Simon ' Champion.' [11] As he justly observes, ' Champion ' was now becoming, indeed had already become, a well-known surname ' (p. 69).

Dealing in another work with ' the Geste of John de Courcy,' [12] I have spoken of the large part played by single combat in legend and romance. There is, however, some reason for believing that ' champions ' were actually employed to decide by ' battle ' an issue between English and French kings. On the Norman Exchequer Roll of 1198, Walter de Ely charges ' In costamento campionum Regis qui fuerunt ducti in Insulam de Andele contra Regem Francie xxx li. per breve Regis.'[13] There is also a curious entry in the *Book of Fees* (ii, 937), which seems to have been overlooked by those who have written on the subject.

Heredes Nicholai Malemayns et Cristiana Leddet tenent in Burton de baronia Alani Dynant, qui habuit terram illam de dono domini Regis Henrici avi (*sic*) domini Regis Ricardi, *qui pugnavit contra pugilem Regis Francie* intra Gysorz et Trie.

Eyton, in his *Itinerary* (p. 283), speaks of ' the usual rendezvous, between Gisors and Trie,' where Henry II and the French King used to meet. In his valuable work on *The Loss of Normandy* (pp. 216, 357-8), Professor Powicke touches on this employment of men ' arte bellandi in duello doctos.' The Pipe Roll of 1181 (27 Henry II) contains a charge by the sheriff of Surrey (p. 153) for the equipment of eight approvers and the hire of champions to teach them to fight (*pugilibus locandis ad eos instruendos*). This entry is of special interest because in the *History of English*

[10] Contigit ergo quod quidam uir stature magne, dictus Phillippus le Champion, diluculo fecit Priorem excitari de lecto suo, dixitque ad eum : *Volo habere ad opus domini mei totum bladum tuum, et totum braesium tuum, et totum lardarium tuum. Trade igitur mihi claues.* (*Liber Memorandorum Ecclesie de Bernervelle*, p. 122.)

[11] A.D. 1248. *Select Pleas in Manorial Courts*, p. 16.

[12] *Peerage and Pedigree*, ii, 258 *et seq.*   [13] *Rot. Scacc. Norm.* ii, 481.

Law [14] we read that Stephen the Englishman (*Angelicus*) appears in Bracton's *Note-Book* (case 40) as a hired champion for the County of Surrey in 1219.

Mr. Neilson, in his interesting treatise, unearths the retaining fee to a bishop's permanent champion, the champions of two abbots, and the Prior of Tynemouth's big champion (*magnus pugil*'). In their *History of English Law*, Profs. Pollock and Maitland observe that ' for civil causes professional pugilists were shamelessly employed ; apparently there were men who let out champions for hire.' [15] As Mr. Neilson writes, ' Hired champions were forbidden, nevertheless, much hiring, direct and indirect, went on : championship, in spite of the law, became a regular occupation, notwithstanding its dangers ' (p. 48).[16] He cites an instance of a contract with a hired champion (p. 49), and I myself found one among the muniments of the Duke of Rutland at Belvoir.[17] It is easy, therefore, to see how, at a time when surnames were taking permanent form, that of Champion or Campion would arise.

[14] Ed. 1895, ii, 664.

[15] Ed. 1898, ii, 633. Richard of Newnham, they observe, was probably a professional champion. See *Bracton's Note-Book*, Nos. 185 (p. 152), 400, 551.

[16] Mr. Neilson writes of the well-known illustration of the ' battle.' ' Highly popular as an illustration of all books touching trial by battle is the picture of a duel in an appeal of theft between Hamo le Stare and Walter Bloweberme, contained in a plea-roll of Henry III. Its most glorified version is that of its first presentation in a note to Upton's *De Re Militari*. It is there so sublimated as almost to defy recognition. Madox gives a good copy. Kendall, for his preface, gave it less accurately. Last of all, photolithography has exactly reproduced it, and made it the frontispiece to the Selden Society's *Crown Pleas*. The shields of the combatants are very like the shield on the seal of Henry the Marshal, and the weapons of their mutual vigorous assault are likewise much the same, save that the tip of horn is pointed at both ends ' (pp. 54-5). No one, apparently, has observed that a figured tile at Boxgrave Priory (*Sussex Arch. Coll.* iii, 239) shows a combat between two men on foot, of whom one, at least, is armed with precisely the same weapon as the combatants in the above picture. The other man, however, appears to be armed with a long hatchet, and the shields of both are different from those in the picture. See also for the *baculi cornuti*, the remarks of Mr. H. W. C. Davis in *Eng. Hist. Rev.* xvi, 730.

[17] *Hist. MSS. Com. Rep.* iv, 49.

Although the legal ' trial by battle ' died out, in practice, at an early date, ' professional pugilists ' were still hired, for election purposes, in modern times. I have heard of this being done when my grandfather was member for Maldon and have even been told that these gentry boasted of those elections which they had successfully conducted.

THE YARBURGH PEDIGREE

THERE are degrees of iniquity in the methods of the pedigree-maker. One of them may assert an affiliation which is nothing but a guess of his own ; another may tamper with the evidence or even forge a document to prove an alleged descent ; a third may invent an entire pedigree, lock, stock, and barrel. But this last is a dangerous game and most dangerous of all when there is mention of facts or dates, or worse still, of records. They give, no doubt, *vraisemblance* to a tale, but the cautious artist should eschew them rigidly, and as a matter of fact he usually did.

Mr. Freeman, who dealt with Burke's *Peerage* in such merciless fashion,[1] insisted that a mere glance at Domesday was enough to blow to pieces some of the fictions it contained. And it is to the Domesday Book that I must refer in the Yarburgh case.

The statement under ' Deramore ' in Burke's *Peerage*, as to the origin of the Yarburghs, is as follows :

> The family of Yarburgh, is one of great antiquity, and can trace an authenticated (*sic*) male succession, from the time of the Norman Conquest. At that period, Eustachius de Yarburgh was Lord of Yarburgh, co. Lincoln, which manor, together with the patronage of the living, still remains vested in his representative, the present Lord Deramore. . . .
>
> *Edmund Yarburgh*, . . . son of Francis Yarburgh, sergeant-at-law, and the lineal descendant of Eustachius de Yarburgh, lord of Yarburgh, *temp. Conquestoris*, etc., etc.

The statement, we see, is quite definite and the descent ' authenticated.' Moreover, if words have any meaning, it is distinctly implied that the manor of Yarburgh has

[1] ' Pedigrees and Pedigree-makers ' in *Contemporary Review*, xxx, 11-14.

descended from 'Eustachius' to 'his representative the present Lord Deramore.' Infinitely rare as is a proved descent, in the male line, from the Conqueror's day, the continuous tenure of a manor is a thing rarer still, but such tenure would give the most convincing proof of the descent.

When, however, we turn to Domesday, there is no 'Eustachius de Yarburgh' to be found: Yarborough (Gereburg), which is assessed at $2\frac{1}{2}$ carucates and $1\frac{1}{3}$ bovates, appears only as an appendage of the royal manor of Gayton. We are reminded of Freeman's fierce attack on Sir Bernard Burke and his *Peerage*:

> The tale is sheer invention, it is mere falsehood, which might at any time be confronted by the simple process of turning to Domesday. . . . When the pedigree was invented, Domesday was still doubtless in manuscript, but is it possible that there is no copy of those precious volumes in the library of Ulster King-at-Arms.[2]

But let us investigate for ourselves the manorial descent of Yarborough. About a generation after Domesday, we have what is known as the Lindsey survey. In this survey, Yarborough (Yerburc) appears with the same assessment (expressed as 2 carucates and $5\frac{1}{3}$ bovates) but the great soke of Gayton-le-Wold, of which it formed part, is now in the hands of the Count of Brittany. Passing to the reign of Henry III, we find that Yarborough (*Yerdeburgh*) was held in 1242-3 jointly with its neighbour, Grimblethorpe, of the Honour of Richmond (representing the Count of Brittany), as half a knight's fee, by Richard, son of John, and Alan, son of Walter, together.[3] Some sixty years later, 1303, we find this half fee split into two quarters, one of them held by Philip Fraunke, the other by the Prior of Alvingham.[4] By 1428, Philip's quarter, after being held by Robert Darcy, was in the hands of Patrick Skipwith [5] (less a third of it, held by John Skipwith's widow). The Yarburghs have not yet

[2] 'Pedigrees and Pedigree-makers' in *Contemporary Review*, xxx, 26.

[3] *Book of Fees*, pp. 1053, 1071. [4] *Feudal Aids*, iii, 133.

[5] M.P. for Lincs, 1433. A younger son of John Skipwith, he founded the Skipwiths of Utterby, the heiress of which place he married.

appeared upon the scene.[6] But when we turn to the concocted pedigree, we find Yarburghs from the Conquest, all
of them marrying, of course, into the best families. From
Eustachius de Yarburgh, in 1066, it took four generations
to reach the days of Stephen (1135-1154), and their wives
were daughters of ' Sir Lambert Munby,' of ' Arthur
Ormsby, Esq.,' of ' Sir Ralph Humberston, knt.,' and of
' Sir William Staine.'[7] I need hardly add that all these
marriages are fiction. After Stephen, the pace slackened ;
it took indeed but three generations to reach the reign of
Richard II (1377-1399), when Richard de Yarburgh
' flourished.'[8] Three generations later we have another
Richard de Yarburgh, ' Lord of the manors of Yarburgh
and Kelstern,' who may probably be identified with that
Richard Yarburgh of Yarborough, gentleman, who was a
feoffee of four different properties in 1431 ;[9] though he is
not entered as the owner of any. As to the manor of
Kelstern, its true history is known. It passed from the
Missendens of Great Missenden to John de Iwardby (or
Ewerby), who married their heiress and who was holding
the manor in 1431.[10] From him it descended to their
grandson, John Iwardby, who died in 1485,[11] and whose
youngest daughter and co-heir brought it to her husband,
Sir Thomas Clifford, and died seised of it in 1558.[12] It is
therefore quite untrue that Richard Yarburgh, or his
descendant, Charles Yarburgh, who died in 1544, were as
alleged, lords of the manor.[13] Richard ' Yerborowe '
appears to have had a small holding in Kelstern in or about
the year 1485,[14] and Charles was buried in its church.

---

[6] *Feudal Aids*, iii, 265, 275.

[7] Burke's *History of the Commoners*, iii, 661, and *Visitation of Linc.* (Harleian Society) in 1562.

[8] *Ibid.* p. 662.   [9] *Feudal Aids*, iii, 345, 347, 352, 354.

[10] *Ibid.* iii, 353.   [11] *Cal. of Inquisitions*, Henry VII, i, pp. 3, 139.

[12] *Lincolnshire Pedigrees* (Harl. Soc.), i, 339.

[13] Burke's *Commoners*, iii, 662.

[14] *Calendar of Inquisitions*, Hen. VII, p. 481.

A John 'Zerburgh de Zerburgh' was a juror for an inquest taken at Louth in 1401-2 for the South Riding of Lindsey,[15] but those among whom he is found do not appear to have been land owners, and the manor of Yarburgh, we know, was then in other hands. It is significant, however, that he does not appear in the pedigree, for in his case a record proves both his existence and his date.

It looks to me as if here again we had to do with the usual Elizabethan pedigree, and if so, it may have been compiled for 'Francis Yarburgh, Esq., of Northampton, serjeant-at-law *anno* 37 Elizabeth,' who founded the Yorkshire line, or for his father, Edmund. It appears, if the transcript can be trusted, as early as 1562 in the Visitation of Lincolnshire made in that year.[16]

[15] *Feudal Aids*, iii, 245.   [16] *The Genealogist*, v, 59-60.

THE HENEAGE FICTION

IT appears that when I was writing on some Saxon houses,[1] I did not deal exhaustively with those families which claim a pre-Conquest pedigree. It was not long ago, a well-informed and serious paper stated, of Lady Heneage, that :

Although her husband is only the first baron, his family held an established place before the Conquest. There was a Sir Richard de Heneage in the reign of William Rufus, who bore witness to a grant of land from Nicholas Bassett to the monks of Brucria (*sic*), and all the way down through history the name occurs. A Heneage was private secretary to Cardinal Wolsey, etc., etc.[2]

This was not the first occasion on which I had encountered this wild tale of the Heneages' position before the Conquest, but the strange thing is, that such obvious nonsense should be still persistently repeated. And what makes it all the stranger is, that it is not to be found in ' Burke ' and that even the old pedigree-makers seem to be guiltless in the matter.

But the story of the William Rufus Heneage is another matter ; this can be traced to its source. Let us place side by side the accounts of the family's origin in Burke's *Commoners* (1838) and Burke's *Peerage* (1907) :

The period of the first settlement of the family in Lincolnshire may[3] be nearly defined by the circumstances of Sir Robert de Heneage being witness together with	The period of the first settlement of the family in Heneage *in co. Lincoln may* be nearly defined by the circumstance of Sir Robert de Heneage being witness, to-

[1] *Peerage and Pedigree*, vol. ii.
[2] *The Standard* (newspaper), 3rd Jan., 1913.   [3] The italics are mine.

Sir Richard de Angemine (of the same county) and several others, to a grant of land from Nicholas Bassett to the monks of Brucria (*sic*). The deed, a very short one, is addressed to Robert Bishop of Lincoln. . . . This document is without date, but must have been either in the time of Robert Bloet, who was chancellor to *William Rufus*, or of Robert, Chesney, consecrated in the 13th of King Stephen; for, when Robert Grosshead was made Bishop of Lincoln in 1235, the dating of deeds was in use [4] (Burke's *Commoners*, iv, 103).

gether with Sir Richard de Angemine of the same co., and several others, to a grant of land *temp. William Rufus*, from Nicholas Bassett to the monks of Brucria (*sic*). (Burke's *Peerage*.)

Now ' Brucria ' is an undetected misprint for ' Brueria,' which has wandered down through Burke's *Peerage* to the paragraph-writer of the *Standard*.[5] And ' Brueria ' is merely the latinisation of Bruern, where Nicholas Bassett founded a Cistercian Abbey, it is said, in 1147. *Exit*, therefore, ' William Rufus.' *Bishop Robert*, to whom the deed is said to be addressed, was consecrated Bishop of Lincoln in September 1147. But the worst is yet to come. Far from being in co. Lincoln, ' Bruern ' lies in the west of Oxfordshire, near the Gloucestershire border, and Nicholas Bassett was a local man who had nothing to do with Lincolnshire. It is obvious that the use of this evidence as proof that the Heneages, even then, were seated in co. Lincoln, must have originated with someone who was blissfully ignorant of the fact that Oxfordshire was included in the diocese of Lincoln then and for ages afterwards. It is also obvious that for him ' Brueria ' had no meaning.

If then, the name of Sir Robert ' de Heneage ' occurs in

[4] As a matter of fact it was still exceptional at that early date.
[5] He has added the error of making ' Robert ' into ' Richard.'

this deed, which may or may not be the case, its date is not
' William Rufus ' and it does not relate to Lincolnshire.   So
much for the hapless ' Burke.' Even under Stephen, to
whose reign the alleged deed would belong, witnesses would
not have a ' Sir ' (*dominus*) prefixed to their names.
Nothing, unfortunately, seems to be known of the deed in
question,[6] so that we cannot test the reading of the names,
but as I have said, the evidence, even if true, could have no
bearing on the settlement of the family in Lincolnshire.   It
is more satisfactory to have traced the story to its source
because, in the standard work on surnames, Mr. Bardsley,
who presumes the name to be derived from some unknown
locality, vouches that very erratic antiquary, Mark Antony
Lower, for the statement that ' Sir Robert de Heneage was
in Lincolnshire *temp.* William Rufus.'

From this alleged early evidence the pedigree in Burke's
Commoners passes, as it were, *per saltum* to its next fixed
point, the possession of the manor of Haynton, by John
' de Heneage ' in 10 Edward III (1336-7), which is followed
by its sale and its repurchase in 21 Richard II (1397-8) from
' John Lord de la Ware ' (*sic*) by ' John Heneage of
Hainton.'

Now there happens to be a very careful modern pedigree
of the family in Canon Madison's *Lincolnshire Pedigrees*,[7]
compiled from ' MSS. C 23 and D 23 Heralds' College and
MS. history of the Heneage family.' [8]   The actual pedigree
begins only with the last-named ' John Heneage of Hainton,'
in 1398, who is described as ' legatee of John, Lord de la
Warr in 1398,' being, I presume, mentioned in the will of
that nobleman, who died at Swineshead, Lincs, in that
year.   He had inherited lands at Hainton from his ancestors,
the Gresle lords of Manchester and of Swineshead.[9]   This

---

[6] The Rev. H. Salter, who has special knowledge of the religious
houses of Oxfordshire, tells me he has ' never heard of it,' though he has
studied Bruern Charters.

[7] *Harl. Soc. Pub.* vol. ii (1903).   [8] Vol. ii, pp. 480 *et seq.*

[9] They formed a manor held as a knight's fee, of the Gresles under
Edward I and Edward II, by the Worth family, whose heiress married
a Knivett.

John Heneage, the true patriarch of the family, is found as John Heneage of Hainton, Lincs, ' gentylman ' in 1431, holding lands and tenements there, valued at £5 a year, of which it is expressly recorded that they were not held by knight-service.' [10]   According to Canon Maddison's pedigree this John died 22nd September, 1439.[11]

Thenceforth, the pedigree seems to be clear enough,[12] and if the family has been seated at Hainton for more than five centuries, that, the reader must always be reminded, is a tenure of exceptional duration.   The category, however, to which it belongs is that of those which, although landowners, long before the days when the new men of the second Tudor became the lords of old acres, owed to his lucrative favour their advancement in the social scale.[13] Leland, who supplies that contemporary evidence which often throws so vivid a light on the real rise of the families, observed, as Mr. Shirley reminds us,[14] that ' the olde Henege lands passid not a fyfetie poundes by the yere,' but that Sir Thomas ' hath doone muche cost at Haynton, where he is Lorde and Patrone, yn translating and new building, with brike and abbay stone.'   It was this Sir Thomas who was a courtier of Henry VIII and died in 1553.   His brother Robert, who died three years later, acquired wealth as auditor of the Duchy of Lancaster and surveyor of the royal woods beyond Trent, and was father of that Sir Thomas Heneage who rose high under Queen Elizabeth, ancestor, through his daughter, of the earls of Winchilsea.   He was also father of that Michael Heneage who was made keeper of the Records in the Tower in 1581.

[10] *Feudal Aids*, iii, 361.   In this interesting return the holders of lands are distinguished as ' knight,' ' squyer,' and ' gentylman.'

[11] It was also with this John ' Hennege ' that the Visitation pedigree of 1592, as printed in *Herald and Genealogist*, vi, 257, begins.

[12] It is somewhat singular that John, son of the above John ' of Hainton,' 1398, did not marry till 1451, many years after his father's death, but even if a generation has been here omitted, this would not affect the descent.

[13] Such for instance, as the Russells and the Cavendishes.

[14] *Noble and Gentlemen of England.*

The Heneage Fiction

In an age fecund with new pedigrees he may perhaps have, in that capacity, endowed his family with their own.

In any case, it is clear that the Heneage ' lineage,' as given in Burke's *Commoners*, and repeated thence in Burke's *Peerage* down to ' John de Heneage,' the last who styled himself *de* Heneage, is one of those fictitious concoctions which should long have been abandoned. Nor do I make that statement on my own authority alone. The contrast between the pedigree given by Canon Maddison (1903) and that which appears in Burke's *Peerage* does but remind us of the gulf on which I insisted at the outset, that gulf which still severs two schools of genealogy.[15] Between the repetition of exploded error and the patient construction of pedigrees from facts and evidence alone, there can be no compromise.

[15] See p. 125.

THE GRANVILLES AND THE MONKS

ALTHOUGH the Granvilles of the West Country and the Grenvilles, Dukes of Buckingham, are apparently distinguished by their names, the distinction is comparatively modern. Dugdale, dealing with the former family, could still write of them as Grenevill,[1] and they themselves consistently used, at least as late as the Restoration, the form ' Grenvile.' The fact that Pepys and Evelyn wrote of them alike as ' Greenvill ' and that Dugdale styled them ' Grenevill ' implies certainly that the name was so pronounced at the time. And, indeed, we have but to pass back from the famous Sir Bevil ' Grenvile ' to his no less famous grandsire, the hero of the *Revenge*, to find him writing his name Greynvile, while the form ' Graineville ' is found in the registers of Buckland Monachorum (1579). These are by no means mere variations ; they take us back to the older and mediaeval form of the name—Greinville, Greynville, Grainville—and afford a valuable clue to its true local origin.

It is strange that when Sir John ' Grenvile ' was raised at the Restoration to the peerage (20th April, 1661) he should have begun to change so illustrious a name, by adopting ' Granville ' as the style of his two lesser dignities. But the change synchronized, we shall see, with his amazing and successful attempt to obtain from the Crown formal confirmation of the gorgeous origin he claimed for his House. Since then there have been no fewer than four peerage dignities created with the style of Granville for descendants of this family. But, not content with thus changing the true form of their name, they endeavoured, like Chinamen, to bestow, in posthumous fashion, the new

[1] *Baronage* (1676), ii, 479.

form on their ancestors. To some extent they assigned them also their newly invented dignities. In the elaborate *History of the Granville Family* [2] (1895), to which I shall have occasion to refer, the name is deliberately and barbarously changed to ' Granville ' throughout the pre-Restoration history in the teeth of every letter and document that it contains.

But although the name of ' Granville ' and ' Grenville ' were thus originally the same, it does not follow that the two families who bore them were of common origin. That the bearing of a common surname involves a common origin is one of the most frequent of genealogical delusions. And this applies to surnames derived from the name of a locality as well as to those originally formed from a christian name, from an occupation, or from some personal peculiarity. The ' Granvilles ' and the ' Grenvilles ' can both be traced back to Norman times, that is to say, to the close of the reign of Henry I. They were then already in the districts in which they are subsequently found, and these districts were far apart. It seems, however, to have been assumed by all who have dealt with the subject that they must have been originally one, although their arms, it is admitted, were altogether different. Collins observed that ' Prince, in his " Worthies of Devonshire," treating of the family of Granville, mentioned the Grenvills of Buckinghamshire to be a collateral branch,' which is also remarked by George Granville, Lord Lansdown, in the account he gave of his family to Moréri ; and he himself thought ' a very reasonable conjecture ' that the ' Gerard de Grainville ' who held three knight's fees, in Bucks, of Earl Walter Gifford in 1166,[3] was a son of Richard de Granville, who came in with William the Conqueror (i.e. a century before), and from whose son, Richard, were descended the Granvilles, Earls of Bath.[4]

---

[2] By the Rev. Roger Granville (a D'Ewes by paternal descent).

[3] *The Red Book of the Exchequer*, p. 312. This entry is unindexed, as is that relative to Richard de ' Greinville ' on p. 288.

[4] *Peerage of England*. This is also stated as a fact in the *History of the Granville Family*, p. 30.

It is, however, pure conjecture and appears to rest on the delusion of which I spoke above.

If, however, there were in Normandy but one place of the name, it might be fairly claimed as the cradle of both houses. But far from this, we find in Normandy Granville —now a fashionable watering-place—to which the ' Granvilles ' traced their name and no fewer than six Grainvilles, two in the Department of the Calvados, one in that of the Eure, and three in that of the Seine Inférieure. And yet it is not to one of these that Norman antiquaries have traced the origin of the English house. M. de Gerville, with local patriotism, claimed for the Department of La Manche the origin of as many followers of Duke William as possible.[5] He knew only the Buckinghamshire Grenvilles, the ' Granvilles ' being then extinct in the male line, and he charged the English peerage books with error in deriving them from Granville, asserting that their true origin was to be found at Grenneville, which was not in the south-west, but the north-east of La Manche. He even stated that the Marquis of Buckingham (1784-1813), visiting, during the French Revolution, the exiled French clergy in Winchester Castle, talked of the Norman origin of his house, regretted that ' son curé de Grenneville ' was not among them and showed himself well acquainted with that place and its Castle. Some years ago there was published a French monograph on the ' Companions of the Conqueror,' by the President of the Historical and Archaeological Society of St. Malo, in which M. de Gerville's work was described as ' manquant trop souvent de précision, de méthode et d'exactitude géographique.' Nevertheless, the learned author repeated under ' Grenneville,' M. de Gerville's statement, making it the ' lieu d'origine des Grennevilles, dont le Duc de Buckingham est le chef.'[6] Unfortunately no ' Grenneville '—described as ' Commune du canton de Quettehou,

---

[5] *Recherches sur les Anciens Châteaux du département de la Manche,* 1825-1830.

[6] *Recherches historiques et topographiques sur les compagnons de Guillaume le Conquérant,* i, 46.

arrondissement de Valognes '—is to be discovered in the list of ' communes ' in Joanne's excellent ' Géographie de la Manche.' [7] Nevertheless Sir Francis ' Palgrave ' had confidently followed M. de Gerville, speaking of Greneville or Grenville as ' not to be confounded with Granville ' and ' unquestionably the cradle of the Grenvilles.' [8] It was certainly, however, no more so than Palgrave was the ' cradle ' of his own house. The adoption of a name and of arms to which one has no claim is a practice of which his own case affords illustration.[9] As Francis Cohen he wished to adopt an old English name, and actually obtained official permission to assume not only the name, but even the arms, of Palgrave. On this extraordinary proceeding there will be found some just comment in the pages of the *Genealogist*.[10] It is also difficult to conceive on what ground the heralds can have made this grant.

In that most misleading work, styled by its author *The Norman People*, the house of Grenville is traced to Greinville (*sic*) in the Cotentin, a fief of the barons of St. Denis le Gaste (p. 268). But there is no ' Greinville ' in the Cotentin, and the connexion of the Giffards with the early ancestors of the Grenvilles, of which he was well aware, points to quite another district as that from which they came.

The fact is that it is no less difficult to trace the minor companions of the Conqueror—those who became in England under-tenants—to their homes in Normandy, than it is in the seventeenth century to affiliate with certainty Englishmen who settled in Ireland or in New England.[11] William's

---

[7] Ed. 1892, pp. 42, 60.   [8] *Normandy and England*, iii, 652, 657.

[9] Compare the observations in court of Mr. Justice Darling on a ' person named Cohen'; using an ancient English name is a practice which in some countries would not be tolerated.

[10] *Genealogist* (V.S.), iii, 285. Sir Francis Palgrave, deputy-keeper of the Public Records, married a daughter of Mr. Dawson Turner, the well-known antiquary, whose wife was a daughter of William Palgrave of Cotishall. But this daughter was not an heir and could carry no representations in blood of the Palgrave family.

[11] It is not generally known how few of the English and Scottish families founded by a settler in Ireland can prove his parentage or his birthplace.

barons do not appear to have selected for their under-tenants mainly, or even largely, those who were in Normandy their neighbours. As Domesday usually records only the christian names of the under-tenants, it is difficult to speak positively, and in some cases they had, we find, followed to England their neighbours or their lords. But the point to bear in mind is that we must not assume that an under-tenant necessarily came from the same neighbourhood as his lord : only evidence can establish the fact. The best of all evidence is that which proves a connexion in Normandy between the tenant and the lord.

The reason why it is necessary to be thus cautious in the matter is that in Normandy we often have to choose between two or more places bearing the same or similar name, when seeking the cradle of a house. There are, as I have said above, at least six Grainvilles from which the Buckingham-shire Greinvills, afterwards Grenvilles, may have come. But the Giffard connexion is our clue. Now the Giffards were best known as Lords of Longueville-la-Giffard, in the little valley of Scie, close to which they founded their priory of Sainte Foy, to which the Manor of Newton-Longueville, on their Buckinghamshire lands, was among their gifts. I was able to show for the first time that from Sauqueville, lower down the valley, there followed them to England Herbrand de Saugueville, who settled on their Manor of Fawley,[12] and whose house under its English name of Sack-ville attained an earldom in 1603 and a dukedom in 1720, only, however, to become extinct in 1843, but there is no Grainville to be found in the valley of the Scie or, indeed, in this district. Walter Giffard, however, was lord of another fief, that of Bolbec—some thirty-three miles as the crow flies from Longueville—which he inherited from his paternal grandfather, Osbern de Bolbec.

In this capacity he confirmed the gifts by Hugh de Bolbec and others, of Bolbec church to the Abbey of Bernay,

---

[12] *Peerage and Pedigree*, i, 286-8, and compare my paper on ' The Essex Sackvilles,' for this branch of the family whose founder was derived in *The Norman People* from Sageville, Isle of France.

by a charter to which William de ' Greinvilla ' and Robert, his son, were witnesses.[13] Now, only some six miles from Bolbec there is a Grainville, lying south of Fécamp, from which William and Robert may be fairly conjectured to have come.   I assign, therefore, to this locality, the origin of the English Grenvilles ; the superficial resemblance of whose name to the alleged Grenneville in the Cotentin appears to have been the sole reason for tracing them to a spot far removed from Giffard fiefs.

Gerard de ' Grainvilla,' who held three fees on the Giffard fief in 1166,[14] was succeeded by his nephew, Eustace de ' Greinvilla,' [15] in or about 1184.   This was probably the Eustace de Greinville whose name is found on the Norman Exchequer Roll of 1200,[16] and who derived it, says Stapleton, from a place in the Pays de Caux.   This would be the Grainville of which I have spoken above.

The Grenvilles attained, like the Sackvilles, an English earldom (1749) and dukedom (1822) after remaining country squires for more than six centuries at Wotton. They only recently became extinct on the death of the last Duke of Buckingham, in the direct line.   It is possible, of course, that the descent may be traced from some cadet, but so far as I know, it has not yet been done.[17]

We will now turn to the family with which I am immediately concerned, the Granvilles of the West Country.   The

---

[13] See *Neustria Pia*, p. 402, and my *Calendar of Documents, France*, pp. xxvii, 137.   The date given in this charter and accepted by M. Delisle is 1061, but I have suggested in the work cited that its confirmation at the council of Lillebonne (by which alone it is known to us) should be dated 1080.

[14] See p. 131 above.

[15] *Pipe Roll*, 31 Hen. II, p. 135.   Robert de Greenvill also occurs under Bucks, p. 138.

[16] *Rot. Scacc. Norm.* vol. ii, p. cxlix.

[17] Various surnames have been claimed as possible corruptions of Grenville or Greynville.   There is just sufficient resemblance between the arms of Greville and of Grenville to suggest that the former may originally have been derived from the latter.   But the Grevilles are traced to Campden, Glos., which is far away from Wotton, and Greville is a distinct place-name in Normandy.

one fact that emerges as to their origin in England is that their earliest ancestors held of the ' Honour of Gloucester.' The lands they held had come to the first earl of Gloucester by his marriage, under Henry I, with the daughter of Robert Fitz Hamon, whose conquest of Glamorgan is a fact, though its details, unfortunately, are doubtful. It is, of course, alleged that Richard de ' Granville ' was one of that band of knights which followed Robert to his conquest under William Rufus and obtained Neath for his reward, but I wish to keep here to what can actually be proved.

The starting-point for the history of this family is undoubtedly the foundation charter granted by Richard de ' Grainvilla ' at Neath Abbey. This Abbey was founded as a daughter-house of Savigny in or about 1129.[18] Richard mentions his wife, Constance, as acting jointly with himself— which supports the view that she was heiress of Neath, but does not mention any children. Among the witnesses to this charter, which was probably granted at their castle of Neath, are Payn de Turberville (of Coyty), Robert de Umfraville (of Penmark), Richard de St. Quintin (of Llanbethian), Maurice (? de Londres, of Ogmore), Robert Fitz Ber[nard], Odo (? Sor of St. Fagan), and Robert ' dapifer,' his father, and Robert de Grainavilla. This conjunction of Richard and Robert de Grainville is curiously confirmed by a document of almost ' the same date, that is to say, of 1128, in my calendar of documents preserved in France ' (p. 521). Richard and Robert de Greinvilla are there found as witnesses on the part of the Earl of Gloucester, and as in the Neath charter Robert's name is last but one among the witnesses, so is it, in this document, the last of all. From this we may infer that his position was considerably less important than Richard's. Another charter in which Richard styles himself the constable of the Earl of Gloucester, was printed by Mr. Francis in his work on Neath (p. 36) and will be found also in the new edition [19] of *Glamorgan*

---

[18] This is the date usually assigned.

[19] By Mr. Geoffrey T. Clark (1910), p. 1680.

Charters.[20] He gives, by this charter, his vill of ' Litaham '[21] to Neath and mentions his wife Constance, brother William, and two nephews, but no children.

There is one more document which must be cited here, for it is of great importance. I printed, apparently for the first time, in my ' Geoffrey de Mandeville ' (pp. 381-3), the curious treaty of alliance between Robert, Earl of Gloucester, and Miles, Earl of Hereford. Its date I there determined as July 1141-December 1143, and most probably June 1142. Among the sworn pledges for the Earl of Gloucester we there find Richard de ' Greinvill,' immediately preceded by ' Geoffrey de Watervill ' (who follows him in the document of 1128), and followed (among others) by Odo Sorus, Gilbert de Umfravill, and Richard de St. Quintin. This appearance of Richard de Grainville as still living in or about the year 1142 absolutely blows to pieces the whole ' Granville ' story.

But before I come to grips with that mendacious story I will advance another objection no less fatal to its truth. It is alleged that this Richard was the Granville's direct ancestor, and that, after founding Neath Abbey, he returned to his ' patrimony ' at Bideford in North Devon,[22] where he lived in great honour and reputation the remainder of his days, though according to an old pedigree of the family, bearing date 1639, it is stated that in his old age he took upon himself the sign of the Cross, according to the devotion of these times, and went towards Jerusalem, in which journey he died.[23] As Bideford was so long and so prominently a possession of the Granvilles, Sir Richard's alleged tenure of it appeared to support the descent. But when we

---

[20] From an inspeximus of 1468.   [21] See below.

[22] On the author's own showing he must have been nearly ninety.

[23] *History of the Granville Family*, p. 26. The story of his pilgrimage appears to rest on an authority by no means good, namely the ' Gwentian Chronicle ' or ' Aberporgwm Brut.' We there read that ' Riccard Grinfil,' who had obtained the lordship of Glyn Neath, returned to Wales after visiting the sepulchre of Christ and founded the monastery of Glyn Neath. . . . He brought with him a man from the land of Canaan,

enquire as to the evidence, we find that it is 'Fuller's Worthies,' where we read, that after the foundation, Richard returned to his own patrimony at Bideford, where he lived in great repute in the reign of King William Rufus,[24] that is to say, long before Neath Abbey was founded.

Now there is no proof that Richard held Bideford ; he does not mention it in his Neath charter, but he does mention, although the fact seems to have escaped notice, two Manors in the fief which he held of the Earl of Gloucester in Devonshire,[25] namely ' Naissa ' and ' Lytheham.' These I make to be Ash Reigny and Littleham by Bideford.[26] The importance of this lies in the fact that Ash Reigny was subsequently held of the Gloucester Honour, not by the Granvilles, but by the Reignys. The case of Neath Castle and lordship is even more striking. It is known not to have descended to the ' Granvilles,' but to have reverted to the chief lords, the Earls of Gloucester. Neath was the advanced post of the Norman settlement in Glamorgan, and exposed as such to the fury of the Welsh. This, I think, favours the view that Richard only obtained it by marriage with the daughter of its Welsh lord. Indeed, so imperfectly Normanised was this part of Glamorgan, that he still had, we are told, a Welsh lord at Aberavon in his rear. That Neath did not pass to his alleged descendants is an awkward fact. Bearing upon this is an important entry, which seems to have been overlooked, on the Pipe Roll of 1207. Under the Honour of Glamorgan, we there read, that the monks of Neath pay a 100 marcs and a palfrey for having the castlery (castellaria) which belonged to Richard de ' Greinville ' and

of the name of Lalys, well versed in the science of architecture, who erected the monasteries, castles and churches here mentioned. . . . Afterwards he went to London as architect to King Henry, and taught the science to many of the Welsh and English.' This, it will be seen, places the pilgrimage before the foundation of Neath Abbey and indeed the MS. dates his return 1111.

[24] *History of the Granville Family*, p. 22.

[25] ' In feodo quod teneo de se in Devensira.'

[26] Not to be confused with Littleham by Exmouth.

for all his land between the Tavy and the Neath, save the holdings of the King's burgesses.[27]

Putting all the evidence together, we find: (1) that Richard, in his charters, makes no mention of children, (2) that Neath and Ash Reigny alike escheated, after his death, to his lord, (3) that in the return in 1166 of the Earl of Gloucester's knights his important holding (seven fees) is entered as ' Feodum quod fuit Ricardi de Greinville.' [28]   It is clear that this fief did not descend to the ' Granvilles.'   In 1212, their only holding, of the Honour of Gloucester, in Devon, was half a fee in Bideford,[29] which was subsequently returned as held by Richard de Greinville's heir.[30]   My suggestion is that Richard, the founder of Neath Abbey, left no children, and that the ' Granvilles ' descended from that Robert de Grainville who occurs in conjunction with Richard, and who is found in 1166, holding a single fee of the Earl of Gloucester.[31]

It is of some interest to note that Bideford, Littleham, and Ash, are all found in Domesday, among those lands which had been held by Mathilde, William's queen, and before her by Briktric.   For it is known to students of these subjects that Briktric's lands were eventually given by William Rufus to Robert Fitz Hamon, from whom they descended to the Earls of Gloucester.   The Grainvills, obtaining them from the first earl (or, just possibly from Robert himself) had only to cross the Bristol Channel from Barnstaple Bay to reach that ' Castle Perilous ' in the vale of the Neath.

It was not till the seventeenth century—possibly, not till the Restoration—that the great Granville story made its first appearance.   But it burst full-blown upon the world. In the full flush of Royal favour, earned partly by his own

[27] Pipe Roll, 9 John, m. 21b.

[28] *Red Book of the Exchequer*, p. 288.   Richard de Grenville in name, under Dorset, on the Pipe Roll of 1130.

[29] *Ibid.* p. 559.   [30] *Testa de Nevill*, p. 177.

[31] *Red Book of the Exchequer*, p. 291.

services and partly by those of his kinsman, Monk, Sir John Grenville obtained, in addition to the earldom of Bath (with a viscountcy and barony of 'Granville'), the reversion to his kinsman's (Monk's) dukedom of Albemarle, the reversion to an earldom of Glamorgan, in consideration of his alleged descent from Robert Fitz Hamon, lord of Glamorgan, and finally—all in the same year, 1661—permission to use the titles of his ancestors as Earl of ' Corboile,' Thorigny and Granville. The amazing document containing the second and third of these concessions sets forth the whole of the alleged illustrious descent.[32]

Whereas it appears unto us that our right trusty and right well-beloved cousin, John, Earl of Bath, Our Grome of the stole, and First Gentleman of our Bedchamber, derives his title in a direct line, as heir-male unto Robert Fitz Hamon, Lord of Gloucester and Glamorgan in the reignes of King William the Conqueror, King William Rufus, and King Henry the First, and who was the son and heir of the lord Hamon dentatus, Earle of Corboile and Lord of Thorigny and Granville, in Normandy, whereby he justly claims his descent from the younger son, as we ourself do from the eldest of Rollo, the first Duke of Normandy, Our com'on ancestor. In consideration whereof . . . We are graciously pleased to promise and declare, that in case the Earldom of Glamorgan should at any time fall into the hands of the Crown, during our raigne . . . we will not again confer the said Earldom upon any other family but restore (*sic*) the same to that of the Granvilles, by creating the said present Earl of Bath also Earl of Glamorgan . . . and we are further graciously pleased for the considerations aforesaid, to allow and permit the said Earl of Bath to use also these other titles of Honour, as Earls of Corboile, Thorigny and Granville, as was formerly

---

[32] This document dated 26th April, 1661, under the royal sign manual and countersigned by Sir Edward Nicholas, Secretary of State, whatever may be its precise character and authority, is always spoken of as a warrant but is not transcribed in the Secretary of State's Entry Book. It is printed as above in *Collect. Topog. et Gen.* vii, 193-4, where Sir C. G. Young, Garter, copied it from the College of Arms MS. i, 27, fo. 120. It was doubtless ' recorded ' in the College of Arms as the authority for the use of these titles by the family. One may perhaps compare the mysterious and extraordinary royal warrant of 2nd Jan. 1767, confirming the Perrot baronetcy alleged to have been created in 1716 (or 1717). See *Complete Baronetage*, v, 33-37.

done by his ancestors and though the same hath been discontinued of late [33] by some of his said ancestors, yet we do hereby give full power and authority to the said Earl of Bath, not only for himself and his posterity, to use the same, but in case he shall hereafter erect in memory of his father, or any other his former ancestors, any monument or inscription concerning him or them, to use the name stile and dignity of Earle of Corboile, Thorigny, and Granville, in as full and ample a manner as his said ancestors, formerly and before Normandy was lost from the Crown of England, the said family of the Granvilles being then also sufferers with the Crown and then also dispossessed for their loyalty out of their said inheritance of the said Earldom and Lordships within the said Dutchy of Normandy.

The supposed Norman honours, thus tardily revived, were taken very seriously by Lord Bath's nephew, George Granville, who, on the extinction of the Bath Earldom in 1711, became heir-male of the family, and was raised to the peerage, within a year, as Lord Lansdown of ' Biddeford.' [34] To his relative John, Lord Gower (senior co-heir of the earls of Bath) he wrote, 3rd November, 1714 :

I am entitled, by the virtue of King Charles' warrant, to assume the Earldom of Corbeil, as the direct male-descendant from Sir Bevill. I cannot think a patent would be refused me, if it was represented to the King as an article that would give peace to the family. I would not have you indifferent in either of these articles, nor look upon them as vanity.[35]

Instead, however, of obtaining the coveted title from the King, he fell into disfavour for his Jacobite tendencies and was sent to the Tower for two years in 1715. Eventually he left the country for France in 1721, whereupon the old ' Pretender ' revived for him the family earldom of Bath and, a month later (3rd November, 1721), created him, as ' George Granvill, commonly called Lord Lansdown,[36] Earl of Corbeil and Lord Thorigni and Granville in France

[33] It had never existed.

[34] This was one of the eight baronies created on the opening day of 1712.

[35] *Fifth Report Historical MSS. Com.* p. 188.

[36] The title was thus described as being post-Revolution.

and Normandy, . . . Marquis Monk and *Fitzhemon*, and
Duke of Albemarle.' As these titles were especially limited,
the marquisate of ' Fitzhemon,' as a Jacobite title, may be
said to have existed till his nephew's death in 1776.

In 1714 he had erected [37] a stately monument to his famous
grandfather, Sir Beville, with an epitaph beginning :

> Here lyes all that was mortall of the most noble and truly
> valiant Sir Bevill Granville . . . Earl of Carbile, and Lord of
> Thorigny and Granville, in France and Normandy, descended
> in a direct line from Robert [38] (*sic*) second son of yᵉ warlike
> Rollo, first Duke of Normandy, who . . . was at length slain
> with many wounds, at the battle of Lansdowne July yᵉ 5, 1643.

Thus was his gallant grandfather made somewhat
ridiculous by having these ' bogus ' titles posthumously
thrust upon him.

Lord Lansdown subsequently erected a column also to
Sir Bevill on Lansdown Hill, near Bath, where he fell
in the hour of victory. On it he placed the Royal arms,
supported by those of Granville and of Monk, as jointly
concerned in the Restoration. So cherished by the ' Granvilles ' was the manner of this victory that, although the
first Lord Bath had selected, for his second title, the
Viscountcy of Granville of Lansdown, his son styled himself Lord Lansdown in spite of having been summoned
in his father's barony of Granville. As Lord Lansdown
he was married (1678) and his wife as ' Lady Lansdown',
was buried in Westminster Abbey.[39]

When he was created by the Emperor for his youthful
gallantry against the Turks, a Count of the Holy Roman
Empire (27th January, 1684), it was as Charles Viscount
Lansdown that he received the King's formal approba-
tion of that distinction (21st July, 1684). When his line
ended, the heir-male was created, we have seen, Lord Lansdown, and, although the title died with him, it was revived

---

[37] In Kilkhampton church.
[38] This is at variance with the story itself as now told.
[39] Chester's *Registers of Westminster Abbey*, p. 224.

half a century after, for that Earl of Shelburne who had married the daughter of the youngest co-heir of that Earl Granville, who was the descendant and the younger co-heir of the Earls of Bath. Thus it is that the Marquisate of Lansdown still commemorates in its style Sir Bevill's famous victory.

There was another member of the Granville family who made the most of the story and who contrived to suck thereout no small advantage. This was Dennis Granville, a younger son of Sir Bevill, who became Dean of Durham. This very interesting example of a Restoration divine was at once an ardent churchman, an unblushing pluralist, and so extravagant in his private life that all the revenue that he drew from the church was insufficient to pay his debts. A man of the most fervent piety, battling to restore weekly communion and other ordinances of the church, mortifying his flesh by applying the discipline, not indeed to himself but to his nephew,[40] he contrived to hold simultaneously the Deanery and Archdeaconry of Durham, with two livings in the Diocese, one of them a peculiarly good one. As he was also chaplain to Charles the Second, that worthy patron of his family, he had duties up in London at the court, which he did not fail to discharge. Yet he was either proud of his pluralism or destitute of the sense of humour. For we find him writing to one of the curates who performed his duties in his absence—he styles them ' Fellow labourers in the Gospel of Christ '—and reminding him that, in his charge of ' one of the most considerable parishes of England,' he had ' in one person your Rector's, Dean's and Archdeacon's continual example in your eye.'[41]

His father-in-law and bishop, the saintly Cosin, although heart and soul with him, as a high churchman, in his views,

---

[40] ' Method with Mrs. Finch and Mary to prepare them the better for the sacrament. . . . To whip the boy, if it can be possibly contrived this morning after prayers, though it be a great mortification to my nature in some respects, to convince Moll that I am in earnest.' *Surtees Soc.* vol. xlvii, p. 34.

[41] *Surtees Soc.* vol. xxxvii (Letters of Dean Granville), p. 121.

resented the behaviour of his young son-in-law, for whom he had provided rich preferment and who was Archdeacon at five and twenty. ' I know not,' he wrote, ' what to do with Mr. Grenvyle, who is still at Oxford, idling away his time, and suffering his curates to be non-resident . . . as he himself is.' The editor of his ' Remains ' could only plead that London, where he had great connexions, and Oxford not unnaturally offered far higher attractions to a man of his time of life than anything which either Durham or his country parsonages could afford.[42] In 1670 we read that ' Mr. Greenvill intends to continue with his wife at London not only this winter, but another spring and fall, if not longer.' [43] But, at least, the cause of the church had triumphed : better a pluralist absentee than a Puritan rector in his cure. It was, however, a bad scandal when, in spite of his splendid ' income,' he was publicly arrested for debt in the cloister of his own cathedral.[44] He had already brought the influence of Monk and even of the King himself to bear upon the poor bishop, who was sternly admonished to pay up his daughter's marriage-portion. Now he had desperate hopes of the Deanery, the revenue from which might free him, it was hoped, from the embarrassments which pressed upon him.[45] The Dean had ' one foot in the grave ' or, at least, was ' most infirme of his legg.' [46] But the Dean's leg recovered.

It was ten years before the Dean's leg aroused fresh hopes. And meanwhile, alas, Durham had a new bishop. And the new bishop had a nephew. With a nepotism worthy of Laud himself the good man strove to secure for his own relative the prize. His letters on the subject, the editor (the Rev. George Ornsby) observes,[47] are both curious and amusing, for he was trying to persuade Lord Bath that the office was not really worth his needy brother's acceptance. For the moment the struggle was premature : the Dean's

---

[42] *Surtees Soc.* vol. xxxvii (Letters of Dean Granville), pp. xviii-xix.
[43] *Ibid.*   [44] *Ibid.* p. xx.   [45] *Ibid.* p. xxii.
[46] *Ibid.* p. 152.   [47] *Ibid.* p. xxxiv.

leg again proved a cruel disappointment. We find the bishop writing to the earl :

> When these changes may happen, God knows. For the Dean hath lately been very much indisposed with a lame leg, yet he is recovering to a wonder and is very hearty.[48]

Yet in the same letter he strove to arrange a ' deal ' with the earl, if his nephew—a modest pluralist, who had but a stall in Durham Cathedral and the non-resident mastership of Sherburn Hospital in conjunction with that of Trinity College, Cambridge—could have the coveted Deanery, the earl's brother should have Sherburn, as a further source of income, with certain useful privileges at Court, while the bishop would also throw in a prebend for the earl's nephew and the reversion of a good living for a friend.

It was all in vain. The powerful aid of the King was again successfully invoked, but Sancroft, to his credit, objected to the dean-expectant remaining archdeacon as well. ' Greenvill,' he is said to have protested, ' was not worthy of the least stall in Durham Church, but a debtor is a desperate man.' To the primate he pleaded in self-defence :

> It is so notorious that I greatly need it, that I can in no good conscience, while I am in debt, consent to the parting with what I can honestly keep.[49]

And he did keep, not only the archdeaconry, but his own two livings as well.

It is pleasant to turn from all this, to the Dean's ready sacrifice of ' the best deanery, the best archdeaconry, and one of the best livings in England ' at the Revolution, in order to follow his Royal master into exile. The famous doctrine of non-resistance became with him, an obsession, and he bitterly denounced his brethren who accepted the rule of William. The wretched bigot whom he served and for whom he made his sacrifice retained him as a chaplain-in-ordinary,[50] but characteristically refused to let him

---

[48] *Ibid.* p. 184.   [49]*Ibid.* pp. 187-8.
[50] *Stuart Papers* (Hist. MSS. Reports), i, 174.

minister to his fellow-heretics at St. Germains.[51]   Obliged at last to withdraw to Corbeil, on the Seine, this pious soul discovered ' an act of God's goodness,' to him, in conducting him, unawares, to the seat of his alleged ancestors.   For him the Granville story became a joy indeed.

> After living three years at Tremblet, *alias* Tremblay, in the Fauxbourg of Corbeile, *alias* Corboile upon the river Seine, . . . I have lately and happily discovered that this town . . . hath been the seat of my ancestors and . . . is that Corbeil whereof there were antiently Earles (who were, as many others in France, little soveraine Princes) from one of whom I have made out my descent in a strait line by confronting my Pedigree sent me out of England with the written Antiquities and records of the towne, greatly to my honour and satisfaction, which is made beyond all dispute, as was so acknowledged by my Father (i.e. James II) himself, as he passed by us, by my comparing my arms in my seal with Count Hamon's on his tomb, who sent two sons with his cosen germaine William the Conqueror into England. . . . You will find mention made of this famous Hamon Dentatus and his two renowned sons that assisted King William the Conqueror in the year 1066 at the battaile of Hastings to win the Crown of England. . . .   The making out my descent as above hath made me known to some noble familyes at Court, now flourishing, allyed to the Counts of Corbeil, who can do kindnesses in a strait, and are likely (in case) God takes away my F[ather] to get my annuity now allowed me continued by the K. of France.[52]

The eager Dean had not even grasped who his ancestors were, for he here mixes up Hamon, Count of Corbeuil, living (it is said) about 1012, with Hamon Dentatus, who was alleged to be the Count's great-grandson and who was slain in 1041 !

Of the count he writes thus :

> I cannot forbeare to add an act of God's goodness to me in conducting me and fixing me in this Province of Bry. . . .   My house is in the Faubourg of Corbeile . . . from the antient earles whereof potent men I am descended in a right line, and one of

[51] *Surtees Soc.* vol. xxxvii, p. xliii.
[52] Letter of 4th August, 1710 (*Surtees Soc.* vol. xlvii, pp. 195-6.)

my ancestors being a man of great piety and valour, having founded here two collegiate Churches, is in great veneration, and being buried in one of them, I have lately discovered his tomb, which is very magnificent. And being now proclaimed to be their founder's kinsman, receive many civilities from the people more than before. I pray you . . . require for a copy of our pedigree, and bring it over. It was some good angel which led me here to the place I sought, thinking it was in Normandy, where I could never find it, I found there the other places named in the pedigree.[53]   May I never want such a good spirit to conduct and inspire me.[54]

The pious hope was realised. ' A fresh providence '—assisted apparently by the Dean himself—led a ' lusty ' Countess to invite him to stay for fishing.

I may by my providential discovery to all here that I am not only originally French, but descended from a cosen germaine even of a Queen of France, sister to the Emperor Otho, be enabled to play a good after game and obtain by a petition to the Grand and most generous Monarch, backed with the recommendations of my Father etc. (who encreases in strength dayly) more than my lost salary.

And as a step to this project a fresh providence seems to concur. From making out publicly my descent from the aforesaid famous Count, *in high veneration, almost adored for a saint*, I am made known to some noble familys, and received but yesterday from a very noble old Countess of 84 years old, but lusty and strong, a kind invitation to her castle . . . to stay with her a week or a fortnight, to divert myself in her ponde and river that goes thorow her Park.[55]

The Granville story with its earldom of ' Corbeuil,' brought him, we see, pleasure and even the hope of profit as well as honour and glory.

---

[53] This is a very interesting passage, for it will be seen on referring to the ' warrant ' of Charles II, that it most distinctly speaks of ' Corboile,' as well as Thorigny and Granville, as being in Normandy.   This discovery by the Dean must have enlightened his family, for his nephew in 1714, and again in 1721, both in the inscription he set up and in his Jacobite creation, inserted the word ' France ' (' in France and Normandy ').

[54] Letter of 4th May, 1701 (*Surtees Soc.* vol. xlvii, p. 195).

[55] *Ibid.* p. 198.

On the death of his brother, Lord Bath, whose son promptly followed him to the grave (August 1701), the Dean wrote that he was ' going home to Corbeil to mourne (*sic*) for the great mortallity in the successors of Count Hamon ' (of Corbeuil), referred to his ' ever honoured father, the 29 E[arl] of C[orbeuil] ' and observed that his sister ' can only behold two Earles of C[orbeuil] dead.' [56]   As the year drew to its close the sanguine writer is found hoping ' for my profitt as well as to my satisfaction, my extraction and descent from the Earls of Corbeil being like to be amply set forth on this occasion,' though he was ' a prisoner in mine house or rather own town, near the tomb of my great ancestors.' [57]   In 1702 he began to sign his letters ' Corbeil ' and even ' De Corbeil,' and prattled ' of one special providentiall good turn.' ' Soon after I had discovered last summer,' he writes, ' the tomb of my renowned ancestor Count Hamon . . . we discovered the name of an ancestor of the said old Countess, related to, as we fancyed, Count Hamon.'   This brought him into favour with that ' gallant, heroick lady ' and procured him boundless hospitality.[58] Still sanguine of turning his alleged descent to profit, he wrote in Pepysian vein (16th June, 1702) :

My head being mighty full of new projects (on my discovery that this Corbeil where I live was the Corbeil whereof Hamon Dentatus, my ancestor and their founder, was Earle, and that the said Earle was descended from Charlemagne), which are like to be greatly impeded, if not wholly dashed, by want of money . . . for I am a private country man living at Corbeil, the seat of my forefathers.[59]

' I am preparing,' he wrote further, ' a petition to his Majesty on discovering my descent from the Kings of France.   Whereof I do not talk much unless it hitts.'   But his hopes were always disappointed.   ' My bold projects, on the tomb of my Ancestor, do not yet succeed.   I had

[56] *Surtees Soc.* vol. xlvii, pp. 198-200.   He means the father and the son.

[57] *Ibid.* pp. 202-3.   [58] *Ibid.* pp. 205-6.   [59] *Ibid.* pp. 206-7.

hopes . . . from a great man who would have shown some favour to a founder's kinsman, but my expectation yet produces nothing.' [60]

At Corbeil, as at the Court of St. Germains, he was plagued by the priests' attempts to convert him to the Church of Rome, so late as 20th November, 1702, we find him writing :

> I cannot be so rude as not to return any answer at all to the letters and papers they send me with civility and good meaning, however their zeal be ill-grounded, and proves too a kind of per-secution, . . . I do therefore, for the honour of my family, descended from their noble founder and benefactor, like a gentle-man receive their visits as well as papers, behaving my self, remembering I have a sword by my side, like a cavalier rather than Divine . . . having never been good at such kind of fighting.[61]

The battle he loved to fight, as a Granville and a cavalier, was that on behalf of his ' Father ' and his King, to whom resistance was an act of sin.   James had died in September 1701, but his heir had recognised his fidelity to the cause by allowing him ' a salary, paying him as one of our domestic servants and promising to be mindful of his services and sufferings on our happy and wished for Restoration.' [62] A year later the Dean died, remembering all that the Restoration had done for his family and for himself, and dreaming, like the exile of St. Germains, that a King would again return.

No less keen himself, on the great Granville story, was the Dean's nephew and friend, George, Lord Lansdown, who, we have seen, claimed, on becoming the heir-male, that he was entitled to the earldom of Corbeuil.[63]   As a young man, addicted to verse, he had indulged in the fashionable panegyric on his cousin Charles, Lord Bath's

[60] *Ibid.* p. 209.

[61] *Surtees Soc.* (Letters of Dean Granville), vol. xxxvii, p. 240.

[62] 29th April, 1702 (*Stuart Papers*, i, 174).   [63] See p. 141 above.

son and heir, who took part in the bombardment of
Granville, 1695.

> Tho' built by gods consumed by hostile flame
> Troy bury'd lies, yet lives the Trojan name ;
> And so shall thine, tho' with these walls were lost
> All the records *our ancestors could boast.*

> *   *   *   *   *   *   *   *

> Those arms which for nine centuries had brav'd
> The wrath of time on antick stone engrav'd
> Now torn by mortars, stand yet undefac'd
> On nobler trophies, by thy valour raised.
> Safe on thy eagle's wings they soar above
> The rage of war or thunder to remove,
> Borne by the bird of Caesar and of Jove.

George ' Granville,' it is clear, believed that the arms of
his house, borne by his cousin—as a Count of the Empire—
an Eagle's breast, had been carved on the walls of Granville
since the year 795 or thereabouts.   This belief far surpassed
that of the Dean, his uncle, who had merely found them on
the monument of a man who was living in 912—some two
centuries and a half before arms came into use.   The
Grenville family, as a matter of fact, had no more to do with
' Granville ' than with ' Corbeuil,' but ' Granville ' was
thenceforward the form they affected for their name, whence
it has become familiar as that of an earldom.

As for their arms, these are full of interest and, indeed,
mystery.   The three golden charges on a field of ' gules '
have been very variously described.   ' Brackets,' ' lance-
rests,' or simply ' rests,' ' sufflues,' ' rudders,' ' clarions,'
and ' clavicords,' have all in turn been suggested.   Even
Papworth hesitated between ' organ rests,' ' sufflues,'
' clarions,' and ' clavicords.'   To Planché is due the credit
of observing that, ' if a rest, it is certainly not a rest for a
lance, as some writers describe it, because it appears as a
charge long before the invention of the lance-rest.' [64]   He
himself considered that a ' clarion ' was the right name, and

[64] *The Pursuivant of Arms.*

that these charges ' were originally a badge or coat of the Clares,' who succeeded to the earldom of Gloucester. Yet he could not but perceive the resemblance of the charge to a mouth-organ, and he pointed out that the Clares were Lords of Glam*organ*. Mr. Oswald Barron tells me he considers that this was the real origin of the charge.

To put the matter beyond question I consulted the Rev. F. W. Galpin, an expert on ancient musical instruments. He was good enough to write as follows :

I have no hesitation in confirming your opinion that the Heraldic device, of which you have sent me sketches, is the Syrinx or Panpipes . . . illustrations of the Syrinx are not at all uncommon in Mediaeval MSS. It was considered a Biblical instrument—Jubul's ' organ ' in fact—and Iduthun or some other of David's musicians is afterwards shown with it as in the Anglo-Saxon Psalter in the University Library, Cambridge, (early 11th cent.). In a Psalter of the 12th cent. at St. John's it appears amongst the instruments of ' Musica Sacra,' as opposed to those of ' Musica Profana. . . .' In an 11th cent. MS. (Brit. Mus. Harl. 603) a large Syrinx is shown hung up in a tree as an illustration to the 137th Psalm (verse 2), where the Vulgate read ' *organa* nostra,' not ' harps.'

A specimen of this instrument from the Basque Provinces, in Mr. Galpin's own collection, has a striking resemblance to the heraldic charge.

From this it is clear that the ' Granville ' charge depicts that most ancient instrument—the Hebrew *ûgâb*—and alludes therefore to Glam*organ*.[65] The ' Granville ' coat was usurped by the modern family of Grenfell,[66] and when a differenced coat was granted them anew, not long ago, these charges had to be blazoned and were styled ' organ rests,' which they are not. They are, as I have said, mouth-organs.

[65] It is amusing to find Mr. Fox-Davies in two successive entries (p. 431), under ' Granville ' in his *Armorial Families*, giving this charge (1) as ' three clarions or (for Granville) ' and (2) as ' three rests or (for Granville).'

[66] Founded by Pascal Grenfell of Marazion, Cornwall (*d.* 1810). See Burke, *Landed Gentry*.

When we leave mere guess-work, and leave also the attribution, by late heraldic writers of this coat to the earliest earls of Gloucester, we are confronted with the sure evidence of seals and are left to draw from that evidence what deductions we please.   It is usually alleged that the arms of Neath Abbey were those of its founder, Richard de Granville, but it is certain that arms were not in use till some time after the foundation and, indeed, after Richard and his family had ceased to be connected with the Abbey.   It has been justly observed by Dr. De Gray Birch that the above allegation, made in the *New Monasticon*, cannot be correct, because precisely the same arms are found on the seal of the sister house in Glamorgan, Margam Abbey, with which Granville had nothing to do.[67]   Moreover, Keynsham Abbey in Somerset, founded by William, Earl of Gloucester, bore, as he says, six of these mysterious charges in its arms, to which I may add that at Neath Abbey the armorial tiles show us six as well as three of the ' clarions ' in the shield.   It is only possible, therefore, to connect them with the Earls of Gloucester, founders of two of these abbeys and patrons of the third.[68]

We can understand, therefore, how old heraldic writers came to assign this coat to Robert and William, Earls of Gloucester, though there is no trace of it on their seals. But why the Greinvilles, alone among their followers, should have borne it, remains wholly obscure, the more so as they were not even directly descended from the Glamorgan baron, the Lord of Neath.[69]

The only difficulty in dealing with the great ' Granville ' story and its absurd ' Earldom of Corbeuil ' is presented by the fact that there are two versions.   This is kept out of sight in the Rev. John Granville's book (1895), but it is

[67] *Hist. of Margam Abbey*, p. 332.

[68] For Neath Abbey reverted to the Earl of Gloucester, as Lord of Glamorgan, on Richard de Greinville's death.

[69] The coat appears on the seal of a charter granted by an early Richard de Granville to Bideford.   (*Hist. of Granville Family*, p. 33.)

clear that the version sanctioned by the ' warrant ' of
Charles II, and believed by the Dean of Durham and his
nephew, Lord Lansdown, is quite distinct from that
which Mr. Granville has given. The old story, which is
still found in Burke's *History of the Commoners* (1836), was
that Rollo, the first Duke of Normandy, had by Giselle,
daughter of the French King, Charles the simple, two sons,
William, his successor, and Robert, the younger, created
' Earl of Corbeil,' of whom the Granvilles were the heirs-
male. From this Robert, through Hamon Dentatus, Earl of
' Corboile,' and Lord Thorigny and Granville in Normandy
(which titles they held before Normandy was lost to the
Crown of England),[70] the Granvilles were said to descend as
the heirs-male of his (alleged) ' second son, Richard de
Granville, who fought at Hastings.' The eldest son,
Robert Fitz-Hamon, having only left a daughter, Richard, it
was claimed, ' as heir-male, was Earl of Corbeil [71] and
baron of Thorigny and Granville.' This, which is clearly
the authorised version, was that which George, Lord Lansdown gave to Moréri, who thus sets it forth in his *Grand
Dictionnaire Historique*.[72]

Granville, ou plutôt Grenevil ou Grainevill (Richard), Comte
de Corboile [73] (*sic*), baron de Torigni et de Granville en Normandie, etoit (dit un auteur Anglois) issu de Rollou, premier
duc de Normandie, qui eut pour fils Guillaume, surnommé
' Longue epée ' . . . auquel on ajoute Robert, comte de Corboile
(*sic*), etc., qui eut entr' autres enfants, Hamon, surnommé Dentatus ou le Dentu qui fut père de Robert Fitz Hamon, comte de
Corboile, baron de Torigni et de Granville et de Richard *dont
nous parlons*.

[70] Warrant of Charles II.

[71] Mr. Granville writes, that ' all Fitzhamon's titles, according to
Norman law, descended to his brother Richard de Granville and were
borne by him and his posterity till Normandy was lost to the Crown of
England.' (*Op. cit.* p. 22.) But Norman law would, on the contrary,
have made them descend to his daughter, and it is quite untrue that
they were borne by Richard and his successors.

[72] Ed. 1759, v, 340-342.

[73] This is the spelling in Charles II's ' warrant

This descent was at least consistent, but as Rollo had no son Robert, and, indeed, no children by Giselle,[74] it had of course to be abandoned, lock, stock, and barrel.

Very different is the story told by Mr. Granville. Representing the above version as merely an error of Lord Lansdown, and ignoring the Dean's belief in it, he disposed of the fact that it is found also in King Charles' ' warrant,' by tampering with the text of that document and altering the word ' son ' to ' branch.' The text was thus made to read : ' the youngest *branch* . . . of Rollo.' [75] By the side of the old version I have here placed the very different descent which he substituted for it :

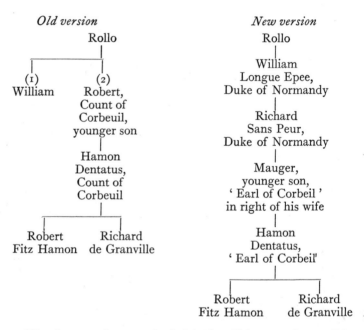

Old version	New version
Rollo	Rollo

Old version

Rollo

(1) William   (2) Robert, Count of Corbeuil, younger son

Hamon Dentatus, Count of Corbeuil

Robert Fitz Hamon   Richard de Granville

New version

Rollo

William Longue Epee, Duke of Normandy

Richard Sans Peur, Duke of Normandy

Mauger, younger son, ' Earl of Corbeil ' in right of his wife

Hamon Dentatus, ' Earl of Corbeil'

Robert Fitz Hamon   Richard de Granville

The descent given on the left is, it will be seen, impossible for reasons of chronology as well as for those already given above. As for that on the right, I have not been able to

[74]*Hist. of the Granville Family*, p. 270.   [75] *Ibid.* p. 352.

discover from what source it was concocted. The 'earldom' of Corbeuil is now alleged to have descended as follows :

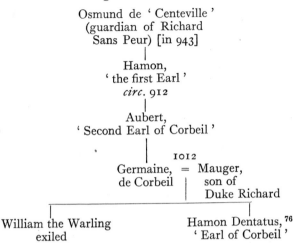

Osmund de ' Centeville '
(guardian of Richard
Sans Peur) [in 943]
|
Hamon,
' the first Earl '
circ. 912
|
Aubert,
' Second Earl of Corbeil '
| 1012
Germaine, = Mauger,
de Corbeil | son of
| Duke Richard

William the Warling   Hamon Dentatus, [76]
exiled   ' Earl of Corbeil '

It would be a waste of time to disentangle this early genealogy, but one must explain that Hamon, ' the first Earl,' was that Count Hamo, the pious founder, in whom Dean Granville exulted as his ancestor, and whom he confused with ' Hamo Dentatus.' The Count's date was not 912, but about 950, when he founded a collegiate Church at Corbeuil for the fugitive relics of two bishops of Bayeux. This church, however, had to be refounded by Count Burchard,[77] after its virtual destruction. Corbeuil was ceded to the Crown by Count Burchard's heir, according to Père Anselme, in 1012.

What one would like to know is, where Mr. Granville derived his statement that ' Hamon Dentatus ' was the younger son of Mauger, a statement for which no authority is given. I suspect that when the story was hatched in the seventeenth century, its author, wishing to exalt ' Hamon Dentatus ' (of whom hardly anything is known), identified

[76] *Hist. of the Granville Family*, pp. 15, 16.

[77] *Gallia Christiana*. For Burchard see Palgrave, *Normandy and England*, iii, 74.

him with Count Hamo (or Aime) of Corbeuil, living long
before him. Dean Granville, we have seen, did so, and so
did the 'warrant' of Charles II. When this view had to
be abandoned, it became necessary at all costs to provide
another explanation of his alleged,[78] but quite fictitious,
tenure of the 'earldom.' The only possible way of doing
so was to make him a younger son of Mauger, who succeeded
his elder brother, William 'the Warling,' when the latter
was exiled in 1049 and lost his father's rich *comté* of Mortain.[79]
But Hamon had been slain *before* this, namely, in 1047, so
that even if the pedigree were true he could never have
succeeded to Corbeuil. We thus obtain further proof that
the story of his earldom is sheer falsehood. And in the
next generation we can prove yet another statement contrary to the fact. All versions of the tale make Robert
Fitz Hamon to be son of 'Hamo Dentatus.' Such indeed
was the general belief, although William of Malmesbury
definitely styles Hamo as his 'avus.' But we know now
that Robert was a son of 'Hamo' dapifer and a grandson
of 'Hamo dentatus.'[80] This completely alters the pedigree
at the point from which the 'Granvilles' claimed that they
had branched off.

That Richard 'de Granville' who 'came over to England
in the Conqueror's army'[81] (1066), and founded Neath
Abbey (about 1129), was a younger brother of Robert Fitz
Hamon is part of the original story, but is a separate invention from that which made his father Earl of Corbeuil.
The above dates do not exhaust his chronological marvels,
for Mr. Granville makes him, maternally, a nephew of
'the Emperor Otho' (son of Henry 'the Fowler'), who
mounted the throne so far back as 936.[82]

[78] *Hist. of the Granville Family*, pp. 15, 16.

[79] Mr. Granville, following Palgrave (iii, 28, 224), calls it 'Mortaigne,'
meaning Mortagne, a wholly different place.

[80] Hearne, *Textus Roffensis*, xcvii; Dugdale, *Mon. Ang.* i, 164;
Davis, *Regesta*, i, No. 451.

[81] *Hist. of the Granville Family*, p. 18 (1066).

[82] *Ibid.* p. 37; cf. for the chronology, *Genealogist* (N.S.), xii, 285-6.

The Granvilles and the Monks

It appears, however, that after all Mr. Granville was not the inventor of the present version of the story. I find that eleven years before his book was published, a paper was read before the Devon Association (July 1884) by a local antiquary, Mr. Charles Worthy, in which the same version was given.[83] In this paper it is stated of the founder of Neath Abbey, without the least hesitation, that in the year 1147, ' being then of advanced age, he took the vow as a Crusader, and started for the Holy Land.' [84] As his alleged father, Robert Fitz Hamon, had been slain no less than a hundred years before he was certainly of ' advanced age.' Of Robert himself, Mr. Worthy wrote quite gravely :

> I find him styled ' Robert Fitz Hamon, by the grace of God, Prince of Glamorgan, Earl of Corboile, of Thorigny, and Granville, Lord of Gloucester, Bristol, Tewkesbury and Cardiff, Governor of Wales, near Kinsman unto the King and General of all his Highness' Army in France.' [85]

One need not waste further time on Mr. Worthy's paper, but what was the Devon Association about, to allow the publication in its volumes of such nonsense as this ?

The question is one which I am anxious to raise. A private individual has a perfect right to issue, as his own adventure, a history of his family which bears no one's *imprimatur* but his own. The case is altogether different, when a learned, or presumably learned society, supported by subscriptions given for the advancement of accurate knowledge, fathers a genealogical paper which moves us to laughter or contempt. And when that paper is written to glorify the writer's own family, the case is even worse. So recently as 1903, the Devon Association published a paper of great length by the Rev. W. Wykes-Finch on ' The Ancient family of Wyke of North Wyke, co. Devon,' [86] than which I know of nothing more outrageous in its claims.

[83] *Trans. of the Devon Assoc.* xvi, 678-693.   [84] *Ibid.* p. 680.
[85] *Ibid.* p. 679.   [86] *Trans. of Devon Assoc.* xxxv, 360-425.

For the writer began by thus criticising the author of a previous paper on ' the Wykes of South Tawton.' [87] :

> It is feared that he did not realise the importance of accuracy in such writings, nor the seductive fertility of the soil on which he was working in the production of statements that have much to do with the domain of the imagination.   Probably in nothing do men more slip, or allow preconceived ideas to dominate their conclusions than in the writing of family history.   Too often a pleasing assumption speedily becomes a boasted fact.   The imagination is feasted with indulgence, and sentimental adornment imposes on the unwary and sometimes deceives the very elect.   A single minded devotion to the investigation of truth gradually falls into abeyance ; the desire to convert the pride of fiction into unassailable fact grows apace, and the result becomes worse than misleading . . . it would be unfortunate to allow the paper to be handed down to posterity as historically correct.

I quote this passage in full, because it cleverly prepares the reader for acceptance of the writer's own statements as free from such imaginative error, while, in truth, his criticism recoils with peculiar force upon himself.   It is also because ' it would be unfortunate to allow the paper to be handed down to posterity as historically correct,' that I in turn propose to show its true character.

The writer starts not from a record, but from a statement by Risdon that ' North Wyke was the land of William de Wigornia *alias* Chamberlain, in the reign of Henry III ' (i.e. 1216-1272).   ' We readily see,' he proceeds, ' that William de Wray, William de Chevereston, and William de Wigornia (Wig) are one and the same person ' ;   he then assumes the date, ' in or about 1227,' for Risdon's statement of tenure, and promptly informs us, of William, that ' if we give due weight to all the facts and circumstances that affect our enquiry, no reasonable doubt can remain in our minds that he was either the son, or grandson, of Robert, Earl of Mellent and Worcester (Wigornia).'   For this ' pleasing assumption ' there is not the slightest ground, but in the writer's hands, to quote his own words, it ' speedily becomes

[87] *Trans. of Devon Assoc.* xxix.

a boasted fact.' As he truly observes, ' The desire to convert the pride of fiction into unassailable fact grows apace,' and page after page is devoted to urging ' how probable it is,' that ' we shall find it difficult to stop short of the conclusion,' that ' we cannot reasonably suppose otherwise,' that ' we may reasonably conclude ' that ' Henry de Pontaudemer ' was Earl Robert's third son,' and finally, that as ' he could not transmit his name if a son,' . . . ' his posterity would receive some other cognomen, which probably would be " de Wigornia " or " de Wig." ' Thus we arrive at the conclusion that William de Wigornia, who held North Wyke in 1227 (*sic*), was his (Earl Robert's) son or grandson : to the same conclusion came Mr. Charles Worthy, and its correctness could not well be doubted, even if there was no further proof (*sic*).[88] All this wild guess-work is but introductory to a proposition so crazy that one wonders how it could be seriously advanced. For, to continue the above quotation, ' I would suggest that Luke Fitz John's manor of Teign *Wyke* got its affix from him, as did " Wyke South Teign " *its* prefix. If, as I strongly suspect, this was so,' etc., etc. The proposition in short, is that ' Wyke ' and ' Worcester ' are the same names, *because* Worcester was Latinised as ' *Wigornia* ' which was sometimes abbreviated by busy scribes as *Wig* !

One might almost despair of conveying to the mind of the ' general reader ' the full grotesque absurdity of such a proposition as this. To claim that the grandson of an Earl of Worcester would probably be styled ' William de Wig ' and would give his name to Teign as ' Teign *Wyke* ' is surely even madder than it would be to suppose that the Bishop of Worcester, because he uses the ancient style ' Wigorn[*ensis*] ' is also known as Bishop ' Wig,' or the Bishop of Rochester as Bishop ' Roff.' Yet it is strenuously advanced. We find the author writing :

[88] Yet on one page we read that William was probably a son of Henry de Pontaudemer, and therefore a grandson of Robert Comes de ' Wigornia,' while on another he is definitely given on the contrary as ' grandson of the most potent Lord of his time, Waleran, Comes de Wigornia.'

During the thirteenth century Wigornia is often written ' Wig ' in the charters and records of that period.   This is seen in Noake's Worcester, and is very general in the episcopal Register of Bishop Giffard. . . .   And it can readily be established *as a fact* that during this century ' Wig ' (or Wyg and Wyk) or Wik, were indiscriminately written and identical.

The worst of it is that the writer realised that ' Wig ' was but an abbreviation, and yet he treated it as identical with ' Wyke,' which was a complete word.

' I might go on,' we read at last, ' adding evidence to evidence . . . clearly demonstrating that the circumstances and arguments and facts I have adduced are only *compatible* with the deduction that the founder of the Wyke family of North Wyke, " William de Wigornia " *alias* Chamberlain, was either a son or grandson of Robert, Earl of Mellent and Worcester.   The conclusion is irresistible, and the proof as complete, I think, as one of the problems of Euclid.'   As illustrating this clerical idea of ' proof,' one of these decisive pieces of ' evidence ' is that the writer has been ' informed ' that ' an old yeoman family ' had possessed ' some MSS., either original or copies,' which ' showed that the ancestor of the Wyke family not only " came over with the Conqueror," but held high office and command under him.'   These MSS. could not be found, and yet, the writer claims they ' can and do bear testimony, to the fact that the Wyke ancestor at the battle of Hastings was high in the favour of William and of kin to him ; and tradition bears the same testimony.'   And ' *no doubt* ' the Wyke writings would have shown, had they not been lost, ' that identity of William de Wigornia with the son *or grandson* of Comes de Wigornia,' [89] which the author is determined to assert. Such is the ' evidence,' such the ' proof,' claimed as complete by the reverend gentleman.

May we not say in his own words that ' it is to be feared that he did not realise . . . the seductive fertility of the soil on which he was working in the production of statements

[89] The italics are mine.

160

that have much to do with the domain of the "imagination"'?
As he justly added, ' probably in nothing do more men slip,
or allow preconceived ideas to dominate their conclusions
than in the writing of family history.'

The name of ' William de Wigornia ' is by no means
unique at that period. Of those who bore it, one was a
burgess of Bristol, who occurs in 1230 and 1233, and who
traded in wine with Worcester.[90] The obstinate resolve of
the writer to claim his ' William de Wigornia,' *alias* ' Chamberlain,' as a son ' or grandson ' of an earl of Worcester and
as founder of ' the ancient family of Wyke,' was due to his
eagerness to assert for his own maternal grandfather a
' descent ' in the *male-line* from ' Bernard the Dane '
without a break. Words almost fail him as he thinks of :

> The warrior line of ' Bernard the Dane,' a Saxon (*sic*) warrior,
> who accompanied his cousin Rollo as second in command, on
> his invasion of Normandy. The descendants of Bernard, all
> through to the Wigornias (*sic*), had a renown in the battlefield
> and in the council chamber unsurpassed probably by any family
> that has ever taken part in any affairs of state.

Although himself only a County Councillor for Worcestershire, he cannot forget that his ancestor, Waleran, was
undoubtedly the most princely subject that ever held official
position in the County of Worcester. . . . No subject could
boast of a more illustrious birth. He claims of ' this great
Norman family ' that ' its illustrious career from Bernard
to the close of the life of Earl Waleran has never been
excelled, probably never equalled, by any family, as warriors
or statesmen.' In fact, ' but for the force of character, its
power to govern and administer, we might never have heard
of the Norman Conquest and so never have been blessed
with the marvellous blood-mixture. . . .' The reader will
think that we are coming to the patent medicine at last.

---

[90] Per manus Rogeri Aylard et Willelmi de Wygornia, burgensium
nostrorum Bristollie (*Cal. of Patent Rolls*, 1225-1232, p. 346), ' Pro
quodam burgense Bristol' . . . permittat Willelmum de Wigornia
ducere x dolia vini usque Wigorniam de Bristoll.' (*Cal. of Close Rolls*,
1231-1234, p. 245.)

But no, we are merely reminded that for this prodigious family we might never have hoped ' to make the English tongue, the universal language of mankind.'

Eloquent alike on the greatness of their princely Norman ancestors, the modern descendants of these nobles are, alas, also alike in finding the names of those ancestors a sore puzzle. Mr. Smith ' Carrington,' I have shown, discovered that ' William called Longsword, *Duke of Aquitaine*, succeeded as second duke of Normandy ; [91] Mr. " Granville " claimed Maliger (*sic*) or Mauger, third son of Richard the Fearless,' as the ' direct ancestor of the Granvilles,' quoted William of Jumièges as ' Guillaume Gemmet,' and made a ' Count of Chartres ' into an ' Earl of Chartiers,' Mr. Wykes-Finch tells us that Bernard, ' second in command . . . in the invasion and conquest of Normandy, . . . married a daughter of . . . de Sprote of the royal family of Burgundy. His son added *inter alia* Potatou to his paternal inheritance.' But the scribal Latinisation of surnames is, as ' Wigornia ' showed us, the chief stumbling-block. The author makes ' Humphrey de Vetulis ' marry ' Albreda de la Haye,' evidently quite unaware that he was really styled ' de Vieilles (de Vetulis).' His sons he names ' de Bello Monte,' similarly unaware that this is merely Latin for ' de Beaumont.' If ' William de Wigornia ' founded the house of ' Wig,' surely ' Roger de Bellomonte ' must have founded that of Bell !

Such then are the two Devon stories which the Devonshire Association has seen fit to publish in its learned Transactions. For the ' Granvilles,' an unbroken male descent from Rollo, Duke of Normandy ; for the Wykes, an unbroken male descent from Rollo's ' cousin and second in command,' Bernard the Dane. The former could at least claim a fairly respectable antiquity ; but the latter was a modern concoction without a shadow of excuse.

The ' Granville ' story probably arose in that middle period of the seventeenth century when much antiquarian

[91] *Peerage and Pedigree*, ii, 247.

work was being done both here and abroad, and the publication of chronicles and documents was providing the pedigree-maker with material. We hear of ' an old pedigree of the family, bearing date 1639,' [92] in which it may have made its appearance, but I cannot trace it ' in being ' till after the Restoration, more than twenty years later. It is not, as I have said, till then that the form ' Granville ' begins to be used. Dugdale, who usually received such stories with caution, accepts in his *Baronage* (ii, 479) the descent from Rollo, through ' Hamo Dentatus . . . who was Earl of Corboil ' ; but he only cites for this the family's pedigree (' Ex stemmate '), and he was bound, I presume, by the King's acceptance of the story.

Great as was the favour bestowed on Sir John ' Granville ' and his brothers under Charles II, the actual part taken by Sir John in the Restoration of the King was less potent to obtain it than his lucky relationship to George Monk, the prime agent in that event. The King's lasting gratitude to ' the General ' who had enabled him to return and the greatness of Monk's reward contrast strangely with Charles' neglect of those who had fought and suffered in his father's cause. Among the latter, Sir Bevill Grenville had pre-eminently deserved well of the Crown, but his sons relied rather on their kinship to that soldier of fortune, whose skill and caution had succeeded in removing the apparently insuperable obstacle presented by Cromwell's army to the triumph of the Royal cause.

The two families were on excellent terms, and George Monk's brother, Nicholas, had been presented by Sir John Grenville to the good living of Kilkhampton. When the Restoration pitchforked Nicholas into the see of Hereford, Sir John gave the living to his younger brother, Dennis, who promptly succeeded, however, in obtaining fatter preferment.[93]

[92] *Hist. of the Granville Family*, p. 26.
[93] See p. 143 above.

Family Origins

The relationship of the Grenvilles and the Monks was this :

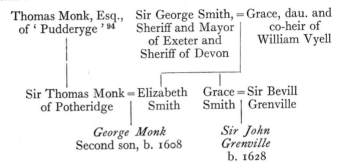

Thomas Monk, Esq., of ' Pudderyge ' [94]	Sir George Smith, Sheriff and Mayor of Exeter and Sheriff of Devon	=	Grace, dau. and co-heir of William Vyell

Sir Thomas Monk of Potheridge	=	Elizabeth Smith	Grace Smith	=	Sir Bevill Grenville

George Monk Second son, b. 1608			*Sir John Grenville* b. 1628

The Monks of Potheridge, though not wealthy, were a family of great antiquity ; so early as 1183, ' Willelmus Monachus de Puderigge ' is found on the Pipe Roll under Devon, and when George Monk, originally but a younger son, soared to a dukedom, the barony of ' Monk of Potheridge ' was chosen as a minor title. The lordly addition of ' Beauchamp and Teyes ' exposed him no doubt, to ridicule, but he was careful to secure in the preamble of his patent, a recital of his female descent from the Beauchamps, Earls of Warwick, the title of whose English earldom was then borne by the Riches, but whose Norman Comté of Aumale in its quaint Latin form of ' Albemarle ' became the style of his dukedom.

The position of the cousins was wholly changed by the events of 1660, and though Sir John Grenville was created Earl of Bath (1660), the duke was now the great man. It

[94] Thomas Monk was so described in the inscription to his widow, ' Catherine Monke, gentlewoman,' who died 2nd of Nov. 1595, on her tomb in Parkham Church, Devon.' It appears that (in a spirit, perhaps of economy . . .) one Roger Gyffard, of Halsbury, thought proper to have this lady's tombstone raised, turned it over, and on the reverse had inscribed the names of his two wives . . . and his daughter.' (*Fourth Report on Hist. MSS.* p. 469.) This was only discovered in the last century. The above Roger was the second son of that great Devon cavalier, Col. John Giffard of Brightleigh, who led the pikemen of Devon to battle at the ' Granville ' victory of Lansdown Hill and, whose eldest son was Lord Halsbury's direct ancestor.

was he who obtained from Charles II in 1661 the extra-ordinary warrant promising the reversion of his dukedom, should his male-issue become extinct, to the Earl of Bath, and his son, the second duke, renewed this request to the Crown. The earl, hoping to succeed to the whole Monk inheritance, wrote to the latter in his later days, in this servile strain :

... that I may kiss your Grace's hands at London ... and will be always ready to observe your commands ... with all other due respect to your Grace. ... My wife joins me in the presentment of our most humble services to my Lady Duchess and your Grace.[95]

The wretched Duke did his best to make his elderly cousin heir to the Newhall estate,[96] bestowed on his father at the Restoration, but his famous mad Duchess had other views. When she had got him safe in Jamaica, she induced him, possibly in one of his drinking bouts, to execute a fresh will (4th July, 1687) increasing the provision for herself and leaving most of his estate to a kinsman, Colonel Thomas Monk, whom he asked the King to create Lord Monk of Potheridge. Shortly afterwards he died (6th October, 1688).

Although Lord Bath welcomed the Prince of Orange and took an active part in supporting the Revolution, he does not seem to have sought from William the dukedom of Albemarle,[97] and the title was conferred as an earldom on that King's favourite, Keppel, in 1697.

The Earl had enough to do with his struggle to secure the estate left to him by the Duke's earlier will. For many years this ruinous contest was fought with bitter obstinacy.

[95] *Buccleugh MSS.* (Hist. MSS. Com.), i, 345 (Letter of 1686).

[96] In Boreham, Essex, his father-in-law, the Duke of Newcastle, described Newhall, in 1684, as the best house, the best seat, and the best furnished of any subject's house in the kingdom and ... more convenient for anybody that takes physic than if it was within four miles of London. *Ibid.* p. 340.

[97] A Dukedom of Albemarle was bestowed on his Jacobite nephew, George, Lord Landsdown (see p. 142), in 1721 by ' King James III,' in avowed fulfilment of Charles II's promise.

On the one side were the Duchess (with her second husband, the Duke of Montagu [98]) and Colonel Monk ; on the other, the Earl of Bath and Sir Walter Clarges (nephew to the first Duke of Albemarle's low-born wife). A further complication was introduced by the allegation that this wife when she married the duke had a husband living,[99] and that consequently, Christopher, the second duke, was illegitimate. This point was raised by the real heirs of the Restoration duke, namely, the descendants of his elder brother, Thomas, who had left a daughter, Mrs. Pride.

So late as 1703 Sir Walter Clarges was furiously denouncing this allegation and apparently endeavouring to influence a jury before whom the case was to come.

' The last of this month, I am to have another trial with Sherwin, upon that scandalous attempt of bastardising the last Duke of Albemarle, to try whether Christopher, the late Duke, or Mr. Sherwin, is right heir to Duke George, and whether the present duchess, if she be still living, was and is, Duchess of Albemarle, or only my Lady Elizabeth Radford.[1]

This scandalous case, they have four times brought on already, and as often miscarried in such their vile pretensions . . . a reproach to Westminster Hall and a scandal to common justice, that the memory of people so long after their deaths, and people of such consideration to[o] should undergo such barbarous

---

[98] He married her in 1691, after wooing her to gratify her craze, as the Emperor of China !

[99] This appears from the evidence of the cases of Sherwin *v.* Sir Walter Clarges (1700) and Pride *v.* Earl of Bath (1 Salkeld, 120). She was daughter of John Clarges, a farrier in the Savoy. This ' Madame Sans Gene ' was sempstress to Monk, used to bring him his linen, and married him early in 1653, when the death of her first husband, Thomas Radford, a farrier, was apparently not proved. The same point was raised in a recent peerage case, the claim to the barony of Fitz Warine, in which it was unsuccessfully attempted to displace the marriage of Sir Bourchier Wrey, seventh baronet, to ' a beautiful Irish nursemaid '— Burke called her ' Mrs. Ellen Riddle widow '—on the ground that her former husband was living at the time.

[1] The meaning of this is that if Duke Christopher was a bastard, he was only entitled to his mother's married name of Radford. His wife, Lady Elizabeth Cavendish, was kept shut up by her second husband so that it was doubted if she were alive. Hence the words ' if she be living.' At his death in 1709, Lord Glenorchy applied from Edinburgh for ' the keeping of her ' as profitable for him.

reflections, when nothing like it was ever brought in question during the course of their whole lives.

All he asked of his correspondent was ' to speak to two gentlemen of the jury, to be present at the trial.' He would be ' mighty glad,' he said, to trust his fate ' in the hands of men of their fortunes and credit, since I am satisfied my adversaries are supported and countenanced by another noble Lord who would come at the Duke of Albemarle's estate any way although he is of kin to it by none.' [2]

The last will of Duke Christopher had led not only to the bitter struggle for what was left of his estate, but to a clandestine marriage. So curious and so typical of one of the scandals of the age was the story of this marriage that it seems worth telling. The Colonel Monk, whom we have seen associated with the Duke's widow in the lawsuit, had a son and heir, whose prospects led him to be entrapped into a marriage from which, at the ripe age of fourteen, he asked the House of Lords to relieve him. According to the preamble of ' Monk's Marriage Bill ' (July 1689)

Christopher Monk, the eldest son and heir of Col. Thomas Monk, being placed about October with one, Mr. Foubeart near the Haymarket, for education [3] by the directions of the trustees of Christopher, late Duke of Albemarle, . . . and it being reported that he had left Christopher Monk most of his estate after the death of the Duchess, one Mathew Hungerford, of Lime Street, London, a pastry-cook, insinuated himself into young Christopher's acquaintance, and by frequently enviting him to his house and giving him small sums of money, got into his good opinion and afterwards seduced him to meet him at a tavern on 12 February last, where having made Christopher drink to excess,

[2] Letters of 12th April, 1703. *Duke of Portland's MSS.* (Hist. MSS. Com.), ii, 183-4.

[3] This is referred to by Sir John Reresby, in Feb. 1681-2, as ' Monsieur Faubert's academy in London.' . . . ' A gentleman that kept the French academy in London, one Monsieur Faubert' (*Memoirs*, pp. 237, 240). Its name is preserved in Foubert's Passage, Regent Street. Evelyn wrote, 18th Dec., 1684, of going ' to see the young gallants do their exercise, M. Faubert having newly railed in a *ménage* and fitted it up for the academy. There were the Dukes of Norfolk and Northumberland, Lord Newburgh, and Duras, a nephew of Lord Feversham.'

Mathew and his wife and daughter Sarah, with others, their confederates, carried him to Pancras Church, and by the wife Mary, personating and pretending to be his mother, they procured him to be married to their daughter Sarah . . . and afterwards sent Christopher back to Mr. Foubeart, charging him to stay there as before, and frequently bribed Christopher by money and promises, not to discover what had been done for six or seven years, by which means the matter was concealed for two months from Christopher's relations and friends, and the exact time of his attaining the age of fourteen years elapsed, without his making any solemn renunciation of his marriage, which, in strictness of law, he was bound to do.

Curious evidence was given before the House of Lords Committee. Sir Charles Porter, Counsel for the 'pastry-cook,' asserted that ' Mr. Hungerford ' was a gentleman of the ancient family of Hungerfords, and had been a considerable merchant,[4] and his elder brother had £800 a year. It was not proved in evidence that the boy was actually drunk when married, or indeed that he was under fourteen,[5] or that Mrs. Hungerford passed herself off as his mother. On the other hand it was deposed by the clergyman of the first church to which they were taken that he had refused to perform the marriage. Two witnesses stated that ' they heard Mr. Monk say that he would have £15,000 with Sir Thomas Stringer's daughter, but that he would sooner have this gentlewoman.' The wretched youth vainly protested that ' he cannot own her for his wife, and he shall ever endeavour to get loose from it.' The committee reported against the Bill.[6] One could not have a better illustration of the state of things described by Lecky, when writing of Lord Hardwicke's Marriage Act (1754):

[4] He was probably the Matthew Hungerford of Reigate, Surrey, gent, who had licence 2nd Sept. 1668, to marry Sarah, dau. of Abraham Browne of Charlton, Kent.

[5] His father had licence to marry Mary Treherne, 16th Aug. 1673, and married her next day. Christopher seems to have been born 25th Feb. 1673-4.

[6] *House of Lords MSS.* (Hist. MSS. Com. Twelfth Report, app. vi, pp. 220-223).

The Granvilles and the Monks

In such a state of the law atrocious abuses had grown up. . . . Young and inexperienced heirs, fresh from college or even from school, were thus continually entrapped. A passing frolic, the excitement of drink, an almost momentary passion, the deception or intimidation of a few unprincipled confederates were often sufficient to drive or inveigle them into sudden marriages, which blasted all the prospects of their lives.[7]

[7] *England in the eighteenth century.*

THE MAULEVERER CONCOCTION AND OTHERS

THE pedigree of the Mauleverer family, which was compiled, or rather concocted, in 1591, was one of those great armorial rolls which are so typical of the period, and to it was appended the official seal of Lancaster Herald.[1] For two reasons this pedigree is deserving of special attention. In the first place, it illustrates the amazing lengths to which an official herald would go in spinning a pedigree of great elaboration, marriages and all, from his own brain. In the second, it contrasts in strange fashion with the scrupulously truthful and painstaking pedigree which the Yorkshire squire, for whom it was made, constructed for himself from his own evidences some ten years later. The latter pedigree agrees, moreover, with that which he entered at the Yorkshire Visitation of 1584-5, which was made by that estimable herald, Glover, Somerset, some six or seven years before Paddy's[2] performance.

We might divide perhaps into four classes the bulk of spurious pedigrees. There are those that rested on garbled versions of perfectly genuine documents, such as Philpot, the herald, was an adept at constructing,[3] those which rested on alleged transcripts of wholly imaginary documents,[4] those which rested on actual forgeries expressly concocted for the purpose,[5] and lastly, those which rested on nothing

---

[1] It is printed from the original in *Misc. Gen. et Her.* ii, 77.

[2] Paddy was then Lancaster Herald.

[3] See my criticism of his Pelham and Finch pedigrees.

[4] Such as I have dealt with in my paper on ' The Brodrick Charters ' (see above).

[5] Such as the Lambert Charters dealt with in my paper on ' A great forgery.'

but sheer fantastic fiction. Of these last, the Mauleverer concoction is, if not the best, at least an astounding example.[6]

In 1601 Mr. William Mauleverer of Arncliffe—an estate derived from the marriage of his ancestor with a Colville heiress under Henry VI—sets himself to arrange ' My Petiegree collected and contrived out of myne ancient and new evidences.'[7] He arrives at the conclusion that his ' earliest ancestor ' was a certain Robert Mauleverer, whose son William occurs in deeds, 1336-1348. The Visitation of 1584-5 begins with this same William Mauleverer of Potters Newton living ' 19 Edward III ' (1335-6). So at least two and a half centuries have elapsed since the Conquest before the pedigree begins, and the family, when it does begin, are not of much position. When Lancaster herald set to work he had soon altered all that. He started in the most approved fashion with a knightly Mauleverer at the Conquest.

> Sir Richard Malleverer came into England with William yᵉ Conqueror who maid him master of yᵉ forests, parkes and chaces Trent northward.

Beneath him, on his shield of arms are the three silver greyhounds (levriers). His son, Sir John, marries ' Bendreda, daughter of Sir Henry Hirst, knight,' a ' genuinely armigerous person,' as Mr. Fox-Davies would say, although of the Conqueror's time. For his enviable coat, ' gules, a fess indented or ' has for warrant, at the foot of the roll, ' the official seal of Lancaster Herald.' This knightly pair had three sons, and our herald knows not only their names, but the names and arms of their fathers-in-law, Sir Thomas Gravenor, Sir George Perpoint, and ' Mr. Brigveild esq.' (? *temp*. William Rufus). It is passing strange that he could only invent a name for one of the wives ; for why should his fertile imagination have been exhausted by ' Dianis ' ?

We seek for references and we find none ; we look for

---

[6] It is said to have been exhibited among a collection of old pedigrees, at the rooms of the Society of Antiquaries, in 1862.

[7] *Coll. Gen. et Her.* ii, 78.

dates and we find but one (10 Henry III) in all this precious production. Yet our herald's knowledge enables him to supply, in each generation, the names of the sons and of the daughters, together with the names and the arms of the families into which they married—even in those early days, when family arms were unknown. Nor does his invention cease when the true pedigree begins. It is not till we reach the Robert Mauleverer who was still living in 20 Henry VI, (1441-2) and whose son married the Colville heiress, that we can connect the pedigrees. For the early stages of the true one were too humble for our herald ; he substituted men of knightly rank, for whom he selected wives from ancient Yorkshire houses.

Bad enough was the imaginary pedigree that traced the Yarboroughs to the Conquest, and found their patriarch ensconced in the folios of Domesday Book. But for sheer cold-blooded fiction, for persistent and elaborate inventions, with nothing to suggest it, this pedigree, efficiently sealed as it was by Lancaster Herald, would be difficult to beat. There were, of course, heralds and heralds, and it must not be said that I treat them all as tarred with the same brush. One of the most amusing concoctions so far as imaginary brides are concerned is that which is printed in Joseph Foster's *Yorkshire Visitations*, 1584-5 and 1612, as that of Clervaux. But owing to his tiresome system of combining pedigrees from different sources, it is difficult to say whether it is taken from the 1612 Visitation or who is responsible for it. For we must always remember the College of Arms naturally disclaims responsibility for those Visitations which are found in the British Museum. Still, whoever may have been their ' onlie begetter,' the names are too good to be omitted. The daughter-in-law of the Conqueror's companion,' Sir Hamon Clervaux,' has, alas, no Christian name, but she was the daughter of ' Jordan Busby,' whose arms are duly given. Subsequent brides of the house of Clervaux bore, we find, the delightful names of 'Amaretta,' ' Oswalda,' Timothea,' ' Herodia,' and ' Janathela.'

The Mauleverer Concoction and Others

Hitherto, I believe that modern concoction, the notorious Coulthart pedigree, has been considered to bear the palm for invention. In his article ' The bonny house of Coulthart,'[8] Mr. Oswald Barron, with his merry pen has once more laughed it to scorn. ' Deriving in uninterrupted male succession from the era of Julius Agricola,' the Coultharts derived their origin from ' Coulthartus, a Roman lieutenant, who fought under Julius Agricola at the foot of the Grampian mountains.' It may fairly be said that this pedigree has its pendant in one which, if it does not extend to quite such a remote period, provides us at least in full detail with an ' uninterrupted male succession ' from the first century of the Christian era.

William Mauleverer, who signed their true pedigree in 1584, was the genealogist of the family ; but it would have been extraordinary indeed had he escaped the temptations of his age. His waverings have their interest. In 1581, at the age of twenty-four, he prefixes some verses to the well-known fiction, which generally passes as the pedigree of Mauleverer. In 1584, he signs the true pedigree in the Visitation of Yorkshire. The fictitious pedigree is in fact brought down to 1587, and in 1591, it is emblazoned on vellum, certified ' *par me, Lancaster Harold at Arms* ' and sealed with that unscrupulous herald's coat. In 1601, at the age of forty-five, Mauleverer reverts to the truth and elaborates with proofs *in extenso* for every generation ' my pettiegree collected and contrived out of myne ancient and newe evidences.' It had been well had the Elizabethan heralds' contrivances been triumphantly refuted by every family in the same way. From the entry of 1584 it would seem that Mauleverer rather amused himself with the tempter's suggestions than adopted them against the evidence of his own cartulary.[9]

[8] *Ancestor*, No. IV (1903), pp. 61-80.

[9] This article is probably unfinished. There are a few notes at the end, the essential parts of which have been incorporated in the article. —W. P.

THE GARTER PLATES AND PEERAGE STYLES

' GARTER-PLATES,' as they are loosely termed, are the metal plates affixed to the stalls of Knights of the Garter in accordance with one of the statutes of the Order made by Henry VIII. This statute ran thus :

Item, it is agreed, that every Knyght within the yere of his Stallation shall cause to be made a Scauchon of his Armes, and Hachementis in a plate of Metall suche as shall please him, and that it is shall be surely sett upon the back of his Stall. And the other that shall come after shall have their Scochons and Hachements in like manner ; but their plates of Metall nor their Hachements shall not be soo large nor soo greatte as they of the first Founders were, excepte Strangers, which may use their plates and fashions at their pleasure.

These plates, therefore, constitute contemporary records of a stall's successive occupants and of the arms they bore. Their existence has been much more widely known since Sir W. H. St. John Hope produced his notable volume, *The stall plates of the Knights of the Order of the Garter* (1348-1485), in 1901. Their heraldic interest was the subject of that work, and it might be supposed that only for antiquaries would they possess importance.

This supposition, however, would be wrong. My object in this paper is to form an estimate of the value, on the claims to ' baronies by writ,' of the peerage styles which they attribute to the Knights who held the stalls. These elaborate styles begin only at a date later than the period covered by the work mentioned above. It is from about the middle of the sixteenth century that we find a tendency to develop these ornate styles by assigning to the holders of the stalls, as minor dignities, baronies which either had never existed or were not theirs by right. But this anticipates the conclusions which I hope to establish.[1]

Neither in Cruise's well-known work nor in Sir Francis Palmer's *Peerage Law in England* (1907) can we find any mention of the use in peerage cases of these plates as evidence. A period, however, of no less than 220 years is covered by those cases in which their evidence has been used. As recently as 1912, the Printed Case on behalf of the claimant to the barony of Furnivall, contained an illustration of the stall-plate of Henry, Duke of Norfolk (1685), which was taken from the Mowbray and Segrave case, which was vouched as proof of the proposition that he ' was styled Lord Furnivall.' And in 1692, on the claim to the barony of Howard of Walden,[2] three stall-plates were adduced on behalf of the Earl of Suffolk, to prove that the baronies by writ did not pass away with heirs-general, but were retained by the heir-male, if he were an earl, with his earldom. Incidentally one may observe that this, which is known as the doctrine of attraction, was a strange doctrine to advance as late as 1692. The arguments in the Howard of Walden case seem to have been unknown to the writers of our text books, for Cruise considered that the doctrine that an earldom attracted a barony was entirely exploded, at latest in the Fitz Walter case (1668), and seems to be followed in this by Sir Francis Palmer [3] (p. 164). It is certainly remarkable that in the Fitz Walter case the judges report (in 1626) on the three baronies claimed by the Earl of Oxford as heir-male, was most properly cited as decisive on the question (Collins, p. 287). Yet in 1692 it was argued anew, as we have seen.

[1] I have already touched upon this subject in my paper on ' The abeyance of the barony of Mowbray.' (*Studies in Peerage and Family History*.)

[2] *House of Lords MSS.* (Thirteenth Report on Hist. MSS. Com. part v, pp. 486-7).

[3] Sir Francis dates the case 1660 and cites a wrong place in Collins' book. The case seems to have been decided in 1670.

Indeed, although the decision on the Earl of Oxford's baronies was then, as it is now, familiar to antiquaries and students, we find the wrongful assumption by the earls of these baronies, in spite of that decision, actually treated as evidence that they continued to possess them. The statement takes this form :

The Baronies, notwithstanding, accompanied the Earldom, and Aubrey de Vere, the present Earl of Oxford, when installed Knight of the Garter, with the title of Earl of Oxford, . . . also proclaimed his baronies of Bolebec, Sanford and Badelesmer in the presence of the King, and [these] are also engraven upon his plate at the back of his stall at Windsor, which we do esteem also a precedent.

The allegation as to the stall-plate is perfectly correct ; the earl is there described as ' Aubrie comte d'Oxford, baron Bulbec, Samford, et Balidismere . . . enstalle le quinziesme jour d'Avril 1661.' [4] There could not well be a clearer case of dignities which had been ascertained not to be vested in a certain earl being formally attributed to his son and successor by proclamation ' in the presence of the King ' and upon his stall-plate.

Let us take the next ' precedent ' of those invoked in 1692. The Earl of Derby, Lord Stanley, Strange of Knocking and of the Isle of Man,' who had died in 1594, leaving three daughters and co-heiresses, had been succeeded in the earldom by his heir-male.

The Baronies, notwithstanding, were used and enjoyed by William, Earl of Derby, brother and heir-male to the said Ferdinand, and being chosen Knight of the Garter (at his installation, according to the custom) the said William's titles and stile were proclaimed in the presence of Queen Elizabeth in 1601, which were William Stanley, Earl of Derby, Lord Stanley, Strange of Knocking and of the Isle of Man, and were also engraven upon his plate under his armes at the back of his stall, and continue still to be used by the present Earl of Derby, without the least dispute which we do esteem a good precedent.

[4] I take all these stall-plate inscriptions from Pote's *History and Antiquities of Windsor Castle* (1749).

Here again the allegation as to the stall-plate is correct. It is only right, however, to add this, though the baronies were really vested in the late Earl's three daughters in 1601,[5] it had not been ' ascertained ' so early that this was the law, and indeed, in 1628 the then earl's son and heir was actually summoned as Lord Strange, under the erroneous supposition that this barony was vested in his father.

The third of the precedents cited in 1692 was that of the Earl of Rutland, who was allowed in 1616 by James I to style himself Lord Ross of Hamlake, Trusbut and Belvoir,' while the heir-general was confirmed in the ancient barony of Roos. It is alleged of the earl that when ' installed Knight of the Garter, his style was proclaimed in the King's presence, and engraven also upon his plate set up at the back of his stall at Windsor, with the Baronies of Rosse of Hamlake, Trusbutt and Belvoir.'

The statement as to the stall-plate cannot be verified, as it seems to be absent from Pote's work. There is no reason, however, to doubt the allegation, for it is also found in Collins' well-known *Proceedings, Precedents,* etc. (p. 213). This ' precedent,' however, is not of much consequence. The only one, indeed, of real importance is that of the Earl of Oxford's baronies. But my object has been to show that the inscriptions on these ' garter-plates ' were invoked as evidence in a peerage case, even so far back as 1692.

From this case I now pass to that of the earldom of Shrewsbury (7 H.L.C.), decided in 1858, and that of the barony of Berkeley (8 H.L.C.), decided in 1861. In the former the evidence of a ' garter-plate ' seems to have been admitted to prove the identity of a particular person, but not admitted as proof of a peerage style. In consequence of this ruling the evidence of a ' garter-plate ' had to be withdrawn from the Berkeley case, though the redoubtable Mr. Fleming, who was engaged as counsel in that case, appears to have disputed the fact when it was duly recalled in the Mowbray and Segrave case (1877).

[5] That is to say, if they were all indeed baronies, as Strange was.

M 177

This case to which I now come is by far the most important in its bearing upon these stall-plates as evidence of peerage styles. I have persistently and rigorously criticised the decision, on that occasion, of the Committee for Privileges, and the evidence and the reasoning on which it was based. Here I shall deal only with the weight attached by the committee to the evidence of two stall-plates as proof of the peerage styles. The Petitioner's object was to prove that the abeyance of the baronies of Mowbray and Segrave had been determined at an early date in favour of the Howards, one of whose co-heirs he was. As the evidence of this determination was by no means satisfactory,[6] his counsel endeavoured to eke it out by citing two stall-plates. The first of these bore the inscription :

Thomas Howard, comte d'Arundell et Surrey, seigneur Howard, Fitzallen, Mavtravers, Mowbray, Segrave, Bruse et Clun, chevalier de tres noble ordre de la jartierre, enstallé le 13 jour de May 1611, en la presence du roy et du prince du Gaules.

The second was that of the Duke of Norfolk who was installed in 1685. Its inscription ran :

Henry Duc de Norfolc, et Conte Marefcal D'Angleterre Conte d'Arvndel, Svrrey, Norfolc et Norwich, Baron MOW-BRAY, Howard, SEGRAVE, Brvse (de Gower,) Fitzalan, Warren, Clvn, Oswaldestre, Maltravers, Greystock, Fvrnival, Verdon, Lovetot, Strange (de Blackmere) et Howard (de Castle Rysing). . . . Enstallé au Chasteau de Windsor le xxii jour de Juliet l'an M.DC.LXXX.V.

The second of these inscriptions is of special importance, not merely on account of its elaborate character, but also because the word ' baron ' is more emphatic than ' seigneur ' and must denote a peerage barony and no mere feudal lordship.

In these inscriptions, I have placed ' Mowbray ' and ' Segrave ' in capital letters for the convenience of the

---

[6] See my paper on ' The determination of John Mowbray abeyance ' in *The Law Quarterly Review*, vol. x, p. 37, and *Studies in Peerage and Family History*, p. 435.

reader. In the Mowbray and Segrave case the question as to these stall-plates was whether they were, or were not, evidence that these two baronies were rightly vested in these nobles among whose titles the above inscriptions record them. If they did prove the fact, then the abeyance of these two baronies must have been determined in favour of the Howard co-heirs in or before the year 1611.

What then is the test, the obvious test, that anyone trained to deal critically with documentary evidence—might I not almost say that any intelligent man—would apply to these inscriptions ? He would examine, in the first place, their internal evidence. That is to say, he would set himself to ascertain if they were trustworthy by examining the other peerage styles which they assign to the Earl of Arundel in 1611 and to the Duke of Norfolk in 1685. If they proved to be untrustworthy in respect to any of these, it is obvious that they might be so also in respect to the styles of Mowbray and Segrave. But, if he wished to establish his conclusion upon a broader basis, he would undertake a general examination of the stall-plates of the sixteenth and seventeenth centuries in order to make a thorough test of the value of such evidence. But was this test, this obvious test, applied in the Mowbray and Segrave case, either by the Attorney-General or by the Law Lords on the Committee ? It does not seem to have even occurred to them that the evidence should be so tested. We shall see below that what led them to attach importance to this evidence was no test at all, but simply what they thought probable, in other words, mere speculation, or, to put it bluntly, guesswork. In this, however, they doubtless acted in accordance at least with the principle on which is based the law as to the evidence of ' inscriptions,' as stated in the works of Cruise and Sir Francis Palmer. That principle is mere presumption, and the result, in this case, of acting upon it affords grim comment on the legal conception of evidence, on the legal idea of proof.

The ' garter-plate ' evidence was presented to the

committee by Mr. Fleming, petitioner's counsel, as follows :

In the Garter-plate which your Lordships will find facing page 266 of the Minutes, the person restored is styled ' Seigneur Howard, Fitz-Alan, Maltravers, Mowbray, Segrave,' and so on.

(*Lord Chancellor.*) What is this Garter-plate ?

(*Mr. Fleming.*) It is the Garter-plate erected upon his installation as a Knight of the Garter and made by the Garter King-at-Armes in pursuance of his duty as Garter King-at-Armes.

(*Lord Chancellor.*) Erected in St. George's Chapel ?

(*Mr. Fleming.*) Yes ; the tracing was brought here from thence.

(*Lord Chancellor.*) At what date was that ?

(*Mr. Fleming.*) In 1611. Seven years after the Act of Restoration.

Of the Duke of Norfolk's stall-plate Mr. Fleming observed that :

He was elected a Knight of the Garter in 1685 ; and upon his Garter-plate again the titles of Mowbray, Howard, Segrave, and Braose of Gower are repeated.

(*Lord Chancellor.*) At what page is that ?

(*Mr. Fleming.*) The Garter-plate is facing page 203 ; it also was copied from St. George's Chapel at Windsor. He is styled ' premier Duc, Conte et Baron D'Angleterre.' I do not know whether it would be possible to have stronger evidence.

Counsel's meaning appears to have been that the words ' premier . . . baron ' refer to the barony of Mowbray.

The Lord Chancellor, who seems, from the above passages, to have paid special attention to this evidence, interrupted the address of the Attorney-General by calling his attention to the subject.

(*Lord Chancellor.*) What have you to say as regards the Garter-plate or Garter-plates ? There are two of them I think.

(*The Attorney-General.*) With regard to the Garter-plates, I should have thought that they were evidence, but it seems to have been decided in the Berkeley case that Garter-plates were not evidence.

(*Lord Chancellor.*) Not evidence of what ?

(*The Attorney-General.*) Not evidence of the description of the person ; that is to say, supposing upon a Garter-plate a particular nobleman is described as having a particular title, the Garter-plate is not evidence of that. I will read to your Lordships what was said about it in the Berkeley case. I find my learned friend Mr. Fleming was in that case, and he offered a tracing of the arms and inscription on a plate erected in St. George's Chapel, Windsor, for James Earl of Berkeley, on his installation as Knight of the Garter, on the 30th of April, 1718. This was tendered in evidence but objected to. My learned friend Mr. Fleming says that such a piece of evidence was admitted in the Shrewsbury case.

(*Lord Chancellor.*) What was it tendered for ?

(*Mr. Fleming.*) To show the styles.

(*The Attorney-General.*) Your Lordships will see when I read a line or two further on. My learned friend Mr. Fleming said that it was offered to prove the style by which he was described on his election as Knight of the Garter. The Committee thought that it was not admissible. In the Shrewsbury case it was admitted as proof of the Pedigree.

At this point I break off in order to draw attention to Mr. Fleming's statement that the ' garter-plate ' was ' made by the Garter King-at-Armes in pursuance of his duty as Garter King-at-Armes.' We saw at the outset that the statute of Henry VIII directed the newly-elected knight to cause to be made a plate ' as shall please him ' and does not even mention Garter in connection with the matter. Nor did Mr. Fleming adduce any evidence as to the alleged practice in 1611. When a dispute arose at this point as to what had really taken place in the Berkeley case, the responsible officer of the House observed that :

From that time downwards it has been supposed that a Garter-plate being a mere statement of the Peer of the time, and not being made officially or under that obligation which is imposed upon Peers when they present their Pedigrees to the House, did not obtain an official sanction.

(*Lord Chancellor.*) That makes it rather more important to know what I asked just now, namely, what was the precise point that it was tendered to prove in that case.

(*The Attorney-General.*) There is very little said about it.

My learned friend Mr. Fleming says : ' It is offered to prove the style by which he was described on his election as Knight of the Garter.'

(*Lord Chancellor.*) What style ? Perhaps it was offered to prove that he was an Earl ; it would not prove that he was an Earl ; that is not the way to prove that a man is an Earl. But supposing it is offered to prove this in a case where a Peerage is in abeyance between two co-heirs, and where the sovereign has the right to determine that abeyance in any formal mode the Sovereign likes, that, in the face of the Sovereign, in the chapel which is the peculiar chapel of the Order of which the Sovereign is the chief, there is a plate put up visible to the Sovereign's eyes, and remaining there with an inscription upon it which is tantamount to saying that the abeyance has been determined in favour of one of the co-heirs ; is not that a very strong piece of evidence, after all the parties are dead, that in some way or other, of the sufficiency of which the Sovereign is satisfied, the abeyance has been determined ?

(*The Attorney-General.*) I should have thought so but for that decision in the Berkeley case.

(*Lord Chancellor.*) That decision may not in the least degree interfere with it. I cannot imagine that a Garter-plate would be evidence that a particular person had a particular title of honour, not coming by way of the determination of an abeyance, but coming specially to the person mentioned ; it would be no evidence of that.

(*The Attorney-General.*) I should have thought that if a Garter-plate is put up in St. George's Chapel, Windsor, and that Garter-plate states upon the face of it that the person whose plate it is, has a particular title, and courts denial to that statement in the very place where it would be seen by the Sovereign and those who would be interested in the facts, that would be evidence.

Let us consider for a moment what this reasoning involves. We are dealing with that seventeenth century in the course of which our peerage law was slowly taking form—or, as a lawyer might say, was being ' ascertained.' The very doctrine of abeyance, as is well recognised by those who have written on the subject, was so imperfectly established that the judges even so late as the year 1626 stated the law ' in terms which would certainly now be regarded as

erroneous or misleading.'[7] Nevertheless, Lord Cairns—
and, we shall see, Lord Blackburn—to say nothing of the
Attorney-General, seem to have discovered by that light of
nature which may prove so dangerous a guide, that, as early
as 1611, the king would examine as an expert the styles in
an inscription on a stall-plate, to satisfy himself whether it
implied that an abeyance had been determined either by
him or by his predecessors—in accordance with a doctrine
which had not even, at that time, taken form.   More than
three centuries have elapsed since that date, and yet, though
we possess to-day incomparably greater facilities, it is not
by any means an easy task to disentangle the peerage
styles in these stall-plate inscriptions or to trace their origin
and history.   Some, like the Earl of Oxford's baronies, had
passed away from the family ; some were still in abeyance ;
others, again, had never existed as peerage baronies at all.
But the task which would have baffled even an expert
presented no difficulty in Lord Cairns' view, to the king ;
the Lord's anointed, as he deemed himself to be, had doubtless received at his hallowing, this miraculous gift, together
of course with the power of healing ' the King's evil.'

We will now resume the quotation from the Mowbray
and Segrave minutes.

(*Lord Chancellor.*) Supposing you had proved a petition to
the Sovereign, which stated to the Sovereign : ' Your Majesty
has been graciously ' pleased to determine the abeyance in favour
of the Petitioner ;   your ' Petitioner gratefully expresses his
thanks,' and supposing it was proved that the petition was
presented to the sovereign and was received by the Sovereign,
would it not be evidence that the abeyance had been determined ?

(*The Attorney-General.*) My own view is that it would be
evidence and strong evidence ; but finding the decision in the
Berkeley Peerage Case I thought it right to mention it.   I should

---

[7] Palmer, *Peerage Law in England*, p. 101. The learned writer
observes that these and their points in the law relating to the abeyance
have only come to be settled by slow degrees—some of them by decisions
as late as the nineteenth century. See also Pike, *Constitutional History
of the House of Lords*, pp. 131-138, where it is contended that the ' earliest
case, in which anything like the doctrine of the abeyance was recognised
was, it is almost certain . . . in the reign of Charles II.'

think that it would be evidence, and if so . . . my learned friend's noble client would have the evidence of the Garter-plates in two cases in which one and another of his ancestors are described as Lord of Mowbray and Segrave, showing that in some way or other the abeyance must have been determined in favour of that noble family.

All this, the reader will observe, is mere supposition and guesswork. Of any attempt to test the evidence there is not a trace. Now both the stall-plates in question include among the dignities they name the barony of ' Bruse.' Better known as Braose (although derived from Briouze in Normandy). This was the name of that baronial house which was Lord of the Sussex Rape of Bramber, where Bramber Castle preserves its fame. The last Braose was summoned to Parliament from 1299 to 1322, but if a barony was vested in him, it fell into abeyance at his death in 1326. How was the Sovereign to know in 1611, or indeed in 1685, whether there had been a peerage barony, and, if so, whether and when it had been called out of abeyance ? As a matter of fact, no one, I believe, has ever suggested that it was. Again, ' Verdon ' is among this style on the plate of 1685— in the case of this barony also there had been summonses (to two barons) between 1299 and 1307 ; but if a peerage barony was created it had been in abeyance since 1316. How was the King to know, *proprio motu suo*, in 1685, whether there had ever been a peerage barony of the name, and, if so, whether and when it had been called out of abeyance. Was it by divine afflatus ?

Are we to gather from the decision in the Mowbray and Segrave case that these stall-plates are evidence that the abeyance believed to exist in the baronies of Braose and Verdon has been determined ? If not, how could they be held to afford such evidence in the case of ' Mowbray ' and ' Segrave ' ? But, as it might be urged that Braose and Verdon are not proved peerage baronies and were therefore, wrongly included, we will take a decisive case of a peerage barony in abeyance. The Nevill barony of Latimer is well known to have fallen into abeyance in the year 1577.

The Percy heirs of Northumberland were its senior co-heirs and, as is justly observed in Courthope, 'have been frequently but erroneously styled Barons Latimer.' Earl Algernon (1632-1668) became a Knight of the Garter in 1635, and his stall-plates styled him 'Baron Percy, Lucy, Poynings, Fitz-Pain, Brian et *Latimer*.' Of all this gallant array, Percy was the only barony to which the earl was entitled ! Here, however, I am not concerned with any of these styles but Latimer. Some years ago Mr. Francis Coutts claimed to be a co-heir to this barony, then, it was alleged, in abeyance. His claim was established and the barony was ' called out ' in his favour. What then becomes of the garter-plate evidence that the barony had been called out of abeyance in favour of the Earls of Northumberland between 1577 and 1635 ? The period is here narrowed down to fifty-eight years and it was relatively easy to ascertain when the stall-plate was made, whether the abeyance of the barony had indeed been determined. Yet the evidence to which Lord Cairns attached so much importance and which the Attorney-General thought ' strong evidence ' is here proved to be worthless.

The whole trouble arises from the fact that the Law Lords and the Attorney-General applied to this evidence the wrong test. They ' thought ' as a matter of speculation, that it ought to be good : if they had tested its statements, they would have found that it was bad. The former, in their judgments, gave their reasons as follows :

(*Lord Chancellor.*) . . . I think that that is very much fortified by two Garter-plates, which on a question of this kind, without saying how far on other questions Garter-plates can be evidence, appear to me, put up as they are in St. George's Chapel, the Chapel of the Order of which the Sovereign is the head, very strong evidence that in some way or other the Sovereign had terminated the abeyance of the Barony.

(*Lord O'Hagan.*) . . . I wish to say that I agree with my noble and learned friend also in this ; under these circumstances and for the purpose I cannot conceive that these Garter-plates should not be admissible in evidence. A Garter-plate is a thing of a very remarkable and striking character ; it is used on a very solemn occasion ; it may have been put up in the presence of the Sovereign himself or herself—at all events it has remained in a place where its existence and effect must have been fully known to all persons about the Court of the Sovereign.

(*Lord Blackburn.*) . . . It is quite clear that the mere fact that a Duke of Norfolk put upon his Duchess' coffin-plate a statement that she was the wife of the Lord Mowbray and Segrave, is no evidence at all.[8] But when you come lower down to the two Garter-plates it is a more serious business. I think that those Garter-plates put up solemnly at the installation of a Knight of the Garter in the presence (for, I think, we must take it to have been in the presence) of the Sovereign that the person holds those titles ; and when the King, for the time being, saw the Garter-plates put up (and we must take it that he did see them) and did nothing to repudiate that assertion, it is strong evidence, what one may call circumstantial evidence, that the Crown did tacitly assent to the claim to possess those titles thus asserted.

The only difference between the Law Lords seems to have been that, while Lord O'Hagan considered the Letters Missive of Richard III to be of themselves sufficient evidence that the abeyance had been determined, the Lord Chancellor, who took the same view, considered their evidence to be very much fortified ' by the very strong evidence ' of the Garter-plates, Lord Blackburn doubting if the Garter-plates would be by themselves decisive, but holding the Letters Missive to be quite conclusive upon the matter.'

My own point is that the stall-plates are neither ' strong evidence ' nor, indeed, evidence at all. This indeed was the view taken by Lord Redesdale, who was in the chair and who observed :

As to the Garter-plate, I confess I do not think it is very strong evidence of anything but what Garter-King-at-Armes chose to think at the time, and if you accept what Garter thinks at any particular moment as being the fact in regard to a Peerage, I think you admit him to a higher position with reference to the determination of Peerages than he ought to have, in fact you put him on an equality with the decisions of the Committee for

[8] What Lord Blackburn imagined to be a coffin-plate inscription was a formal ' funeral certificate,' and, as such, evidence.

Privileges. I therefore, myself, do not accept that as evidence with regard to determination of the abeyance.

The conclusion is sound, but it is not based upon the strongest ground of all, namely, that the styles of baronies found on these stall-plates are absolutely untrustworthy and represent merely the 'plumes of honour' with which certain nobles decked their genuine titles.

Of the Ratcliffes, Earls of Sussex, five in succession (1529-1629) were made Knights of the Garter. All of them are styled on their stall-plates 'seigneur d'Egremont (or Aigremont) et Burnell,' though the barony of Burnell fell into abeyance in 1420 and is not known to have been called out of it, while Multon (of Egremont), if a peerage barony, had been in abeyance since 1334. To two of the earls the barony of Botetourt is also assigned on their stall-plates, though they do not appear to have been even descended from the Lords Botetourt, whose barony, in any case, was not called out of abeyance till 1764. William, Marquis of Northampton, Queen Catherine Parr's brother, who was installed 3rd June, 1559, was styled on his stall-plate, 'Marqvys de Northampton, conte d'Essex, baron de Kendall, seigneur de Marmion, Saint Quintyn et de Parre,' though he is believed to have been only restored (in January preceding) to the marquisate of Northampton. In any case he was not Lord Marmion and St. Quintyn, though he may have been a co-heir, through the Fitz-Hughs, of the Marmions of Witringham. However, his sister and co-heir's descendants, the Herberts, Earls of Pembroke, continued to use these styles, and within four years of his death his nephew Henry, Earl of Pembroke, was installed and styled 'seigneur Marmion et Saint Quentin' on his Garter-plate. The latter's son and successor improved upon this, for, when he became K.G. in 1603, he was styled on his stall-plate 'seigneur Parr et Ross de Candall, Marmion et St. Quintin,' though he was certainly neither Lord Parr nor Lord Roos of Kendall (which is the title intended).

The careful student of peerage history will recognise,

indeed, on these stall-plates, those wrongful assumptions of peerage titles with which he is already familiar. George, Earl of Cumberland, installed in 1592, is styled ' baron Clyfford et de Skypton, seigneur de Westmorland, Vipont, Bromflet et Vesey.' ' Loraine ' is among the baronies included in the styles of Walter, Earl of Essex, in 1572. A prolonged controversy is brought to mind by the attribution of the barony of ' Roos de Hamlake, Trusbut, et de Belvoir ' to two successive Dukes of Rutland on their stall-plates (1714 and 1722). For this barony, which was allowed to the Duke of Rutland and his son, as heirs-male, by a special patent in 1616, is considered to have become extinct in 1632. It was, however, retained among their titles by the dukes [9] well into the latter half of the eighteenth century. The climax, however, is reached, no doubt, in the six baronies assigned to the Earl of Northumberland in 1635 when he was only entitled to one of them.[10] It is remarkable that Sir Hugh Smithson's son, the second Duke of Northumberland, is given the styles of all these six baronies in his private divorce act so late as 19 George III,[11] and that they are all also assigned to his mother in the Westminster Abbey Register of burials.

One more instance may be given. The ' Garter-plate ' of that magnificent cavalier, William (Cavendish), Marquis (afterwards Duke) of Newcastle, must have been set up when he was installed, 15th April, 1661. It is pointed out in the *Complete Peerage* (Ed. G.E.C. VI, 22), that among the styles which it attributes to him are the baronies of ' Ogle, Bertram and Bolesover.' He was clearly entitled

[9] See *Complete Peerage* (Ed. G. E. C.), vi, 405, note b, where it is observed that the well-known divorce of John Manners, afterwards (1679) 9th Earl of Rutland, and subsequently (1703) 1st Duke of Rutland, was granted to him in 1669 under the designation of Lord Roos, to which he was not entitled.

[10] When the Latimer case was recently before the House, I thought that attention should be drawn to the quasi-recognition of the Latimer title by the Royal assent to this Act. But it was not done.

[11] The account of his monies spent on this occasion imply that the heralds were present in force. His style would doubtless be proclaimed by them.

to the barony of Ogle as his mother's son and heir, but it is not known in what right he claimed the barony of Bertram.[12] I cannot but think that this is yet another assumption typical of the practice that I am discussing. For the Ogles had owed their importance largely to a marriage with the heiress of the Bertrams of Bothal (not to be confused with the Bertrams of Mitford), who brought to them that castle with the territorial barony. Thence it passed with their own heiress to Cavendish. But there is nothing of this in the *Complete Peerage* of G.E.C., nor is the assumption of the imaginary peerage barony by the Duke mentioned under Bertram in Mr. Gibbs' new edition.

[12] See *Complete Peerage* (as above), where its alleged creation with his marquessate is mentioned and it is stated to be not found among his styles in his monumental inscription.

THE BARONY OF FERRERS OF CHARTLEY[1]

THE complete success of the Crown's contention on the recent claim to the barony of Fitzwarine, with regard to its origin, descent, and precedence, clearly justifies a similar contention on the Ferrers claim, for the two cases resemble each other closely. (*A*) There is no attempt to prove a sitting in the original line of the alleged Lords Fitzwarine or that of the alleged Lords Ferrers, reliance being placed, in both cases, on the fact that the husband of the heiress of the line sat in Parliament. (*B*) In the case of the alleged Lords Fitzwarine there was a continuous absence of writs of summons from that to the 'second lord' in 1336 to that which was produced for the husband of the heiress in 1455.

With regard to the alleged Lords Ferrers there is (according to the Printed Case) a continuous absence of writs of summons from the writ to the 'first lord' in 1311 to that which is produced for the husband of the heiress in 1462. The absence of writs, therefore, in the case of Ferrers extends to no less than 151 years as against 119 years in the case of Fitzwarine.

The Ferrers case is one of those on which great stress was laid in the seventeenth century as proving that though a man might be summoned to Parliament his heirs were not of necessity summoned after him. On such cases Prynne based his contention, in his *Register of Parliamentary Writs*, that writs of summons were not intended to create hereditary dignities. Stubbs, dealing with this contention,

[1] This article is based on Dr. Round's Report to the Treasury Solicitor on the Barony of Ferrers. Dr. Round left a note desiring that this Report should be included in his volume of essays.—W. P.

has suggested that in some cases the cessation of writs might be explained by a minority (*Const. Hist.* 1878, iii, 439 *note*). This might explain the Ferrers case, for, after the death of the first and only ancestor summoned, there were two minorities extending, apparently, from 1312 to 1330.

It should be observed that it has been claimed that the ' second lord ' was summoned in 16 Edward III (1342), but this claim was abandoned, doubtless because it was discovered that the summons of this date (25th February, 1342) was not to a Parliament, but to a Council. This distinction is emphasized by comparing the long list of those summoned to this Council with that of those summoned a year later (24th February, 1343) to a true Parliament.

The absence of writs for a century and a half presents a difficulty, which an attempt has been made to explain away by urging the frequent absence of the alleged lords ' on foreign service.' The answer to the argument is clear ; there was nothing in the fact of a man being summoned to serve, say, against the Scots to prevent his also being summoned to Parliament. A document tested at Newcastle-on-Tyne, 1st July, 9 Edward III (1335), records that Robert de Ferrers, who is about to set out for Scotland with the King, has letters of protection till 1st November following, that is for four months (Scotch Roll, 9 Edward III, m. 27). This document is explained by another, also on the Scotch Roll of 9 Edward III (see *Lords' Reports*, vol. iv. pp. 442-3), which records a summons to Robert de Ferrers, with others, dated at Nottingham 27th March, 1335, to be at Newcastle-on-Tyne on the Trinity Sunday following (11th June). Five days later there were issued, also from Nottingham, writs of summons to a Parliament at York on the morrow of the Ascension (26th May) following. There was obviously nothing to prevent Robert de Ferrers attending at York on that date, on his way to the subsequent muster at Newcastle-on-Tyne, and, as a matter of fact, of the last eighteen names recorded on the Scotch Roll as summoned to that muster, fifteen (including Henry de Ferrers of Groby) were also summoned to the Parliament at York, and only Robert de Ferrers and two others were omitted (*Ibid.* p. 445). *See* Appendix A.

There was also nothing in the fact of his summons to the Scottish campaign to prevent him from being summoned by the writs of 22nd January, 1335-6, to attend the Westminster Parliament of 10th March, 1336 (*Lords' Reports*, vol. iv, p. 454). Although *Henry* de Ferrers, John de Willoughby, Adam de Welle, and the others, who had been summoned to the Scottish campaign, were all, as before, summoned to this Parliament, yet Robert de Ferrers was omitted.

Conversely the summons to his father, John de Ferrers, in 4 Edward II, to attend the muster against the Scots at Berwick on Tweed, on 8th September, 1310, had not precluded his being summoned in the same regnal year by a writ of 16th June to attend a London Parliament at the beginning of the following August (*Lords' Reports*, vol. iv. pp. 202, 206). Nor did the fact that he went to Gascony as seneschal early in 1312 (Gascon Rolls, 5 Edward II, m. 6 : *Cal. of Close Rolls*, 1307-1315, p. 401) preclude his being summoned to Parliament twice in the same regnal year (*Lords' Reports*, vol. iv. pp. 209, 212). Proof is required here, not that an alleged Lord Ferrers served abroad once or twice in the course of his alleged tenure of the dignity, but that his absence was so continuous that he could not have attended any Parliament and was not summoned on that account.

Yet in the case of the ' fourth baron,' who was in possession of the fief and of age from 1353 to 1367, there is only proof of his being abroad on two or three occasions, while in that of the fifth baron, who was of age and in possession for some thirty-two years, there is actually only one document to support the argument, namely, that which proves that on 18th July, 1378 (2 Richard II), he was about to leave England on the King's service and received the usual letters of protection, accordingly, *for a year*. Moreover, ' Robertus

de Ferrers chivaler,' mentioned in 1378, is not identified
with this alleged ' lord,' and appears to be more probably
Robert de Ferrers of Wemme (*jure uxoris*), who was continuously summoned to Parliament from 1375 to 1390, than
his nephew and namesake, Robert de Ferrers (of Chartley),
who was still a minor at the time, being only, apparently,
eighteen, and whose lands were in the King's hands. If
this is so, there disappears the only proof that the latter ever
left England, while, as I have said, there is, in any case, no
such proof, during his thirty-two years of actual possession
(1381-1413).

Edmund, his successor, the ' sixth baron,' was in possession for twenty-two years (1413-1435), and yet only two documents are adduced to prove that he was leaving England,
one of 12th July, 1415, and one of 9th March, 1417-8, these
being obviously for the Agincourt campaign and for the
second invasion of Henry V.   There is nothing to suggest
that Edmund was permanently employed abroad.   As for
William, the ' seventh lord ' (1435-1450), it is not even
suggested that he ever served abroad.   The endeavour to
explain the absence of summonses to all the six alleged lords
after the death of the ' first lord,' by their occasional service
abroad in common with other tenants-in-chief, fails.

With regard to proofs of their sitting, there is none even
alleged ; all that is known is an extract from the Acts of the
Privy Council in which William de Ferrers, ' seventh baron,'
is named among the peers as Lord Ferrers of Chartley.
This may be good evidence of reputation ; it is obviously
not proof of sitting.

The allegation that Walter Devereux was summoned ' in
right of his wife ' rests on even weaker grounds than the
similar allegation in the Fitzwarine case, which was recently
rejected by the Committee.   In the first place the absence
of summonses to his wife's ancestors extends continuously
over a century and a half and over the lives of all the seven
alleged ' lords ' except the first.   In the second place, there
is evidence that Walter Devereux was not summoned to

Parliament till after the accession of Edward IV and then only as one of a batch of new creations bestowed on the King's Yorkist followers. This creation of peers is of historical importance. Stubbs observes that, in consequence of the havoc of the Wars of the Roses, ' the King was already taking measures for replacing the missing dignities with new creations ' (*Const. Hist.* 1878, III, 194). He had originally summoned but one duke and four earls, with thirty-one barons. But about this time he created two dukes, two more earls, and, in one batch, eight barons, none of whom had been summoned before. Their writs were issued simultaneously on 26th July, 1461. These men are known Yorkists, such as Lord Hastings and Lord Herbert. Walter Devereux himself is expressly stated in the grant of 20th February, 1462, to which we are coming, to have been an ardent supporter of Edward against the Lancastrians. (See *Calendar of Patent Rolls*, 1461-7, pp. 153, 486.) As early as 20th July, 1461, before he received his first writ of summons, he had been granted ' the King's brewhouse called " le Walsshman " outside Ludgate,' as ' the King's servant, Walter Devereux of Ferrers, knight.' (*Ibid.* p. 126.) It is obvious that this grant was not made to him *jure uxoris* and that the words ' of Ferrers ' were merely part of his style. When, therefore, a writ was issued to him six days later as ' Walter Devereux of Ferrers, knight ' (*Lords' Reports*, IV, 956), the inference is that the words ' de Ferrers ' were similarly only part of his style, as holder of the Ferrers lands, and in no way involved the fact that he was summoned ' in right of his wife.'

This conclusion is confirmed by actual record evidence. On 20th February, 1462, he received a grant which is printed in the Appendix to the *Lords' Reports* (V, 345), and which is abstracted in English in the official *Calendar of Patent Rolls* (1461-7), p. 153, and again in a fresh and later form on p. 486. This grant is headed on the Roll, ' Pro Waltero Devereux milite,' and in its opening recital he is simply styled ' dilectum militem nostrum Walterum

Devereux.' But the really important point is that the King employs the phrase that he has raised him ' in statum baronie et magnatis nostri,' and that in the later grant of 1466 he again speaks of ' Walter Devereux, king's knight, whom the king has raised to the rank of baron ' (*Cal. of Pat. Rolls*, 1461-7, p. 486).

Now this is exactly the formula which is also applied to Sir William Herbert, seventeen days before, when he received (3rd February, 1462) a grant of lands for his services to the Yorkist cause. The King employs the phrase, ' quem in statum baronis et magnatis regni nostri . . . ereximus' (see Appendix B). As there is no question that Sir Herbert's creation was a new one, the application of the same formula to Sir Walter Devereux implies that his also was new.

As bearing upon this point, the Act of 4 Henry VII (1489) repealing the attainder of this Walter in 1 Henry VII (7th November, 1485) should be very carefully considered. His son John had been summoned to Parliament, 1st September, 1487, and is spoken of in this act as already Lord Ferrers. Yet it is provided by the Act that he and his heirs shall be ' restored, abled, demed, and adjudged to have all suche name of honour, estate, dignite and pre-eminence and the names of the same . . . as by and after the deth of the seid late Lord Ferrers . . . he should have had or done or hereafter shuld doo if the seid acte or actes agenst the same late lord Ferrers had never be made ne hadde.'

It is clear that this cannot refer to the dignity of Lord Ferrers which John already enjoyed (he is styled ' John, Lord Ferrers,' 24th April, 1488, in *Cal. of Inq.* Henry VII, vol. ii, p. 156) in virtue of his writ of summons in 1487, and, as the words clearly refer to a peerage dignity and its precedence, they must relate to a peerage dignity descendible to him from his father (not from his mother) and must have been intended to give him the precedence of the barony created for his father by the writ of 1461.

The obvious objection to this view is, that in 1678, on the

termination of the abeyance, Lord Ferrers was placed 'next below the Lord Berkeley' and above Lord Fitzwalter, who sat as 'the last baron of the reign of King Edward the First' (*Printed Case*, p. 16). Whatever weight ought to be attached to such placing of peers—on which point there is a useful note in *Complete Peerage* (old edition), I, 21—it is certain that no consistent basis for such placing can be discovered. In 1548 Walter (Devereux), Lord Ferrers, who was created Viscount Hereford in 1550, sat below the Lords Dacre of the North and of the South, whose earliest writs of summons were substantially later than the earliest Ferrers writs (*Lords' Journals*, I, 423). It is probable that the placing of 1678 was based upon the records of sitting in the *Journals* from 1478 to 1548, but there is nothing to suggest on what was based the placing of the peer who sat in 1478, for there had been no Ferrers writ since 1311, and not a single sitting on record.

The discrepancy between the precedence of the holders of ancient baronies and the dates of the earliest writs was thus commented upon by Mr. Fleming in the Mowbray and Segrave case (1877) :

'My Lords, it never has been held that the earliest Writ of Summons affords the proof of the precedency of a Peer. Of course, I do not speak of recent writs, but the Writs of Summons of the reigns of the Plantagenet Kings have never been held to be the proof of the creation of a Peerage for the purpose of fixing the precedence. Now, my Lords, the Act of 31st Henry VIII, required the Peers to be placed according to their ancientry that is to say their antiquity. . . . I point out to your Lordships how they sat. Bergavenny is put first. Now there is no writ of Summons to Bergavenny before the 16th of Richard II. The next to him is Audley. There is a Writ of Summons to Lord Audley of the 25th of Edward I. The 16th of Richard II was in 1392, the 25th of Edward I was in 1297, therefore, regarding those two the Writs of Summons were not taken as the guide. Now both Lords Audley and Zouche are placed before Lord Berkeley. Audley was of the 25th Edward I. (I am speaking of the Writs of Summons as they appear in the records.) Zouche was of the 2nd Edward II and Berkeley was of the 23rd Edward

I. Therefore, they were not placed according to the dates of the Writs of Summons. Then Dacre was placed above Cobham. The first Writ to a Dacre was in the 14th Edward II, and the first Writ to a Cobham was in the 6th Edward II. Then Cobham, Maltravers, and Talbot are placed before Ferrers. The first Writ of Summons to a Lord Ferrers was in the 28th Edward I, that is to say, 20 years before Cobham, and nearly 40 years before Maltravers or Talbot. Grey de Wilton was placed after Lord Cobham and several other Peers, though there was a Lord Grey de Wilton summoned in 1295, and the ancestors of the others who were placed before him were not summoned until the reign of Edward II, or Edward III . . . what I am now upon is this, that the Writs of Summons which are recorded do not form a criterion upon which the precedency of Peers has ever been determined or fixed, and that the ancient usage as to the order in which the Peers have sat, has been the sole guide for the precedency.'

There are well-known cases of precedence in the House having been allowed in error and reduced at a later time, when the error had been discovered or the law affecting peerage dignities more clearly ascertained. The two leading cases are those of the baronies of Strange and Clifford (Cruise, 1823, pp. 225-234), in which the precedence of the ancient baronies was allowed to the parties summoned in 1628 because the doctrine of the ' attraction ' had not then been exploded and, indeed, was not exploded till the reign of Charles II. After the law on the subject had been more clearly ascertained this precedence was corrected and the baronies were treated as new creations of 1628. Another precisely similar case is that of the summons in 1722 of Algernon Seymour in the barony of Percy, under the erroneous impression that he had inherited from his mother the ancient barony of Percy, the precedence of which was allowed to him. This precedence was again wrongly allowed to this dignity in 1777 and 1817, though it has never been formally corrected, and it is now recognised to be erroneous. The barony of Audley is another case in which precedence was wrongly allowed after the restoration by letters patent *temp.* Charles I. (See *Lords Reports.*)

The question, therefore, as it seems to me, is whether the precedence allowed to the barony of Ferrers under Henry VIII and in 1678, the reasons for which are not known, is sufficient to outweigh the evidence which has been adduced to show that, according to the law as now settled, a new barony was created by the writ of 26th July, 1461.

The reason why, in my opinion, the Crown is bound to fight the point is, that, otherwise, it would stultify the position it took on the Fitzwarine claim with entire success. Since the decision of the House in the Earldom of Norfolk case, the law as now ascertained must be applied retrospectively, even if at variance with the view that may have been taken before such ascertainment. The doctrine that a barony by writ is not created until there has been a sitting in Parliament under the writ, although now settled law, was not even enunciated until the days of James I, and did not secure acceptance till the days of Charles II. But it is now applied retrospectively to every claim to a barony that was created by writ in the thirteenth, fourteenth, or fifteenth centuries. Tried by this test, the claim that a barony was vested in Anne, wife of Walter Devereux, on the death of her father, William de Ferrers, in 1450, breaks down at once. It would break down even if her ancestors had been continuously summoned. But when we find that, of the seven alleged Lords Ferrers, only the first had been even summoned, the claim is seen to be not only legally, but even historically, baseless. The precedence allowed to the Lords Ferrers, after 1461, even if at variance with the law as now settled, is incomparably less so than was the full and unquestioned acceptance of the Earldom of Norfolk created by Edward II in 1312, the validity of which was not questioned till, in 1907, the House of Lords pronounced it null and void. If that acceptance and the sitting in the House under that creation went for nothing, *a fortiori* the precedence allowed, before the law was ascertained, to the barony of Ferrers must similarly go for nothing.

The Barony of Ferrers of Chartley

The only other point to which I desire to draw attention is the renewed attempt to use Visitation evidence as proof of a pedigree at a period long antecedent to that at which the Visitation was taken.   In this case a Visitation of 1620 is cited as proof for a series of events ranging from 1469 to 1489, although Mr. Wollaston urged in the Burgh case that in the majority of the Visitation cases the details very seldom go beyond what was within the personal knowledge of those who entered the pedigree (*Minutes*, p. 53).   The objection which I have frequently raised to this use of Visitations is now greatly strengthened by the fact that the visitation evidence which was put in similarly in the St. John case as proof, contained two serious blunders which were actually at variance with the Proposition which it was supposed to prove.

APPENDIX A.   (See pp. 191-2.)

Writs of Summons (27th March, 1335) for military service at Newcastle on Trinity Sunday, 1335 :	Writs of Summons (1st April, 1335) to Parliament at York on the morrow of the Ascension, 1335 :
Henrico de Ferrariis	Henrico de Ferrariis
Johanni de Wylughby	Johanni de Wylughby
Ade de Welle	Ade de Welle
Willelmo de Eyncourt	Willelmo de Eyncourt
Rogero Bavent	Rogero Bavent
Rogero de Kerdeston	Rogero de Kerdeston
Thome Tregoz	Thome Tregoz
Alexandro de Hilton	Alexandro de Hilton
Johanni de Ros	Johanni de Roos
Hugoni de Nevill	Hugoni de Nevill
Johanni de Verdon	Johanni de Verdon
Johanni de Haustede	Johanni de Haustede
Petro de Uvedale	Petro de Uvedale
Antonio de Lucy	Antonio de Lucy
Willelmo de Bohun	
Egidio de Badlesmere	
Roberto de Ferrariis	
Jacobo de Audele	Jacobo de Audele

APPENDIX B.　(See p. 195.)

Pro Willelmo Herbert milite (3rd February, 1462) :

Nos . . . memorie reducentes intime dilectum militem nostrum Willelmum Herbert quem in statum baronis et magnatis regni nostri suorum exigencia meritorum ereximus suorum servientium benevolorum et amicorum comitiva ad suos grandes sumptus et expensas copiosa suffultum se multimodis periculis in nostro servicio magnanimiter exponentem circa nostram personam regiam in variis preliis et exercitibus tam contra magnum nostrum adversarium Henricum sextum nuper regem Anglie pretensum ceterosque suos malivolos complices et fautores quam contra Henricum nuperime Exoniensem ducem et Jasparem Pembrochie et Jacobum Wiltes dudum comites aliosque rebelles proditores contra nos hostiliter guerram levantes maxima cum diligencia attendisse. . . . De gratia nostra speciali premissorum ex nostra certa sciencia intuitu concessimus et pro nobis et heredibus nostris per presentes concedimus eidem Willelmo. (Patent Roll 1 Edw. IV, pt. 4, m. 16.)

Pro Waltero Devereux milite (20th February, 1462) :

Nos . . . memorie reducentes dilectum militem nostrum Walterum Devereux quem in statum baronie (*sic*) et magnatis nostri (*sic*), suorum exigencia meritorum eripimus (*sic*) . . .

De gratia nostra speciali ex nostra certa sciencia premissorum intuitu concessimus et pro nobis et heredibus nostris per presentes concedimus eidem Waltero. (*Ibid.* pt. 5, m. 1.)

THE BAYEUX INQUEST OF 1133

AMONG the great inquests concerning military service there is one peculiarly deserving of attention on account of the early period to which it can be shown to relate. If its true nature had been recognised it would hardly require discussion, but by an almost incredible error, it has been wholly misunderstood.

There is printed on pp. 645-7 of *The Red Book of the Exchequer* a return headed, ' Nomina militum, tenentium de ecclesia Baiocensi.' It was also printed in Bouquet [1] from the *Red Book* text with ' conjectural emendations partly derived ' from what the editor of the *Red Book* describes as ' The original Inquisition.' [2] He speaks of this return, at the outset, as ' The list of Knights holding of the church of Bayeux in the year 1133.' [3] But the first point to strike the student, on examining this list, with its thirty-eight entries, is that of the men it names, several are well known to have died before 1133 and to have flourished in the days of William Rufus, if not, indeed, of his father. For among them there are famous men. The first and largest holder is Robert Fitz Hamon, who flourished under William II and died in 1107. Richard, earl of Chester, was drowned in 1120, and Ranulf, *vicomte* (of the Bessin) could only be so described before he succeeded Earl Richard on his death (1120). ' Eudo Dapifer,' prominent under the second William, passed away in 1120. Philip de Braiose had succeeded, under William II, his father William, the

[1] Martin Bouquet (De Wailly, Delisle et Jourdain). *Recueil des Historiens de la France*, xxiii, 698-9.

[2] Hubert Hall, *Red Book of the Exchequer* (Rolls Ser.), II, ccxxxiv, 645.

[3] *Ibid.* ccxxxiii.

Domesday lord of the Sussex Rape of Bramber; and Henry de Portu was the son and successor of that great Domesday baron, Hugh de Port. But, indeed, Domesday barons are themselves here as well; here are Hugh de Montfort, and Roger de Courceulles (*Corcella*), both of them lords of great fiefs, and here too is ' Aeloudus,' the chamberlain, who, as ' Adelald,' the chamberlain, held largely of the bishop when Domesday was compiled.[4] But we note that this entry runs ' *Feodum Aeloudi camerarii* ' (as do several others), which, as in the returns of 1166, is, the formula applied to a *former* holder of knight's fees.

It is evident that ' Henry de Warewic,' with two fees in St. Vaast, was Henry, first *earl* of Warwick, who held that dignity at least as early as the days of William Rufus.[5] The name which follows his is that of Roger de Beaumont, possibly his long-lived father.[6]

Again the first entry runs : ' Robertus filius Hamonis x milites *tenebat*,' and the second : ' Feodum Grimoudi de Plessis *erat* feodum viij militum.' We knew that the fee taken from Grimoud had been given to the bishop by William so far back as 1074. Let us see then if we can discover why the return to an inquest which was admittedly, made on the death of a bishop of Bayeux in 1133, should record not the names of the knights then holding, but of those who held the fees more than thirty years before.

When we learn the object of this inquest, the answer becomes quite simple. The stormy and chequered career of the famous Bishop Odo had proved disastrous to the see ; while his brother kept him in prison its great patrimony suffered badly at the hands of grasping magnates. With the help of his nephew, Duke Robert, he was able, before his

[4] It is interesting to note in the Bayeux Cartulary (l'Abbé V. Bourrienne, *Antiq. Cartul. Eccles. Baiocensis* (Soc. de l'Hist. de Normandie), i, 31), ' Tethaldo fratre Adelaldi [camerarii] ' as a witness to a Bayeux Cathedral deed of 1092, for ' Tedaldus ' is found as a tenant of the bishop, in 1086, in Bucks.

[5] Hall, *op. cit.* 646.

[6] There was, at least, a Roger de Beaumont living and a tenant-in-chief in 1086 (*Domesday Book*, pp. 80, 168).

death in 1097, to regain many of the lost possessions, but his weak successors were not able to vindicate the rights of their church till the coming of a strong bishop, in the person of Philip de Harcourt, King Stephen's Chancellor, in 1142, set a fresh complexion on its fortunes. His vigorous representations to the Pope produced a series of orders to everyone concerned; he was himself directed by Celestine II to enforce restitution of the lost possessions of his church; [7] and on Celestine's death, he obtained from his successor, Lucius II, at Rome, a series of bulls confirming the rights of his church. The date of this was May 1144. In these documents, the time referred to as that when the church of Bayeux was in full enjoyment of her rights is always that of Bishop Odo.[8]

The papal instrument which enables us to advance a step farther is that which was addressed to Geoffrey Plantagenet, then Duke, 16th May, 1144. For in it Lucius holds up, as a precedent for his imitation, the action of Henry I, who honoured the church and preserved its rights. He then proceeds :

Pervenit ad nos quod . . . sollicitus per legitimos homines

[7] 'Pervenit ad nos quod possessiones et bona Baiocensis ecclesiae a perversis illius terrae hominibus, praedecessorum tuorum incuria et negligentia distracta sint et alienata, et a multis contra justiciam occupata . . . tibi mandamus quatinus eos, qui possessiones et jura ipsius ecclesiae venditione, donatione, seu permutatione, contra justiciam et ejusdem ecclesiae utilitatem illicite detinent, districte commoneas ut ea tibi et eidem ecclesiae, cujus juris esse noscuntur, sine dilatione restituant' (Lateran, 9th Jan. 1144). Bourrienne, *op. cit.* i, 223.

[8] 'Ut Baiocensis ecclesiae bona ita semper debeant inconcussa stabilitate servari sicut bonae memoriae Odonis, ejusdem ecclesiae episcopi, tempore fuisse noscuntur.' *Ibid.* i, 188. . . . 'donationes, venditiones, seu quaslibet alienationes de bonis vel possessionibus Baiocensis ecclesiae, per episcopos qui post Oddonem in eadem ecclesia praefuisse noscuntur factas, quoniam, sicut accepimus, dilapidatores bonorum Baiocensis ecclesiae extiterunt, et tam thesaurum quam possessiones fere ad nichilum redegerunt evacuamus et irritas esse censemus. Unde . . . mandamus ut vos . . . possessiones et bona . . . eidem episcopo cum integritate reddatis, sicut per legitimos testes juramento probari fecerit Baiocensem ecclesiam tenuisse, tempore Oddonis episcopi in dominicatura vel in feudo.' *Ibid.* i, 199.

illius regionis possessiones Baiocensis ecclesiae fecit recognosci et, *sicut tempore Odonis episcopi fuerant*, sacramento probari.[9]

This we shall find is a direct reference to the Inquest of 1133. For Geoffrey, in consequence of the Pope's action,[10] followed in King Henry's footsteps.

Juramento antiquorum et legitimorum hominum, qui rem noverant, fecimus recognosci jura, possessiones, consuetudines, libertates supradictae ecclesiae, quascunque habuerat *in tempore Odonis episcopi, vestigiis regis Henrici inhaerentes qui hoc idem juramento antiquorum hominum fecerat recognosci post mortem Ricardi episcopi filii Sansonis.*

Here we have the very phrase which is applied to itself by the return to the Inquest of 1133 :

Nomina illorum qui juraverunt se verum dicere de feodis militum tenentium de ecclesia Baiocense et servitiis eorum *post mortem Ricardi filii Samsonis.*[11]

I have laboriously proved that we clearly ought to read ' juraverunt ' with ' post mortem,' and that the actual subject of the return (' de feodis militum tenentium,' etc.) was the state of the knight's fees of the bishopric *under Bishop Odo.* This is why the sworn testimony of aged men (antiquorum hominum) was required.

It is again spoken of in the charter of Duke Henry, who thus refers to the same Inquest :

provide Henricus rex, avus meus, instituit ut juramento antiquorum hominum *qui rem norant*, recognoscerentur tenedurae jam dictae ecclesiae sicut fuerant *in tempore praedicti Odonis*, tam in dominicis quam in feodis militum, vavassorum, et rusticorum ; *ipsius equidem tempore haec omnia jurata sunt et recognita*, et saepe dictae ecclesiae praecepto ejus resignata.[12]

It is then certain that the aged jurors of 1133 were deposing to the state of things in the time of Bishop Odo, who had died

---

[9] Bourrienne, *op. cit.* i, 253. Eugenius III, succeeding Lucius II in 1145, had renewed the papal command.

[10] *Ibid.* i, 45.

[11] Hall, *op. cit.* 647. In the Norman text the passage runs : ' statim post mortem Ricardi episcopi filii Sansonis.'

[12] Bourrienne, *op. cit.* i, 21.

so far back as 1097. If it be objected that their recollection would be somewhat hazy as to details after thirty-six years, the answer is that Henry II, in his great Norman Inquest of 1171, required the jurors to make their returns of the ducal demesne lands as they had existed at his grandfather's death thirty-six years before.[13] The information asked for in 1133 was not nearly so detailed as that which the Domesday jurors supplied after the lapse of twenty years, and Henry I had similarly obtained in the first Winchester survey, sworn information as to ' the time of King Edward,' at least forty years after that sovereign's death.[14] This method of obtaining information was of course regularly employed under our Norman kings and is of great importance in the history of our institutions. The Conqueror did for the church of Ely what his son did for that of Bayeux ; he ordered a sworn inquest as the preliminary to restitution.[15] As the oldest inhabitant totters into court to depose to-day to the state of things existing in his youth, we are carried back to the ancient practice under our Norman kings, when written evidence was scarce, and oral testimony employed. It was that very aged man (' vir antiquissimus ') Ethelric, the former Sussex bishop, who was brought on to Pennenden Heath in a waggon by the Conqueror's command, to declare what had been the ancient customs of the land.

The strange thing is that l'Abbé V. Bourrienne, editor of the *Livre Noir* (1902),[16] was evidently unacquainted with that version of the return to this Inquest, which was printed from

---

[13] ' Rex Henricus senior fecit investigari per Normanniam terras de quibus rex Henricus avus suus fuit seisitus die qua obiit.'

[14] ' Henricus Rex, volens scire quid Rex Edwardus habuit omnibus modis Wintonie in suo dominico, burgensium suorum sacramento hoc comprobari jussit.' For the date, see my paper on the survey in *Victoria County History, Hampshire,* i, 528.

[15] ' Eligantur plures de illis Anglis qui sciunt quomodo terre jacebant prefate ecclesie *die qua rex Aedwardus obiit,* et quod inde dixerint ibidem jurando testentur. Quo facto restituantur ecclesie terre que in dominio suo erant die obitus Ædwardi,' etc. *Inquis. Com. Cant.* p. xviii.

[16] Bourrienne, *op. cit.*

Léchaudé d'Anisy's collections in 1834 [17] and again by the editors of Bouquet [18] in 1876. That he should not have known of the *Red Book* list (1896) is but natural : it is hard enough to keep in touch with what is appearing in one's own country on any given point of historical or archaeological research ; but to be well acquainted with that which appears in other countries is not practically possible.

At this point I would endeavour to explain the exact genesis of the Norman text of what M. Guilhiermoz has justly termed ' La précieuse enquête faite vers 1133.' [19]

In the treasury of Bayeux Cathedral, there was preserved before the Revolution, among the title deeds of the see, a small register of six folios, of which the earlier portion is devoted to what purports to be a sworn return to an Inquest ordered by Henry I concerning the services due from the barons, knights, and vavasseurs holding of the see.[20]   Of this Inquest M. Guilhiermoz writes that it

> ne nous est connue que grâce à une fort mauvaise copie moderne ; cette copie a été publiée telle quelle par M. Léchaudé d'Anisy.[21]

This is not perhaps absolutely exact. The ' copie moderne ' was a transcript made in 1637 and officially collated by a notary, and I think it possible that the errors may, in part at least, have existed in the original register. Mr. Hubert Hall observes of the short list representing this Inquest in *The Red Book*, that :

In the edition of Bouquet, this list is printed from the Red

---

[17] *Mémoires de la Soc. des Antiq. de Normandie*, viii, 425-431.

[18] Bouquet, *op. cit.* 699.

[19] Guilhiermoz, *L'Origine de la noblesse en France au moyen âge* (1902) p. 292, note.

[20] ' Henricus Rex Angliae (*sic*) fecit inquiri de feodis baroniarum (*sic*) militum et vavassoriarum (*sic*) tenentium de ecclesia beatae Mariae Baiocensis et de servitiis eorum ; videlicet qui servitia facere debebant ipsi Regi per manum episcopi et quae de jure facere debebant ipsi episcopo.   Hoc autem factum est coram Roberto comite Glocestriae filio Regis, qui ad hoc audiendum ab ipso rege missus est apud Baiocas.' *Mémoires de la Soc. des Antiq. de Normandie*, viii (2), 425-6.

[21] Guilhiermoz, *op. cit.* p. 292, note.

Book of the Exchequer with valuable conjectural emendations partly derived from the *Original Inquest*, of which a greatly improved text is printed as an Appendix to the Exchequer list.[22]

And he again refers, somewhat inexactly, to the above transcript from a register as the ' original return.' [23] But we must distinguish between an original return and a transcript from a register, which register itself contains but a transcript, and that, as I shall show, very imperfect. A true ' original return ' is, for instance, the *carta* of the Bishop of Chichester (1166), which is still preserved in the Record Office.[24]

Again in the above quotation, Mr. Hall speaks, we see, of ' a greatly improved text of the Original Inquest.' But M. Guilhiermoz, more accurately writes that the text of the transcript (1637)

a été publiée telle quelle par M. Léchaudé d'Anisy : au contraire, les éditeurs du *Rec. des hist. de France* ne l'ont reproduite dans le tome xxiii qu'en y apportant de nombreuses corrections, qui ne nous paraissent pas toutes également heureuses.[25]

In short, the only text is that of the 1637 transcript,[26] to which the editors have appended more or less conjectural emendations.

It is important to be quite clear on this point, because I am going to contend that the register from which the transcript was made did not contain the full text of the original return and that the proof of this is found in *The Red Book* list. Its editor holds that his list ' was probably compiled ' from ' the original Inquisition ' (by which he means the Bayeux register) : [27] I hope by a comparison of the two to demolish his view.

[22] *Red Book*, p. ccxxxiv.   The italics are mine.   [23] *Ibid.* pp. 645-7.

[24] *Red Book of the Exchequer*, pp. 199-200, and frontispiece to vol. i.

[25] Guilhiermoz, *op. cit.* p. 292 note, where he criticises them.

[26] The editors had before them two copies of it by Léchaudé d'Anisy and one by M. Le Prevost.

[27] ' The original Inquisition, from which it was probably compiled, is carefully printed in Bouquet, xxiii, 699, from d'Anisy's and Le

Family Origins

As the entries in the *Red Book* list and in the Bayeux text are almost identical in order, we are struck by the great discrepancy between those which follow :

Bayeux text	The Red Book
(Bouquet, *op. cit.* p. 700)	(p. 646)
Robertus de Novoburgo tenet feodum duorum militum in Sancto Vedasto ; et Belm [28] comes Mellenti feodum duorum militum propter Friebois.	Henricus de Warewic, in Sancto Vedasto, ij milites, Rogerus de Beumont, in Hispania, ij milites. Willelmus Camerarius, ij milites praeter Friebois.

The student will at once perceive, if he knows something of early genealogy,[29] that the holding of Robert de Neufbourg is that of his progenitor (Henry de Neufbourg), Earl of Warwick in the corresponding entry, and that the Count of Meulan, on the left, similarly represents his predecessor Roger de Beaumont on the right. But the *Red Book* list interpolates a wholly additional entry, ' Willelmus Camerarius ij milites.' This entry is of great importance, because it is found only in the *Red Book* and is wanting in the Bayeux text. Its omission in the latter seems to me a clear case of parablepsis, and I here enclose in square brackets the words which must have slipped the scribe's notice after the first ' ij milites.' [30]

Prevost's transcripts.' (*Red Book*, p. 645.) What is really meant is d'Anisy's and Le Prevost's personal *copies* of a transcript (in 1637) from a register which was *not* the original Inquisition.

[28] See remarks on this below.

[29] It is true that Professor Haskins—whose admirable studies on Norman institutions (thanks to the Carnegie fund) are so far in advance of anything previously attempted—writes (*American Hist. Rev.* 1903, viii, 620 note) of the Bayeux text, ' The Returns. . . . Upon them is based the summary of services due from the bishop of Bayeux contained in the *Red Book of the Exchequer*'' (Ed. Hall, 645-7 ; *Historiens de France*, xxiii, 699, and that he similarly styles the *Red Book* list ' a summary of the returns in the Bayeux text in *Eng. Hist. Rev.*' (1907), xxii, 643, and again speaks of ' the actual returns of 1133 . . . and the abstract of them in the *Red Book* ' (*Ibid.* p. 644), but he must have heedlessly followed Mr. Hall's statement although his own versions disprove it.

[30] Whether the recurring phrase was ' ij milites ' or ' feodum duorum militum,' the parablepsis would arise in the same way.

Roger de Beumont[31] in Hispania ij milites [Willelmus Camerarius, ij milites] praeter Friebois.

But who was William 'Camerarius'? I make him, without any hesitation, to be William 'Camerarius de Tancarvilla,' i.e. Lord of Tancarville and Chamberlain of Normandy.[32] That this identification is right is proved by the fact that in later days the famous 'Chamberlains of Tancarville' were still holding of the See of Bayeux two knight's fees.[33]

We have now seen clearly that the *Red Book* list contains the names of earlier holders, and the Bayeux transcript those of their successors in 1133. What is the inference to be drawn? It is, surely, that in the true 'original return' to the Inquest there were given, not only the names of those who held in 1133, but also the names of their predecessors 'in the time of Bishop Odo.' This would be exactly parallel, for instance, to the return of the knights holding of the See of Winchester which was made in 1166.[34] That return gives not only the names of those then holding, but also the names of their predecessors 'in the time of King Henry.' In each case, the interval that had elapsed was rather over thirty years.

From that return with its double lists, the *Red Book* scribe must have derived his list of the earlier holders, while the Bayeux Register selected on the contrary the holders in

[31] With regard to the 'Belm' in the Bayeux text, the editors of Bouquet suggest 'belun,' which they would read with 'Sanctum Vedastum.' But I feel no doubt that it was a fragment of Belmont (Beumont).

[32] On the great chamberlainship of Normandy, vested in the *seigneurs* of Tancarville see *The King's Serjeants*, pp. 115-6, where I have illustrated their tenure of the office in the twelfth century. So close and so prolonged was the association of 'Tancarville' with the office that when Sir John Grey was created, by Henry V, Earl of Tancarville in Normandy (1418), he styled himself on his seal, 'Conte Tancarville . . . grand chamberlain hereditaire de Normandie.'

[33] In the second portion of the 1637 transcript from the same Bayeux Register we read: 'Le Chambelleng de Tanquerville, deux fiefs de chevalier à Tour et à Oistreham,' etc. Ouistreham is at the mouth of the Orne, and Tour is between Bayeux and Trévières.

[34] *Red Book of the Exchequer*, pp. 204-7.

1133. That the former ' compiled ' his list from the text in the Bayeux Register is, I must repeat, impossible, for however much we may allow for error in the 1637 transcript (on which we have to depend), it is obvious that the *Red Book* list contains information which cannot have been in the Bayeux Register. Those who are familiar with the texts of the *Red Book* and the *Testa de Nevill* have observed doubtless, in those volumes, cases in which an indolent or a hurried scribe has similarly cut down a return, taking from it only certain names, to the confusion and misleading of those who do not grasp the fact. It is thus that Mr. Hall, the *Red Book's* editor, has been misled as to the serjeanties.

So far as one can test them, the names in the *Red Book* list are compatible, as I suggest, with the ' time of bishop Odo,' except that of Richard, Earl of Chester. This Richard did not succeed till 1101, four years after the bishop's death ; but the jurors of 1133 may have forgotten that he had not succeeded so early as 1097. In some respects, the *Red Book* list is the more accurate of the two : it has, for instance, ' Ranulfus Vicecomes ' (i.e. of the Bessin), while the *Bayeux text* reads : ' Istae sunt terrae quas tenuit Raymondus (*sic*) vicomes Baiocassini ' and repeats this erroneous name in two places. Its ' Petitvilla ' (now ' Petiville ') and ' Monte Mart[ini] ' (now ' Montmartin ') [35] are similarly most accurate as compared with the ' Petra Villa ' and ' Monte Aperto ' of the Bayeux text. So also its ' Escorceviele ' (i.e. Ecorcheville) is right, and the ' Esnotheville ' of the Bayeux text is wrong. Thus far, then, the *Red Book* text is far superior to what its editor terms ' the original return.' And yet on one point of infinitely more importance, the former is seriously wrong. Mr. Hall gives what he terms ' the few important variants ' in footnotes, but he has overlooked the most important of all,

[35] The fee at ' Montmartin ' heads the later list of holdings in the Bayeux transcript (p. 43), and occurs in the *Livre Noir* (Bourrienne, *op. cit.* i, 33) as held of the bishop by William de Moyon in 1151-2.

possibly because the editors of Bouquet [36] had also failed to note it. For historians, the vital thing in this early evidence is the record of the service due from the bishop and of the way in which it was rendered. Here are the two versions:

Bayeux text	*Red Book*
Episcopus Baiocensis debebat Domino Normanniae decem milites ad servitium regis Francorum, et . . . decem milites episcopatus faciebant hoc servitium per unum militem per quadraginta dies. Dixerunt etiam quod idem Episcopus debebat servitium viginti (*sic*) militum in marchis Normanniae per quadraginta dies ubicumque rex vellet. Et istud servitium faciebant quinque milites per unum.	Episcopus Baiocensis debet invenire x optimos milites ad servitium Regis Francorum per xl dies; et ad eos procurandos debet capere in unoquoque feodo militis xxs Rothomagensis monetae. Cum autem inveniet Duci Normanniae xl (*sic*) milites per xl dies debet capere in unoquoque feodo militis xls praedictae monetae et nihil amplius.

The details of this arrangement in the passage on the left show quite clearly that the service due from the bishop in Normandy, to the Duke, was twenty knights, not forty. And this is confirmed by the deposition of Robert, Earl of Gloucester, that from ten knights' fees he owed the service of one knight to the King of the French, and of two to the Duke of Normandy. The figure ' xl,' given in the *Red Book* version, would upset the whole scheme.

It will be observed that here again there is information in the *Red Book* text which is not found in the Bayeux Register, namely, the bishop's right to levy from each of his knights fees, a fixed sum for the support of the knights he was bound to furnish. This then is further proof that, as I have shown above, the *Red Book* text was compiled from an independent source and not from the Bayeux Register. But the latter supplies additional information as to ' the

---

[36] Among whom was no less famous an authority on these subjects than M. Delisle himself.

bishop's service ' which is not found in the *Red Book*. It also mentions the very interesting duty of his knights to give him an aid from each fee when he went to Rome on the business of the See, or when the cathedral had to be repaired or if his palace in the city were burnt.

Having thus cleared the ground, one may note the value of this Inquest for the history of our Norman houses. Four at least of the baronies or ' wards ' (*custodia*) connected with Dover Castle [37] bore names which occur in the *Red Book* list of knights. These are Crevequer, Maminot, and Port, with that of the Constable, who appears in that list, as Hugh de Montfort, a chief tenant of the See. Among the knights of the Dover baronies we find Philip de Colombières (west of Bayeux), a name familiar with the records of the see. Of the military tenants of the bishopric in 1133 (entered in the Bayeux transcript), some bore famous names. Apart from the Earl of Gloucester, to whom we shall come below, and the Earl of Chester, Vauquelin de Corcella, was holding in Courseulles and Bernières (sur mer), and Henry

---

[37] *Red Book*, pp. 706 *et seq.* 717 *et seq.* Professor Haskins in his learned and most valuable paper, on ' Knight Service in Normandy in the eleventh century ' (*Eng. Hist. Rev.* xxii, 636-649), has traversed, I find, the same ground as myself with regard to this Inquest. Unfortunately I had not noticed his paper when my text was written.

He justly insists on the importance of the early five-knight and ten-knight units on the bishop's fief as ' confirming ' my view that the Normans were familiar with such units at the Conquest ; but he criticises me for relying on Wace, in my *Feudal England* (p. 260), as my ' only authority ' for the fact. Reference to what I actually said will show the reason why I cited Wace, namely, that I was definitely opposing Mr. Freeman's theory (p. 230), and that I therefore appealed to Wace, as his own favourite authority (*Norm. Conq.* 1875, iii, 295-8) against that theory. My words were, ' we have only to refer to Wace ; for in the ' Roman de Rou,' *as quoted by Mr. Freeman himself*, we find,' etc., etc. (p. 260). Moreover, when Prof. Haskins seeks to score a point, by contrasting my citation (*ut supra*) of Wace with my attack on his authority, as ' a mere late compiler,' for the palisade at the battle of Hastings, I must point out that Wace, as a canon of Bayeux and presumably familiar with its records, must have been personally familiar with the ten-knight unit, as he knew it and read of it, while he could not personally have known anything of the old English formation in ' shield wall ' at the battle of 1066. It is my essential contention that on the latter subject he merely misunderstood the words of William of Malmesbury.

de Port [38] held Commes adjoining his own Port-en-Bessin, which lay like Bernières on the coast. Gilbert and Henry de ' Lacey ' were holding in Lassy and Campeaux [39] and Hugh Bigot in (les) Loges and Savenay (Courvaudon). The names of Marmion and of Walter Gifford will also strike the English reader, but perhaps the most remarkable is that of Richard de Lucy (Luceys), for this is perhaps its earliest occurrence. It is found in conjunction with that William de ' Moon '—more correctly de ' Moiun,' who held Montmartin of the bishop in the middle of the twelfth century, [40] and who, as William de Mohun is known to us as Lord of Dunster.

The connexion, through Bishop Odo of Bessin, with the Kentish baronies, leads me to make the novel suggestion that the Baronia Fouberd [41] or ' Custodia Roberti de Dovra,' [42] of which Chilham was the head, was held by a family which took its name, not, as we all have supposed, from Dover, [43] but from Douvres (in the Bessin), east of Bayeux and north of Caen. The Kent family had for its distinctive name ' Foubert ' (*Fulbertus*), and it is at least an odd coincidence that we find this exceedingly rare Christian name at Douvres in the time of Henry II. [44] The clue may seem rather faint, but to me at any rate it is very suggestive.

The document to be specially studied in connexion with

[38] His barony was in Hants, but he held in Kent under the Bishop of Bayeux.

[39] The text is here very corrupt : ' Feodum de Laceys in Capella.' The Earl of Gloucester's charter (see below), thirteen years later, enables us to emend it.

[40] Bourrienne, *op. cit.* i, 33.   [41] *Red Book of the Exchequer*, p. 708.

[42] *Ibid.* 616, 719.

[43] Dugdale *Baronage*, i, 461 ; Courthope's *Historic Peerage*, p. 166. A family, resident in Kent, would not take its name from Dover without good reason ; and in the case of this family there seems to have been no reason for it.

[44] ' Quadam terra apud Doveram quae dicitur terra thesaurarii, et nominatim terra Fouberti.' (Bourrienne, *op. cit.* i, 144.)

the Bayeux Inquest is one that touches English History, namely, the Earl of Gloucester's charter in 1146. It forms an addition to that group of charters which belongs to the stay of the Empress Maud at Bayeux.[45] The earl— known, we must remember, as Robert ' de Caen ' from his birthplace—had in the Bessin the chief seat of his power beyond the Channel. Of the Bayeux lands alone he was by far the largest holder. It was in his presence that the Inquest was made, and he himself deposed that he held ten fees ' de honore Ebreceii ' and was hereditary standard-bearer of the See, in addition to which he had the eight fees of Robert Suhard, and the seven which Malfilastre (Malus-filiaster) had held. The ' Honour ' was that of ' Evrecy,' which had been held by his wife's father [46]—and if we may here believe Wace—by Hamo Dentatus, the famous rebel of 1047.[47] When Philip de Harcourt succeeded, as bishop, the earl's own son, he found the powerful earl his most difficult problem. He told Eugene III at Rome that Robert was detaining from him the best part of his See's posses-sions,[48] and the Pope directed the bishops of Worcester and of Bath to enforce restitution.[49]

It was not, however, till September 1146 that the earl made what even then appears to have been a compromise. His charter,[50] made in the presence of the Empress, and of representatives of the bishop as well as of his own friends, shows how large had been his holdings. He resigned to the bishop the fees of Ilbert and Gilbert de Lacey at Lassy and Campeaux, the Malleverer fee at Asnières, which he

---

[45] See *Geoffrey de Mandeville*, pp. 133, 417-8, and my *Ancient Charters*, p. 46.

[46] So also the *Red Book* list : ' Robertus filius Hamonis x milites tenebat de honore Ebricensi ' (p. 645). Mr. Hall identifies this as the Honour of ' Evreux ' (p. 1164).

[47] Mr. Freeman, working from a bad text of Wace, made the name ' Mezi.' There was, however, a Maisy in the district.

[48] ' Saepe conquestus est quod Robertus, comes Gloucestrie maximam partem bonorum Baiocensis ecclesiae sibi auferat, et tam in feudo quam in dominio violenter detineat.' (Bourrienne, *op. cit.* i, 237.)

[49] *Ibid.*   [50] *Ibid.* pp. 48-50.

had extorted from the bishop Richard who had died in
1133, and the whole fief of ' Eudo Dapifer ' (d. 1120) at St.
Clair and at Mathieu (*Mattonum*), with a guarantee that he
would exercise his influence with Duke Geoffrey to secure
the bishop's possessions of Mathieu for five years.[51]   This
holding at Mathieu is specially mentioned in the Inquest
of 1133.[52]

Then follows the curious provision that if the heir of
Eudo should recover his inheritance, he is to hold these lands
directly of the bishop.[53]   The peculiar interest of this is that
the second charter of the Empress to Geoffrey (de Mandeville), Earl of Essex had recognised his right to Eudo's
inheritance,[54] while the earlier charter (1141) had ' restored '
to him (apparently as his right) all the lands of ' Serlo de
Matom ' (i.e. Mathieu).[55]

In return for all this, the bishop had to allow the earl to
retain for life the fiefs of Roger Suhard [56] and of Malfilastre.[57]
And in addition, the bishop granted him possession of all
the land held by Ranulf, Earl of Chester of the church of
Bayeux until the Duke of Normandy (i.e. *Geoffrey*) should

[51] With the saving clause that this was not to involve him in expense
or in war (' absque meae pecuniae donatione, et sine guerra facienda ')
we may compare the phrase, ' sine pecuniae donatione ' (*bis*), in the
second charter of the Empress to Geoffrey de Mandeville (see p. 170 of
my book).

[52] ' Hoc est feodum episcopi Baiocensis apud Mathonium.'   (Bouquet,
op. cit. xxiii, 702.)   Pope Eugene defined it as ' Quartam partem
Matomii quam Eudo Dapifer ab antecessoribus tuis in feudo noscitur
tenuisse, et ibidem feudum quatuor militum.'   (Bourrienne, *op. cit.* i,
195.)

[53] ' Et quando heres Eudonis dapiferi hereditatem suam recuper-
averit, de Baiocensi ecclesia et de episcopo haec predicta feoda in
capite tenebit.'   *Ibid.* 49.

[54] ' Et do ei totam terram quae fuit Eudonis Dapiferi in Normannia
et dapiferatum ipsius.   Et haec reddo ei ut rectum suum ut habeat
et teneat hereditabiliter.'   (*Geoffrey de Mandeville*, p. 167.)

[55] ' Serlo de Maton ' had witnessed a charter of Duke Robert, relating
to a monastery near Bayeux, in 1089.   (Bourrienne, *op. cit.* i, 13.)

[56] ' Unde loquela inter me et episcopum fuit.'

[57] See p. 214 above.

recognise the right of an heir of the earl, which heir should thenceforth hold directly of the bishop.[58]

This land must have included the five fees which had been held by Richard, Earl of Chester, as well as the seven and a half which had been held by the *vicomtes*. The earl, therefore, had done well, thanks to his influence and power ; he had secured these twelve and a half fees in addition to the twenty-five which he returned himself as holding in 1133 and which he now retained.

Among the witnesses on his part, to this great compromise, were his brother Reginald, Earl of Cornwall, and Osbern Oitd[eniers], one of his knightly tenants.[59]

The earl's strong position in the Bessin doubtless exercised an influence on the Norman campaign which he undertook with Count Geoffrey and his Angevins in 1142. Miss Norgate, who attempted its reconstruction, was baffled by the name of ' Brichesart ' among those of the places they captured ; [60] but this is Briquessart in Livry (in the Bessin), the Norman stronghold of the Earls of Chester, where the mound and ditches of their ancient castle remain as a monument of their power.[61]

[58] ' Tenere terram quam Rannulfus, Comes Cestriae de eadem Baiocensi ecclesia tenebat . . . donec talis haeres adveniat quem dux Normanniae justum heredem Rannulfi Comitis Cestriae recognoscat. Et postea idem heres eandem terram de ecclesia Baiocensi et de ipso episcopo in capite teneat.' This is new and interesting information, for the Earl of Chester was not dead, but was playing a great part in England this very year (see my ' King Stephen and the Earl of Chester ' in *Eng. Hist. Rev.* x, 88-9). Geoffrey must have forfeited the Norman possessions of the earl when he took part with Stephen. See *Gesta Stephani*, Ed. Howlett, p. 117.

[59] See *Geoffrey de Mandeville*, pp. 374-5, 382.

[60] *England under the Angevin Kings*, i, 339.

[61] I have been unable to find any continuation of this article. Dr. Round apparently left it unfinished.—W. P.

RELIEFS

IT is not the least of the many services which *The History of English Law* has rendered to English history that it has defined with legal exactitude the distinction, in the twelfth century, between the two classes of tenants holding in chief of the Crown. Long though historians and antiquaries have disputed the matter, Profs. Pollock and Maitland speak with no uncertain voice :

> So far as the land law is concerned there seems no difference between tenure by barony and tenure by knight-service, save in one point, namely the amount of the relief. . . .[1]

Gneist, who devoted to this subject special attention, wrote as follows :

> In comparatively early times, by *barones* were pre-eminently meant the *barones regis* ; that is, the *tenentes in capite*, who from the first were divided according to the amount of their property into greater feudatories and lesser Crown Vassals.[2]

He denied that these ' barons,' co-extensive with the tenants-in-capite, held any ' distinction in rank ' or ' definite and legal distinction ' of tenure.[3] Returning to the subject, he divided ' the Crown vassals into two classes : (1) ' The class of the greater vassals,' (2) ' The lesser Crown vassals,' who ' differ in no way from the greater in respect of their tenure.' And these classes he respectively styles *Barones majores* and *Barones minores*.[4] When we turn from Gneist to Dr. Stubbs, we find the latter quoting, apparently

---

[1] *Hist. of Engl. Law* (1898), i, 279.

[2] Gneist, *Constit. Hist. of Eng.*, i, p. 289 ; cf. p. 126.   [3] *Ibid.* p. 290.

[4] *Ibid.* pp. 333-338. It is true that on p. 335 he contrasts the *barones majores* with the ' squireless knights ' ; but this cannot obscure his view, as emphatically expressed on p. 291.

with approval, the remarks of the great German scholar on ' the distinction of *majores* and *minores barones*.'[5] Yet, on looking closer, we discover that the military tenants-in-chief, include, in his opinion, not merely the greater and the lesser barons, but another and distinct class, the knights. In his chapter on ' Administration during the Norman period,' he classes the ' barons ' and the ' knights ' apart,[6] describing the latter as ' the lowest class of tenants-in-chief who are likely to have presented themselves in the national council.' So again, in dealing with the council under ' administrative and representative institutions,' he first describes the ' greater barons,' and then observes that ' the entire body of tenants-in-chief included, besides these the minor barons, the knightly body and the socage tenants of the Crown.'[7] Lastly, Profs. Pollock and Maitland, while dividing, like Gneist, the ' military tenant(s)-in-chief of the crown ' into ' two classes ' only, the ' greater ' and the ' lesser ' barons, detect, we have seen, unlike that scholar, a difference of tenure between the two.   The ' greater men ' held by ' barony,' the ' smaller men ' by ' knight's ' service.[8]

Though, as we have seen, these writers differ on certain points they are all agreed at least in making the relief the dividing line between the greater and the lesser ' barons.' Even Dr. Stubbs, who, one might have thought, would have connected with his class of ' knights ' the relief for the knight's fee, connects it on the contrary with all those below the greater barons.   It is, in his opinion, a distinctive mark of the latter that ' the greater barons . . . made a separate agreement with the Crown for their reliefs.'[9]

Gneist emphatically made the relief the distinction between *barones majores* and *minores*,[10] and observes that

[5] Stubbs, *Constit. Hist.* i, 366 note.   [6] *Ibid.* pp. 365-368.

[7] *Ibid.* pp. 564-5.   [8] *Hist. of Engl. Law*, i, 259-260.

[9] *Const. Hist.* (1875) i, 564.   So too, on p. 366, he accepts with Gneist, ' the difference of relief between a hundred shillings for the knight and a hundred marks for the baron ' as a distinction between ' the two classes ' of ' majores and minores barones.'

[10] *Ibid.* p. 290.

the former ' in the rating of the *relevia* . . . had the undesired honour of a higher scale.' [11]   That this is also the view of Profs. Pollock and Maitland, is evident from the passage quoted at the outset of my paper.

It has been urged that the tenants-in-chief in the twelfth century did not include a separate class of ' knights.'   Their first appearance is in Magna Carta.   It will be desirable on this point to place side by side the parallel clauses from the charter of Henry I and that of John.

Henry I	*John*
si quis baronum, comitum meorum,[12] sive aliorum qui de me tenent, mortuus fuerit, heres suus non redimet terram suam, sicut faciebat tempore fratris mei, sed justa et legitima relevatione relevabit eam; etc.	si quis comitum vel baronum nostrorum sive aliorum tenencium de nobis in capite per servicium militare, mortuus fuerit . . . heres . . . habeat hereditatem suam per antiquum relevium ; scilicet heres vel heredes comitis de baronia comitis integra per centum libras ; heres vel heredes baronis de baronia integra per centum libras ; heres vel heredes militis de feodo militis integro per centum solidos ad plus ; etc.

If we view these provisions of John's charter in isolation and endeavour to make the text here its own interpreter, we observe (1) that those to whom they apply are the tenants-in-chief by *knight service* ;   (2) that these are divided into three categories, earls, barons, and ' others ' ;   (3) that the holdings recognised are only two, viz. the barony and the knight's fee.   It is important to observe that in this chapter of the Great Charter no distinction is made betwen ' greater ' and ' lesser ' barons and that no knights (*milites*) are mentioned by name.

[11] *Ibid.* 335.

[12] The *Red Book of the Exchequer* text reads : ' baronum meorum comitum.'

The difficulty presented by these provisions is that no one has been able to give a satisfactory explanation of the difference between the two holdings here specified, when their holders were all alike tenants-in-chief by knight service. The barons' returns of their knights (*Cartae baronum*) in 1166 imply that all this class stood on the same footing and that the *milites* were not among them, but were the under-tenants whom they had enfeoffed upon their lands. The above difficulty was already felt in the seventeenth century, when Selden considered that the holdings of tenants-in-chief were originally alike in *status*, but were subsequently differentiated, some being classed as ' baronies ' and others as ' knight's-fees.' [13] Madox on the other hand boldly assumed that the difference in *status* of the two holdings went back to the Norman Conquest, that ' William I enfeoffed his Barons of their Baronies, or his Knights of their Knights Fees.' [14]

While I do not presume to hope that I shall solve the difficulty by which historians and antiquaries have been so long baffled, I shall endeavour to elucidate the problem to the best of my ability and to clear away some of the confusion by which it is at present surrounded. For it affects an important development of our constitutional history.

That problem is the *status* and fate of those lesser tenants-in-chief who ceased to attend the Great Council. Were these lesser barons known as *barones minores*, or as *milites* ? And if the latter, is it possible to trace any connexion between these *milites* and the representative ' knights ' of the shire ' ?

The first point I desire to make is that, in spite of the freedom with which the commentators on the Charter have applied both these terms to the lesser tenants-in-chief, they are not so applied in the clause that we are considering, or, indeed, so far as I can find, anywhere else.

---

[13] Selden's position is set forth fully by Hallam in his *Middle Ages*.

[14] *Baronia Anglica* (1736), p. 26. So too we read that lands were granted by him to be held ' in Baronage, in Knight service or in Serjeanty,' etc. (p. 27).

Reliefs

There has been, if I may venture to say so, on the part of the commentators on the Charter too much glossing and too much assumption. When we examine the text itself we find (1) that in the second chapter—dealing with reliefs—the two classes below the earls are the 'baron' and the 'knight'; (2) that in the fourteenth chapter dealing with the summons to the Council—the two classes below the earls are the '*majores barones*' and all those (others) who hold of us in chief.' It has been assumed but not proved that in both 'chapters' and for both purposes the line of division is the same. And it follows, as a consequence of this assumption, that

> The *barones* of one clause of the great charter seem to be the *barones majores* of another. . . . It seems that the *baro* who has a *baronia* in the one clause is the *baro major* who is to have a special summons in the other clause.[15]

Nor is this the only consequence which follows from that assumption. For it involves, we find, the still more improbable equation of the 'knight' (*miles*) who held a knight's fee in Chapter II with the 'alleged' *barones minores* of Chapter XIV.[16] I use the term 'alleged' because, in spite of the freedom with which the phrase is used by the commentators on the Charter,[17] it is not found in that chapter or indeed anywhere else in the text of the document.

[15] Maitland, *The Constit. Hist. of Engl.* pp. 66, 80.

[16] Hallam, *Middle Ages* (1860), iii, 7 ; Davis, *England under the Normans and Angevins*, pp. 325, 380 ; McKechnie, *Magna Carta* (1914), p. 200.

[17] E.g. Stubbs, *Const. Hist.* (1875), i, 366 : 'the great distinction of *majores* and *minores* which appears in *Magna Carta*. . . . The distinction of *majores* and *minores barones* . . . appears perhaps in legal phraseology first in the *Dialogus de Scaccario* and *Magna Carta*' ; Gneist, *Hist. of the Engl. Const.* (1886), i, 289-290 ; Maitland, *Const. Hist. of England*, p. 80 ; Davis, *England under the Normans and Angevins* (1905), p. 380 ; McKechnie, *Magna Carta* (1914), pp. 251-2 : 'The Crown-tenants on one side of this fluctuating line were *barones majores* ; those on the other *barones minores.*'

This is no mere verbal quibble : the phrase *barones majores* does, indeed, imply that there were lesser barons, but it certainly does not involve the gloss that ' all those (others) who hold of us in chief ' were *barones minores* ; they might—and judging from Chapter II they would— comprise at least the ' knights ' as well as the lesser barons, in which case these classes were distinct and the ' alleged ' equation disappears.

Let me endeavour to make the point absolutely clear. The ' tenants-in-chief' by ' knight service ' include accord- ing to Chapter II, (*A*) barons, (*B*) knights. Chapter XIV introduces a further distinction by speaking of *majores barones*. This no doubt implies the existence of *barones minores*, but it does not affect the ' knights,' who would remain as before, distinct from all ' barons ' whether ' greater or ' less.' Therefore *miles* cannot be used as the equation of *baro minor*. Putting the point differently, the line in Chapter II (which is concerned with reliefs) is drawn to include the lesser barons with the greater ones ; but in Chapter XIV (which is concerned with separate summons) it is drawn athwart the baronage, and by excluding the lesser barons creates (so far as summons is concerned) a fresh class. Again the phrase 'all (others) who hold of us in chief ' (in Chapter XIV) may include in addition to the lesser barons not merely the knights, but others such as tenants by serjeanty. Stubbs, indeed, admits in one place,[18] when speaking of the ' greater and lesser barons,' that ' the entire body of tenants-in-chief included besides these (i.e. the greater barons) the minor barons, the knightly body, and the socage tenants of the Crown,' [19] all of whom, he deems, were entitled to be summoned by the general summons as provided in Chapter XIV. It is true that he writes in another place of the phrase, ' Barones secundae dignitatis ' (who are admitted to be identical with the ' barones

[18] Stubbs, *Const. Hist.* (1875), i, 565.

[19] The tenants by serjeanty should be named before the socage tenants.

minores ') that ' Hallam rightly understands this to refer to
the knightly tenants-in-chief,' [20] which virtually accepts
the wrong equation ; but this only illustrates the need of
greater clearness in definition.

No one, I think, will suspect me of imperfect appreciation where our great historian is concerned, but his work
occasionally betrays a certain vagueness of conception, a
lack of clearness in definition, which perhaps is sometimes
met with in the work of English scholars. For instance,
we first find him treating of ' the great council ' in Norman
times and recognising the barons (greater and less) and
the ' knights ' as distinct classes among ' its members.' [21]
But when he turns to the composition of this same great
council ' under Henry II and his sons,' he appears to lose
sight of the essential distinction between these two classes.
This, I think, was due to the influence upon him of Gneist,
to whom we may clearly trace the fundamental error of
confusing the line drawn by the Charter (Chapter II)
between the ' baron ' and the ' knight ' with that which it
draws (Chapter XIV) between the ' greater baron ' and the
tenants-in-chief below him.

By the ' interval between the two classes ' Stubbs here
obviously means the distinction of *majores* and *minores
barones*. Yet the *Dialogus de Scaccario* (vol. i, p. 10), so
far from making that distinction, actually denies that there
was any, so far as relief was concerned.[22] Here, again, the
identity of the ' knight ' with the minor baron is wrongly
assumed. In the *History of English Law*,[23] Pollock and
Maitland, it will be found, have fallen victims to the same
confusion ; they write vaguely of ' the greater men ' and
' the lesser men,' and evidently treat as identical the two
lines of division which we have to keep distinct.

Another error, traceable to Gneist, is the connexion of

[20] Hallam, *op. cit.* p. 182 note.   [21] Stubbs, *op. cit.* i, 366.

[22] ' Quidam enim de rege tenent in capite que ad coronam pertinent
baronias, scilicet, *majores* seu *minores*,' etc., etc. Cf. ii, 24.

[23] Ed. 1895, i, 259-260.

the distinction between ' greater ' and ' lesser ' baron with two passages in Domesday.

Gneist	Stubbs
' At the time of Domesday Book the maxim held good, that only vassals (*taini*), who possess six *maneria* or less should pay *relevium* to the Vicecomes. Those possessing more than six *maneria* pay immediately into the Exchequer (at all events this principal is expressly mentioned in two counties).[24]	' It may indeed be fairly conjectured that the landowners in Domesday who paid their relief to the sheriff, those who held six manors or less, and those who paid their relief to the king, stood in the same relation to one another [25] (as the greater and lesser barons).

Prof. Adams similarly refers to the antiquity of the distinction drawn in Chapter XIV of the Charter.[26]   Now the two passages in Domesday to which Gneist refers relate only to Yorkshire and to Derbyshire and Notts, and I have explained in *Feudal England* (pp. 72-3) that the practice described is part of that duodecimal system which is peculiar to the ' Danish ' district in the northern portion of England.   It would not consequently be met with outside that district, that is to say, in the larger portion of the country.   It could, therefore, have nothing to do with the later distinction between ' greater ' and ' lesser ' barons.

This point is of some importance if—improbable though it may seem—we have here the origin of Stubbs' statement that the ' lesser ' tenants-in-chief paid their reliefs to the sheriff, but the greater direct to the Crown.[27]   This statement is repeated without question by Maitland,[28] by Pollock

[24] *History of the English Constitution*, i, 143-4 ; *Domesday Book*, 280b, 298b.

[25] *Const. Hist.* i, 366 note.

[26] *Origin of the Engl. Const.* p. 226 note.   See the difference in the payment of relief in Domesday 1280 (Vinogradoff, *Society in the Eleventh Century*, p. 308, note 2).

[27] *Const. Hist.* (1875), i, 564-5, 567 ; ii, 182.

[28] *Const. Hist. of Engl.* pp. 65, 80.

and Maitland,[29] and by Prof. Medley.[30] It is, however, at variance with the evidence of the Pipe Rolls, which proves that holders of a single fee or even less are found paying their reliefs as directly to the Crown as a great Baron.

Hitherto I have been endeavouring to prove that the line drawn in the second Chapter between ' barons ' and ' knights ' by the Charter has nothing to do with that which it draws in its fourteenth chapter between the greater barons and the rest of the tenants-in-chief. A different and far more difficult question is that of the identity of the knights mentioned in the second chapter. For the wording of that chapter, as I contend, is sufficient to prove that they cannot possibly have been, as is so loosely assumed, the ' minor barons.' How then did they differ in status from the ' barons,' from whom the amount of their relief distinguishes them so sharply ?

It is usually endeavoured to interpret this ' chapter ' of the Charter by the help of (*A*) Glanville's book, (*B*) the *Dialogus de Scaccario*, both of them written in the latter part of the reign of Henry II.[31] Now what Glanville says is this :

Dumtamen domino suo sicut tenetur suum offerat homagium coram probis hominibus, et suum rationabile relevium, dicitur autem rationabile relevium, alicujus juxta consuetudinem regni de feodo unius militis, centum solidos de socagio vero quantum valet census illius socagii per unum annum ; de Baroniis vero nihil certum statutum est, quia juxta voluntatem et misericordiam domini Regis solent Baroniae capitales de releviis suis domino Regi satisfacere.[32]

[29] *Hist. of Engl. Law* (1895), i, 260.

[30] *Engl. Const. Hist.* (1907), p. 30.

[31] *Hist. of Engl. Law* (1895), i, 289, where it is loosely stated that, ' The Dialogue on the Exchequer tells us that the relief for the knight's fee is 100s. It is, we shall find, most important to note that the Dialogue limits its statement to knight's fees held in chief "ratione baronie cujuslibet " or " de eschaeta".'

[32] Glanville, *Tractatus de Legibus et Consuetudinibus Angliae*, bk. ix, cap. 4.

The obvious difficulty of this passage is that Glanville is here speaking of reliefs due to a lord (*dominus*) and yet includes among them reliefs due from ' baronies ' to the king. Mr. McKechnie claims that ' Glanville's words are ambiguous,' and there seems to be among the latest commentators some difference of opinion as to whether they cover the case of a ' knight's ' fee held in chief *ut de corona*. The authors of the *History of English Law* [33] are alleged to hold that they do, though this is by no means clear. On the other hand, the learned editors of the *Dialogus de Scaccario* consider that the holder of such a fee did not enjoy the privilege of fixed relief,[34] and in this they are followed by Mr. McKechnie [35] and by Professor Adams,[36] who considers him to be right. The view of these writers is based on the *Dialogus*, which undoubtedly limits the privilege to those knight's fees which were held *ut de honore*.

These statements are exceedingly precise and the editors are justified in inferring from them ' that the tenant of a single knight's fee would be a " Baro minor " since the certainty of relief depends not on the extent of the estate held, but of its being held of a mesne lord.' [37] On the other hand this is at direct variance with the second Chapter of the Great Charter, which draws its line of division between ' barons ' and ' knights,' unless we restrict the latter to those who held *ut de honore*. This we shall see appears to be opposed to another chapter of the Charter. Unfortunately, Mr. McKechnie, seeking to produce record evidence that only the tenants of mesne lords . . . had their reliefs fixed, states, by a singular error, that :

Madox (I, 315-6) cites from Pipe Rolls, large sums exacted by the Crown : in one case £300 was paid for six fees—or ten times what a mesne lord could have exacted (*Pipe Roll*, 24 Henry II).[38]

[33] (Ed. 1895), i, 289.   [34] Ed. 1902, pp. 222-3.

[35] McKechnie, *Magna Carta* (1914), p. 197.

[36] *Origin of the English Const.* (1914), p. 214.

[37] *Dialogus de Scaccario* (1902), p. 222.

[38] McKechnie, *op. cit.* (1914), p. 197 note.

The reference is obviously to the entry which Madox cites correctly : ' Tedbaldus de Valeines debet xxx *l* (*sic*) de relevio vj militum (*Mag. Rot.* 24 Hen. II).' [39] The amount therefore, was not £300 but £30, the very amount that a ' mesne lord could have exacted.'

The knight's fees to which the *Dialogus* refers in the above extracts cannot well be those mentioned in the second chapter of the Charter, because the former are specially dealt with in its forty-third chapter. Otherwise it would be tempting to identify the two, as it would dispose of the difficulty raised by the passage in chapter two. Mr. McKechnie, however, does identify the two, but admits that on this hypothesis ' the need for this reference (in Chapter XLIII) to relief is not, at first sight, obvious.' [40] It seems to be clear, at least, that the distinctive privilege of paying only £5 relief on the knight's fee extended to three classes of fees, (1) those specially mentioned in Chapter XLIII, which were held of an escheated honour, such as that of Wallingford, etc. ; (2) those which were held of a fief temporarily in the hands of the Crown, owing to wardship or other cause ; (3) those held of an ecclesiastical fief which was in the hands of the Crown during a vacancy. For all three classes were affected by the same principal, viz. that the king stood in the shoes of the former holders of the fief and could, therefore, only exact from the under-tenants the same dues as their former lords exacted. Speaking of this forty-third chapter, Mr. McKechnie admits that, though it only mentions escheats, the same rule applied to sub-tenants of baronies in wardship (which was analogous to temporary escheat) or of ecclesiastical fiefs during a vacancy. [41]

It is, however, conceivable that, as Mr. McKechnie suggests, John wanted to draw a distinction by which he could treat knight's fees held *de eschaeta* as held of him

[39] *Hist. of Excheq.* (1711), p. 216 ; *Pipe Roll,* 24 Hen. II, p. 75.
[40] McKechnie, *op. cit.* p. 413 note.
[41] *Ibid.* (1914), p. 412 note. Cf. *Hist. of Engl. Law* (1895), i, 261.

ut de corona, and therefore liable, like baronies, to an arbitrary relief. But, at least under Henry II, the Pipe Rolls do not show any trace of such a claim, and confirm the evidence of the *Dialogus.* Nor has any evidence, I believe, yet been produced in support of the suggestion.

With almost monotonous regularity the Pipe Rolls record reliefs on fees held *de eschaeta* at the rate of £5 on the fee. For instance, in 1172, Michael de Preston owes £22 10s. relief on 4½ knight's fees *de escaetis Regis.*[42] Similarly on a lay fief, Nigel, son of the chamberlain, in 1175, pays £57 10s. on 11½ fees held of the ' Honour ' of Richmond [43] then in the King's hands, while on an ecclesiastical fief, Hamo Fitz William pays £18 15s. on 3¾ fees and Robert Bruton £2 10s. on half a fee, held in each case of the See of Canterbury in 1171.[44] It is needless to multiply instances of the rule, but exceptions to the rule are worth noting, though they are not easy to find. And here it may be observed that the evidence of the Pipe Rolls is by no means as easy to use as might be imagined. Extreme care in identifying the fees on which the relief is paid is constantly required, as there is often nothing to show, whether they are held of a fief or an ' escheated Honour ' or directly of the King *ut de corona.* For instance, in 1181, two men are charged thirty marcs relief for two knight's fees which had been Robert of Tilbury's.[45] There is nothing to identify these fees or to explain why the relief was £20, instead of £10. But they can hardly fail to be the two fees which a later Robert of Tilbury held of the ' Honour ' of Rayleigh (forfeited by Henry of Essex) in West Tilbury and Chilter-ditch, Essex.[46]

There is at times considerable difficulty in identifying, without special knowledge, the holding, in respect of which a payment is made ; for instance, in 1182 Gilbert, son of Gilbert de Archis, is charged fifty marcs on succeeding to

[42] *Pipe Roll,* 18 Hen. II, p. 36.   [43] *Ibid.* 21 Hen. II, p. 5.
[44] *Ibid.* 17 Hen. II, p. 142.   [45] *Ibid.* 27 Hen. II, p. 105.
[46] *Red Book of the Exchequer,* pp. 503, 738.

his father's land.[47]　This is an odd sum and it makes us
wonder whether it is paid in respect of a barony or of knight's
fees.　The ordinary sources of information do not assist us,
and we cannot trace his father's holding.　Gilbert, however,
is alleged to hold two knights' fees of the Honour of Tickhill in 1203.[48]　His name is not found in a feodary of the
Honour later in the reign, but we do there find ' Malveisin
de Grava ' as the holder of two fees.[49]　This entry is explained by one on the Pipe Roll of 1209 which shows us
' Malveisin de Hercy and William Ruffus charged 50 marcs
and 2 palfreys for the succession of their wives to the holding
of this Gilbert de Archis, their father.'　This holding was
in Grove, Notts, which thus extended to the Hercys of
Grove.[50]　Now this case might possibly be claimed as
supporting the view that John was trying to extort reliefs
from fees held *de eschaeta* ; but it has been shown that the
holder of these fees had been similarly charged fifty marcs
in 1182 and, moreover, the Pipe Rolls under John show him
regularly paying scutage, not as the holder of a ' barony '
but only as a tenant of the Honour of Tickhill.　Mr.
McKechnie's actual comment on the ' escheat ' portion of
the charter (Chapter XLIII) is this :

> This chapter reaffirms a distinction recognised by Henry II,
> but ignored by John . . . John ignored this distinction, extending
> to tenants *ut de escaeta* the more stringent rules applicable to
> tenants *ut de corona*.　Magna Carta reaffirmed the distinction.[51]

It appears to me that this conclusion is based on the
assumption that, because the Charter limits the rights of the
Crown, it was John who had attempted to extend those
rights.　My own position is that the Pipe Rolls show the
Crown's right to feudal incidents to be already extended
under Henry II.

[47] ' Pro fine terre patris sui,' *Pipe Roll*, 28 Hen. II, pp. 18-19.

[48] *Red Book of the Exchequer*, p. 183.　　　　[49] *Ibid.* p. 593.

[50] See *Tonge's Visit. of the Northern Cos.*, Ed. W. H. D. Longstaffe, Surtees Soc. vol. 41, p. 7 note.

[51] McKechnie, *op. cit.* pp. 411, 413.

We have now seen that Chapter II of the Great Charter cannot apply to any of the three categories of the ' knights ' dealt with by the *Dialogus*, that is to say, not to those who held of a lay or ecclesiastical fief temporarily in the king's hands, because the text forbids it, or to those who held of an escheated Honour, because, in addition to straining the text, such ' knights ' are specially dealt with in Chapter XLIII, which is concerned with escheats.[52] Who then are the ' knights ' that in Chapter II are distinguished so sharply from ' barons ' by the relief on their succession ?

The ultimate and indisputable evidence on which the answer depends is found in the Pipe Rolls themselves, but that evidence has to be combined with that of the various returns of knights' fees, especially the *Cartae baronum* of 1166. It may, however, be said at once that the Pipe Rolls do show a very marked distinction between the arbitrary sums charged as relief on baronies and those of £5 or some multiple thereof charged on the knights' fees. Normally— though not always—the former are further distinguished by the word *finis*, which is rightly used as implying a composition. The difficulty about the latter is that we have to make sure that the fees are held as directly as the ' baronies,' *ut de corona*.

Although we are not here concerned with the reliefs on serjeanties, it is advisable to note that those on the Pipe Rolls confirm Glanville's statement as to their arbitrary character. For instance, in 1163, the charge of a hundred marcs on Ralf Fitz Wigein ' pro relevio terre sue,' [53] was on

---

[52] Possibly the right conclusion here is one which has not yet been suggested, namely, that the Charter nowhere provides for the case of knights' fees *temporarily* in the king's hand owing to a wardship or a vacancy, because the rights of their holders had not been encroached upon by the Crown. Escheats seem to have been recognised as a category apart : the reason for this may have been that in early days, e.g. in the case of the forfeited fiefs of the bishop of Bayeux and the Count of Mortain, the holdings of large under-tenants had actually been converted by the Crown into separate baronies (owing the service of 5 or 10 knights) and appear as such in 1166. These constituted awkward precedents.

[53] *Pipe Roll*, 9 Hen. II, p. 31.

a serjeanty of some value,[54] though the fact is not stated. So also was that of seventy-five marcs (£50), charged to Robert Fitz Hugh in 1186, ' pro fine terre sue.' [55] This *terra* was at Upton and was granted by Henry II. The tenure of his successors, the ' Chanceus' family, proves that it was held by the service of a serjeant for forty days in war, which must not be confused with knight service.

That ' baronies ' were liable to arbitrary relief is admitted on all hands. But in order to ascertain the sums exacted under Henry II, it is not enough to copy the extracts made by Madox ; one has to examine the Pipe Rolls for oneself. And even then, evidence may be missed ; for the phrase *finis terre* is only indexed in some of the printed volumes of Pipe Rolls, though *relevium* is indexed regularly.[56] It is for the former that we have, in the case of ' baronies,' to look. It would be necessary, therefore, to read through the whole of the volumes in order to make one's list exhaustive. The table on page 232, however, will illustrate the nature of the sums paid under Henry II.

The first point to strike one here is that most of these sums are either £200 or £100, 200 marcs or 100 marcs. This is an unexpected result, more so as no relation can be traced between the size of the barony and the relief exacted. Moreover, of these four sums, only two exceed the maximum fixed by the Charter, while one is actually below it. This emphasises the contrast between the arbitrary ' fine ' from a barony and a fixed sum of a hundred shillings due from a knight's fee. When we confine our attention to the figures for a single county, the contrast we shall find becomes striking.

The evidence for Northumberland is of peculiar value for more reasons than one. In the first place, the proportion of single fees held in chief is exceptionally large, and, in the second, we have copious information on the constituents of

---

[54] *Book of Fees*, p. 1279.　　　　[55] *Ibid.* 32 Hen. II, 6.

[56] Neither of them is indexed in the Volumes of Pipe Rolls issued by the Record Commission.

Year.	Baron	Fees.	£	Marcs.
1155?	Robert de Helion - - -	70(?)		100
1158	William Paynel - - -	15(?)		100
1165	Roger d'Oilli - - - -			200
1166	Helias Giffard - - - -		100	
—	Alan de Furneaux - - -			100
—	Walter ' Brito ' - - -	15	200	
1167	Humfrey de Bohun - - -		200	
—	Richard de Siffrewast [57] - -			100
1168	John d'Aiencurt - - -	40		100
—	William de Scalariis - -	15(?)	100	
1171	William Fossard - - -	33½		80
1176	John the constable (of Chester) [58]			400
1177	William Chendeduit - -			200
—	William de Montacute - -	10(?)		100
1178	Robert de Lacy - - -			1000
1180	Hasculf de Tani - - -	7½	100	
1181	Hugh de Gournay - - -		100	
1182	Nicholas de Meriet - - -	2½	20	
1183	Guy de Rochford - - -			40
1186	Hamo fitz Meinfelin - -	15		200
—	Barony of Eaton Hastings -	5		200
—	Hugh de Say - - - -	15(?)	200	
—	Richard Fitz John - - -			200

the holdings together with notable evidence on the use of the word ' barony.' [59] Let us first take a typical five-knight barony, that of the Bertrams of Mitford.[60] In 1166 Roger Bertram certified that it was held by the service of five knights.[61] In 1177, his successor, William Bertram, was called upon to pay ' pro fine terre patris sui ' [62] no less than £200. In 1212, another Roger Bertram is returned as

[57] For Chesham.   [58] For his mother's land.

[59] *Book of Fees*, 200-205, 1111-1130 ; *Red Book of the Exchequer*, pp. 436-444, 562-3 ; *Reports on the Dignity of a Peer*, vol. ii, pp. 91-7.

[60] There was another Bertram barony in the county, that of the Bertrams of Bothal (three knights).

[61] ' Et sciatis, domine, quod feodum meum non debet vobis servitium nisi tantum de v militibus.' *Red Book of the Exchequer*, p. 438.

[62] *Pipe Roll*, 23 Hen. II, p. 83.

holding the ' barony ' by the service of five knights.[63]   Here
then is a clear case of an undoubted ' barony '—by no
means a large one, as baronies went [64]—charged exactly
twice the amount prescribed in the Great Charter as the
rightful and ancient (*antiquum*) relief.   We have thus a
striking illustration of the fact that, as I have insisted,[65] the
feudal extortions remedied by the Charter were not, as is so
often implied,[66] introduced by John, but are found in full
existence under Henry II.   Again we observe that the
sum exacted is rightly styled *finis terre*, not *relevium*, for it
represented, as the *Dialogus* and Glanville's book explain,
a special commutation of the king's right to exact in the
case of a ' barony ' an arbitrary sum.

From this Northumberland ' barony ' we will pass to a
smaller one, the story of which is more complicated and has
to be reconstructed.   In 1163 William de Greinville [67] was
holding what we learn from evidence of three years later
was a ' barony ' held by the service of three knights ; [68]
Next year it had passed to two co-heiresses of whom Ralf
de Gaugy married the elder and Hugh de Allintone (i.e.
Ellington) the younger.   This we learn from the same
evidence, namely, from their respective returns in 1166.[69]

---

[63] ' Rogerus Bertram tenet in capite de domino Rege *baroniam* de
Midford per servicium v militum.' (*Book of Fees*, p. 201.)   ' Rogerus
Bertram *baroniam* de Mytforde per v feoda.'   (*Red Book of the Exchequer*,
p. 563.)   ' Baronia de Mitford.'   (*Book of Fees*, p. 1115.)

[64] Several baronies owed the service of as many as sixty knights.

[65] In my introductions to the later Pipe Rolls of Henry II and to the
Rot. de Dominabus (Pipe Roll Soc.).

[66] E.g. McKechnie, *Magna Carta* (1914), pp. 196, 198.   So also
Petit Dutaillis, *Studies Suppl. to Stubbs' Const. Hist.* (1908), p. 129 :
' Its most salient characteristic is the restoration of the old feudal law,
violated by John Lackland, and perhaps practically its most important
clauses, because they could be really applied, were those, for example,
which limited the right of relief. . . .'   Cf. *Hist. of English Law* (1895),
p. 151 : ' John in these last years had been breaking the law ; therefore
the law must be defined and set in writing.'

[67] *Pipe Roll*, 7 Henry II, p. 23.

[68] *Red Book of the Exchequer*, pp. 438-9, 443.

[69] *Ibid.*   The editor gives (p. 439) the wrong reference for the *carta*
of Ralf de Gaugy and makes the unlucky suggestion by way of emenda-
tion that Ralf may have been the *son* of the elder sister.

The Pipe Roll of 1164 shows each of them paying a sum ' pro relevio terre sue.' [70]   Ralf pays forty marcs and Hugh twenty, so that the whole relief exacted was sixty marcs (£40), though the service due from the barony was only that of three knights.   Hugh, however, admitted that his tenure was baronial,[71] and the entire holding appears in 1212 as a *baronia* in the hands of Ralf de Gaugi.[72]   This exposed it to an arbitrary relief (as the payment is in this case termed) in 1164, namely £40, in lieu of the £15 which would have been payable if the holding had not been a ' barony ' but three knights' fees.

Let us now compare with these ' baronies,' three or four Northumberland holdings, the returns for which were similarly made among the *Cartae baronum* in 1166.   For these were similarly held in chief, though each of them owed the service of one knight at most.

William, son of Siward, who made return in 1166 that he held a knight's fee by the service of one knight,[73] is proved by his tenure of Gosforth, to be a Surtees,[74] and therefore, identical with the William de ' Tesa ' (or ' Tesia ') of 1161-1162.[75]   In 1174 his successor, Randulf ' de Super Teise,' was charged a hundred shillings (£5) *de relevio suo*.[76]   This was a fixed relief on a knight's fee.[77]   The next case is that of Ernulf de Morewic, who returned his

[70] *Pipe Roll*, 8 Henry II, p. 11.   The fact is obscured by Hugh's name being there printed as ' de Clenton.'

[71] ' Ego teneo dimidiam baroniam.'   (See, for its constituents, *Book of Fees*, pp. 203, 1120.)   Compare with this ' dimidia baronia ' the ' baronia integra ' of the Great Charter and observe that the baronial tenure is not affected by subdivision, though Ralf and Hugh each claim to owe the service of ' a knight and a half (only).'

[72] *Book of Fees*, p. 203.   Cf. *Red Book of the Exchequer*, p. 439.

[73] ' Pro feodo et servitio j militis.'   (*Red Book*, p. 440.)

[74] See *Book of Fees*, p. 1120 (' Radulfus super Tayse '), and p. 203 (' Ricardus Surtayse ').

[75] *Pipe Rolls*, 7 Hen. II, p. 24 ; 8 Hen. II, p. 10.

[76] *Ibid*. 20 Hen. II, p. 107.

[77] The service is given (apparently in error) as half a fee (*Book of Fees*, p. 1120), or two-thirds (*Ibid*. p. 203).

holding in 1166, as a knight's fee,[78] ' of the old feoffment.'
In 1177 his successor, Hugh de Morewic was charged a
hundred shillings (£5) for his relief.[79] This Hugh appears
as one of Henry's ministerial officers towards the end of the
reign and it is interesting to note that so early as 1161 he
has a discharge *precepto Cancellarii* of the two marcs
charged to his father,[80] which suggests that he was already
in official employ. The third case is that of Robert Caro,
who returned himself in 1166 as holding five carucates as
one knight's fee.[81] In 1179 Peter ' Carhou ' accounted for
a hundred shillings for his relief.[82]

Even more notable is the case of Godfrey Bayard, who
returned his holding in 1166 as one-third of a fee and who
had been charged the year before 33s. 4d.,[83] that is just a
third of the regulation £5.

The importance of this evidence is that in each of three
cases where the holding was one fee or less, and where the
holding was not part of an escheated honour, relief is
uniformly charged at the rate of £5 a fee. On the other
hand, a three-fee ' barony ' was charged, as we have seen,
£40, and a five-fee barony £200. Moreover, in 1168, an
entry on the Pipe Roll runs : ' Idem vicecomes redd. comp'
de feodis *Baronum et militum* qui de rege tenent in capite
in ballia sua qui cartas de tenemento suo regi non
miserunt.' [84] The sheriff was here dealing, as I said above,
not with the holdings on escheated ' honours,' but with
those which were held ' in capite *ut de corona*.' If we now
pass to the other end of England, we find in Devon,

---

[78] ' Feodum j militis.' (*Red Book of the Exchequer*, p. 438.)

[79] *Pipe Roll*, 23 Hen. II, p. 84.   [80] *Ibid.* 7 Hen. II, p. 24.

[81] ' Pro j feodo militis.' (*Red Book of the Exchequer*, p. 444.)

[82] *Pipe Roll*, 25 Hen. II, p. 28. Cf. *Red Book of the Exchequer*, p. 178.

[83] *Red Book of the Exchequer*, p. 442 ; *Pipe Roll*, 11 Hen. II, p. 27.

[84] *Pipe Roll*, 14 Hen. II, p. 172. The number of fees he assigns to
these barons and knights is Balliol 30, Walter Fitz William 3, Philip
de Humez 2, Odinel d'Umfraville 2, Robert de Bradford 1, William de
(A)mundeville 1.   As a matter of fact, Walter Fitz William had duly
made his return. (*Red Book of the Exchequer*, p. 436.)

Geoffrey del Estre paying £5 in 1183 as the relief on a knight's fee.[85]   There is nothing by which he can be identified in the *Cartae* of 1166, but an analysis of the scutage returns shows that the ' Robertus filius Galfridi ' of 1166 (*Red Book*, p. 258) must have been Robert, son of Geoffrey de L'estre and father of the Geoffrey who succeeded in 1183. Again turning from Devon to Norfolk, we find William de ' Colecherche ' returning his small tenement as held by the service of half a knight.[86]   His son Richard, on succeeding him, paid for his ' relief ' fifty shillings,[87] the sum due on half a fee.   In these two cases we can clearly identify the holdings among those held *in capite* in 1166.

It has, at least, now been clearly established that those who made their returns in 1166, although then treated apparently as being all on the same footing, were not treated alike in the matter of their reliefs.   Those who held, in the cases examined, one fee or less, were only called upon to pay at the rate of £5 on the knight's fee.

[85] ' Pro relevio feodi j militis ' (p. 117).

[86] ' Servitium dimidii militis.'   (*Red Book of the Exchequer*, p. 400.)

[87] *Pipe Roll*, 21 Hen. II, p. 124.

THE PRISE OF WINES

WHEN studying the Pipe Roll of 1186 (32 Henry II) I was much struck by this passage :

Et pro xx tonellis vini Pictaviensis *de modiatione* et pro ij tonellis vini Authisiodorensis *de modiatione*[1] xxij*li* per breve regis. Et pro novis doliis ad imponendum idem vinum xxviij *s.* per idem breve (p. 197).

I venture to suggest that we have here, apparently, the earliest record reference to the King's prise of wines. The two grounds for this suggestion are (1) that 20s. a tun (the prisage rate) is paid for the wine ; (2) that the figure would harmonise with a purchase of the tuns in couples, in accordance with the old prisage definition of ' one tun before and one behind the mast.'

It is obvious that the words ' de modiatione ' must have some meaning, and *modiatio*, as is well known, was the name of the Norman wine-due at Rouen,[2] though that due, no doubt, was distinct in character from our own *recta prisa*. Before proceeding to the evidence that the prise was normally deemed to be the right of taking one tun before and one behind the mast on payment of 20s. a tun, I would point out that if my suggestion as to the above passage is right, it would probably apply to the passage on the previous roll (p. 44) in which Henry of Cornhill accounts ' pro v tonellis vini ad opus regis c solides per idem breve,' and to that on the Roll of 1182 (28 Henry II) in which (p. 159) he receives £42 ' ad emenda xlii dolia vini ad opus regis per

---

[1] The italics are mine.

[2] It is oddly rendered ' multure ' in *Cal. of Charter Rolls*, vol. iv, pp. 67, 724.

breve Rannulfi de Glanvill ' ; for this, as I shall show, was well below the market price of the wine for the King.

In November 1912 Mr. N. S. B. Gras published a critical paper on ' The national customs-revenue in England,' [3] in which he devoted particular attention to the prise of wines and contravened the views of Mr. Hubert Hall as set forth in his *History of the Customs Revenue in England* (1885) and his articles in the *Antiquary* (1882). Mr. Gras informed me that he had overlooked my own contributions to the *Antiquary* (1882) in which I endeavoured to vindicate Stubbs' definition of the prise, denounced by Mr. Hall as his ' gravest mistake of all.' [4] Mr. Gras writes that :

Stubbs originally defined the *recta prisa* with approximate correctness (*Const. Hist.* Ed. 1875, ii, 522), but yielding to the criticism (Hall in *Antiquary*, vi, 65) substituted the incorrect explanation, which has gained acceptance in other standard works (p. 139).

The points at issue between Stubbs and Mr. Hall were (1) the number of casks which the King was entitled to select ; (2) the price which the King had to pay for them. As to the first, no doubt Stubbs was slightly inaccurate ; two definitions are found in records : (*A*) that in the *Liber Albus*, namely, one cask from a cargo of more than nine and less than twenty, and two casks from a cargo of twenty or more ; (*B*) ' one cask before the mast and another behind.' Mr. Hall cites the former as that under which ' prisage was only taken,' [5] but the latter as ' the right of definition of the prisage.' [6] As a matter of fact he cites an Elizabethan customer's account,[7] which treats the two definitions as identical. But the point which is of importance is that they both *are* definitions, quite as much so, in fact, as the scale given by Stubbs. They are, therefore, both of them

[3] *Quart. Journ. of Economics*, xxvii, 107-149. Dr. Round wrote this before Mr. Gras published his larger work on the Customs System (1918).

[4] *Antiquary*, vi, 64.   [5] *Ibid.* vi, 64.   [6] *Ibid.* vi, 65.

[7] *Ibid.* vi, 65 ; *Hist. of the Customs Revenue*, ii, 96 note.

hostile to that ' undefined nature of the prisage,' for which Mr. Hall was fighting.[8]

Perhaps, however, we may infer from Mr. Hall's second passage that the ' head ' and ' front ' of Stubbs' offence was his ' retaining his original estimate of 20s. as the value of the cask of prise-wine.' Stubbs, however, has nowhere spoken of 20s. as ' the value of the cask ' (which was a good deal more), but as ' the price ' at which the Crown was entitled to buy it. Nor does he assert ' that the rate (*sic*) was laid at 20s. on the cask,'[9] or speak of a ' due of 20s. on the cask of wine.' In replying to my own criticism, Mr. Hall admitted ' that prisage was usually taken at 20s. under Henry III, though,' he added, ' Professor Stubbs had no right to make a sweeping definition from the circumstance.'[10] Stranger still, he subsequently wrote in his *History of the Customs Revenue* (ii, 193) that :

At a time when the average price of wine did not exceed 50s. per tun, the denizen who imported 20 casks paid a toll of £3 as the difference between the rate of the *recta prisa* and the current value of the two casks which were taken from him by the Crown.

This calculation, it will be seen, assumes that the Crown took the two casks, in Stubbs' words ' at the price of twenty shillings the cask.' He also wrote of the period extending from Edward I to Edward IV :

It must be remembered, however, that during the greater part of this time the *recta prisa* was taken at the traditional rate of 20s. per tun, regardless of the economical changes in the progress.[11]

It is with this ' traditional rate ' that I now propose to deal.

Mr. Gras finds the first appearance of ' the prise of wines in that document of ' about 1150,' which was edited by Miss

[8] *Hist. of the Customs Revenue*, i, 2 : ' an undefined right of prise forages enjoyed by the Crown, and conspicuous in historical times in the case of the prisage of wines.'

[9] *Antiquary*, vi, 64. [10] *Ibid.* vi, 231.

[11] *Hist. of the Customs Revenue*, ii, 202.

Bateson for the *English Historical Review*.[12] In the case
of a ' hulk u altre nef,' the prise was ' un tunel devant e
altre deriere,' but the price though defined was not fixed.
' It is probable,' Mr. Gras suggests, ' that some time in the
reign of Henry II an assize, now lost, was issued, fixing for
all England the price which the King should pay for his
wine, 15s. in Bristol, and 20s. elsewhere, and likewise
standardising the amount for all ships, at one tun before the
mast and one after ' (p. 137). But the only references he
gives for these figures, are the records of 15-17 Edward I
and 8 Edward II. For the earlier period, he produces no
evidence whatever. Of the two Rouen charters which he
cites from my *Calendar of Documents in France* (pp. 33, 36)
only that of 1199 is in point. It gives one interesting
definition of the prisage at London—' from each ship, two
barrels, one before and one behind the mast at his
selection ' [13]—but it leaves the price to be given obscure.
I have already [14] drawn attention to the importance of
the early Irish evidence which is found in John's charter to
Dublin, granted in 1192 and confirmed in 1200. In that
charter, he reserves to himself :

quod de qualibet navi quam illuc cum vinis venire continget,
ballivus meus, loco mei, eliget duo dolia vini quecunque voluerit
in navi ; unum, scilicet, ante malum, aliud retro malum ad
opus meum pro xl solidis, unum pro xx solidis, et aliud pro xx
solidis ; et nichil amplius inde accipiet, nisi ad gratum mercatoris.[15]

---

[12] *Engl. Hist. Rev.* xvii, 500.

[13] ' Salva nostra prisa vinorum suorum quam habemus apud London
[jam] ad opus nostrum, ad bibendum et donandum ubi nobis placuerit
et non ad vendendum, scilicet, de unaquaque navigata vini duo dolia,
unum ante mastum (*sic*) et aliud retro mastum (*sic*), ad electionem
nostrum.' Cheruel (*Histoire de Rouen*, i, 252) reads ' *vinum* ante mastum,'
and Giry (*Les Etablissements de Rouen*) accepted his reading, though it
obviously makes nonsense. Deville, from whose transcript I worked,
saw the original charter and read the word as ' vini,' which also makes
nonsense. It must have contained six minims and have been intended
for ' unu[m].'

[14] This was in the *Antiquary* for 1882, 'The Great Case of the
Impositions,' vi, 133.

[15] *Historic and Municipal Documents of Ireland* (Rolls Series), p. 53.
The charter was confirmed in the same terms in 1200.

This has hitherto appeared to be the earliest record evidence on the prise, and even at that early date, the definition, we see, is precise, not only as to the number of casks, but also as to the price to be given for them by the Crown. When writing on the subject, I urged that the probable inference from this passage was, that this was then the definition of the prise of wines in England, whence the Anglo-Normans would have introduced it into Ireland. This suggestion would accord, so far as the price is concerned, with the evidence I quoted at the outset from the Pipe Rolls of 1182, 1185, and 1186. In Ireland the definition I have quoted remained precise and unchanged ; for when, in 1327, James ' le Botiller ' petitioned for the ' Prisa vinorum in Hibernia,' as having been enjoyed by his ancestors from time out of mind, he defined it as :

de qualibet navi vinis venalibus carcata infra terram predictam, unum dolium vini ante malum et unum alium retro pro quadraginta solidis mercatoribus quorum vina illa fuerint solvendis.[16]

This petition creates a difficulty which seems to have entirely escaped notice. Mr. Hall writes that :

In the first or second years of Edward III, James Butler, newly created Earl (of Ormonde), on his marriage with a princess of the Blood Royal (*sic*),[17] presented three petitions in Parliament, . . . the third for the restoration of the prisage of wine in Ireland (I, 13).

But his description of that petition differs from the terms of that which is recited in the Close Rolls. It is evident from the description that it must be derived from the Rolls of Parliament, and I found it there duly dated in the margin as of the *ninth* year, 1335.

It is of some importance to date these petitions rightly,

---

[16] Close Roll, Edw. III, part 1, m. 1. See *Foedera* for the Latin text and *Cal. of Close Rolls*, 1327-1330, p. 84, for an English abstract.

[17] This lady, described in the *Genealogist* (i, 79) as ' royalty,' was Eleanor de Bohun.

because they differ materially in their descriptions of the claim. In 1327, James Butler claimed that :

The prise of wines in Ireland pertains to him . . . from each ship laden with wines for sale coming to that land to the cities of Dublin, Drogheda, Waterford, Cork and Limerick for 40s. to be paid to the merchants from whom the wines are taken, of which prise his ancestors have always hitherto died seised in their demesne as of fee from the times aforesaid.[18]

This is clearly a claim to the actual prise itself, not to a mere lease or ' farm ' thereof at a sum payable to the Crown. But eight years later (1335) what he claimed was :

de chescune Neef deux toneaux, rendaunt pour chescun tonel xl s a l'Eschequer, etc.[19]

Although somewhat obscure, this certainly implies, not a right to the prise itself, but only a right to ' farm ' it, accounting to the Dublin Exchequer for 40s. on every tun.

It is difficult apparently to trace the origin of the Butler's claim. I pointed out in the *Genealogist*[20] that James ' le Botiller ' confused the office of Butler, from which he derived his name, with the *feodum* of the prise of wines from which he alleged that he derived it. It is, as I there showed, clear that his father Edmund was in possession in 1310, but only as the actual grantee at the time.[21] Yet Theobald le Botiller, on coming of age in 1290, petitioned the Crown for the prise ' which his father and ancestors enjoyed,' whereupon the escheator reported that his ' father died seised of the franchise, but he knows not by what warrant.'[22] Mr. Hall has discovered the warrant ; ' the grant,' he writes, ' appears to have been made by Edward I in the sixth year of his reign . . . according to the established usage and the known laws of the realm.' The grant in question, namely, that made in the sixth year of Edward I,

---

[18] *Cal. of Close Rolls*, 1327-1330, p. 84.   [19] *Rot. Parl.* ii, 90.
[20] N.S. ii, 188-9.

[21] ' *cui* dominus rex prisam vinorum concessit per totam Hiberniam.' (*Historic and Municipal Docs. of Ireland*, p. 291.)

[22] *Genealogist, ut supra.*

was undoubtedly a lease of the revenues derived from the prescriptive prisage of the Crown, to a royal patentee.[23] No reference is given for this important grant, but a clue is afforded on another page,[24] where ' *Rot. Chart.* 6 Ed. I, m. 2,' is cited for the grant of immunity to the Cinque Ports, with the statement that, ' In this same Roll, the Prisage of wines in Ireland was confirmed (*sic*) to the Lord Butler of Ireland.' But reference proves that no such charter is found on the Charter Roll of 6 Edward I. Nor does the *Calendar of Charter Rolls* reveal it under any other of his regnal years. In Lodge's *Peerage of Ireland*, the root of title is alleged to be a grant ' in fee of his (James) son James and his heirs male, 5 June 1372 ' (46 Edward III), when the grantee certainly was high in favour with the Crown, but no reference is given for this statement.[25]

About the time (1327) when James Butler was claiming, as part of his inheritance, the prise of wine in the ports of Ireland, the Archbishop of York was similarly claiming, as having been granted to the See by Athelstan, the prise of wine in the port of Hull. Letters Close, of 10th March, 1327 (1326-7) directing the King's butler's deputy at Hull ' to permit ' the archbishop to have his prises therein without impediment,[26] recite the return of an inquisition under Edward II by which it was found that ' until 11 Edward I,' the archbishops had enjoyed ' time out of mind '—

their port and prises of wines arriving in the water of Hull, to wit receiving from each ship bringing over 20 tuns of wine for sale in the said water, two tuns of wine, one before and one behind the mast, paying 20s. for each tun thus prised (*priso*).[27]

It is clear from this and from the sequel that what the

---

[23] *Hist. of the Customs Revenue*, i, 13, 14. In the *Genealogist* (N.S. 79), Mr. Hall states that, ' that grant had been made to Lord Theobald Butler, an attached servant of the Crown, during the stress of Longshank's (*sic*) Scottish " campaigns." Was this in his sixth year ? '

[24] *Ibid.* ii, 107.   [25] Lodge, *Peerage of Ireland* (Ed. Archdall), iv, 3.

[26] *Cal. of Close Rolls*, 1327-1330, pp. 51-2.

[27] See *Foedera* for the Latin text, and for the grant of 51 Hen. III, cited therein, see *Rot. Parl.* i, 431-2.

archbishops claimed was to exercise for themselves the King's own right of prise, just as James Butler had claimed it in 1327. Three years later (1330) the archbishop complained that, in spite of this decision in his favour and the Crown's action thereupon, he was deprived of ' prises de vins,' viz. de chescun Nief portant vintz tonels, ou aucuns deux tonels paiant pur chescun tonel vintz souz,[28] by the ingenious device of the wine-ships, which brought twenty tuns or more, discharging outside his jurisdiction, into smaller vessels in which the number of casks was below the limit for prise. The struggle, we find, continued, the archbishop being called on by the King to show ' by what warrant he claims to have the prises of wines in the water and port of Hull.' [29] This is proof that, as I said, he claimed to exercise for himself the right of the prise of wine within ' the water of Hull.' The immediate point, however, is that here again twenty shillings is the fixed price given for the ' prised cask.' In the South of England we discover evidence of great value on the prise in the charter granted to Melcombe Regis in 1280. The burgesses receive ' all the liberties granted to the citizens of London,' with some exceptions such as :

saving the King's ancient prise of wine, that is, of one tun before the mast and one behind it, to be paid at 20s. the tun, as the King and his ancestors have been wont to take the said prise.[30]

Here is the same clear definition coupled with a statement that the prise had been so taken by the King ' and his ancestors.'

Thus far it has been my object to vindicate Stubbs' statement that the Crown took the prise-wine ' at the price of 20s.,' in order to apply it to the Pipe Roll of 1186, from which I quoted at the outset. I now propose to deal with the two allied questions on the subject of the prise : these

[28] *Rot. Parl.* ii, 39. [29] *Cal. of Close Rolls*, 1332, p. 430.
[30] *Cal. of Charter Rolls*, ii, 223.

are (1) the difference in favour of the crown between the price it gave and the value of the wine it took ; (2) the distinction between the wine taken in virtue of the *recta prisa* and the wine which had to be ' bought ' for the Crown.

As to the first, Mr. Gras surely makes one serious error when he states that ' at the time of the assize [31] 20s. per tun would not have been much, if at all, below an average price ' (p. 138). For it was the very essence of the ' prise ' that it should enable the King to take a (defined) amount of wine at well below the market price ; from its very earliest appearance this was its essential feature. Mr. Gras relies on ' John's assize of wines, 1199, practically our only source of evidence,' but his own immediately preceding footnote shows that in 1204 the 20s. per tun for the prise-wine was only three-fifths of what the King had to give for the wine which he acquired by purchase.[32]

With regard to the second of my questions, I would warn the reader that it goes to the very root of the matter. The distinction between the wines in these two categories is a vital point to bear in mind. Mr. Hall, however, writes of ' the sale of prise-wines, both of those which were taken at the rate of one cask on each side of the mast for about half their value, and the others bought up at a rather higher rate, though still considerably below their market value ' (II, 82). It cannot be insisted on too strongly that the phrase ' prise-wines ' (*vinum de prisa*) is applied to the former category *alone*. To learn this, one need not travel beyond the pages of Madox' work (Ed. 1711, pp. 527-8) :

' Lxxiij tonellorum, de quibus xxxj tonelli sunt de prisa, et xlii empti ' (14 John) . . . ' pro v tonnellis Andegavensis (vini) de prisa, et tribus emptis ; et pro xlv tonellis vini Gasconiae de prisa, et cc et xxij tonellis emptis ; et pro ij tonellis *Autisiodorensis* de prisa, et xiv tonellis emptis ; et pro xxxj tonellis Franciscis de prisa et xxiiij tonellis emptis ' (*Ibid.*) . . . ' Et in

[31] This is the last assize of Henry II, of which he postulates the existence.

[32] See also my remarks on the price of wine in 1185 in *Pipe Roll*, 31 Hen. II, pp. xxv-xxvi.

cariagio vinorum Regis tam de prisa quam de empto, scilicet, unius dolii de prisa . . . et unius dolii de empto ' (19 Hen. III) . . . ' Idem r.c. de lxvj doliis, receptis apud Suthampton de recta prisa. . . . Summa doliorum de prisa ccxxxv dolia. Idem r.c. de xxx doliis emptis apud Suthampton. . . . Summa doliorum de empto lxvj dolia. Summa summarum tam de prisa quam de empto cccj dolia ' (49 Hen. III).

These extracts are from the Pipe Rolls, but the Close Rolls tell the same story. In 1230, wines are ordered to be sent to the King, ' xvj dolia vini de prisa regis et xxxvj dolia vini de empto.' [33] In 1232 there is a similar order to Southampton to send ' duo dolia vini de prisa regis et quatuor dolia de empto.' [34] In 1235 John de Colemere, keeper of the King's wines, is directed to place in the cellar at Westminster ' centum dolia vini de prisa regis quam de empto.' [35]

Finally, there is a good case in 1237, where directions are given for payment to Robert Grestein ' pro duobus doliis vini de prisa xl solidos, et eidem Roberto pro viginti et vij doliis vini Andegavie de empto lviij libras et decem solidos.[36] Here we have the additional information that the prise-wine (*vinum de prisa*) was taken by the crown ' at the price of 20s. the cask,' as Stubbs expressed it, while the forty shillings paid for the two casks reminds us of James Butler's claim to the Irish prise in 1327, in which the figures are the same.[37] But indeed one need not travel outside Mr. Hall's pages to find evidence of this distinction. He has made this excerpt :

Poncio de Mora, mercatori, viginti libras, videlicet, decem libras pro decem doliis vini de recta prisa Regis et decem libras pro quinque doliis vini et que una cum predictis decem doliis vini de prisa, etc.[38]

The importance of this extract is that it not only records twenty shillings as the price given for a tun ' de recta prisa,' but shows that the King gave just twice as much for the wine

---

[33] *Cal. of Close Rolls*, 1227-1231, p. 339. [34] *Ibid.* 1231-4, p. 26.

[35] *Ibid.* 1234-7, p. 38. [36] *Ibid.* p. 461.

[37] See p. 242 above. [38] ii, 98 note.

he had to buy. The Patent Rolls supply us with an even
stronger instance in 1261. The King owed to two London
merchants £232 ' for 100 tuns of wine bought of them and
2 tuns of the King's right prise taken (*sic*) from them by
Peter de Gisorciis, chamberlain of London.' [39] Deducting
the £2 paid for the two tuns of prise-wine, the King was here
actually paying 46s. for the bought wine as against 20s. for
the prise-wine.

The two points that I wish to make are : (1) The ' prise-
wines ' (*vinum de prisa*) were those *only* which were taken in
virtue of the King's defined right of prise (*recta prisa*) ;
(2) The bought wines (*vinum de empto*) are carefully kept
distinct ; nor is it the fact that they were only bought ' at
a slightly (or rather) higher rate ' than the wines claimed in
virtue of the prise. With regard to the price given for the
wines ' bought ' for the King, it is a serious error to represent
the price given for the ' bought ' wine as only ' slightly
higher ' than that given for the prise-wine, in order to
approximate the two transactions. Indeed, if the prise-
wines bought at 20s. ' were taken . . . for about half their
value ' (II, 82), the wine which, we have seen, was bought
for twice or even more than twice as much must have
fetched its full value or more.

I do not wish to be dogmatic on the relation of the price
given for the ' bought ' wine to its price in the open market ;
what it really represents is not prise but pre-emption. This
is clearly shown by a valuable entry on the Close Roll :

Mandatum est majori et vicecomitibus Lond' quod non per-
mittant quod aliqua vina Wasconie vel Andegavie que venerunt
usque Lond' vendantur antequam Camerarius Regis Lond' et
Ballivi Regis emerint ad opus Regis ea que Regi fuerint
necessaria (1235).[40]

This resembles the Chester custom entered in Domesday :

si habentibus martrinas pelles juberet prepositus regis ut
nulli venderent donec sibi prius ostensas compararet, etc.

---

[39] *Cal. of Patent Rolls*, 1258-1266, p. 145.
[40] *Cal. of Close Rolls*, 1234-7, p. 219.

The ground is now clear at last for considering the true prise of wines—the *prisa* or *recta prisa* as we have seen it alternatively styled. Mr. Gras writes of the *recta prisa* : ' that the earliest specific occurrence found of this ph[r]ase is of the year 1202 ' (p. 137). This is not quite accurate, for the entry is of 1204.[41] It is defined in the Cinque Ports charter of 1278 as ' recta prisa nostra, videlicet, de uno doleo vini ante malum et alio post malum.' [42] This primitive definition of the number of casks to be taken occurs again and again. Mr. Hall fully admits this and cites the Cinque Ports Charter.[43] But he tells us that :

The right definition of the prisage was used by Baron Clark, who described it as taking for the King one cask before the mast, and another behind.[44]

Mr. Gras makes the comment that here and elsewhere the prise is wrongly described as if it were an out-and-out ' taking,' or seizure, without payment. This criticism seems to be needed, for Hallam, I find, spoke of ' the prisage of wine, that is, a right of taking two casks out of each vessel.[45] Mr. McKechnie also, in his valuable *Magna Carta*, speaks of the casks taken as ' the normal toll,' but says nothing of money being paid for them.[46] Indeed Mr. Gras has pointed out that even so sound a scholar as the late Miss Bateson wrote, that ' it is new to find that the King was expected to pay for the wines of his butlerage.' [47]

What he did pay for them is a point I have discussed above at considerable length. It was there shown by abundant evidence that the standard price he paid was 20s. —' the traditional rate,' as Mr. Hall terms it (ii, 102). That there may have been occasional exceptions to this price at special ports or for special wines I am careful not to deny, for a negative is always difficult to prove. But such exceptions would be insufficient to affect the general proposition

[41] Madox (1711), p. 526 note.   [42] *Ibid.* p. 529 note (a).
[43] *Hist. of the Customs Revenue*, ii, 63, 89, 96.
[44] *Antiquary*, vi, 65.   [45] *Middle Ages*, Ed. 1860, ii, 322.
[46] *Op. cit.* p. 468 ; Ed. 1914, p. 402.   [47] *Engl. Hist. Rev.* xvii, 497.

that the king, in Stubbs' words, was entitled to take a limited
number of casks ' at the price of twenty shillings the cask.'
Thus the salient point that we have to keep in mind is that
the ' *recta prisa* ' was a strictly *limited* right, limited as to
the number of casks, and limited as to the price which the
Crown had to give for them. This, as it seems to me, is
the vital feature which gives to the prise of wines its
exceptional importance in constitutional history.

The later history of the prise of wines is, happily, in no
doubt ; it is recognised on all sides to have been commuted,
in 1302, by the Aquitanian wine-merchants for a toll of 2s.
on every tun of wine ' by way of new custom.' [48] This
commutation was made general for all alien merchants by
the *Carta Mercatoria*.[49] Strictly speaking, it was not only
the *recta prisa* but all ' prises ' (that is, exactions over and
above it) from which exemption was thus obtained. This
' toll ' of ' custom ' of two shillings became known as
' butlerage.' All this is, as I have said, common ground.

This leads us to the last and most important issue. Were
there indeed, as Mr. Hall asserts, ' three distinct phases of
development in the history of ' what he terms ' the taxation
of wines ' ? I say, without hesitation, that there were only
two. The first was that of the *recta prisa*, the ' definite ' or
' restricted ' prisage, which lasted down to the changes of
1302-3 ; the second was that of the subsequent period,
when that prise continued to be taken from denizens as
before, but was commuted in the case of aliens for a ' custom ' of two shillings on every cask of imported wine. That
this is so is proved not only by Mr. Hall's own words, but
by the very passage in which he asserts the three ' phases.'
He speaks at its close—quite rightly—of ' the *recta prisa*
due to the Crown by immemorial usage.' If this was so,
how could it be ' a secondary form ' of an earlier phase, a
' commutation . . . for a fixed toll ' ? It is beyond dispute

[48] *Cal. of Charter Rolls*, iii, 30-31.
[49] *Hist. of the Customs Revenue*, i, 106.

that the defined ' prise ' goes back as far as we have any evidence at all ; the ' commutation ' is a sheer guess.

To sum up, I have now shown what the *recta prisa* was, namely, the King's right to purchase at a *defined* price (not at his own price), a *defined* number of casks out of a cargo of wine. Records prove that its existence was officially recognised by John and it was clearly, as Stubbs states, among the ' antiquas et rectas consuetudines ' sanctioned by the Great Charter. That prise, which was not *recta*, would be, as Mr. Gras observes, (1) of an excessive number of casks ; (2) at a price lower than the defined rate, to which I may add (3) its exaction at more than one port. There is record evidence of restitution being ordered in this last case. And these illicit exactions must not be confused or identified with the ' purchase ' of wines on the King's account by pre-emption.

I have further shown that ' in so far as it forms the analogy on which the general prise theory is founded,' [50] the alleged origin of the *recta prisa* as a secondary form ' of an earlier phase ' produced by a ' commutation ' is not established by any evidence and is mere speculation. Although I am anxious not to indulge in speculation myself, I may point out a salient objection to the theory that the *recta prisa* can be deduced from the principle embodied in ' purveyance.' To ' purveyance ' the products of the realm would be obviously exposed ; but the import of foreign wines stood on a different footing. Excessive demands by the Crown would merely kill the trade ; merchants could not be compelled to import wine into England. This, at least, rests on something more than speculation. For the 23rd Article of the Petition of the barons (1258) runs thus :

Item conqueruntur quod dominus rex de prisis nullam fere facit pacationem, ita quod plures mercatores de regno Angliae ultra modum depauperentur, et alii mercatores extranei ea occasione subtrahunt se de veniendo in terram istam cum suis mercibus, unde terra magnam incurrit jacturam.

[50] Gras, *op. cit.* p. 138.

The Prise of Wines

It would obviously not be worth while for merchants to import wine into England if it were subject to an ' undefined ' right of prise by the King. Some limit of exactions such as the *recta prisa* must have been absolutely necessary to the existence of the trade. This may account for the early appearance of this limit to the exactions of the Crown.

'BURH-BOT' AND 'BRIG-BOT'

It was in 1896 that the late Professor Maitland first advanced his well-known 'garrison theory' of the origin of the borough.[1] In the following year he developed it in his *Domesday Book and Beyond*, but in consequence of the criticism which it had evoked, he modified it somewhat in his *Township and Borough*.[2] His theory was ardently espoused and, indeed, carried further by the late Mr. Ballard, whose confidence in its soundness seemed to be increased rather than lessened by criticism. At the London Congress of Historical Studies, 1913, the present writer read a paper on 'The Garrison Theory of the Borough,' which dealt with the whole subject, but has not yet been published, because the theory seemed to him to have definitely lost favour. The position was well summed up by M. Petit Dutaillis, who, after giving his readers the arguments on which it was based,[3] rejects it without hesitation and quite rightly describes it as 'confronted unfortunately by unsurmountable objections' and made 'even less acceptable as systematised by Mr. Ballard.'[4]

I find, however, that Mr. Chadwick in his *Studies on Anglo-Saxon Institutions* (1905) and Mr. Fisher in his

[1] 'The origin of the borough' (*Engl. Hist. Rev.* xi, 13-19).

[2] Ford Lectures, 1897, published 1898.

[3] 'On a study of Domesday Book which is certainly ingenious and suggestive, he (Mr. Maitland) bases a hypothesis which has been called the "garrison theory"; and he has been followed by another scholar Mr. Ballard, who systematises and exaggerates his theory.' (*Studies supplementary to Stubbs' Constit. Hist.* Ed. Tait, 1908, p. 78.)

[4] *Ibid.* pp. 81, 82. The footnote on p. 81 is of value for its exact references to criticisms of the theory. As the author observes, my own criticisms (in the *Vict. Co. Hist.*) 'more particularly correct the mistakes of Mr. Ballard.'

admirable biography of his distinguished relative [5] (1910) have accepted Mr. Maitland's theory as established beyond question. Mr. Fisher, indeed, as it seemed to me, went even further than the Downing Professor ; he discovered in Domesday, as interpreted by Maitland, various methods whereby ' town walls and town garrisons ' might be carefully maintained, and he wrote of ' garrison men . . . a miscellaneous garrison contributed by shire thegns ' [6] (p. 109).

A new argument for ' the garrison theory ' made, I believe, its first appearance in 1910, and it is with this argument that I here propose to deal.[7] Mr. Ballard having, apparently, failed to discover in the English evidence any further proof of its soundness resorted to the Norman system of ' castle-guard.' [8] ' Norman,' I say, for, as was observed by the late Professor Freeman :

In the eleventh century the word *castel* was introduced into our language to mark something which was evidently quite distinct from the familiar *burh* of ancient times. . . .   Ordericus speaks of the thing and its name as something distinctly French.

With the ' castle ' the Normans introduced their system of defending it by castle-guard.[9] But I need not here labour the point ; for ' the onlie begetter ' of the ' garrison theory,' namely, Mr. Maitland himself, had explicitly insisted that the Old English system of *burh-bot* had been replaced at the Conquest by the system of ' castle-guard,' a system intended

---

[5] *F. W. Maitland,* pp. 108-9.

[6] See also below, p. 261. I do not press the point that according to Mr. Maitland ' the boroughs had put off their militancy ' before the Norman Conquest ; for Mr. Fisher in another passage admits the tendency.

[7] My reason for doing so is that no one else, so far as I know, has yet replied to this argument, and that Miss Reid has even claimed that ' Mr. Ballard's view is supported ' by certain statements in records (*Engl. Hist. Rev.* xxxii, 489 note), which all relate to the system of castle guard only.

[8] ' Castle-guard and barons' houses.' *Engl. Hist. Rev.* xxv, 712.

[9] I have dealt with the system of castle-guard in *Arch. Journ.* (1902), lxix, 144, and the *Commune of London,* pp. 278 *et seq.* See also Haskins, *Norman Institutions,* pp. 19-21.

for the defence, not of boroughs, but of castles. Consequently any analogy between the two is false.

In fairness to Mr. Ballard I will quote his exact words :

We see that in the fourteenth century the barons who owed castle-guard to Newcastle upon Tyne kept houses in the castle, in the same way as the landowners who, in the eleventh century owed burh-bot to Oxford, kept ' mural mansions ' within the city (p. 713).

This is not so. The duty of those who held ' mural mansions ' at Oxford was to repair the town wall ; the duty of those ' barons who owed castle-guard ' was ' to repair and maintain ' quarters in the castle for their knights who performed the service. We read nothing under Oxford, in Domesday, of any obligation ' to repair and maintain and if necessary reconstruct a certain *house*,' as at Newcastle (p. 713). In fact the alleged parallel—to quote a sentence of Mr. Freeman's—' only shows how many people there are quite unable to take in any real likeness or unlikeness.' [10] Mr. Ballard, however, summed up as follows :

It is sufficient to call attention to the support given by the cases of Newcastle, Bamburgh and Dover to the ' garrison theory ' of the origin of the non-dominical burgesses in the boroughs of the eleventh century (p. 715).

The foreign system of ' castle-guard ' cannot possibly give support to the ' garrison theory ' of the English borough and the real moral of this new argument appears to me to be that Mr. Ballard would not have advanced it if he had been able to discover that further actual evidence of which the ' garrison theory ' stands so badly in need.

There is, however, another point which should not be overlooked. Whether we study Mr. Maitland's or Mr. Ballard's arguments, we find that the one case on which they really rely is always that of Oxford. Oxford, Mr. Maitland wrote, ' is here the splendid example ' ; [11] Mr. Ballard went further and evaded the difficulty by recourse

[10] *English Towns and Districts*, p. 235.
[11] *Township and Borough*, pp. 44-5.

to the delusive maxim *Ex uno disce omnes*.[12]   He claimed
that we might safely conclude from the case of Oxford, that
the same system prevailed in all similar towns.   Students
of institutional history should be always on their guard
against attempts to use this argument ; in the case of Domesday it is specially dangerous.   Even if the Oxford evidence
supported the ' garrison theory '—which I do not admit—
it must not be applied to towns for which there is no such
evidence.

I will now make good my statement that Mr. Maitland
had explicitly insisted ' on the totally distinct character of
burh-bot and castle guard.'

It is quite possible that Mr. Maitland's *dicta* on this
subject have been overlooked ; for the index to *Domesday
Book and Beyond* is not helpful.   His chapter on ' the
boroughs ' is of some length (pp. 172-219) and has to be
closely searched.   The index has an entry under ' Castle-
guard,' but under it is no reference to the passages on which
I rely.   These are three in number.   In a paragraph
headed ' *Burh-bot* and Castle-guard ' we read :

> The strand that we have been endeavouring to trace is broken
> at the Conquest.   The castle arises. . . .   The castle is now
> what wants defending ; the knights who defend it form no part
> of the burghal community, and perhaps ' the castle fee ' is in
> law no part of the borough (pp. 191-2).

Again, as to ' the Cambridgeshire landowners ' and the
burh-bot, it is stated, ' newer arrangements, the rise of
castles and of borough communities, have relieved them
from the duty of " borough-fastening " ' (pp. 186-7).
Lastly :

> We have thought of the typical borough as a fortified town
> maintained by a district for military purposes.   But already . . .
> the time has come for knight-service, and castles and castle-
> guard (p. 217).

I have now made it abundantly clear that Maitland
rejected any connexion between the two systems.

[12] *The Domesday Boroughs* (1904), p. 34.

It is more remarkable that Maitland should have insisted on this distinction because, like the other historians of his time,[13] he treated it as axiomatic that a *burh* founded or repaired by Edward the Elder or Aethelflaed was one of those ' mound ' castles which archaeologists are now agreed in holding, were the typical strongholds introduced in the Conquest period by the Normans.[14]   For these were true castles and might as such be associated with a system of ' castle guard.'   Before showing that this was so, I would lay stress on the importance—for historians as well as archaeologists—of a right understanding of this question. For instance, when Professor (later Sir William) Ashley was dealing with the ' garrison theory ' of the borough as set forth by Dr. Varges in 1893-5, his chief criticism of that writer's insistence on the ' town as a stronghold ' (*Festung*), surrounded by ' a circuit of walls,' was that the early *burg* is not proved to have been walled and may have rather resembled the (alleged) English *burh*.   He argued thus :

That *Burg* meant a place of defence, that the oldest towns were in some way connected with defence, we can hardly doubt.   . . .   But it is by no means clear to my mind that we are to think of the earliest *Burgen* as walled towns.   The burhs which Edward the Elder and his sister Ethelfleda were building in Mercia at the very time that Henry the Fowler was building his *Burgen* in Saxony are usually described—and the description seems to be justified by existing remains—as earthen mounds (*sic*) surmounted by wooden stockades.   This might be an equally true description of the German *Burg*.[15]

Mr. Maitland certainly in his *Domesday Book and Beyond* (1897) treated it as axiomatic that the ' burhs ' of Edward and Aethelflaed contained a ' mound ' stronghold. He wrote of the ' burh ' as ' a cluster of inhabited dwellings,

[13] Mr. Tait, for instance, wrote in 1897, of ' those royal or private mound and earthwork fortifications on which the Norman so often superimposed his castles.'   (*Engl. Hist. Rev.* 1897, p. 774.)

[14] See my paper on ' The Castles of the Conquest,' in *Archaeologia*, vol. lviii (1902).

[15] *Surveys, Historic and Economic* (1900), p. 193, reprinted from *Quart. Journal of Economics*, July 1896.

which as a whole was to be made defensible by ditch and mound (*sic*), by palisade or wall ' (p. 186). He then proceeded :

Whatever may be meant by the duty of repairing burgs, when it is mentioned in charters coming from a somewhat earlier time, it must for the future be that of upholding those walls and mounds (*sic*) that the king and the lady are rearing. . . . The man with five hides will know how much of the mound (*sic*) or the wall he must maintain (p. 187).

In his Ford lectures on *Township and Borough* (1898) [16] he was even more precise. He wrote of ' the castle mound ' at Cambridge (pp. 4, 38, 119) :

Just above the bridge rises the mound that is in the narrowest sense the burh (*sic*) of Cambridge. The castle has come and gone ; the old burh (*sic*) remains (p. 37).

Speaking of ' Cromwell's works at the castle,' he observed that Oliver ' timbered the old *burh* once more ' (p. 94). The identity of the *burh* with the castle-mound is here explicitly asserted.

It is strange to find that the authority cited by both the above scholars for this identification is Mr. Green's *Conquest of England*. For not only should we hardly look on that brilliant writer, at the present time, as an authority on this subject, we should ask what was his own authority, and we should find that none is vouched.[17]

There can, I think, be little doubt that Green took his (alleged) identity of the *burh* and the keep-crowned ' mound ' from Freeman's *Norman Conquest*, or that Freeman in turn relied on G. T. Clark, whom he styled ' the great master of military architecture.' Mr. Clark was known to me as a strangely inaccurate archaeologist, but I hastened to call

[16] Delivered, 1897 ; published, 1898.

[17] Sir W. Ashley cited *Conquest of England*, pp. 198 *seq.* (and Boase's *Oxford*) ; Mr. Maitland the same work, pp. 189-207. I find the ' mound ' strongholds mentioned on pp. 197, 200 (' Aethelflaed threw up a huge mound, crowned with a fortress '), 202 (' she reared one of those mounds which marked the defensive warfare of the time, and which still remains to witness to the energy of the lady of Mercia '), 205, etc. ; also 438, 439, 441 (' Aethelfled in 907 . . . raised the mound beside its bridge '), 451.

in question his confident conclusions on the subject, in view of their unhesitating acceptance by such writers as those whom I have named above.

Even when I ventured—four years before Mr. Maitland published the passage on Cambridge castle—to express some doubt as to Mr. Clark's theory, it was only in tentative fashion.[18] Had it not been for the sanction given to Mr. Clark's theories, I should have been more outspoken in my rejection of them, for he could not even grasp clearly what his theories were.[19] Fortunately, Mrs. Armitage, by her exhaustive researches, has disposed once for all of Mr. Clark's contention, and one can now refer the student to her decisive monograph.[20] Its valuable preface sums up the whole controversy on the subject. The historical bearing of the substitution of the Norman ' castle ' for the English ' burh ' is insisted upon and well explained by the author.

Having now, I hope, clearly shown that Maitland definitely rejected the connexion since alleged by Mr. Ballard, between the ' garrison theory ' of the borough and the Norman system of the ' castle-guard,' I will turn to the second part of this paper, namely, Maitland's argument on *burhbot* and *brigbot*. Coupling these two dues as obligations on the land,[21] he holds, as we have seen, that the old *burh-bot*

[18] Mrs. Armitage, of whose notable book I shall speak below, has duly given me credit for being the first to question it. In her *Early Norman Castles of the British Isles* (1912) she wrote : ' Dr. Round was the first to attack (in the *Quarterly Review*, 1894) the assertion of the late Mr. G. T. Clark that the moated mound was a Saxon castle ' (Preface, p. viii). Its fallacy, she stated, ' is now generally admitted by the best English Archaeologists '(p. ix).

[19] Mrs. Armitage refers her readers (p. 48 note) to my demonstration in *Archaeologia*, 1902. Clark attributed the moated mounds to the ' Northmen ' generally, by which he sometimes meant the English invaders, and sometimes the Danes of later days.

[20] *Early Norman Castles of the British Isles* (1912).

[21] ' Land even though given to a church is not to be free (unless by exceptional favour) of army service, bridge work and borough-bettering or borough-fastening. Wall-work is coupled with bridge-work ; to the duty of maintaining the county bridges (*sic*) is joined the duty of constructing (*sic*) and repairing the boroughs. Shall we say the " county boroughs " ? ' (*Dom. Book and Beyond*, p. 186.)

became obsolete on the coming of the Normans, with their system of castles and castle-guard, but asserted that the bridge-work remained unchanged as an obligation on the landowners.[22]   He argued, therefore, that from the method of assessing (long afterwards) the *brig-bot* we could infer the method of assessing the *burh-bot* before it became obsolete.   It is probably little realised how much conjecture and hypothesis have found their way into the work of this brilliant scholar.   Here, for instance, we find him writing, as already partially quoted :

Let us ask ourselves how the burden that is known as *burh-bot* . . . will really be borne.   Is it not *highly probable, almost certain* . . . that if for instance there is but one *burh* in a shire, all the lands in that shire must help to better that *burh*.   Apportionment will *very likely* go further.   The man with five hides will know how much of the mound (*sic*) or the wall he must maintain, how much wall-work he must do.   We see how the old bridge work becomes, etc., etc.[23]   (See p. 257 *supra*.)

What this actually amounts to is a conjecture as to the apportionment of an alleged obligation to maintain an imaginary ' mound.'   If this be thought harsh criticism, we have but to turn over two pages to find it definitely asserted that :

The duty of maintaining the bulwark of the county's borough is incumbent on the magnates of the county.   They discharge it by keeping haws in the borough and burgesses in those haws (p. 189).

Yet, at the foot of the same page, this definite assertion is already weakening ; we only read that :

At all events *we shall hardly go astray if we suggest that* the thegns of the shire have been bound to keep houses and retainers

[22] We see how the old bridge work becomes a burden on the estates of the county landowners.   From century to century the Cambridgeshire landowners contribute according to their hidage to repair the most important bridge of their county, a bridge which lies in the middle of the borough of Cambridge.   Newer arrangements . . . have relieved them from the duty of borough-fastening, but the bridge-work is apportioned on their lands.   (*Ibid.* p. 187.)

[23] *Op. cit.* pp. 186-7.

in the borough of their shire and that this duty has been apportioned among the great estates.

Confidence, however, soon returns. On the next page we learn that the thriving ceorl acquired a town-house

because if he was to be one of the great men of the county, he was bound to keep in the county's *burh* retainers who would do the wall-work, etc., etc. (p. 196).

Or again, ' they kept those laws because they were bound to keep them ' (p. 196).

Now these passages are most important ; they involve the famous ' garrison theory,' as set forth by Mr. Maitland. Nevertheless, a year later, the above confident assertions are claimed by him only as possible, nay, even as a ' guess.' [24] We can hardly be surprised that later writers have been somewhat led astray as to Mr. Maitland's conclusions. Mr. Chadwick, for instance, in his *Studies on Anglo-Saxon Institutions* (1905), accepts as definitive his assertions in *Domesday Book and Beyond*.[25] Even his own brother-in-law, himself a distinguished historian, repeated in his brilliant biography, and accepted without misgiving, Maitland's ' novel theory as to the origin and early history

[24] ' It seems to me possible that the great men of the shire were bound to keep houses and retainers . . . in this stronghold and place of refuge. I do not press that theory upon you.' (*Township and Borough* (1898), p. 44.) ' I have elsewhere committed myself to the guess that the magnates of the shire may have been bound, not only to repair the fortifications of the borough, but also to keep houses and retainers in it.' (*Dom. Book and Beyond*, 190.) ' In support of this " garrison theory," if I may so call it, I made use of an argument which must be abandoned. . . .' ' I ought to have stated in express words that what can be read of certain important towns (Norwich is one) would certainly not suggest the garrison theory and is scarcely compatible with the belief that in these towns the magnates of the neighbourhood have been compelled to keep houses.' (*Ibid.* pp. 210-20.)

[25] ' Professor Maitland (*Ibid.* pp. 189 ff.) has shown that the boroughs must originally have been supported by the districts surrounding them ' (p. 220). ' The word *haga* is frequently used in *Domesday Book* and in charters of the eleventh century to denote a town dwelling attached to some (*rural*) manor. For the history of such dwellings it will be sufficient here to refer to Maitland, *Domesday Book and Beyond*, p. 196 ff., who shows that they were originally occupied by soldiers.' (p. 341.)

of the ' English Borough ' in the form in which it appeared
in *Domesday Book and Beyond*. He appealed to the evidence of Domesday Book, showing ' the contrivances at
once careful and varied for maintaining town-walls and
town garrisons ' ; he spoke of the argument as ' expounded
with beautiful clearness and ingenuity ' and as involving
the conclusion that the town court was the product of
' tenural (*sic*) heterogeneity, for the garrison men would
need a special court to decide their controversies.' [26] The
close of this passage is evidently based on *Domesday Book
and Beyond*, p. 191 :

> They came from different districts and had different lords.
> In this heterogeneity we may also see one reason . . . why the
> borough should have a moot of its own.[27]

Now the origin of the town court (or borough moot) was
naturally one of supreme interest to the Downing Professor.[28]
I need not repeat what he has written in the passages cited
in my footnote, but they will enable the reader to verify my
statement that these passages, where the problem has been
specially dealt with, do not at least support the view that
the ' town court was the product of tenurial heterogeneity,'
and that I have not found in them (or indeed, elsewhere)
the phrase ' garrison men ' employed by the Downing
Professor. Mr. Fisher, indeed, here even goes further than
Maitland himself in upholding the ' garrison theory ' and
seems to ignore or to have overlooked not merely the
damaging criticism to which it was promptly exposed, but
it's author's own subsequent admission that it was merely
a ' guess.' [29]

I must not here let myself be drawn into discussing that

[26] *Frederick William Maitland.* By H. A. L. Fisher (1910), pp. 108-9.

[27] We must remember that what the writer calls the knightly element
in the boroughs was only, in his view, a portion of their population
(pp. 191, 203). What court had the rest ?

[28] See *Domesday Book and Beyond*, pp. 185-6, 209-212, 217 ; *Township
and Borough*, pp. 41, 74-75, 184-5 ; *The Hist. of Engl. Law* (1895), i,
627 *et seq.* See also p. 253 above.

[29] *Township and Borough*, pp. 209-210.

theory anew, beyond referring to what I deem its fundamental fallacy, namely, the confusion of a mason's job—
that of repairing a wall—with the function of a military
' garrison,' probably of all men in the realm the most
professionally warlike.' [30] We first read that the county
thegn ' was bound to keep in the county's *burh* retainers
who would do the wall-work and hoard provisions sent in to
meet the evil day '—and then, in the very next paragraph,
that the thegn's retainer ' was kept in the borough for a
military purpose and was perhaps being fed by the manor
to which he belonged.' [31] The first of these assertions is
supposed to be proved by the Domesday evidence as to
Oxford ; the second is mere conjecture.

But I must return to Maitland's argument from the
brig-bot or ' bridge work.' The evidence is curiously slight.
For no county, indeed, but Cambridgeshire, are we given
any evidence at all as to the persistence of this levy ; for
Cambridgeshire it consists only of a reference ' to the
pontage accounts among the Bowtell MSS. at Downing
College.' [32] The short paragraph dealing with this subject
ought to be here quoted in full. Of ' the one bridge that
gives name to a county,' we read as follows :

The duty of maintaining that bridge lay upon the county ;
The lands of the shire owed it bridge-boot, or to use a later
phrase, they owed it pontage. Many lands had in course of
time secured a chartered or prescriptive immunity from the
charge, but in the middle of the last century, those which were
not free contributed according to their hidage. For example,
in 1752 the Duke of Bedford paid £36 for six hides of land in
Dry Drayton ; it was the boot that they owed to the Great
Bridge.[33]

Two questions here arise : Is the identity of this ' pontage '
with the old English ' bridge-boot ' proved, or merely
assumed ? Is it proved that the liability ' lay upon the
county,' that is ' upon the lands of the shire ' as a whole ?

To me, at least, a liability of £6 on the hide appeared

[30] *Domesday Book and Beyond*, p. 191.   [31] *Ibid.* pp. 191-2.
[32] *Township and Borough*, p. 37 note.   [33] *Ibid.* p. 37.

rather surprising. Cambridgeshire, according to Maitland's reckoning, had 1233 hides which (at £6 on the hide) would imply a levy of £7398 on ' the lands of the shire.' If it should be urged that the exemption of some would throw an additional liability on others, it is obviously doubtful whether such additional liability could be enforced.[34] Happily, however, we are not now dependent on speculation.

The Great Bridge of Cambridge which is so fully discussed in the Hundred Rolls, is the subject of elaborate indictment and enquiry in 1338 and subsequent years. It is one of the cases in which scattered lands were liable for bridge repair cases which led to endless litigation. In this instance lands in about a score of villages were liable and ' communitas ville Cantabr' tenetur reparare unum caput pontis.' [35]

The only case of the kind at all generally known is probably that of Rochester Bridge, of which only ' eleven townships were liable for its repair.' [36] This distribution of the liability is more suggestive surely of that mysterious system under which suit of court ' was a burden on particular tenements.' [37] This, however, can only be advanced as a suggestion.[38] Even, however, if there were evidence (which it seems is not alleged) of the liability having once rested on the county as a whole, this would not of itself prove the identity. Of this we have assumed clear evidence in the case of the sister shire.[39] In 1259 the borough and

---

[34] See *Domesday Book and Beyond*, p. 206.

[35] *Engl. Hist. Rev.* xxxiii, 107.　　　　　　　　[36] *Ibid.*

[37] *History of English Law* (1895), i, 526-9 : ' suit was a burden on particular tenements, a burden not to be increased by any subdivision of those tenements. . . . Somehow or another the court or the king has become entitled to a fixed number of suits, each of which suits is encumbent on a certain tract of land . . . of the size and nature of these suit-owing tracts our evidence only permits us to say that there is no uniformity and that very often a whole vill or manor is represented by a single suitor.'

[38] The writer was unable to examine such evidence as there is in this instance.

[39] Huntingdonshire may be so described from its geographical position and as having the same sheriff. Cambridge and Huntingdon are united by an old Roman road and are only, I believe, some sixteen or seventeen miles apart as the crow flies.

the shire of Huntingdon were at variance concerning the upkeep of Huntingdon bridge. It was fully recognised that the county as a whole (*totus comitatus*) was responsible for keeping the bridge in repair, but as a *quid pro quo* (said the burgesses) for exemption from tolls at Huntingdon.[40] The sole point in dispute was the use of the bridge by the burgesses for the carriage of their crops from beyond it and of dung, which went (the county claimed) beyond what we may term ' fair wear and tear.' What concerns us here is that both sides were agreed as to the origin of the liability, which we have seen was not the ancient *brig-bot*.[41]

Mr. Maitland speaks of the duty of maintaining the county bridges ' [42] without telling us which they were or how we are to distinguish them. Oxford, the alleged brilliant proof of ' the garrison theory,' was surely at least as entitled as Cambridge to have a county bridge,' [43] but I do not know of any evidence that the Cambridgeshire system is found in Oxfordshire. Nottingham, no doubt, had a bridge over the great water of Leen, the upkeep of which was the charge upon the shire, each wapentake being separately assessed,[44] but the actual evidence is late (1458). In Essex—the county with which the writer is best acquainted —there is no trace of such a system. The problem there is complicated by the position of its only ' borough.' Chelmsford, the present county town, is geographically the centre of Essex, is the meeting place of roads and rivers, and stands on the great highway which traverses Essex from the south-west to the north-east of the county. But in Domesday and for long afterwards it appears merely as a rural manor. Its bridge was a local liability only. The ancient

---

[40] ' Dicunt enim quod totus comitatus Huntedon' quietus est de teleon' dando in villa de Huntedon' pro reparacione pontis predicti.' (*Abb. Plac.* p. 148.)

[41] This case is not mentioned by Maitland.

[42] See p. 262 above.

[43] It might of course be urged that the name of Oxford suggests a bridge of later construction than the Cambridge one.

[44] *Records of Nottingham*, ii, 223 *et seq.* Nottingham itself was liable for the repairs of part of the bridge.

and historic town of Colchester is the only one in Essex to which Mr. Maitland's test would allow the position of a county borough.   Situate, however, as it is, in the north-east of Essex, Colchester could hardly be accepted as the county town, nor has it been so recognised.   The question assumed an acute form some years ago, when a cathedral town had to be selected for the new diocese of Essex ; Chelmsford's position won the day.   In Suffolk, similarly, Ipswich and St. Edmundsbury put forward rival claims ; they were both included in the cumbrous style of the new bishop.   Ipswich satisfies Mr. Maitland's test, but it stands near the sea in the south-east corner of the county, so it could not be the county town.   One must not let oneself be drawn too far afield, but something more is here at stake than the question of ' county bridges.'   The sharp distinction between the ' shires ' and the ' eastern counties,' as they ought to be styled, seems to be imperfectly grasped. No one, I believe, but Mr. Chadwick, has gone so far as to group Cambridge with Colchester as ' boroughs of the Eastern Midlands,' [45] but has it not been too hastily inferred that such towns as Ipswich and Colchester, though obviously not in the Midlands, were county towns of the same type as Cambridge, Huntingdon and Hertford ?   Mr. Maitland was deeply interested in ' the great block of shires, which take their names from towns and have a borough apiece.' [46] In his introduction to his remarks on *brig-bot* and the Great Bridge at Cambridge he writes :

It seems to me that throughout a wide tract of England there were in 1086 no boroughs which were not or had not been in some distinct and legal sense the centres of districts, the chief towns of shires.[47]

[45] ' The boroughs of the Eastern Midlands . . . Cambridge and Colchester, perhaps also Norwich and Thetford and Ipswich.'   (Chadwick, *Studies on Anglo-Saxon Instit.* p. 225.)

[46] *Township and Borough*, p. 42.   [47] *Ibid*. pp. 36-7.

THE ORIGIN OF ESSEX PARISHES

WHEN we look at a map we see it divided into ' parishes,' districts which proclaim by their names that they owe their formation to the Church. The so-called ' civil parish ' is, to-day, an administrative unit, but this civil parish is merely an adaptation of that historic and infinitely older unit, the ecclesiastical parish. It seems to be generally agreed that the means by which the ministrations of the church were extended in rural districts was outwards, in missionary fashion, from the diocesan centre, but the names of our parishes, the shapes they assumed and the great variations in their size, have not yet been accounted for.

My old master, Bishop Stubbs, who held for years an Essex living, is, no doubt, our greatest authority on the history and development of the English church ; but his conclusions, though positive enough, were really based on speculation. He held that, as the kingdom or shire of the earliest English days became the sphere of the bishop and so accounted for the diocese, the ' historical township ' became the sphere of a priest and appears in its ecclesiastical form as the parish or portion of a parish. For he admitted that the parish might contain more than one township, if a township was too small to need or too poor to support a priest of its own. This simple theory, however, does not explain the origin of the township itself. This latter point was dealt with by that famous Cambridge scholar, the late Professor Maitland, who was struck by a notable feature of Essex topography, namely, the numerous cases in which adjoining parishes have to be distinguished by suffixes because they had originally borne the same name. He cited those of Layer Breton, Layer Marney and Layer De La

The Origin of Essex Parishes

Haye, with other instances in point, and contended that these phenomena were due to the original local units having been of much greater area than those which we have to-day. His standpoint was directly the reverse of that of Bishop Stubbs ; for while the Bishop was absorbed in the history of the church and its influence on that of the nation, the Professor was bored by the church and revelled in the origins of our law. He even went as far as to deal with the ' parish ' as an upstart and an interloper. ' The parish,' he wrote, ' has done a great deal of harm to English law and English history ; might we not even now give it back to its " priest " ? '

As against this attitude, this view of the problem, I have been led to the conclusion that our parishes, as we see them on the map to-day, owe their origin and their existing names to the building of a parish church. Neither the bishop nor the professor seems to have kept in mind, even if they ever grasped it, the amazing difference in area between the parishes of Essex. This difference is as fatal to the Professor's theory on the one hand as it is to the bishop's on the other. When we find historic parishes, of which a good number contain more than five thousand acres, while some have only a few hundreds, it is obvious that they cannot have been formed on any uniform system and that neither of the theories I have described will square with the facts of the case.

The first conclusion to which I was led was that the formation of a parish was determined by the existence of a church. If a vill—to use the term beloved of Professor Maitland—contained more than one church, it was formed into more than one parish. If, on the other hand, some adjoining vills had but one church between them, they were jointly formed into one parish. My test case was Chignal. Here you have a vill, or township, of which the entire area was only 1389 acres divided originally into three parishes, each with its parish church. This is directly opposed to the bishop's theory that townships were not so divided.

What then is the explanation? Simply that Chignal, territorially, happened to be divided into three manors, and that each of these churches was the church of a manor. In Domesday Book (1086) we actually find that when an Essex church is mentioned, it is not as the church of this parish, but as the church of this manor (*hujus manerii*).

Now let us turn from ancient records to the position of the churches themselves, as we see them standing to-day. West Bergholt is a perfect type of the arrangement normal in Essex. The hall and church are found, as I call it, ' cheek by jowl,' entirely surrounded by the land of the lord of the manor, and away from the people of the village. In the present day we are actually paying the penalty of this arrangement. At Hazeleigh, a small parish near Maldon, the Hall stands close to the old parish church, which is now, we read, disused for service, an iron church having been erected in the centre of the scattered village in 1893. At Bergholt a new church has had to be built more in the centre of the population. At Stanway, to the south, the old church adjoining the hall has been long in ruins and a new church, Stanway All Saints, built in a more central situation. The ruined church of Stanway looks across the Roman River to Little Birch, where the ruined church adjoins similarly the site of the old Hall. In all such cases we have before our eyes actual witness to the ancient system by which the church was originally built, for his own use, by the lord of the manor, in the closest proximity to his Hall. And when he built it he also endowed it, as far as we can now gather, with a small glebe—perhaps from twenty to forty acres. As the direct consequence of this, we find that the advowson descended with the manor for centuries and is sometimes still annexed to it.

The manorial origin of Essex parishes is responsible for the large proportion of ancient family names among the suffixes used to distinguish them from one another. Woodham Mortimer, Woodham Ferrers and Woodham Walter

—the home of the baronial Fitz Walters—preserve the names of three of the greatest of Norman houses. Near Colchester, Layer de la Haye, Layer Breton and Layer Marney are all so distinguished from families that once held them. So also are Wakes Colne and Colne Engaine, while Earls Colne was named from the Veres, Earls of Oxford, who founded Colne Priory. Bergholt, it is true, is now distinguished from its Suffolk namesake by the prefix ' West,' but in earlier days it was more generally known as Bergholt Sackville, from the Sackvilles who were once lords here and at Mount Bures. All over the county we find still upon the map the names of barons and manorial lords. Basset, Peverel, Mandeville, Helion, Gernon, Mountfitchet (for the original Montfiquet you must turn to the map of Normandy), Virley, D'Arcy, Berners, Gray of Grays Thurrock—they are the names of alien lords, stamped upon a conquered land. At times they are difficult now to recognise, as in Stondon Massey, a home of the Marcis, Stapleford Tawney, where Tanis were lords, Mountnessing, which took its name from the Muntenis, Wendon Lofts, Willingale Doe, and even the unhappy Shellow Bowells.

On the other hand, just as Essex parishes are rich in the names of Norman lords, so are they singularly poor in those of patron saints. So far as I can discover, there is, in the whole of Essex, only a single instance in which the name of a parish preserves in proper form the name of a patron saint. This is that of Chignal St. James, and even this form of the name is not of great antiquity ; for as the parish was originally two, it was somewhat irreverently styled ' Chignal Mary James ' by Elizabethan archdeacons. It might be imagined that Belchamp St. Paul's has a name similarly formed from the local invocation, but this is not so ; the patron saint is St. Andrew, and not St. Paul, and the name is derived from the lords of the Manor, the dean and chapter of St. Paul's. The treatment of saints in Essex is, indeed, deplorable ; St. Mary Magdalen lurks in the name of Magdalen Laver and St. Margaret in that of

Margaret Roding, while she is even more effectually concealed in that of Margaretting, *vulgo* ' Margetting.'

Cross the border into Suffolk, and the change begins at once ; Bures St. Mary, and Stratford St. Mary meet us as we pass the Stour ; it is not far to Capel St. Mary, which is so distinguished from Capel St. Andrew. Creeting St. Mary, Creeting St. Olave and Creeting All Saints lay together in the heart of the county ; just north of Bury St. Edmunds we have Fornham All Saints, Fornham St. Martin and Fornham St. Geneveve, the last of which alone among names of this character is found even in Domesday. Northwest of the three Fornhams we come to two ancient parishes, Icklingham All Saints and Icklingham St. James. The climax, however, is reached in north-east Suffolk, where there are seven adjoining parishes, named South Elmham, distinguished only by the names of their saints, St. George, All Saints, St. James, St. Margaret, St. Michael, St. Nicholas and St. Peter. I have now enumerated nineteen of the parish names so formed, and the list is by no means exhaustive. Even as the suffixes formed from the names of patron saints are, we have seen, infinitely more common in Suffolk than in Essex, so, conversely, those derived from the names of feudal lords are infinitely scarcer in Suffolk than in Essex.

That justly famous scholar, the late Prof. Maitland of Cambridge, had examined this subject and many of the names I have cited,[1] but he seems to have overlooked this curious difference between the two counties. Can we account for the difference ? The county border, we must remember, divides not merely two counties, but two dioceses, two peoples, two ancient Kingdoms. Essex land was assessed in hides ; Suffolk land in carucates ; the whole system of land tenure, before the Norman Conquest, differed in the two counties. Essex was a land of manors and their lords ; Suffolk was a land of smaller holdings which were in the hands of free tenants (*liberi homines*). It was by

[1] The surnames of English villages in *Archaeol. Rev.*, vol. iv.

these, apparently, that churches were raised and endowed, with the result that Suffolk parishes rarely preserve the names of manorial lords. In the place of this class of names, they bear those of their patron saints. This, it must be clearly understood, is merely an hypothesis of my own ; it might be considered by others a too speculative theory. If, however, it should be accepted, it might prove of considerable importance, as throwing light on the system of land tenure in these two counties before the Norman Conquest.

In Essex—as, of course, elsewhere—some parishes had their origin in subdivision of others which were already in existence. In certain cases this can be proved ; in others it can only be suspected. The parish has always been a fissiparous organisation, but the fission was, of old, a slow business so far as we can ascertain. It began normally with a chapel of ease, of which there seem to have been a large number in the county, though some of them never developed or even passed out of existence, doubtless from insufficient endowment. There is one Essex parish which proclaims its origin by its name. This is that of Chapel, beyond Fordham, containing not far short of 1200 acres. It is known that a chapel was there consecrated, about 1360, by the bishop of the diocese, but Chapel, or, as it was then called Pontisbright, remained in the parish of Great Tey for a long time after that. We thus see that Great Tey must have originally contained some 3800 acres. There is extant a curious will of 1558-9, in which the testator describes himself as ' of the parishe of Pontesbright, in the Towne of Muche Taye,' and desires to be buried in the ' churcheyarde of Pontesbrighte."

Another Essex parish which began with a district chapel is that of Pleshy, a small parish which adjoins High Easter. As its origin seems to be quite unknown to Essex archaeologists, I may explain that it began with a chapel, built there by the Earl of Essex, in the days of Henry II. The inhabitants of Pleshy advanced the usual plea, namely, that the mother church of Easter—that is High Easter—was far off, and the road bad and long for carrying the dead there, especially in winter. So the chapel was duly consecrated by the bishop of London and the tithes and offerings of the inhabitants of Pleshy assigned to it. But the baptismal chrism and the oil for anointing the sick was to come from the mother church.

The chapelry status of some parishes is more difficult to account for. Why, for instance, should Hempstead, a parish of nearly 3600 acres, have had a church which was merely a chapel of ease to Great Sampford, the parish adjoining it on the south, of which the acreage was only 2260 ? Why, again, should the bishop of London, under Henry II, have collated to his church of Wickham Bishops with its chapel, as he terms it, the church of Langford ? No one, I believe, has ever suspected that Langford church was at any time dependent on Wickham Bishops, nor was the bishop lord of Langford or owner of its advowson. The case of Stanway presents a difficulty of its own. Morant, the historian of Essex, was inclined to believe that there were originally two parishes, because he found mention of Great and Little Stanway ; but this is no proof at all of the existence of two parishes. In Essex, even a hamlet was sometimes divided into ' Great ' and ' Little,' and the neighbouring parish of Fordham is actually divided by the river from ' Little Fordham,' which is not in Fordham, but in Aldham. Morant admitted that, from at least 1366, presentations were made to the church of Stanway—the one now in ruins—with the chapel of St. Albright annexed ; but it is certainly remarkable that, about 1220, we find St. Albrights occurring as a separate parish (*parochia Sancti Athelberti*).[1] The names of St. Albright and St. Athelbert (or Ethelbert) denote the same saint. St. Albright's Stanway is of further interest from its position on the London road. Whatever may have been its early history, that position was probably due to the needs of the population

[1] *Cartulary of St. John's Colchester*, p. 531.

272

attracted by that great highway. The same cause was at work at Witham, though in that case the town which sprang up on the London road, away from the church, had to wait till the last century for its chapel of ease. Brentwood is known to have had its origin in a roadside settlement with an early chapel, within the parish of South Weald. The great parish of Romford, a market town, had nothing but a chapel till modern times, and even this was not built, it is said, till 1323, nor was the coveted right of burial conceded till later still. Billericay, a market town in the south-east of the county, is another parish which owes its origin to the great thoroughfare on which it stands. As its status was only that of a hamlet in Great Burstead, on the border of which it stood, all the rights of the parish church were reserved, when the bishop of London re-consecrated its chapel in 1693. This chapel did not develop into a separate parish church till 1844. At Epping there was only a chapel of ease for Epping town on the high road, which similarly stood on the border of its great parish, till 1832, when a church was built ; but this did not become parochial till 1889, when it took the place of the old church, at Epping Upland, as the parish church. Again there is reason to believe that Braintree was originally only a portion of Rayne, which had its origin as a town in the intersection of important highways. Its notable church was not built till the town was gaining importance.

It is of singular interest to trace the double development by which, with the increase of trade and traffic, a new population with urban interests, had to be provided for by the church, while on the other hand, the provision of parishes in purely rural districts, proved sometimes excessive. Although the parochial organisation and the endowments of the church were of so stereotyped a character as to make re-adjustment a work of extreme difficulty, it proved impracticable at last to retain an outgrown system. Some churches were abandoned and allowed to tumble down ; some livings of which the endowments were insufficient for modern needs were either combined or held jointly ; in some parishes the church adjoining the old manorial hall was either replaced by a new one nearer the centre of population or supplemented, as in medieval times, by a chapel of ease. But it was not until the tremendous change in the balance of the country's population, which began with what is termed ' the industrial revolution,' that really drastic alterations had to be made in a system of such immemorial antiquity, and so encumbered by sentiment and by the existing structures and by vested interests that any real alteration might well have seemed impossible.

INDEX

Archaeological Soc., sphere of an, lxiii.
Archer, T. A., xxvii.
Archery, liv.
Archis, Gilb., son of Gilb. de, 228, 229.
Architecture and Local History, lxiv.
Ardres, lords of, l.
Argall, Rich., lix.
Argentine, Giles de, lvi.
Argles, Rev. G. M., xiii.
Argyll, Archibald, Duke of, lxvi.
— John, Duke of, xxxv, xxxvi.
Arklow, barony of, lv.
Armitage, Mrs., 258.
Armorial bearings, use of, lv, 150.
Arms, College of. *See* College of Arms.
— double coats of, 60.
Arques, relief of, l.
— Will. of, xlix.
Arthur, Sir Geo., xxxii.
Arundel, Earldom of, lxix, 99, 178, 179.
— and Surrey, Thom., Earl of, garter plate, 178.
' As established by law,' xxxii, lv.
Ashingdon, lxii (2).
Ashley, Sir Will., 256.
Ash Reigny (Naissa), 138, 139.
Asnières (Normandy), 214.
Atholl, Duke of, xxxvi, xxxvii, lxxi.
Attainders, reversal of, lxxiv.
Atte Watre, Will., of Ewell, 26, 32.
Audley, barony of, lxxii, 197.
— fam. of, 80, 82 *n*, 83, 87.
— Eliz., w. of Nich. de, 95, 95 *n*.
— Geo., 86.
— Hen. de, lvi.
— James de, lvi, 87, 96, 96 *n*, 199.
— Joan, w. of Nich., 79.
— John, Lord, 83, 84, 86.
— Mary, w. of John, Lord, 86.
— Nich. Lord, 79, 95, 95 *n*, 96.
— Lord, 86, 196.
— Lord, of Walden, lxiv.
Augmentations, Court of, 62, 63.
Augmentations of honour, 35.
Aunay (Normandy), 115.

Aylard, Roger, 161 *n*.
Aylett, Dr. Rob., lix, lxii, 107, 107 *n*.

Bachepuz, charter of, lii.
Bacons, arms of, 53.
Badlesmere, barony of, 176.
— Giles de, 199.
Bagot, Sir Will., lvi.
Baker, Geo., 60.
Ballard, Adolphus, 252-8.
Balliol College, xiii-xvi.
— fee of, 235 *n*.
Ballon, fam. of, li.
Bamburgh, garrison theory at, 254.
Bampton, Rob. of, lviii.
Bannockburn, li.
Banwell (Somers.), 39.
Barbery (Normandy), St. Mary's Abbey, 115, 116.
Barclay, Janet, lxvi.
Bardolf, Hugh, lvi.
— Will., lvi.
Barker, pedigree of, lxvii.
— Sir Christopher, garter, 61, 64.
Barking, Bishop of, xlv.
Barnstaple, barony of, 78.
Barnwell Priory, 117 *n*, 118 *n*.
Baron, description of, lvii.
Baronage, The Official, lxvi.
Barones Majores, 217-22.
Barones Minores, 217-22.
Baronetage, Committee of the, xxxiv.
— Hon. Soc. of the, xxxiv.
— Rights of the, xxxiii.
Baronetcies, reports on claims to, lxxiv.
Baronets of Chas. II, lxxiv.
— Protection Soc., xxxiii.
— Roll of, xxxiv, xxxviii.
Baronies by writ, 174, 175, 198.
Barons, distinction of, 217.
— and knights in the Great Charter, lxx.
— and Peers, articles on, xlvi, lix.
— Letter to the Pope, article on, lii.
Barron, Oswald, 151, 173.
Barry, Phil. de, lvi.
— Rob. de, lvi.

Index

Bristol Channel, 139.
Britanny, Count of, 122.
British Academy, xxxviii.
British Museum, docs. removed from, xlii.
British Record Soc., xx.
Brito, Walt., 232.
Brodrick, ap Rodric, Alan, 104, 105, 106.
— Alice, wife of Thom., 105.
— Edw., 104, 105, 106.
— Geo., 104, 104 n.
— John, 105.
— Sir Rich., 104 n.
— St. John, 104.
— Thom., 104, 105.
— Sir Thom., 103.
— Walt., 104.
— Will., 105, 106.
— Charters, 103-8.
— pedigree, 103, 104.
Bromflet, barony of, 188.
Bronescombe, Walter, Bp. of Exeter, 83.
Bronwydd (Cardigan), 81, 84, 89, 90, 91, 99.
Broughton fam., 13 n, 100.
Bruces in Essex, lxv.
Bruern, Bruera, Brueria (Oxon), monks of, 125, 126.
Bruse of Gower, barony of, 178.
Bruton, Rob., 228.
Buci, fam. of, lxix.
Buckingham, Anne, Duchess of, 67, 68.
— Duke of, 68.
— Grenvilles, Dukes of, 130.
— Staffords, Dukes of, 67.
— Marquis of, 132.
Buckinghamshire Domesday, lxix.
Buckland Monachorum (Devon), 130.
Buissei, Bart. de, 19.
— Jordan de, 19, 20, 20 n.
— Roger de, 19, 20, 20 n.
— Will. de, 19.
Bully (Normandy), 17, 38.
Bulmer (Yorks.), 55, 57.
— fam. of, 54-59.
— Bertram de, 56-58.
— Emma de, w. of Geoff. de Neville, 56, 58.

Bulmer, Steph. de, 58.
— Thom. de, 58.
— Will. de, 55, 56, 58.
— de Brancepeth, 56, 57.
— de Wilton, 57 n.
Burchard, Count, 155.
Burci, fam. of, 85 n.
Bures St. Mary (Suff.), 270.
' Burg,' description of, 256.
Burgh, barony of, report on, lxxvi, 199.
Burgus and civitas, xvii.
' Burh-bot ' and ' Brig-bot,' 252.
Burke, Sir Bernard, 4, 7, 8, 9.
Burke's Dormant and Extinct Peerage, lv.
— Landed Gentry, xvi, lxx, 11.
Burley, Sir Simon, lvi.
Burne and Burneham (Sussex), Henry I at, lxviii.
Burnell, barony of, 187.
Burstead, Great (Essex), 273.
Burton Abbey Surveys, lix.
Burton (Northants), 118.
Bury, Adam de, Mayor of London, 27.
— Rose, dau. of Adam, 27.
Bury St. Edmunds, St. Edmundsbury (Suff.), 29, 265.
Busby, Jordan, 172.
Busli, Bully, Builli, fam. of, 16-20.
— Bart. de, 19.
— Ernald de, 16, 18, 19.
— Jordan de, 18-20.
— Rich. de, 18-20.
— Rog. de, 15, 16, 19, 20.
— Walt. de, 19.
— Will. de, 17, 19. See also Bussei.
Bussei, Jordan de, 20.
— Rog. de, 20.
— Walt. de, 19. See also Busli.
Butler, office or sergeanty of, lix, 242.
— Edm., 242.
— James, 241, 242, 243.
— James, son of James, 243.
— Theobald, lvi, 242, 243.
— Earldom of Carrick, lxvi.
Buttington, liv.
' Bygades ' (Essex), lxiv.
Bysshe, Sir Edw., garter, 6, 103.

Family Origins

Cade, Rob., 41.
— Will., lix.
Cairns, Lord, 183, 185.
Calne (Wilts.), ix.
Calvados (Normandy). *See* Cour-
seulles.
Camaes (Pembroke). *See* Kemes.
Cambrian Arch. Assoc. Congress,
98, 98 *n*, 99, 101 *n*.
Cambridge (Cantabrigiensis), l,
265.
— bridge of, 259 *n*, 262-4.
— Castle of, 257.
Camden, Will. Clarenceux, xvii,
64, 69, 86, 88.
Camerarius. *See* Chamberlain.
Campeaux (Normandy), 213, 214.
Camulodunum (Colchester), lxiv.
Canfield (Essex) Castle, lxiv.
— Little, lxii, 49 *n*.
Canterbury, See of, 228.
— St. Augustine's, lviii.
— and York Soc., xx.
Capel St. Andrew (Suff.), 270.
— St. Mary (Suff.), 270.
Cardigan, Shire of, 92 *n*.
Cardross, Lord, 111.
Carew, fam. of, lii, 90 *n*.
— Odo or Other, 90 *n*.
Carlisle charter, lxxiii.
Caro, Carhou, Peter, 235.
— Rob., 235.
Carrick, Earldom of, lxvi.
Carrington, Carington, fam. of,
61, 68.
— Earl, xxxvi, xxxvii.
— Sir Mich., 11, 41.
— Smith, 162.
— Imposture, li.
' Cartae of 1166,' l.
Carucage, The Great, of 1198, lvii.
' Carucata Terrae,' lviii.
' Carucate,' The, lxvii.
Castle, lvii.
— and Tower, xlix.
— guard, lii, lv, 253-8.
— mound, 256.
— staff of, lix.
— ward and cornage, li.
— watchmen, lix.
Castleacre (Norf.), 48.
Castles, Early Norman, lx.

Castles, English, lxviii.
— of the Conquest, liv.
Caswell, Geo., x.
— Susan Constantia, x.
Catherine Parr, Queen, 187.
Cattiwade Bridge (Essex), lxv.
Cavendish, Manor of, 23.
— Overhall, 24, 32.
Cavendish, Caundish, fam. of, 22-
32.
— Agnes, 27, 28 *n*.
— Alice, dau. of Sir John, 24,
24 *n*, 28 *n*.
— Andrew, 27.
— Augustine, 28 *n*.
— Christine, dau. of Steph., 27.
— Eliz., w. of Will. (Bess of Hard-
wick), 23.
— Lady Eliz., 166 *n*.
— Geo., 22, 31, 32.
— Hen., 28 *n*.
— Isabel de, 27.
— Joan, w. of Sir John, 30.
— John, 24-30.
— John, bro. of Steph., 25.
— John, grandfather of Rob., 31.
— John, s. of John, 24.
— John, s. of Thom. de, 26, 27.
— Sir John, 22-32.
— Marg., dau. of Andrew, 27.
— Marg., dau. of John, 27.
— Martin, 24.
— Mary, 31.
— Matilde, w. of Sir John, 28 *n*.
— Maud de, 27.
— Rich., 24, 26, 26 *n*.
— Rob., 24, 27, 28 *n*, 31.
— Rog., 27, 28.
— Rose, w. of Andrew, 27.
— Rowland, 28 *n*.
— Steph., mayor of London, 23-7,
32.
— Thom., 24-31.
— Walt., 27, 28, 31.
— Will., 22, 22 *n*, 25, 27, 28 *n*, 30,
31, 32.
— Will., Duke of Newcastle, 188.
Cawdor, Lord, 98 *n*.
Cecils, ancestry of, 5.
Cemaes. *See* Kemes.
Centeville, Osmund de, 155.
Cesterwald (Essex), lxv.

Churchscot in Domesday, lviii.
Cicé, Comtes de, 114.
Cinglais, forêt de (Normandy), 115.
Cinque Ports, charters, l.
— prisage at, 248.
Clare, fam. of, lv, lvi.
— Gilb. de, lvi.
— Rich. de, lvii.
— Walt. de, lvii.
Clarges, John, 166 *n.*
— Sir Walt., 166, 166 *n.*
Clark, Baron, 248.
— G. T., liii, 257, 258.
Clarke, Thom., 107.
Clavering, fam. of, 37, 39.
Clerkenwell, priories of St. Mary and St. John, liv.
Clervaux, Amaretta, 172.
— Sir Hamon, 172.
— Herodia, 172.
— Janathela, 172.
— Oswalda, 172.
— Timothea, 172.
Cleveland, Duchess of, 77.
Clifford, barony of, 188, 197.
— Sir Thom., 123.
Clopton, Joan, d. of Sir Will., 30.
— Sir Will., 30.
Clothing Trade in Essex, lxiii.
Clun, barony of, 178.
Cobham, barony, report on, lxxii.
— Lord, 197.
Cockayne, Geo. Edw., Clarenceux, xxxvii.
Cocket Wick (Essex), lxiv.
Coggeshall (Essex) Abbey, lxi.
— clothiers of, lxiii.
— in Domesday, lxii.
Cohen, Francis, 133. *See also* Palgrave.
Coins of Norman kings, lxi.
Coke, Sir Edw., arms of, 61.
— Rob., arms of, 61.
Colchester, xxiii, lviii, lxiii, lxv, lxvi, 265.
— arms of, lxii.
— Bank, ix, x.
— Battle of, xxv.
— Becket at, lxiv.
— Berryfield in, lxiv.
— Bishop's Soke, lxiii.

Colchester. Borough of, to-day, lxvi.
— Boroughfield in, lxiii.
— Castle, ix, xvii, xxiii, xlix, liii, lxi, lxii.
— chantry, lxii.
— charters, lx, lxiv.
— County Hospital in, xxxix.
— Court Rolls, lxiv.
— demolition of Norman buildings, liv.
— Domesday of, xvii, xxii, liii.
— election meetings at, xxiv.
— Grammar School, lxii, lxx.
— Haymesocne in, lxiv.
— Hist. and Antiq. of Castle of, xvii.
— Holly Trees House in, ix.
— Holy Trinity and Bere Churches, lxv.
— mint, lix.
— parishes and churches, lxvi.
— portreeve of, lxii.
— Roman road from Mersea, lxiv.
— St. Botolph's Bridge, lxiv.
— — Priory, lxi.
— St. Helen's Chapel, xxv, xlix.
— St. John's Abbey, Charters of, lix, lxii.
— St. Martin's House in, ix.
— St. Peter's Church, lxiv.
— Siege of, lxi.
Colecherche, Rich., son of Will. de, 236.
— Will. de, 236.
Colemere, John de, 246.
Colenso, Bp., xiii, xv.
Collapse of Cobdenism, xxxi.
Collectanea Gen. et Herald., xx, xxi, lv.
College of Arms, xli, lxxii, 9, 10, 11, 12, 53, 60, 72, 103, 172.
Collins, Arthur, *Peerage* by, 7, 8.
Colne, Earls (Essex), 269.
— Engaine (Essex), manor, lxii, 269.
— Wakes (Essex), 269.
Colombières, Phil. de, 212.
Colville, fam. of, 51, 172.
Combat, Trial by, arms used at, 119 *n.*
Combe Martin (Devon), 74.

Index

Index

Index

T   289

Index

Index

Index

Index

PRINTED IN GREAT BRITAIN
BY ROBERT MACLEHOSE AND CO. LTD.
THE UNIVERSITY PRESS, GLASGOW

Index

Barsham, North (Norf.), 49.
Basset, Alan, lvi.
— Nich., 125, 126.
— Sir Phil., lvi.
— Ralph, lvi.
— Rich., lvi.
— Thom., lvi.
— Will., lvi.
Bateson, Mary, 240, 248.
Bath, Bp. of, 214.
— Chas., Lord, 149.
— Earl of, 140, 143, 148, 164, 165, 166.
— John, Earl of, 140.
Battle Abbey Custumal, lxvi.
— roll, 74, 76, 77.
Baud fam., lxiii.
' Baud's Buck,' lxii.
Bavent, Rog., 199.
Bayard, Godfrey, 235.
Bayeux, Cath., 206.
— Church, 201-216.
— inquest of, 201, 204.
— knight of, 201, 202.
— standard-bearer of, 214.
— tapestry, lvii, lxi, lxvii.
— Bp. of, 202, 211.
— Odo, Bp. of, 202, 203, 204.
— Rob., nephew of Odo, Bp., 202.
Baynard, pedigree of, lxvii.
— Falk, lvi.
— Rob., lvi.
Baynton, Sir Andrew, lvi.
Beachley and Buttington, liv.
Beauchamp, Guy de, Earl of Warw., lvi.
— Hen. de, Duke of Warw., lvi.
— Sir John de, Lord, lvi.
— Rob. de, lvi.
— Thom. de, Earl of Warw., lvi.
— Walt. de, lvi.
— Will. de, xlix, lvi.
Beaufort, Thom., Duke of Exeter, lvi.
Beaumont, Rob. de, Count of Meulan, lvi.
— Rob. de, Earl of Leicester, lvi.
— Rog. de, 162, 202, 202 n, 208, 209.
— Waleran de, Count of Meulan, lvi.

Becket, Gilb., Archbp., at Colchester, lxiv.
— — sisters of, lxv.
Becontree Heath, lxiv.
Bedfordshire, Domesday of, lxix.
Belchamps, The (Essex), lxv.
— St. Paul (Essex), 269.
Bellringers, bequest to, liv.
Belvoir, barony of, 188.
— Castle, origin of, lix.
Bemfleet (Essex), Jarvis in, lxv.
Bémont, Chas., xxvi.
Bendish Manor (Essex), lxvi.
Bentinck, Will., Earl of Portland, lxvii.
Bentley, Great (Essex), lxiii.
Berber Corn Festival, lxx.
Bereford, Rich. de, lvi.
Beresfords, origin and arms of, lii.
Bergavenny. See Abergavenny.
Bergholt Sackville (Essex), 269.
— West (Essex), x, xxxviii, 268, 269.
— — Horsepits in, lxv.
— — Scarlets in, lxv.
Berkeley Castle, lxii, 7.
— peerage case, 177, 180, 181.
— Lords, 7, 99, 196.
— James, Earl of, 181.
Berkshire, Domesday of, lxix.
Bernard the Dane, 161, 162.
— the King's scribe, lviii.
Bernay Abbey (Normandy), 134.
Bernières sur mer (Normandy), 213.
Bertie, Rich., arms of, 63.
Berties, rise of the, li.
Bertram, Rog., lvi, 233 n.
— of Bothal, barony of, 188, 189.
— of Bricquebec, Rob., baron of, 116.
— — Jeanne his w., 116.
— — Rob. their son, 116.
— — Will. their son, 116.
— of Mitford, barony of, 189, 232.
— — Rog., 232.
— — Will., 232.
Bertrand, Rob., 116.
Besant, Sir Walt., l.
Bessin (Normandy), 213, 214, 216.
— Ranulf, Count of, 201, 210.